I0806689

PASSAGE to CHINA

A PHOTOGRAPHIC CELEBRATION OF THE SILK ROAD

LIZA GERSHMAN

Skyhorse Publishing

Copyright © 2017 by Liza Gershman

All rights reserved. No part of this book may be reproduced in any manner without the express written consent of the publisher, except in the case of brief excerpts in critical reviews or articles. All inquiries should be addressed to Skyhorse Publishing, 307 West 36th Street, 11th Floor, New York, NY 10018.

Skyhorse Publishing books may be purchased in bulk at special discounts for sales promotion, corporate gifts, fund-raising, or educational purposes. Special editions can also be created to specifications. For details, contact the Special Sales Department, Skyhorse Publishing, 307 West 36th Street, 11th Floor, New York, NY 10018 or info@skyhorsepublishing.com.

Skyhorse® and Skyhorse Publishing® are registered trademarks of Skyhorse Publishing, Inc.®, a Delaware corporation.

Visit our website at www.skyhorsepublishing.com.

10 9 8 7 6 5 4 3 2 1

Library of Congress Cataloging-in-Publication Data is available on file.

Cover design by Jane Sheppard
Cover photos by Liza Gershman

Print ISBN: 978-1-5107-2320-7
Ebook ISBN: 978-1-5107-2324-5

Printed in China

For Alastair and Nancy.

Thank you for helping me get to 40 by 40.

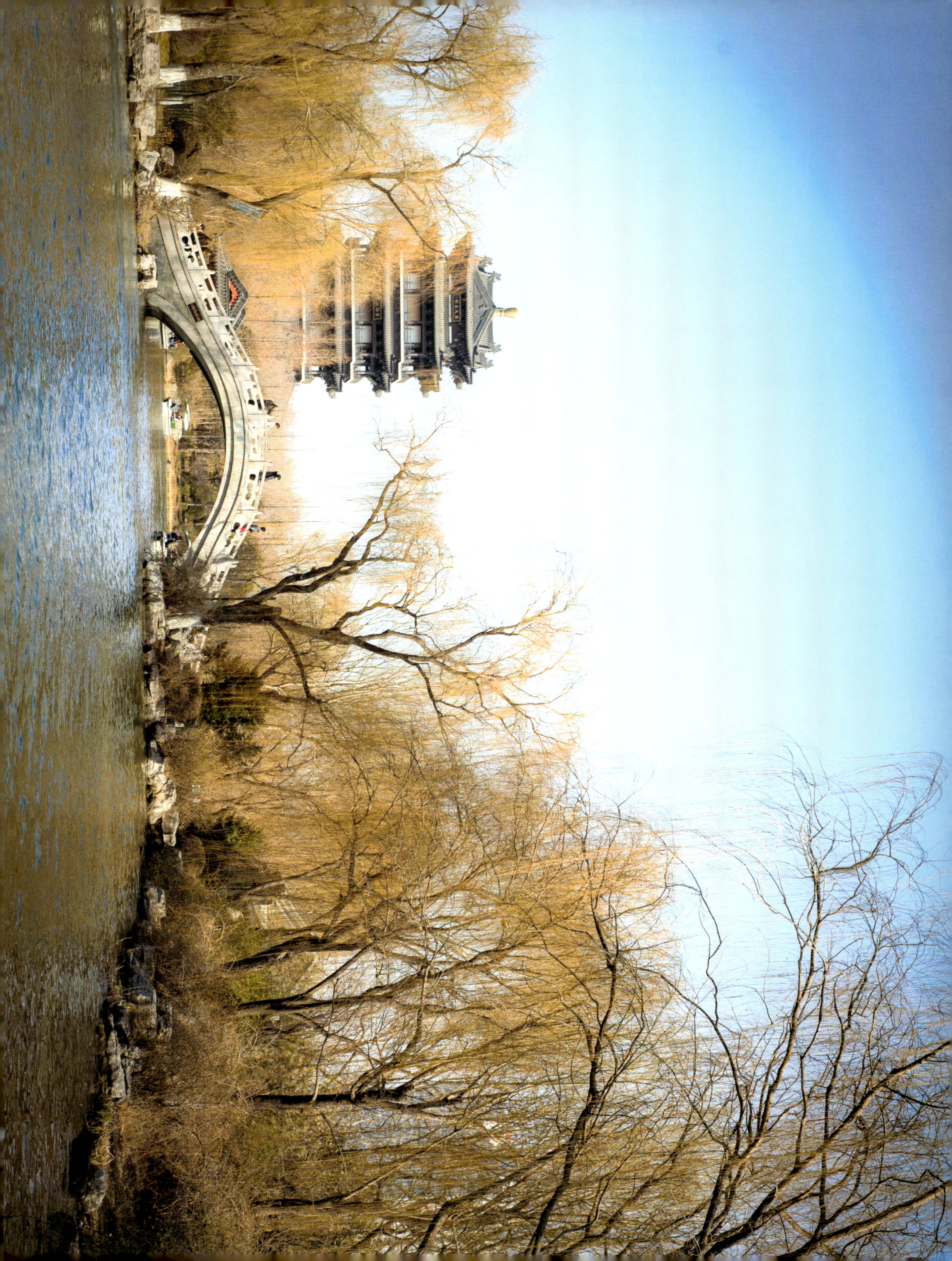

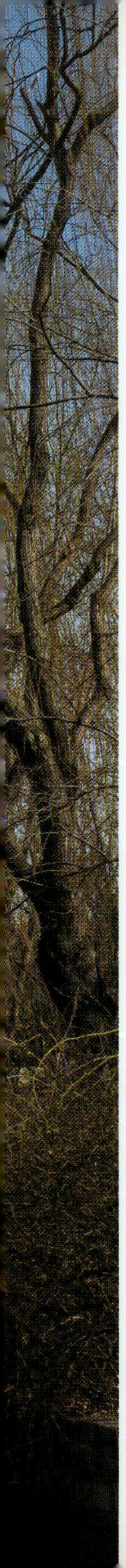

Contents

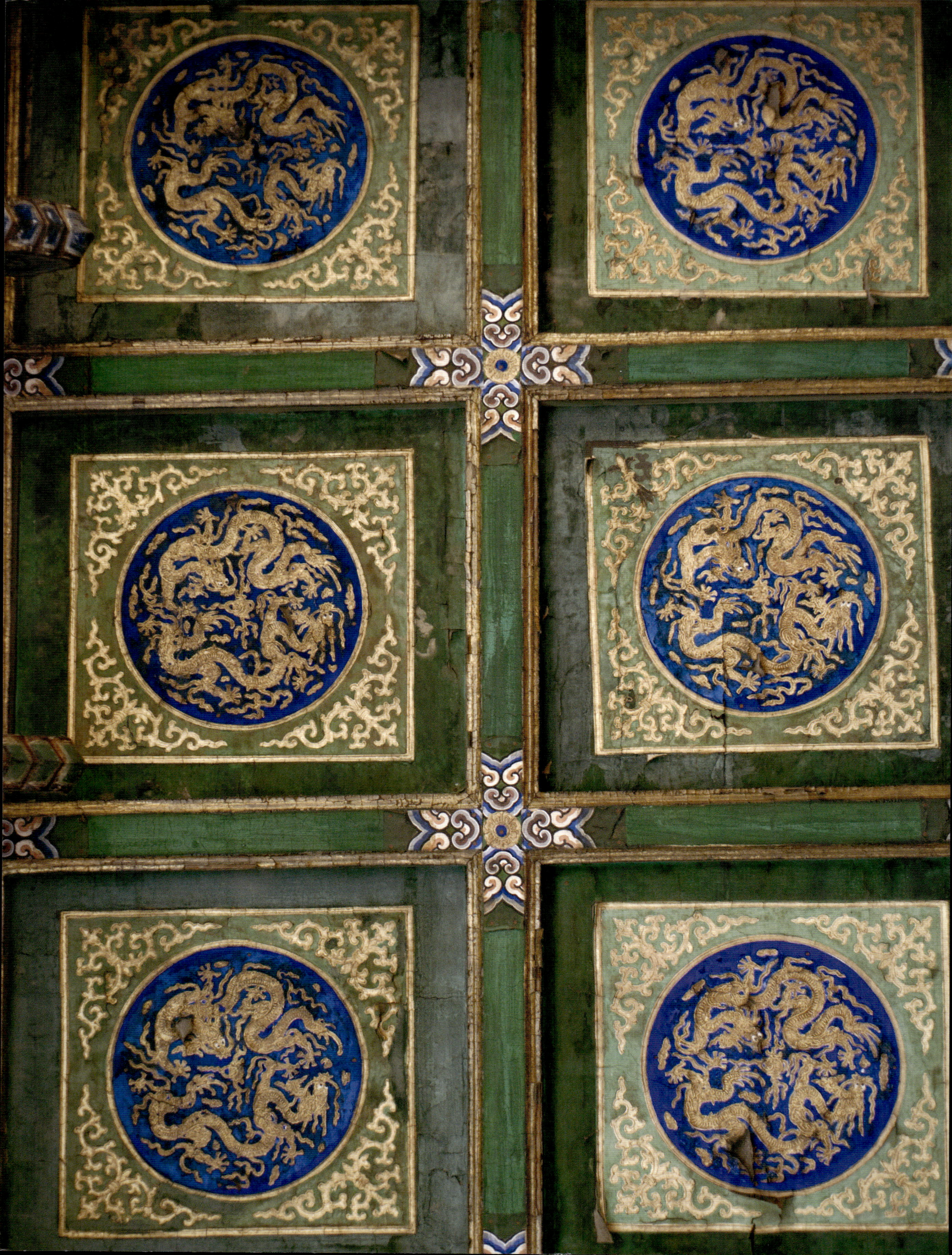

Introduction

For a dreamer like me, the wonders of the ancient world have dazzled my imagination as far back as I can remember. The sights, the smells, the exoticism of something that differs from my home; that is what I yearn for . . . and where I long to be.

China's Ancient Silk Road conjures up romantic images of camel caravans, ornate palaces, exotic spices, and mystery.

If you only a have a short time to visit China, the ancient Silk Road—central to the country's global presence and a cultural essence, woven by mystery, legend, and thousands of years of history—is where you should begin.

Silu is the Chinese name for the Silk Road. This trade route—a network of roads between China and the Mediterranean—circulated culture and valuable goods between Central Asia, West Asia, Africa, and Europe, connecting economics, culture, and commerce between the Western and the Oriental worlds for more than 1,600 years.

Route

With a distance of approximately 4,000 miles by land between China and ancient Rome, filled with foreboding deserts and fierce mountains, traveling between the two regions was a treacherous and often life-threatening trip. Xian, once called Chang'an, was the start to the Silk Road, by way of the Hexi Corridor, stretching to Dunhuang, where the passage forks into three routes: the Southern Route, the Central Route, and the Northern Route. The three disparate routes continue through the Xinjiang Uygur Autonomous Region, extending farther into India, Pakistan, and the ancient city of Rome.

The "Silk Road on the Sea" and the "Southern Silk Road" are also of great importance to trade; however, the original Silk Road that we focus on here was instrumental in opening up a world that had never been experienced before, linking the spirit of the East to the development of the West: China to Rome.

History

China was the first country to produce silk, and this process was first thought to have been invented by the wife of the Yellow Emperor, Leizu, around the year 2696 BC. Leizu is credited with creating the first loom, and therefore also the first silk cloth.

Named the Silk Road in the nineteenth century by German geographer Ferdinand von Richtofen, Silu, the trade route along an ancient road, was mainly used for trading China's valuable natural assets, mainly silk. The Romans discovered this silk as they conquered civilizations, and interest in its origin began. A sort of relay system from one trader to another brought silk through the deserts and mountains of Eurasia. It was an immeasurably dangerous route; beyond the innumerable natural barriers were human barriers, such as pirates.

With an increasing demand for silk in Rome, soldiers set out with gold, silver, and precious gems to conquer or trade with what they called the “silk people.” Most soldiers never returned, falling prey to conditions of the land. Those who made their way farther East were thwarted at the great desert door and forced to retreat. Through these times of exploration and failure, civilizations began to sprout up along the route, creating structures that eventually led themselves to encampments, residents, places of worship, and more, finally connecting Rome and China after attempting to do so for hundreds of years. This became the start of a new world for both the East and the West; it was a connection of precious goods and resources, but also an amalgamation of diverse cultural ideas.

From the time of the Han Dynasty, when Zhang Qian opened up the Silk Road, until the great collapse of the Yuan Dynasty, this trading passageway thrived. China became dependent on its silk trade during the Yuan Dynasty. This is when Genghis Khan conquered the small states to spread his empire, and for the first time in history, dramatically disparate cultures and economic centers were united, as the Silk Road linked China, India, Persia, Arabia, Greece, and Rome.

Although Marco Polo was not the first European to reach China, he was the first to leave a written account of his experience, and was therefore the most famous explorer of his time. His tales inspired many others, such as Christopher Columbus, to embark on similar paths.

What happened to trade along the ancient Silk Road? Much of it stands today, however it has become merely a shadow of what it once was. Myriad geopolitical changes, the rise of the shipping industry, and widespread epidemics like the bubonic plague ultimately degenerated person-to-person trade in the region and the use of the route. Today, city centers continue to produce and sell goods, but the connectors between one country to the next have faded with the shifting threads of time.

Today

Much of the Ancient Silk Road passes through present-day war zones and countries once shrouded under the impenetrable Iron Curtain. Mongolia sits to the East, and Azerbaijan to the West. This area is vastly undeveloped, with migratory inhabitants, and seminomadic farmers, and much of the imagined “action” and excitement of the alluringly mysterious Silk Road is centered around Uzbekistan and Kazakhstan cities and mainland China. Even to this day, China offers the most protected and visited site on the route, with 3,100 miles of the “Silk Routes Network of the Chang’an-Tianshan Corridor” prominently featured in the UNESCO World Heritage List.

This portion of China, rich with centuries of culture, includes remote sections of the Great Wall, markets, temples, palaces, and more.

In addition to the region's rich and fabled history, much of the allure is found in its relative inaccessibility. For travelers and visitors, it's still fairly difficult to access China, and even more so the Silk Road. A travel visa is required from the United States, and it can take weeks to obtain permission to visit. If you plan to visit, be sure to give yourself a few weeks for the approval process.

In addition to stringent travel restrictions, visiting the area can be problematic since the region's culture remains fairly untouched by the modern Western world. Internet access is incredibly limited, signage is in Chinese, there is a daily hustle and bustle of thousands of people, and there's a dramatic language barrier for English speakers without a guide.

On the route between Beijing and the Shandong region, ghost cities the size of Manhattan rise up in all directions. The high-speed rail from Beijing traverses hundreds of miles of uninhabited countryside, shantytowns filled with factory workers, and more. This distance has enabled inhabitants of the Silk Road, hours from any major city and *worlds* away, to continue to practice ancient ritual, worship at thousand-year-old temples, and walk the streets of what feels to be a relatively untouched and unchanged region, culturally speaking.

Ancient traditions abound there, and Chinese philosophers like Confucius continue to be honored and revered with a clear and deep cultural respect from the people of the Silk Road.

The Future

Even today, China's trade initiatives between East Asia and Europe are in play. In 2013, Chinese President Xi Jinoing began talks to create a New Silk Road, focusing on infrastructure to connect the continents. The projected cost to China is more than $16 billion, with pledges from other countries for more financial support. Those infrastructure developments are now underway, and railway, road, and pipeline expansion are all aspects of the new Silk Road Economic Belt. This new expanded route will include trade routes to Poland, Georgia, Azerbaijan, Kazakhstan, Russia, Tajikistan, Sri Lanka, and Indonesia, making it the largest global trade route in our age. When complete, the project, according to Wade Shepard's interview with *Want China Times* for Forbes.com, will be valued at an unprecedented $21.1 trillion. It will offer a new way for manufacturers to transport goods to consumers on both sides of Eurasia through an overland rail connection via Russia (the trans-Eurasian rail), which has already begun. Why is this so significant? The expense of air transportation and the duration of sea travel will no longer be barriers to massive global trade. Food, textiles, and even televisions are the first steps in daily train exchanges between the continents, and the products are increasing at a rapid rate. First, in 2012 they began with a few trains each day, and two years later more than five hundred trains per day were running back and forth. However, according to a main trading company called New Silk Way Logistics, in the beginning, fewer than 10 percent of the trains going Eastbound were loaded with goods for a return trip. Now, we see an influx of European products in China that includes luxury goods, chemicals, cars, and food, and we are truly only in the beginning. The monetization of this trade route is the pavement for enormous global wealth in big business, and with any luck, at least some of that will reach those who truly need help. One can only hope that positive social outcomes flourish from something that has such potential for personal, political, and corporate consumption. What begins as a thirst for goods and connects us physically by nature must spur international diplomatic connections as well. One can never underestimate the East's thirst for the West, and vice versa. Will this trade future be secure, reliable, and effective? Only time will tell as a thriving economic trade history repeats itself in the Modern Age, a new Silk Road mirroring the Silk Road of the past, and centering once again in Chinese cultural roots.

Suggested Ten-Day Trip Itinerary

Day 1: Fly to Beijing.

Day 2: Arrive in Beijing and transfer to hotel in Beijing. Taste Chinese delicacies, like fried grasshopper and silkworms on a stick—for the more adventurous—and Beijing's famed Roast Duck.

Day 3: Climb the Great Wall and visit a jade and cloisonné factory. Stay in Beijing.

Day 4: Morning: visit the Forbidden City (Palace Museum); Afternoon: visit Tian'anmen Square.

Day 5: Afternoon: Take the high-speed rail and travel at 180 miles an hour. Reach Jinan in less than two hours. Private van transfer to Zibo, one of the ceramic centers of China. Stay in Zibo.

Day 6: Visit Zibo ceramics, explore handblown glass and other local crafts and craftsmen. Tour Zhoucun Ancient City. Private van transfer to Qufu. Stay in Qufu.

Day 7: Tour Qufu, hometown of Confucius. Visit Confucius Temple, family residence, and family cemetery. Stay in Qufu.

Day 8: Private van transfer to Tai'an. Visit Mount Tai, one of the five Sacred Mountains of China. Transfer to Jinan. Stay in Jinan.

Day 9: Lantern Festival (dependent on time of year) at the Baotu Springs Garden. Tour the charming Daming Lake and other local sites. Stay in Jinan.

Day 10: Leave for Beijing in the morning via high-speed rail, and then transfer to Beijing Capital Airport. Depart in the afternoon.

Sources:

China.org.cn
"China's New Silk Road" by Wade Shepard for Forbes.com
"China's New Silk Road Hinges on a Small Pakistan Port" by Faseeh Mangi for Bloomberg.com
"Europe Finally Wakes Up to The New Silk Road" by Wade Shepard for Forbes.com
"Silk Road: Trip of a Lifetime" by Chriss Moss for telegraph.co.uk

Extended Itinerary

Day 11: A visit to the Silk Markets in Beijing

Day 12: A trip to the modern city center of Beijing, where you can see firsthand the fast-paced life of Chinese city locals as they interact with technology and fashion; it's like nothing you've seen before.

Why Go Now?

- Very few nonlocals
- Feels like a passage back in time
- Largely underdeveloped region

Challenges

- Strict visa requirements for entry to China
- Mostly local language spoken
- Can be difficult to navigate the infrastructure

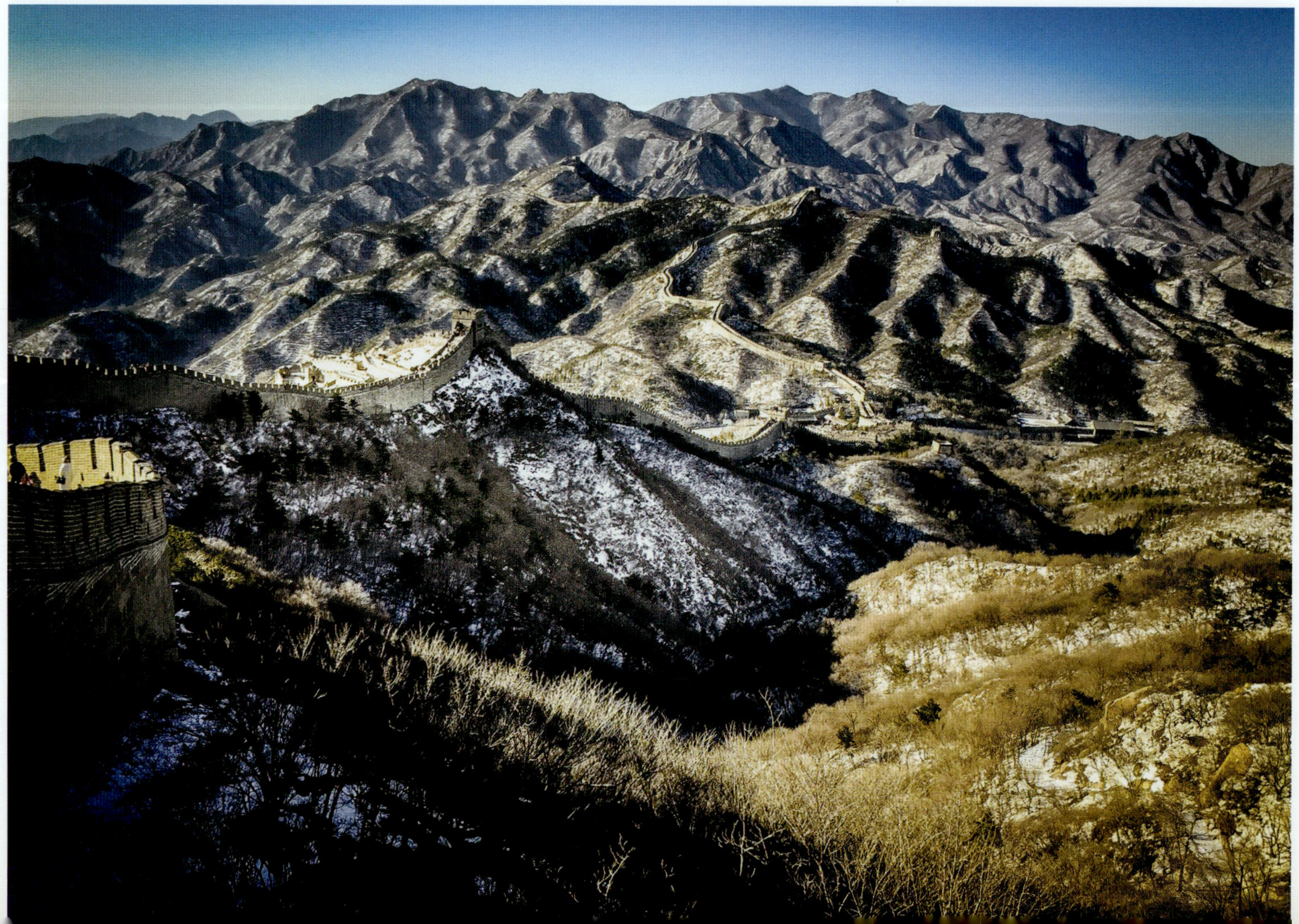

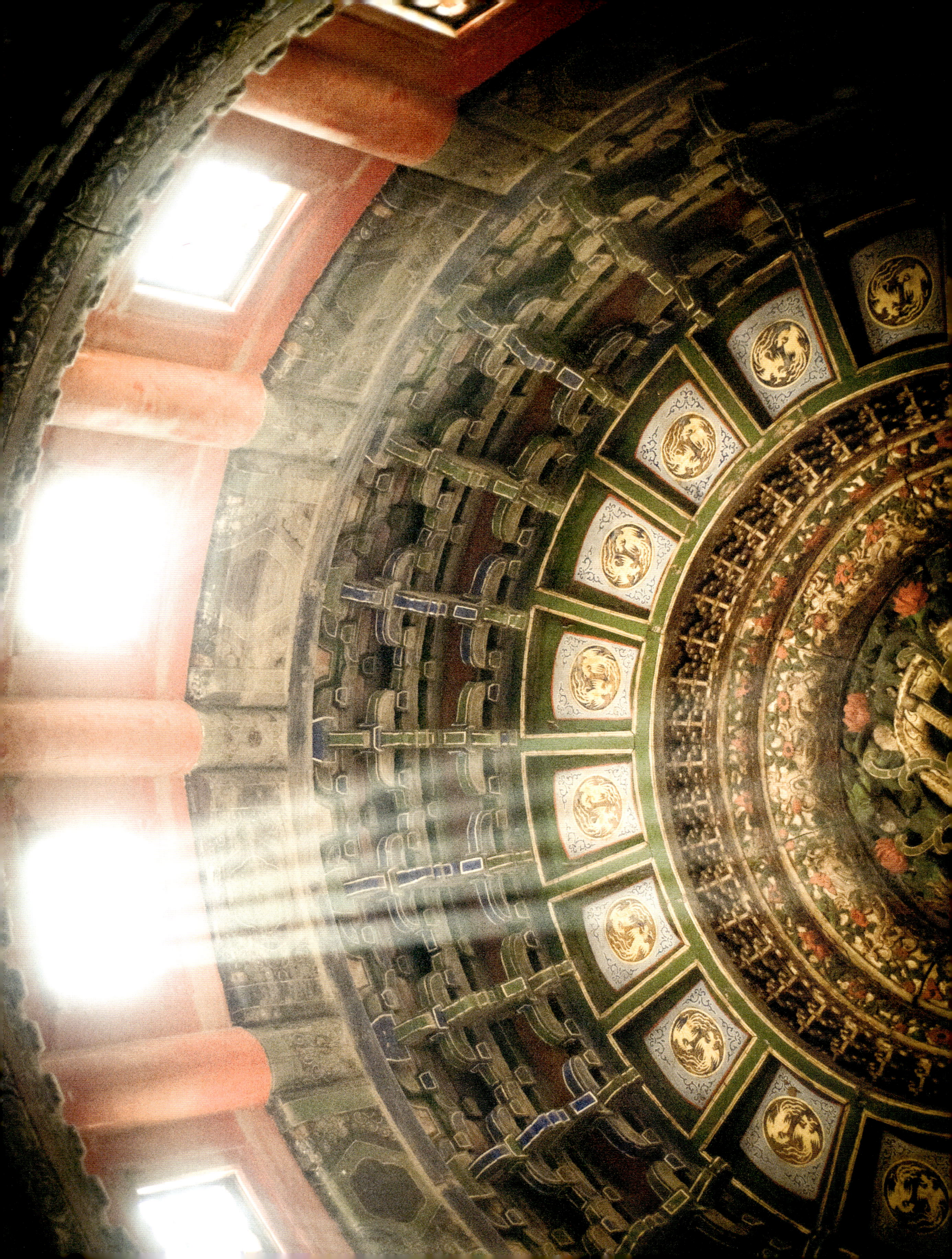

Art & Architecture Along the Silk Road

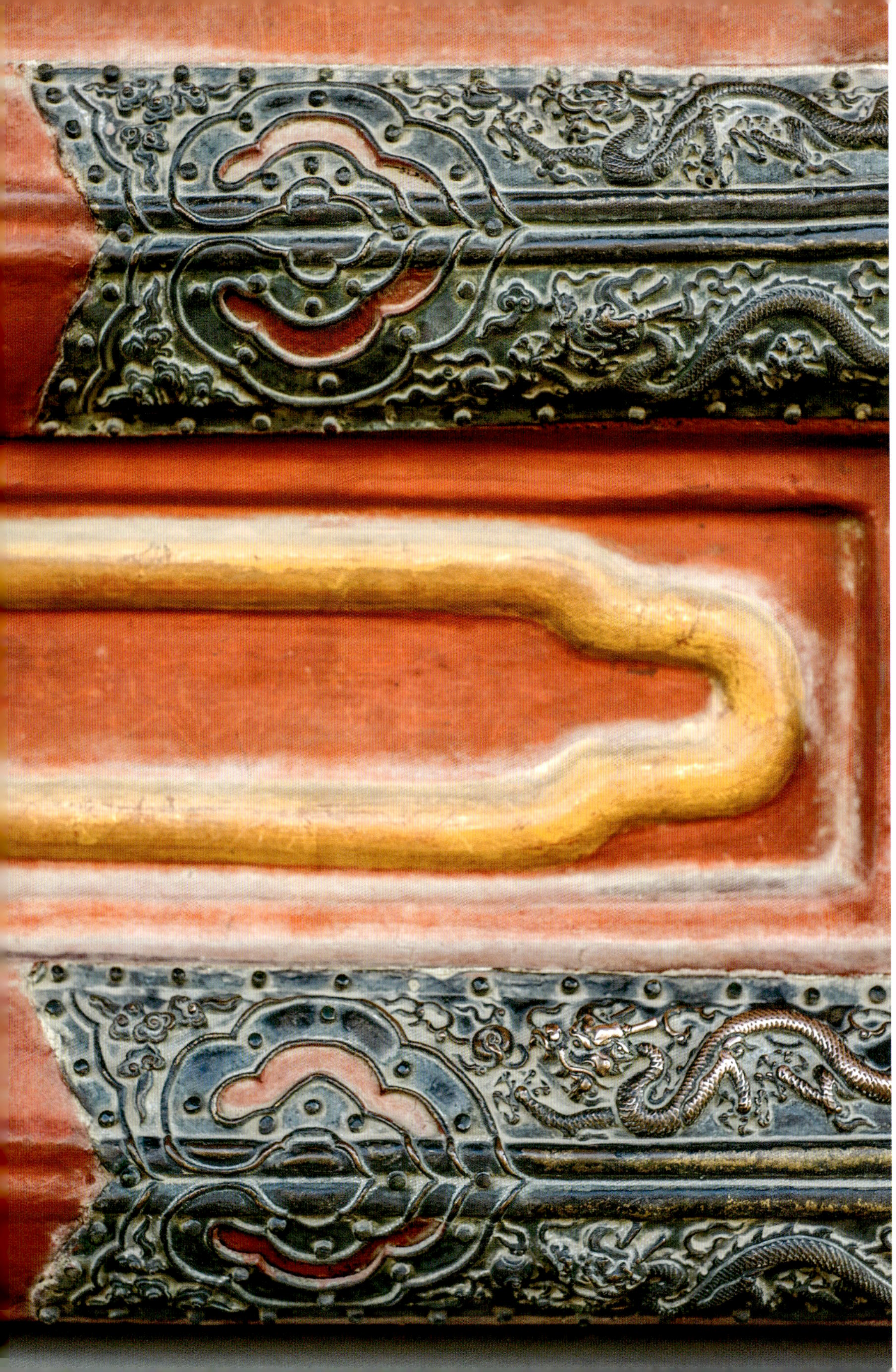

Palaces are filled with fine hand-carved and painted details, like this large wooden door from the Imperial Palace in Beijing.

Beautiful tile and pagodas are a hallmark of Chinese architecture. During the Chinese Dynasties period, pagodas served as a resting place and a place where people would go to drink tea or read poems. Pagodas are a tiered tower with many eaves (areas of roofing that overhang the building's walls). Although they come in many sizes and varying structural shapes, they often attract lightning strikes. Predominantly found in Asia, pagodas are traditionally used for religious worship, especially in Buddhism. The original pagodas were sacred and housed religious relics and writings.

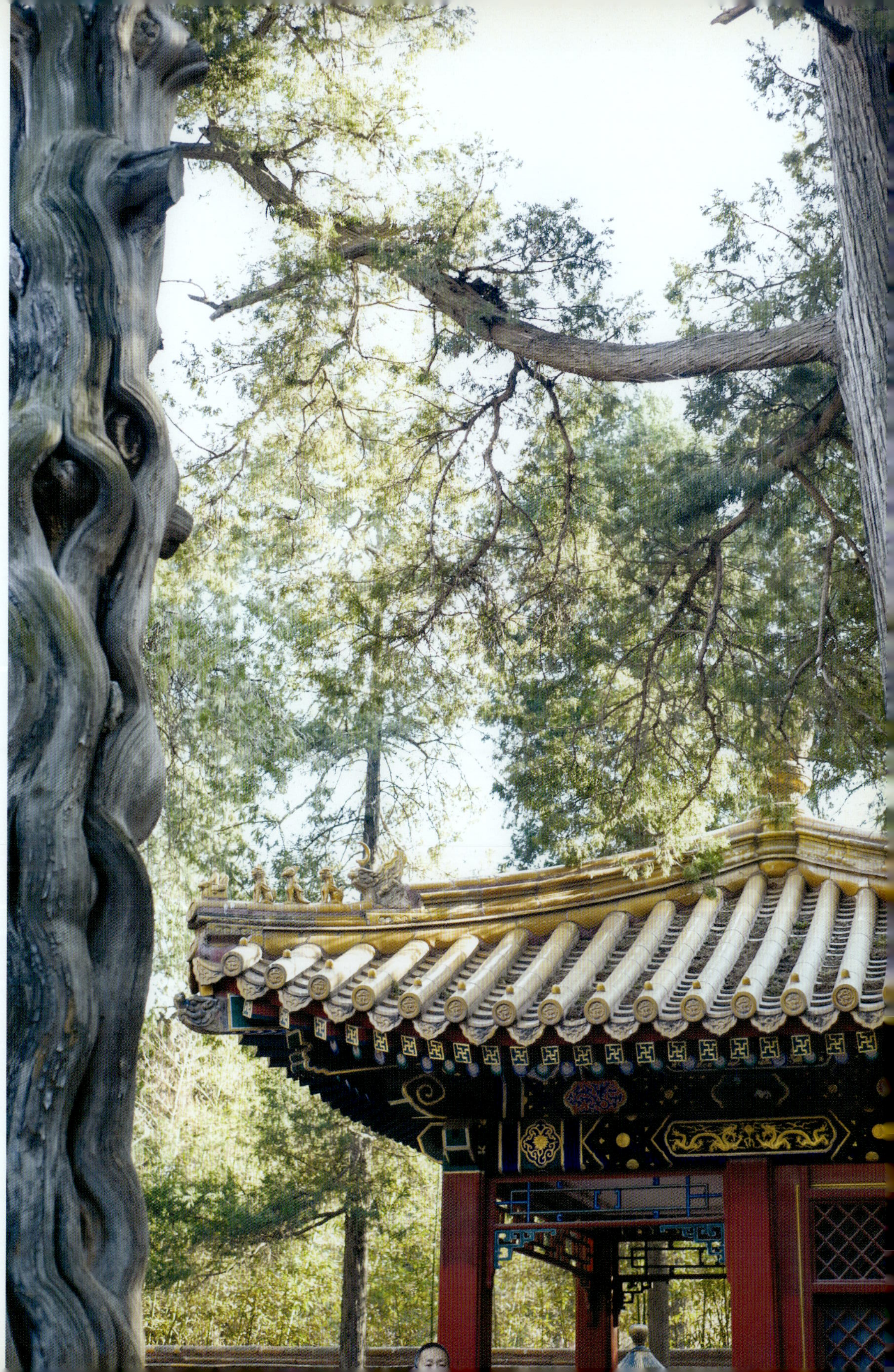

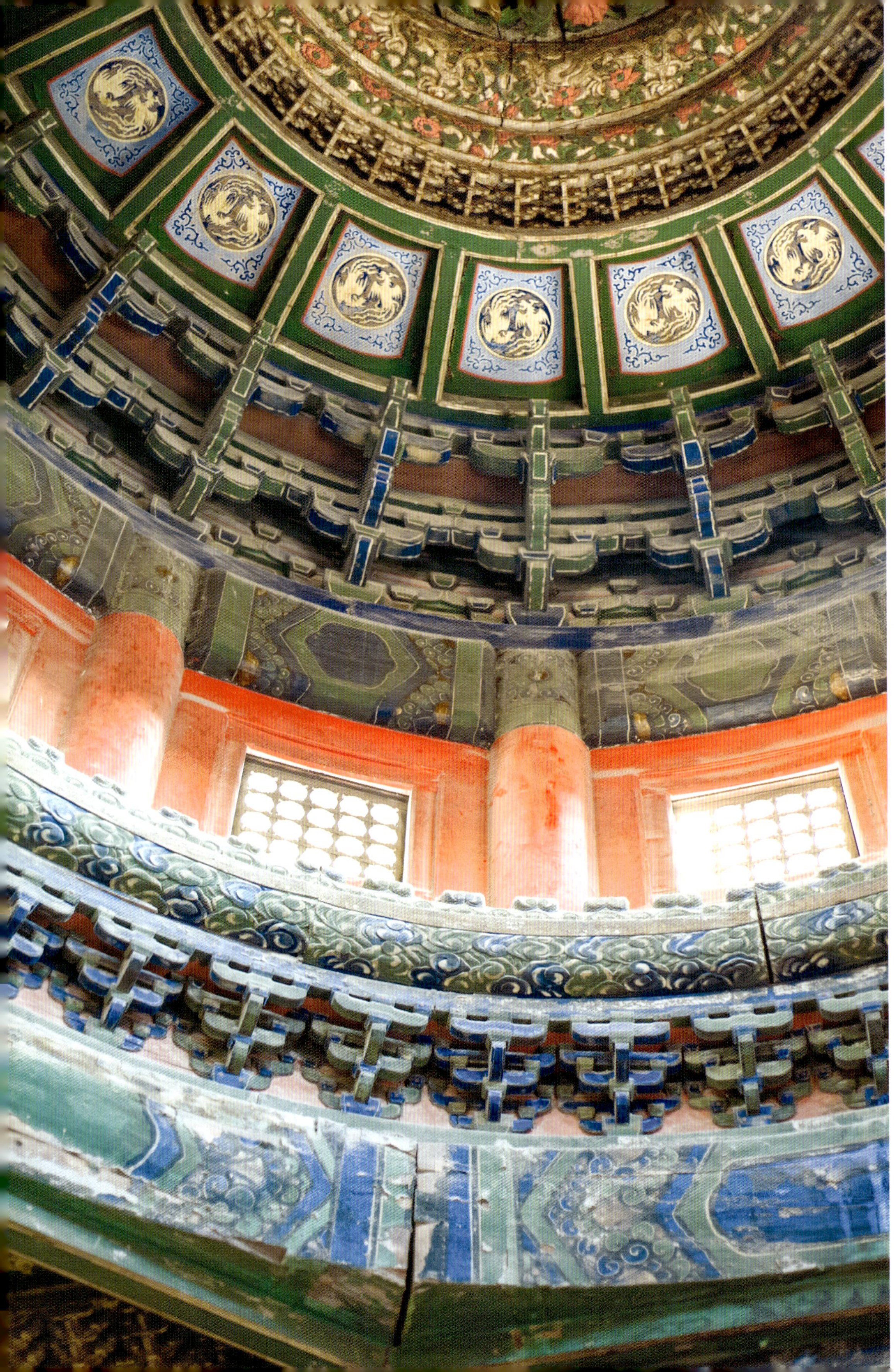

The ceiling of a room in the Imperial Palace. Although little is known about this specific ceiling, much of the palace, which is located within the Forbidden City, was constructed from wood found in the Chinese countryside, marble from quarries outside of Beijing, and brick. Construction started in 1406 and took fourteen years and more than a million workers to complete. Images of the phoenix are carved to indicate that this area was a recreational space for the emperor's wives.

This key rests in a large lock on one of the many doors inside the Imperial Palace. The palace consists of a series of hallways, courtyards, and buildings that are massive in scale. The key's handle is approximately six inches in length.

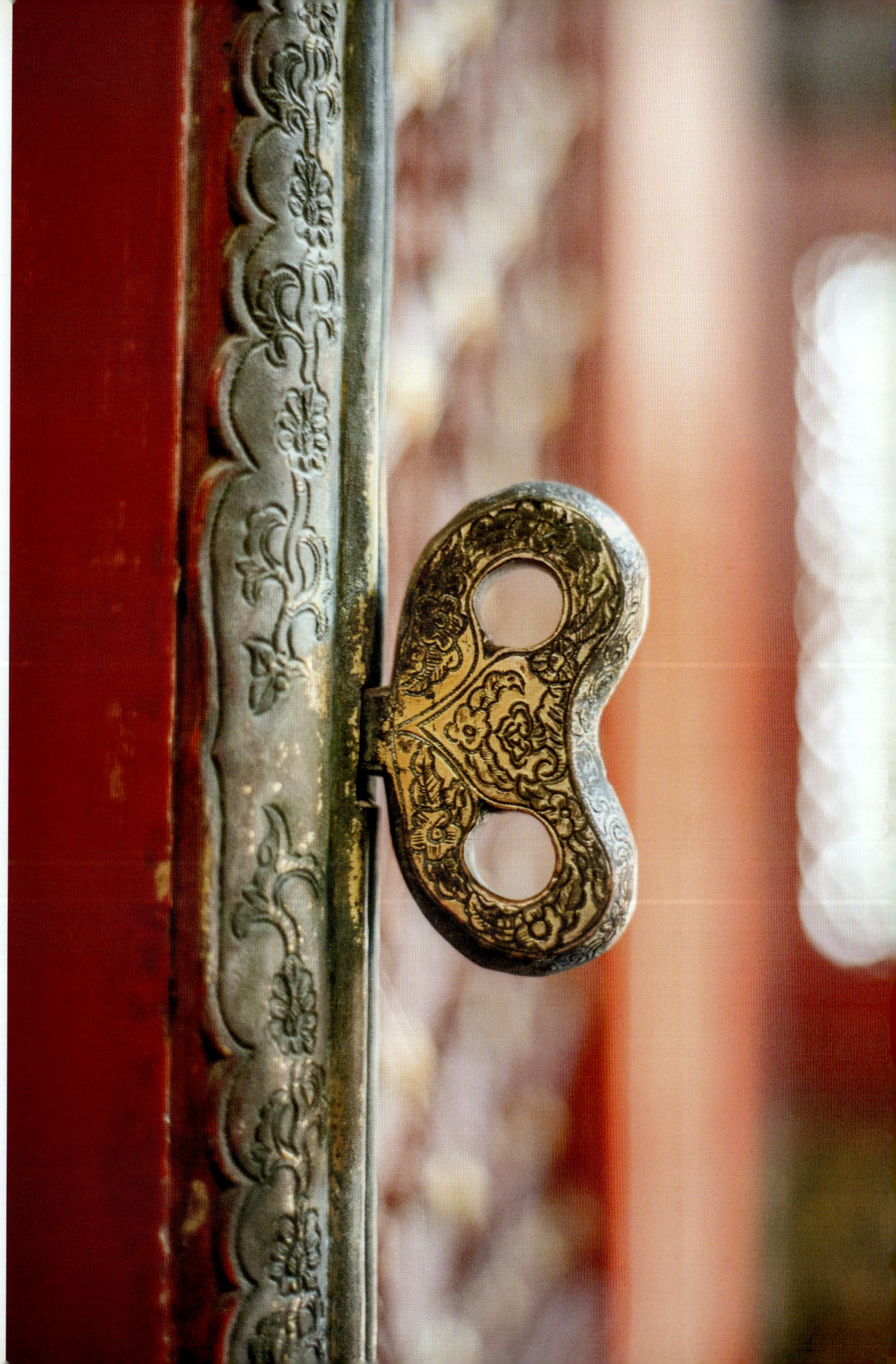

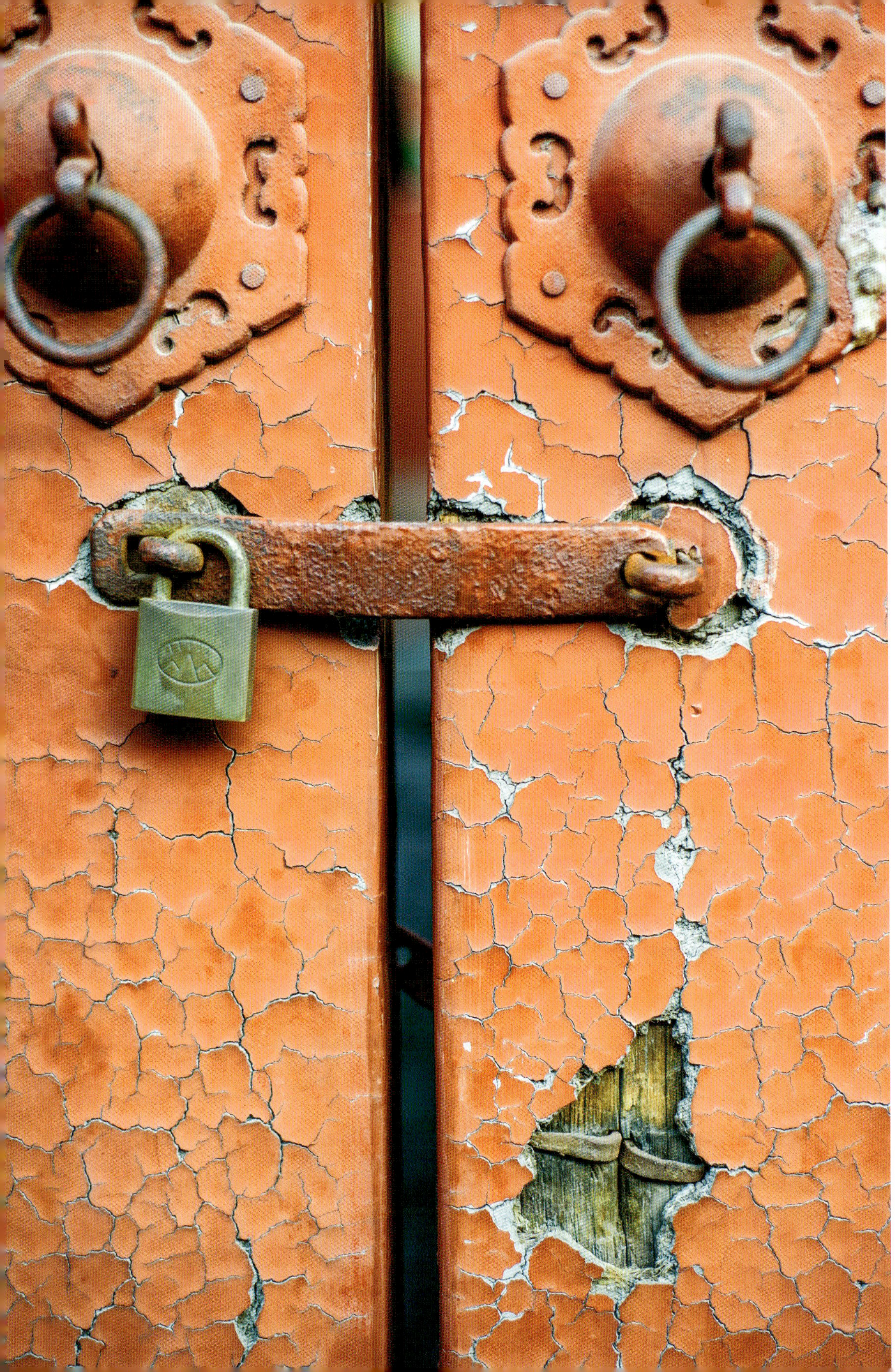

One of the many ancient doors inside of the Imperial Palace. For security, the palace was constructed in such a way that any passage or courtyard could be locked to keep the remainder of the vast area safe from intruders. The palace is so large that only a small portion of it is open to the public.

This door from the Imperial Palace in Beijing is an example of China's most prolific color: red. Colors in Chinese culture are considered auspicious or inauspicious. Black, red, white, and yellow are found in traditional Chinese art; each of these colors corresponds to and represents the five elements.

Red symbolizes joy, good fortune, and fire. Red is the primary color of celebration and is seen throughout clothing, lanterns, and more. Red symbolizes happiness in Chinese culture, and it is a very large part of everything visual. Although red clothing is forbidden at funerals, the names of the dead were once written in red.

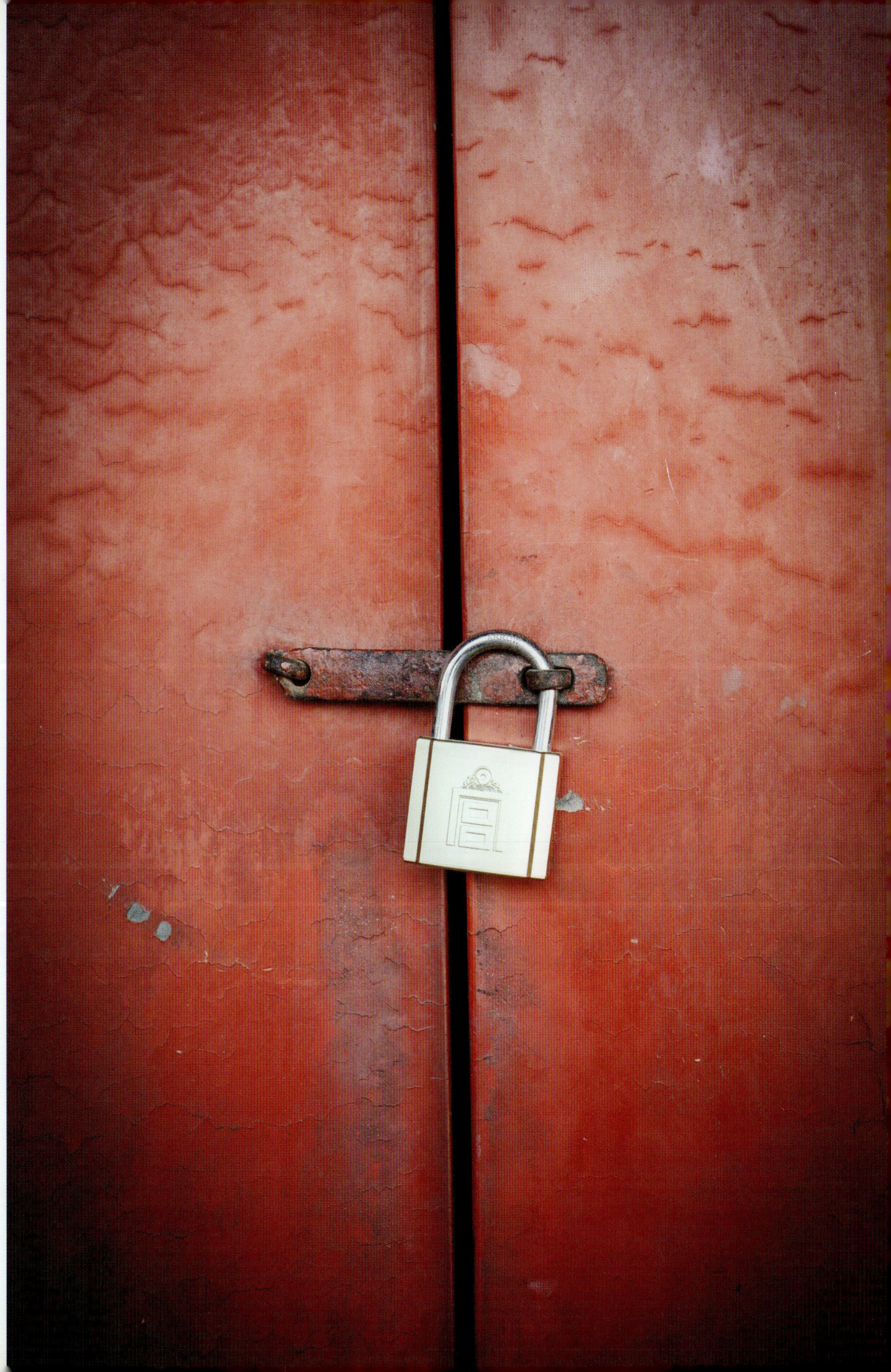

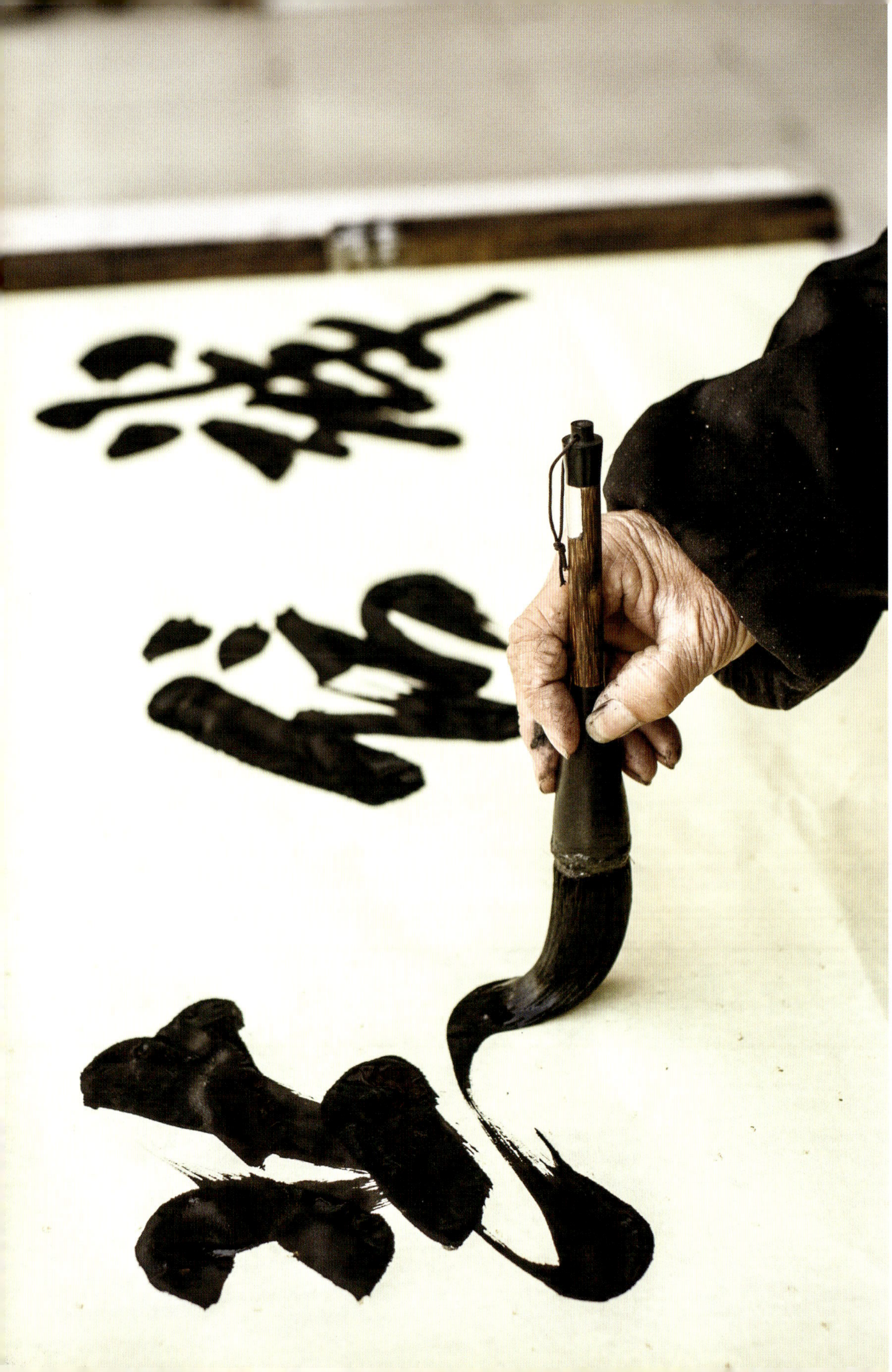

The tools used in traditional Chinese calligraphy include a writing brush, ink stick, ink slab, and paper. The nib of the brush can be made from various materials, such as wool, horsehair, rabbit hair, goat hair, and even weasel hair. The art has been practiced for more than two thousand years in China. The ink used is a combination of soot, also known as lampblack, and binders. The ink comes in the form of sticks, which the artist will rub on an inkstone together with water to create the proper consistency of ink. Although calligraphers today may use different ink colors, traditionally, only black ink is used in Chinese calligraphy.

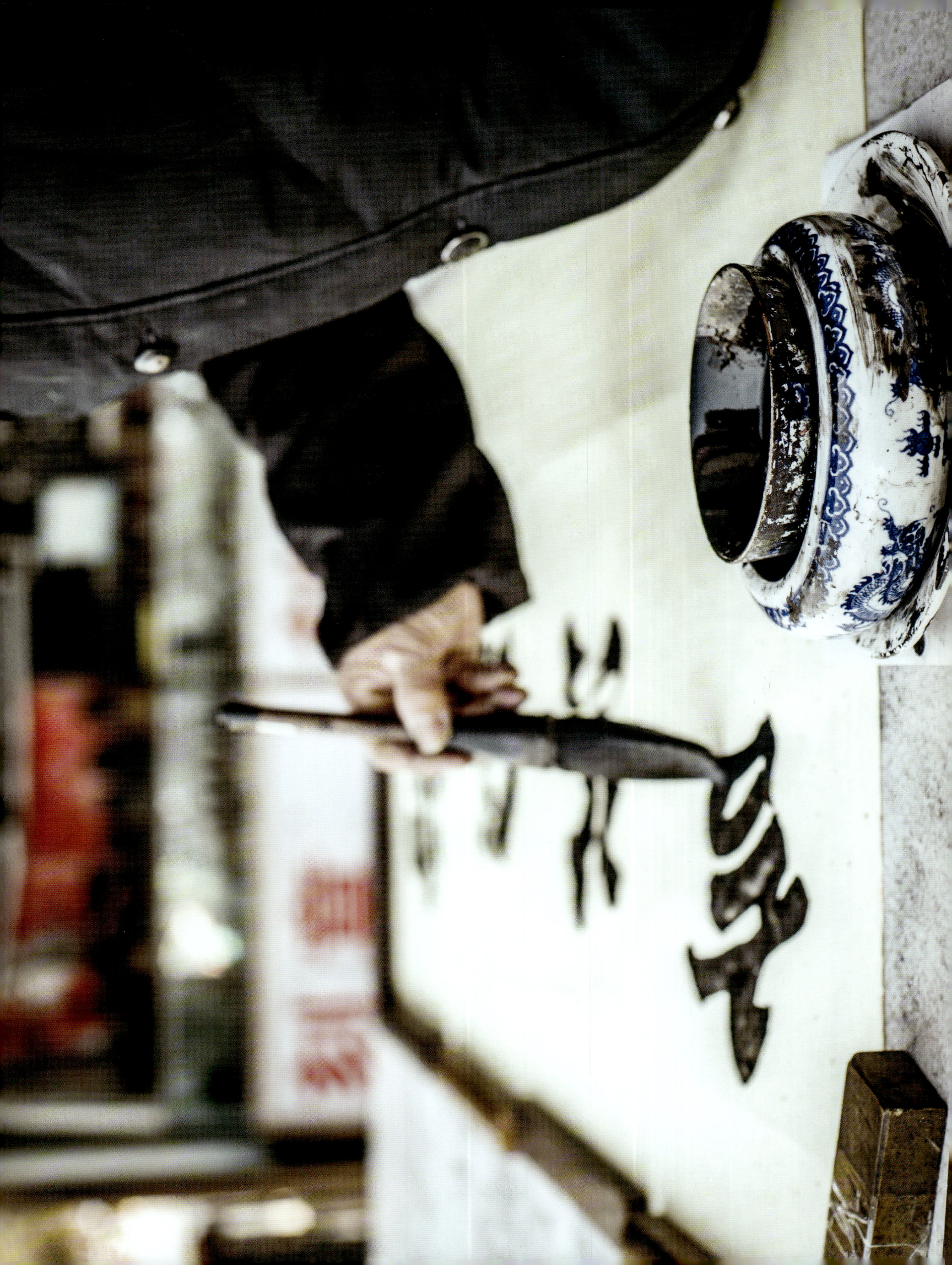

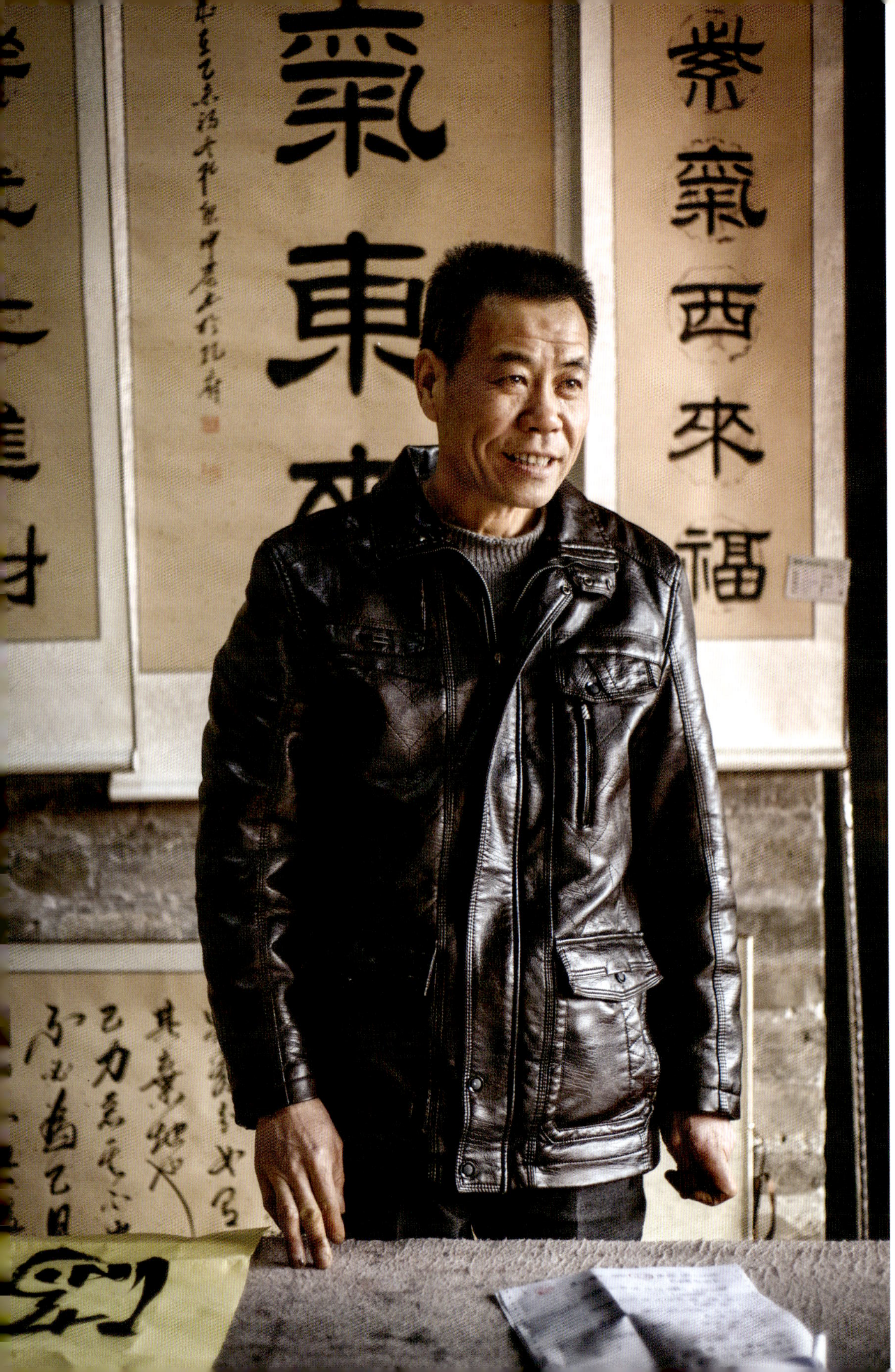

This famed calligraphy artist is a direct descendent of the revered philosopher Confucius. We watch as he draws our names and wishes on a traditional scroll. We wished for vitality, prosperity, joyfulness, and love.

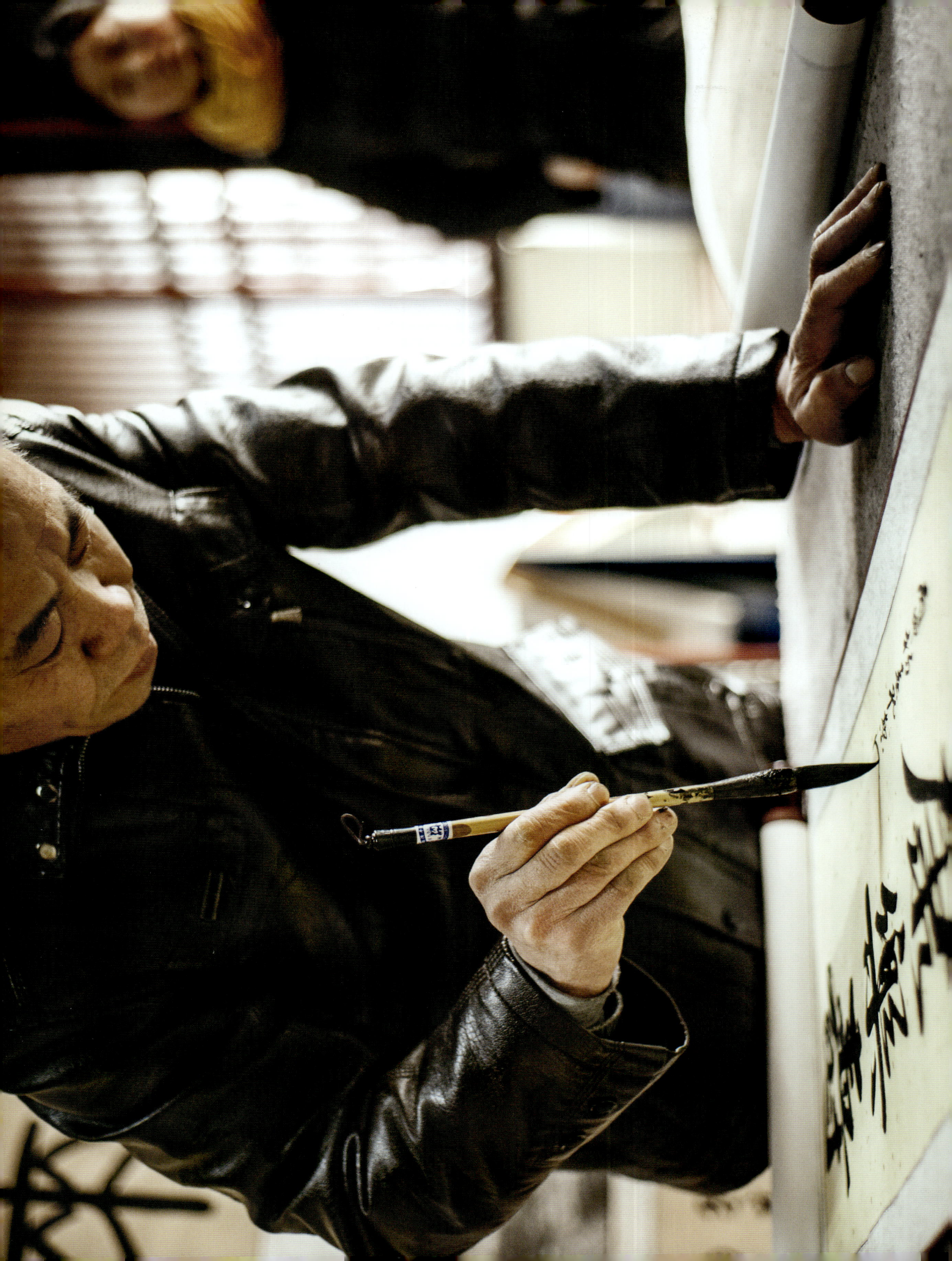

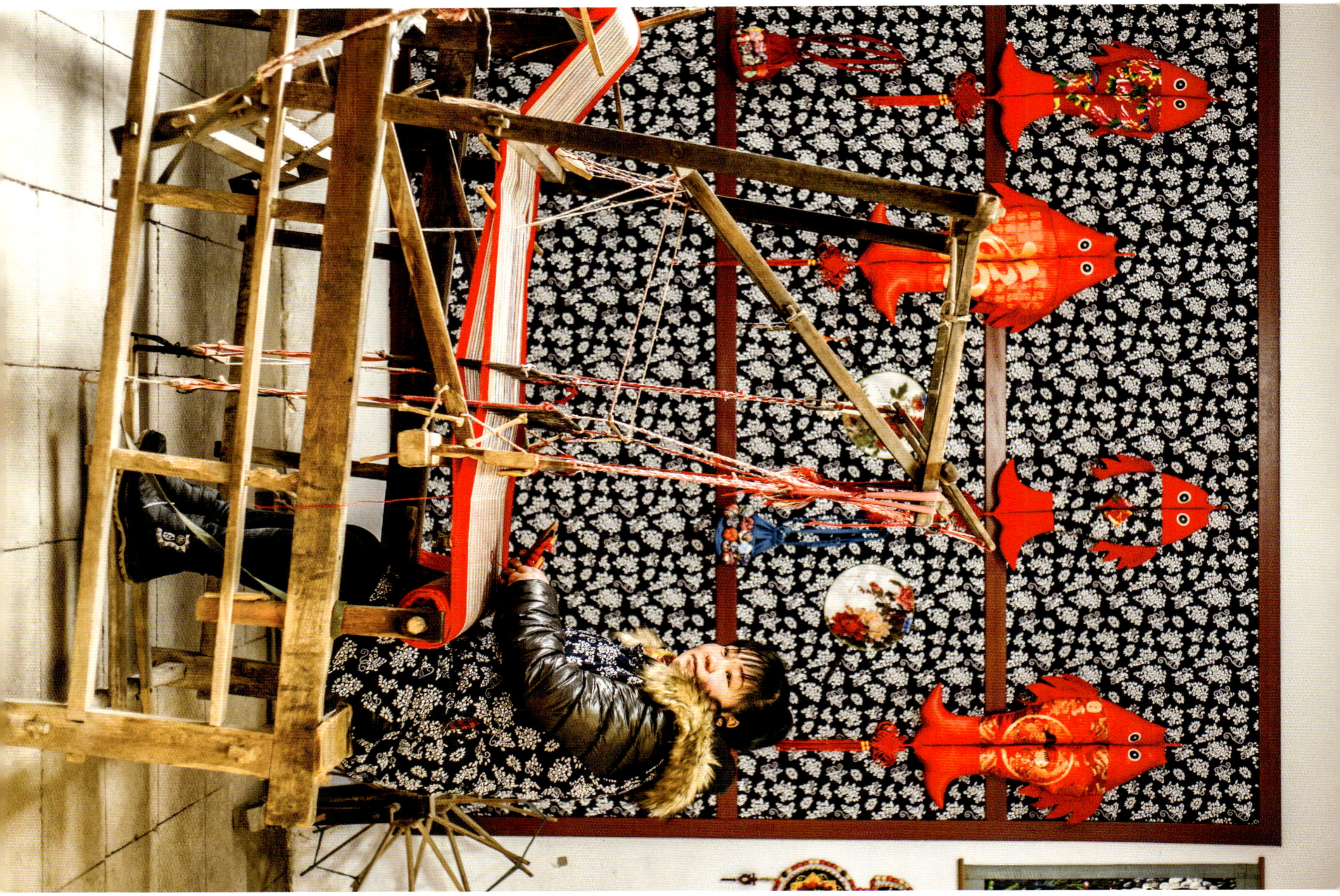

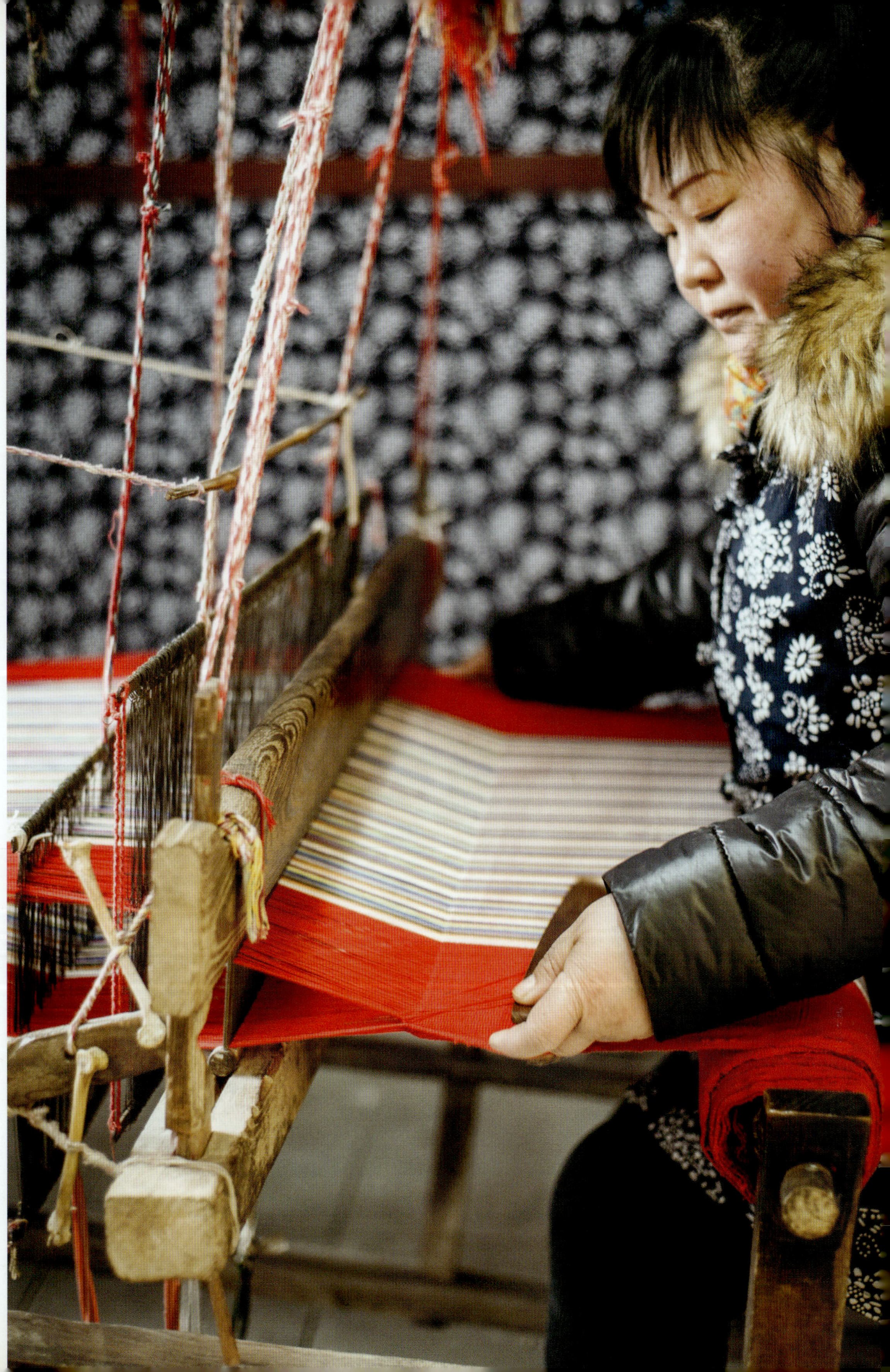

A local artisan weaves on a classic loom in her shop along the Silk Road in Jinan.

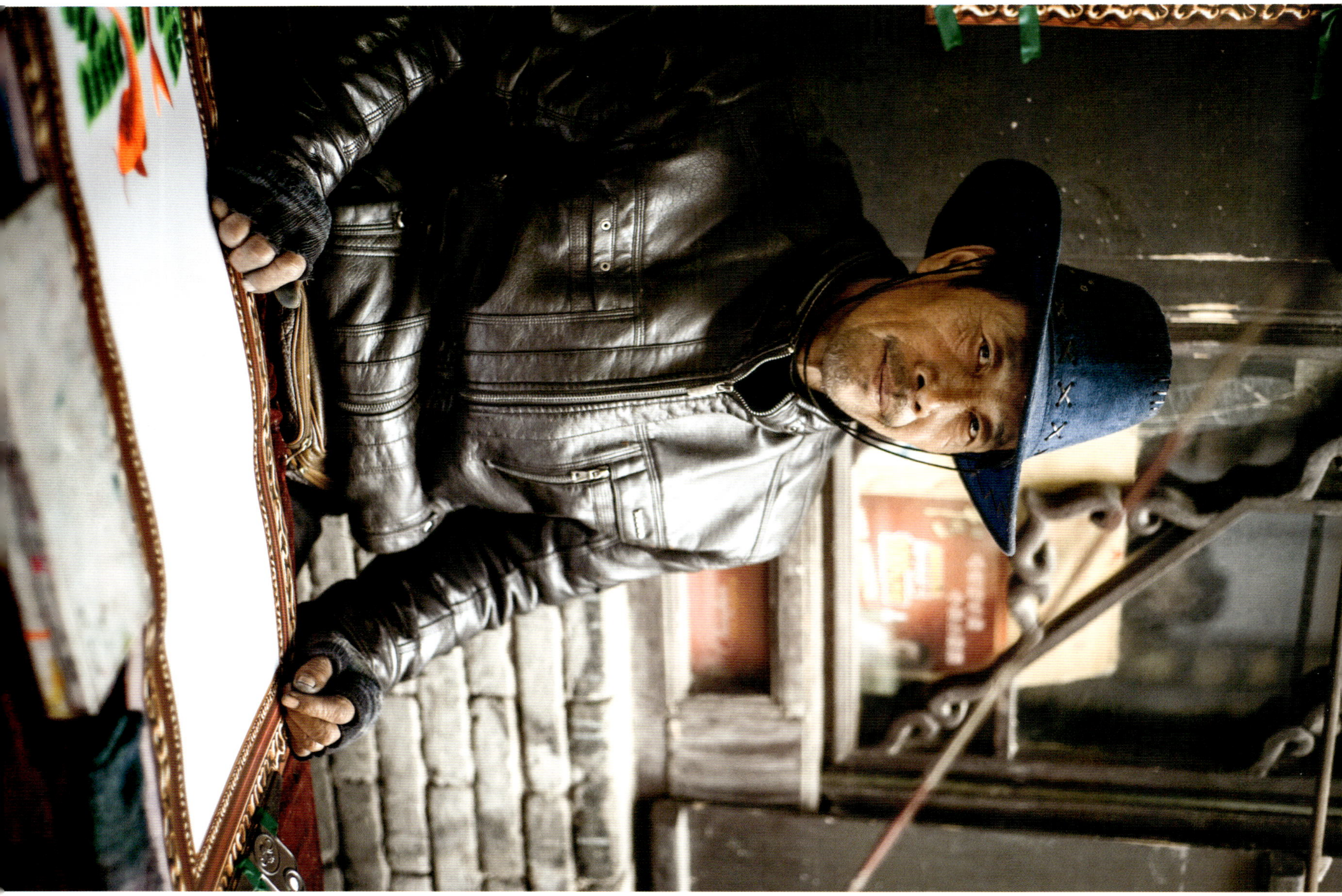

This artist is using Chinese pigments to draw birds and flowers. Within the same piece of art, these birds and flowers are represented in the shape of Chinese characters.

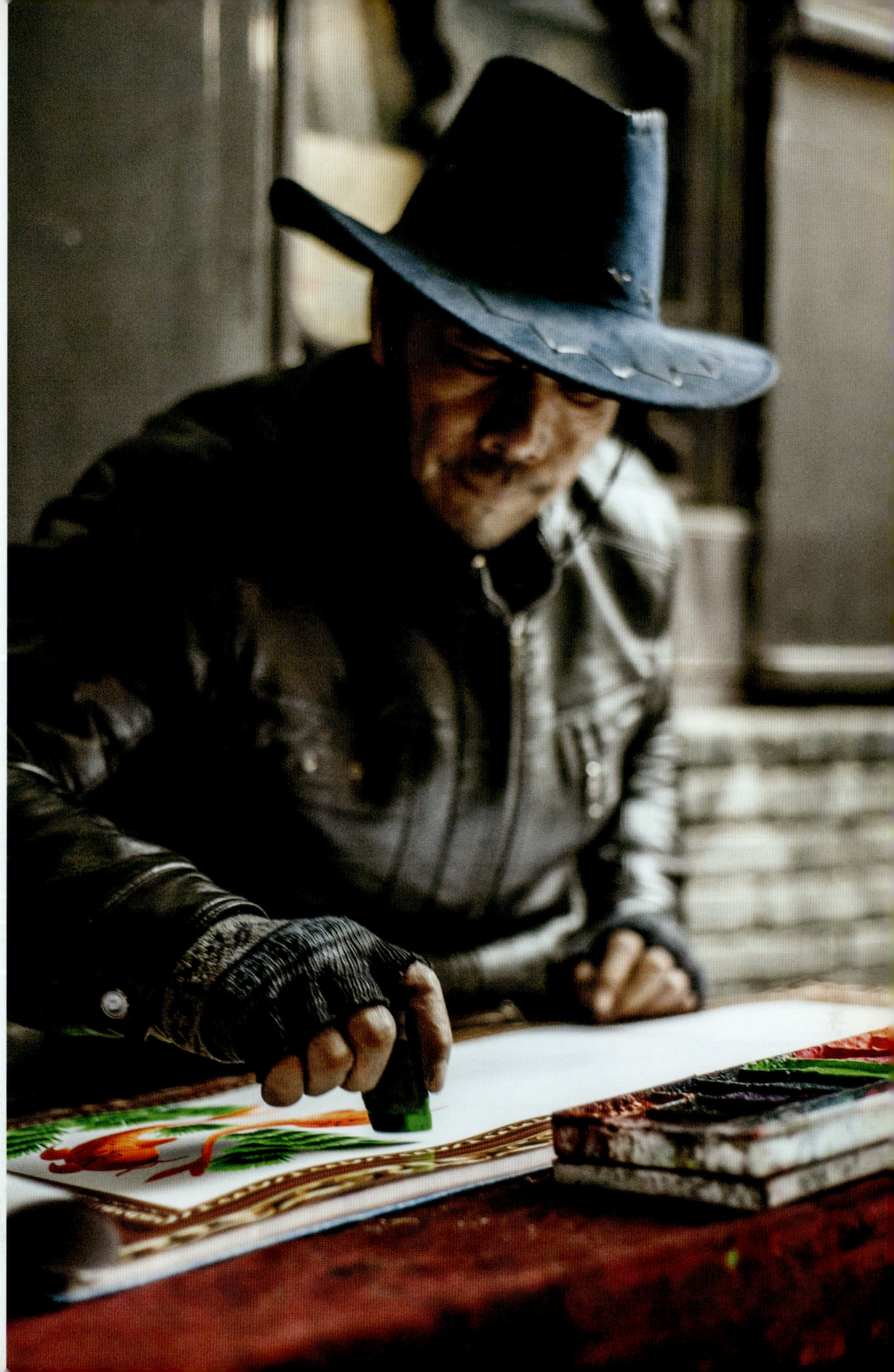

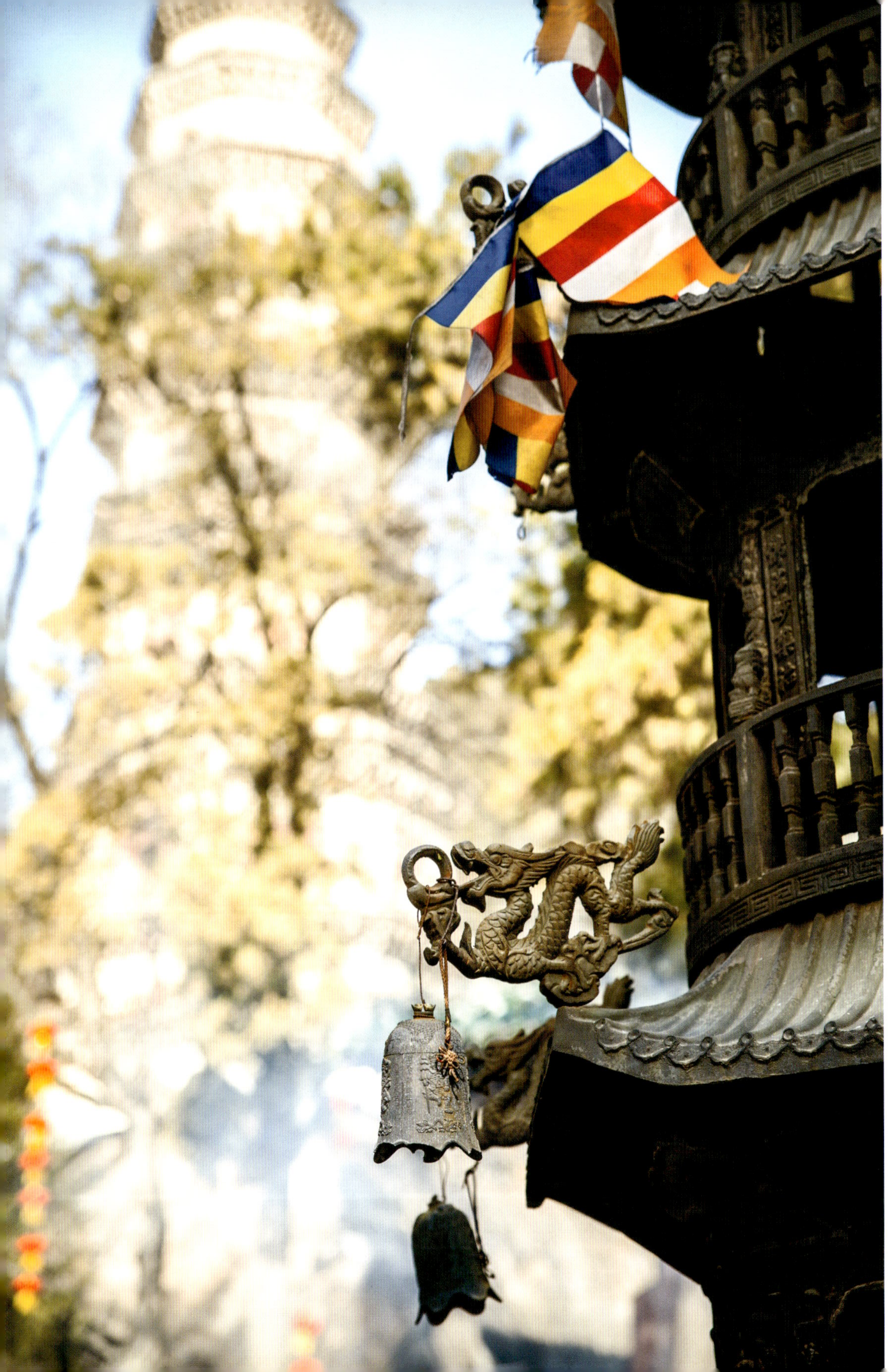

Popular in Chinese mythology and folklore, dragons can be seen throughout the country in art, in architecture, during festivals, woven into clothing, and the dragon is one of the symbols in the Chinese zodiac. Chinese dragons do not breathe fire, and they do not have wings. They are a cultural symbol that represents prosperity and luck.

Although similar to Japanese bonsai, where trees are grown in containers, the art of penjing in China actually came first and was the basis for bonsai. One difference is that the penjing artist may include natural stones in the design. The designs may also be less formal and present more of a landscape scene.

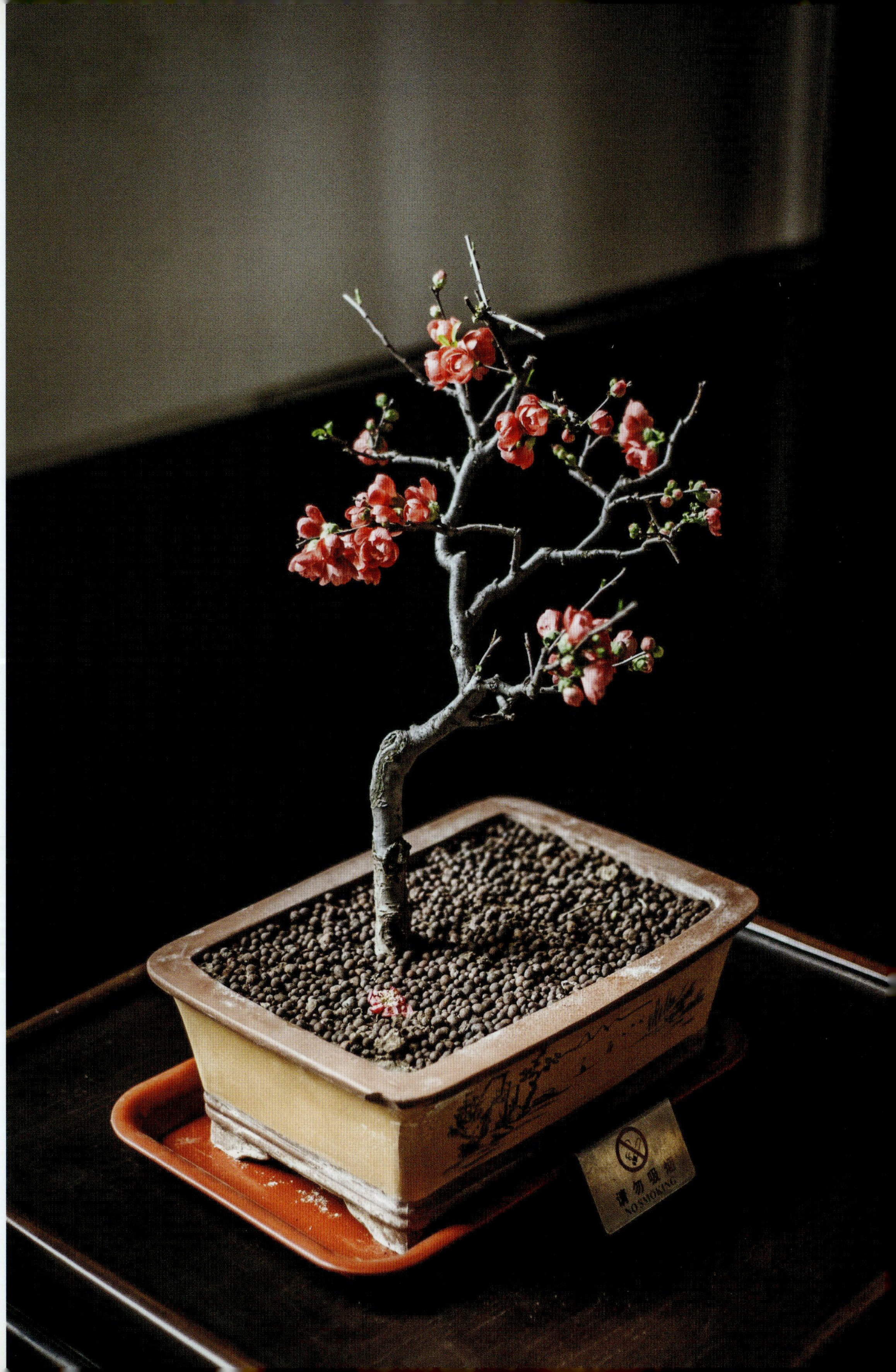

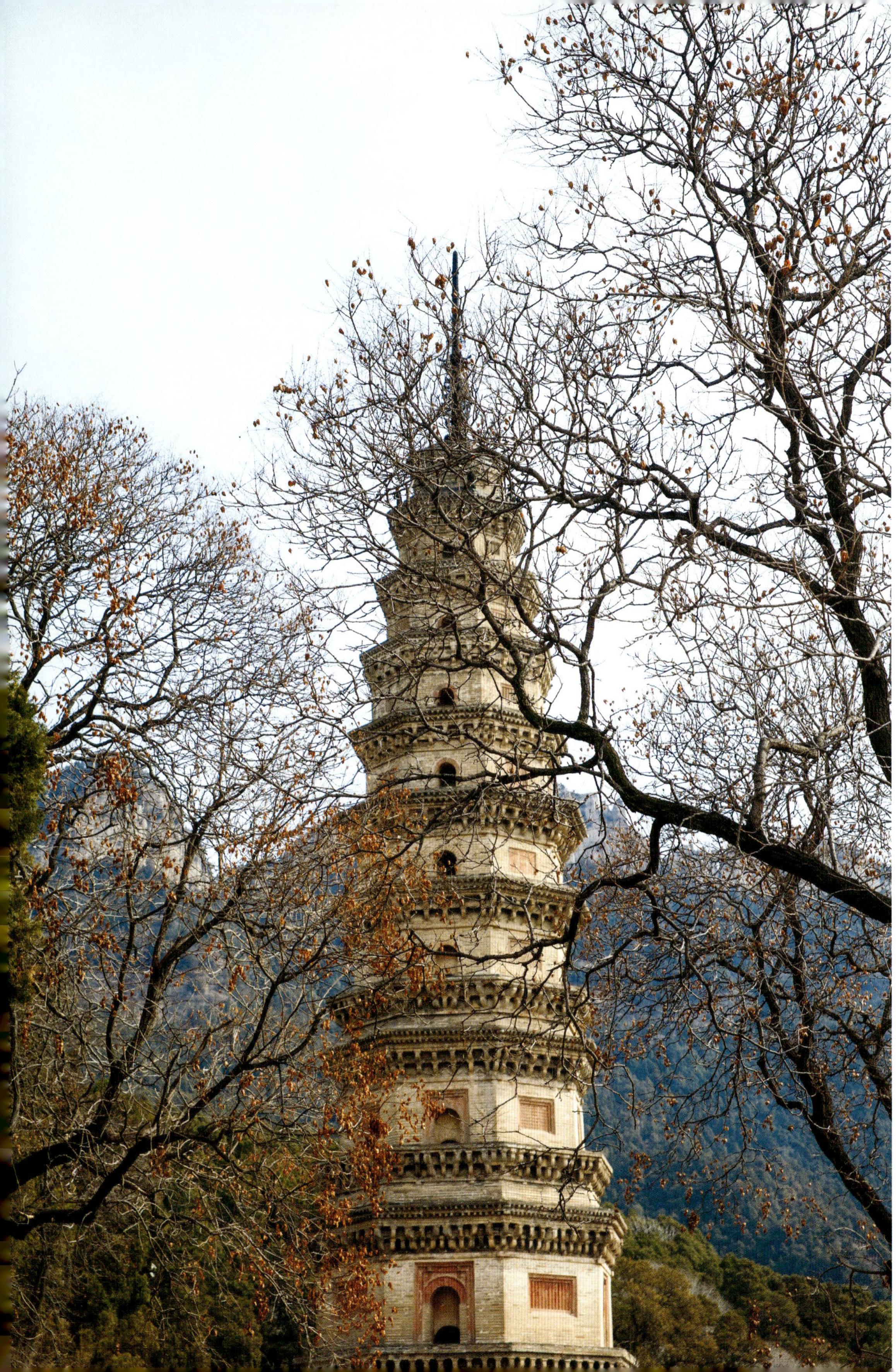

One of the most recognizable structures at Lindyan Temple is the Pizhi Pagoda. Constructed of brick and stone in an octagonal design, it stands just over 177 feet high.

Lingyan Temple, like many others, sits amid stunning scenery in Jinan, located in the Shandong region of China. Lingyan literally means “Temple of the Spiritual Rocks,” and the weight of this meaning can be felt while you are there. The numerous pagodas and pavilion-style structures date back to the eighth century, to the Tang Dynasty, and housed more than five thousand Buddhist monks during its heyday. Many of the 167 structures have been well preserved, and one can see that no two are identical.

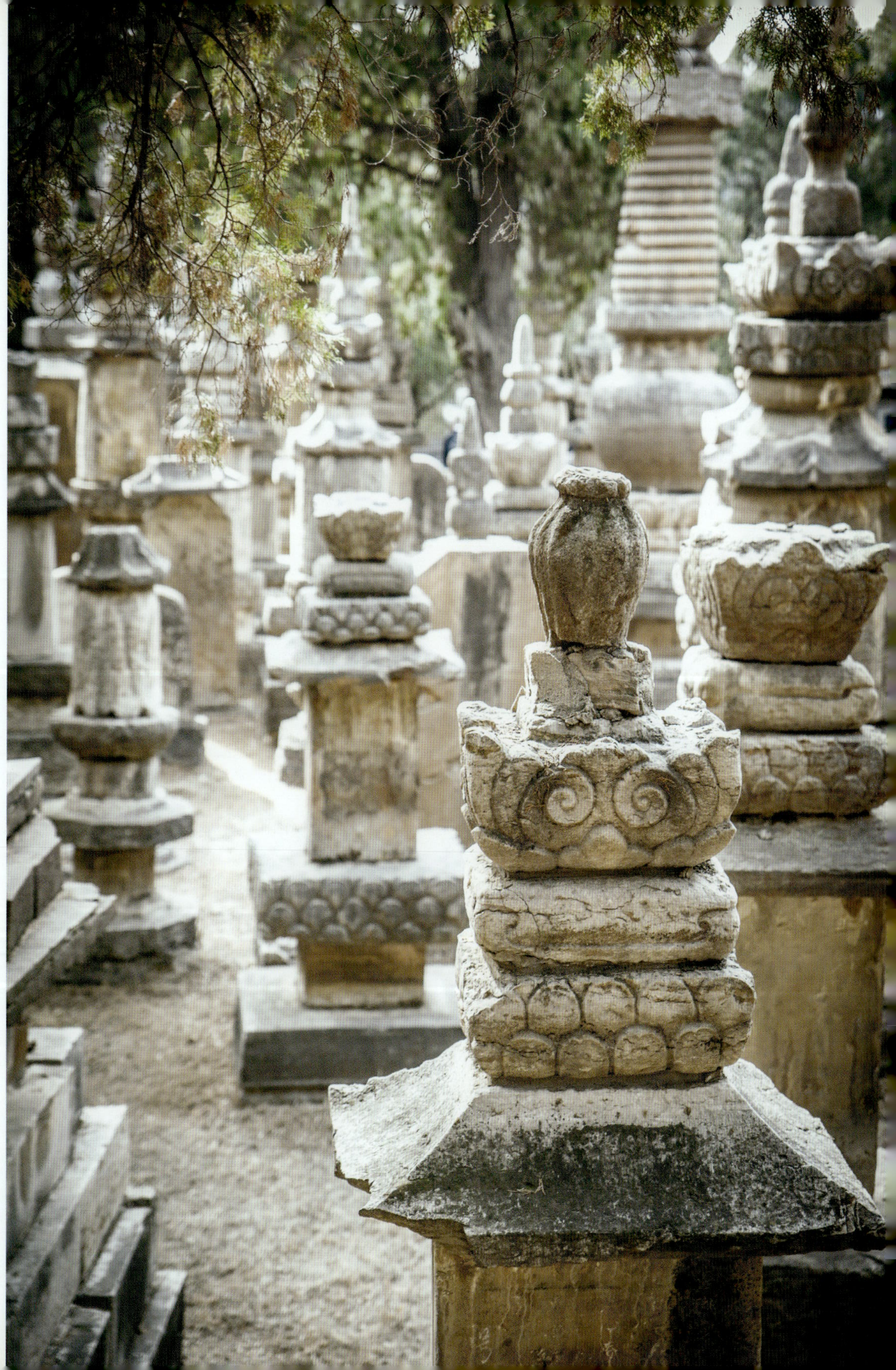

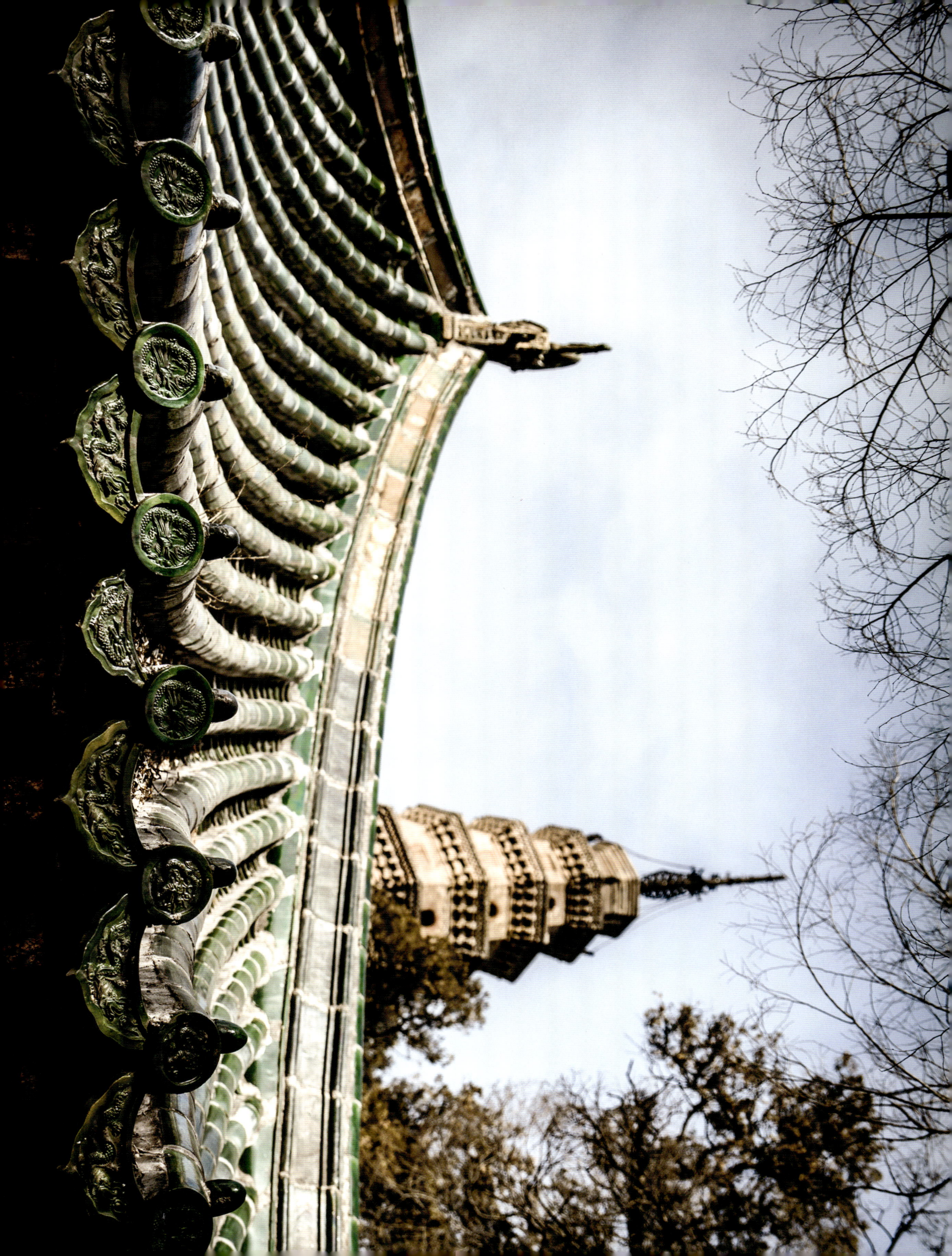

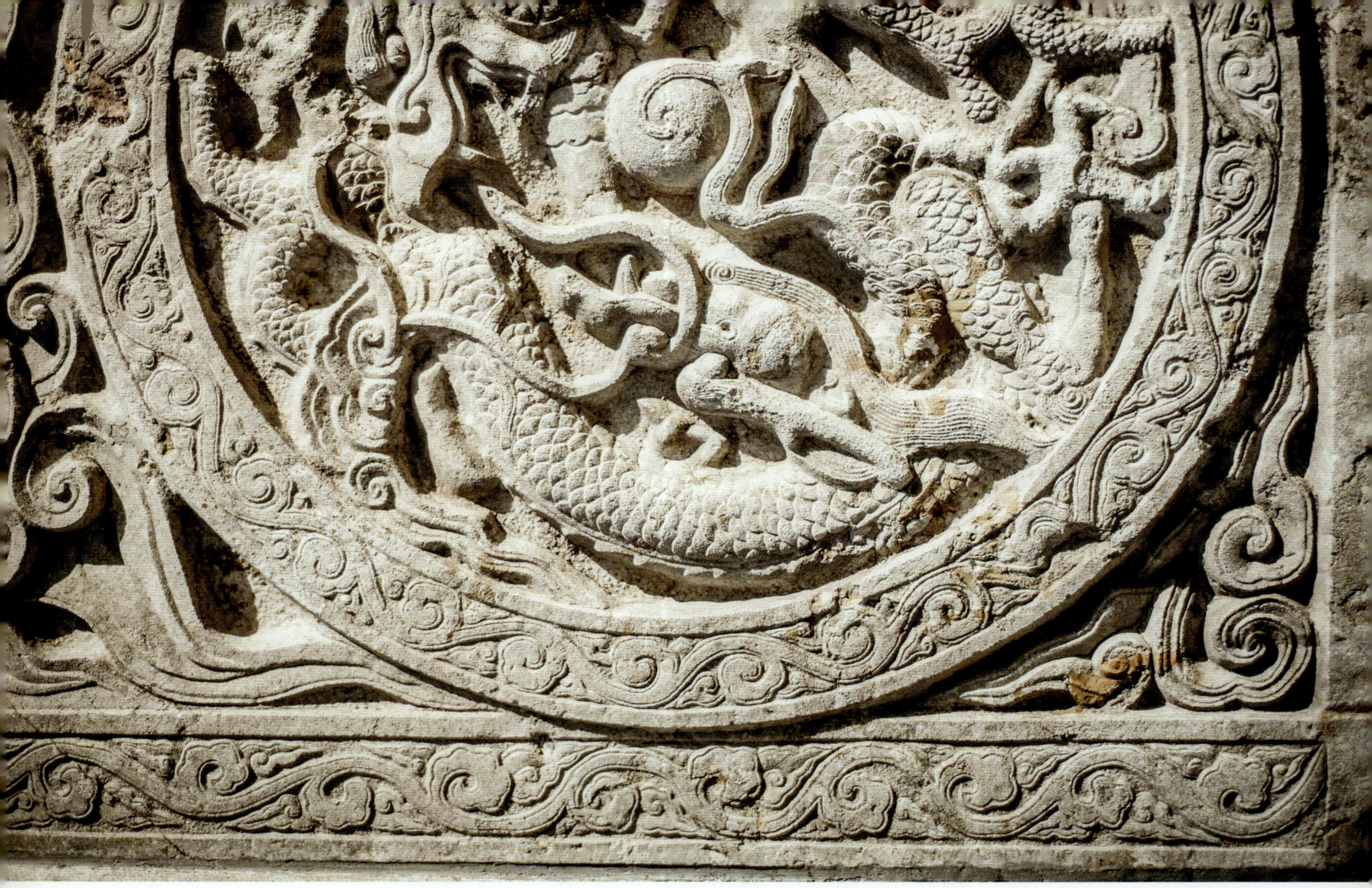
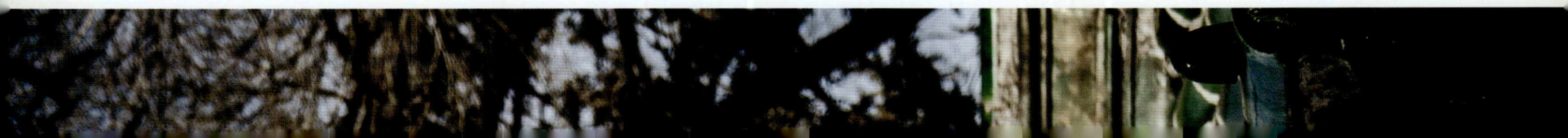

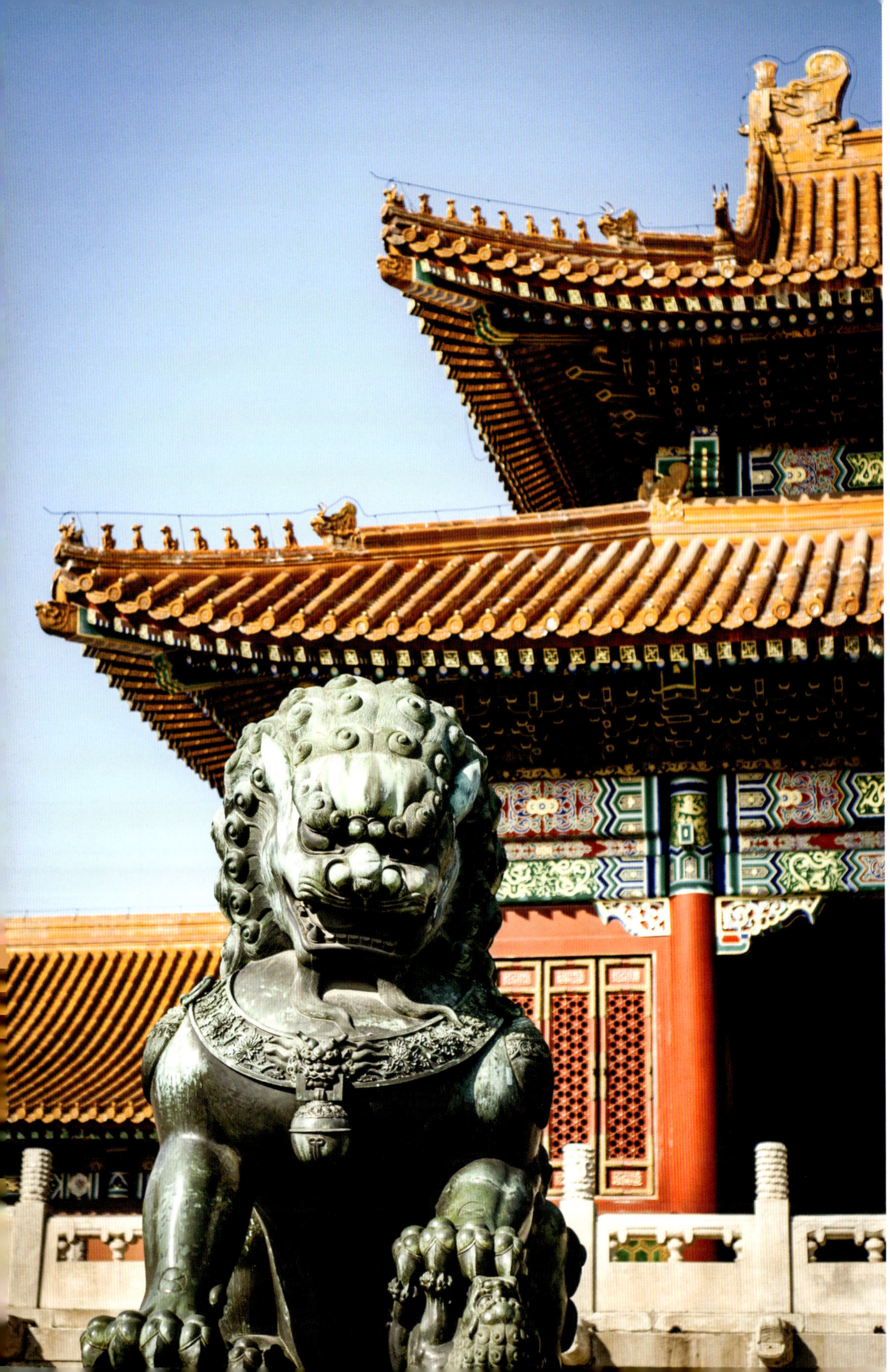

Part of the Imperial Palace in Beijing. Although not technically part of the Silk Road, the Forbidden City was home to emperors during the Ming Dynasty, which would have purchased many of the products produced along the Silk Road.

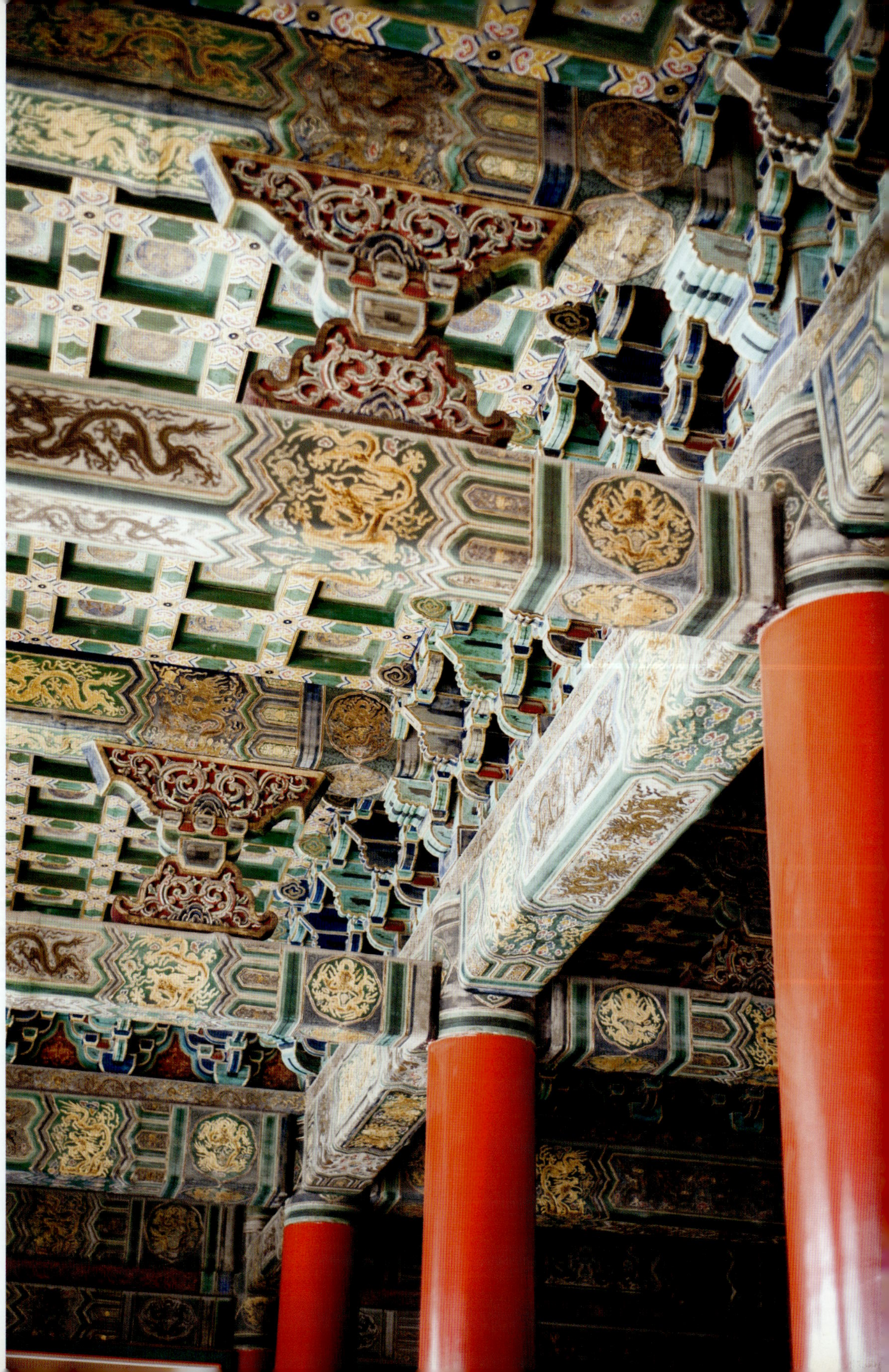

Another section of the Imperial Palace. The colors and designs are indicative of Ming Dynasty art and architecture. The palace and buildings in the Forbidden City span more than 180 acres and consist of an impressive and foreboding 980 buildings in total.

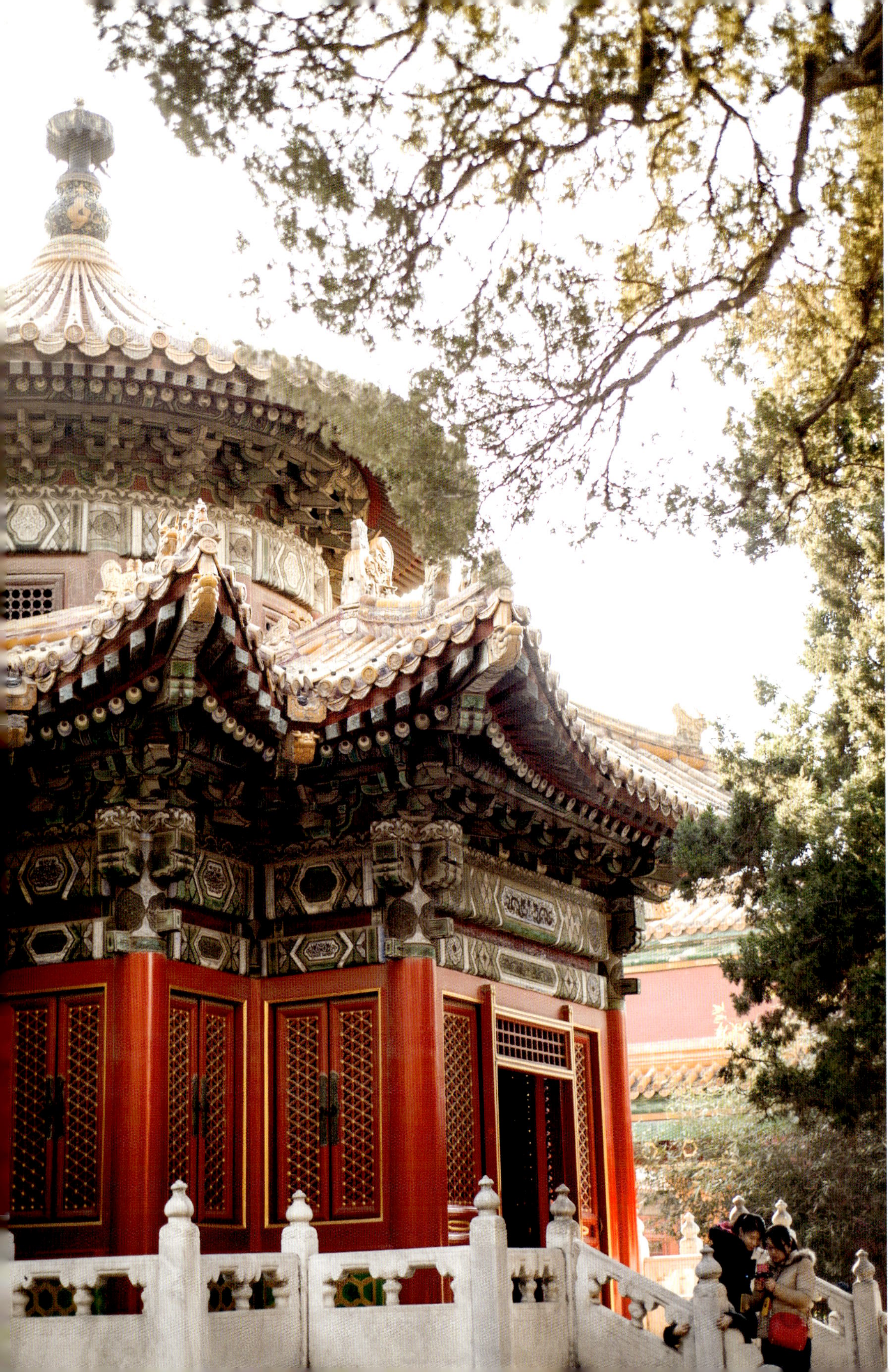

An example of the beautiful design and architecture of the Forbidden City, this pagoda has been carefully preserved for thousands of years. Note the intricate detailing on the roof, the precise cutouts that allow for light to filter through, and the carefully painted designs. This is a wonderful example of Chinese craftsmanship.

The Forbidden City allows visitors to explore inside this pagoda. Here the details truly come to life. Although photos can't fully capture the vibrant colors, they do provide a sense of the beauty of the design and attention to detail that make every inch of the Forbidden City a sight to behold.

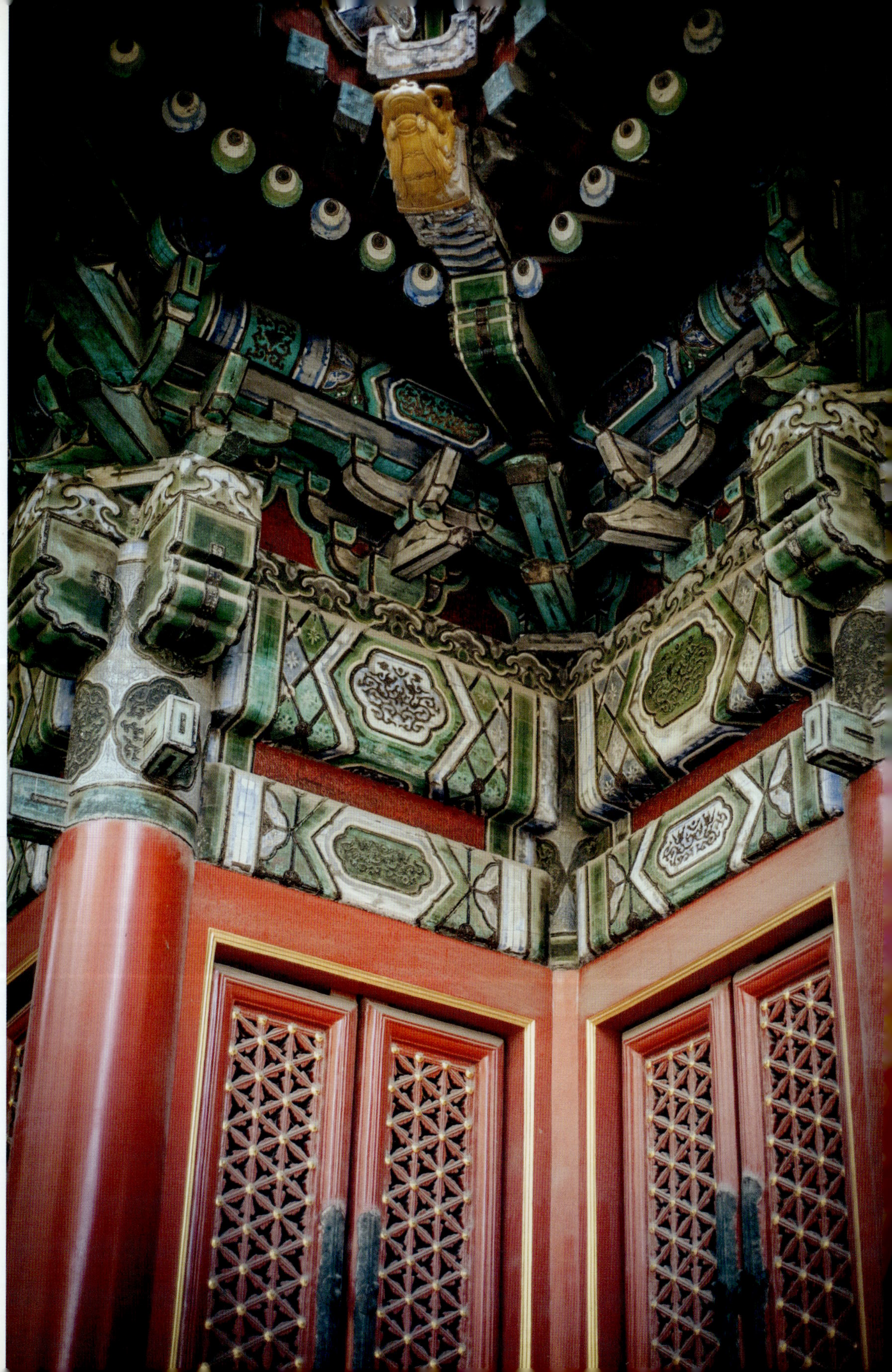

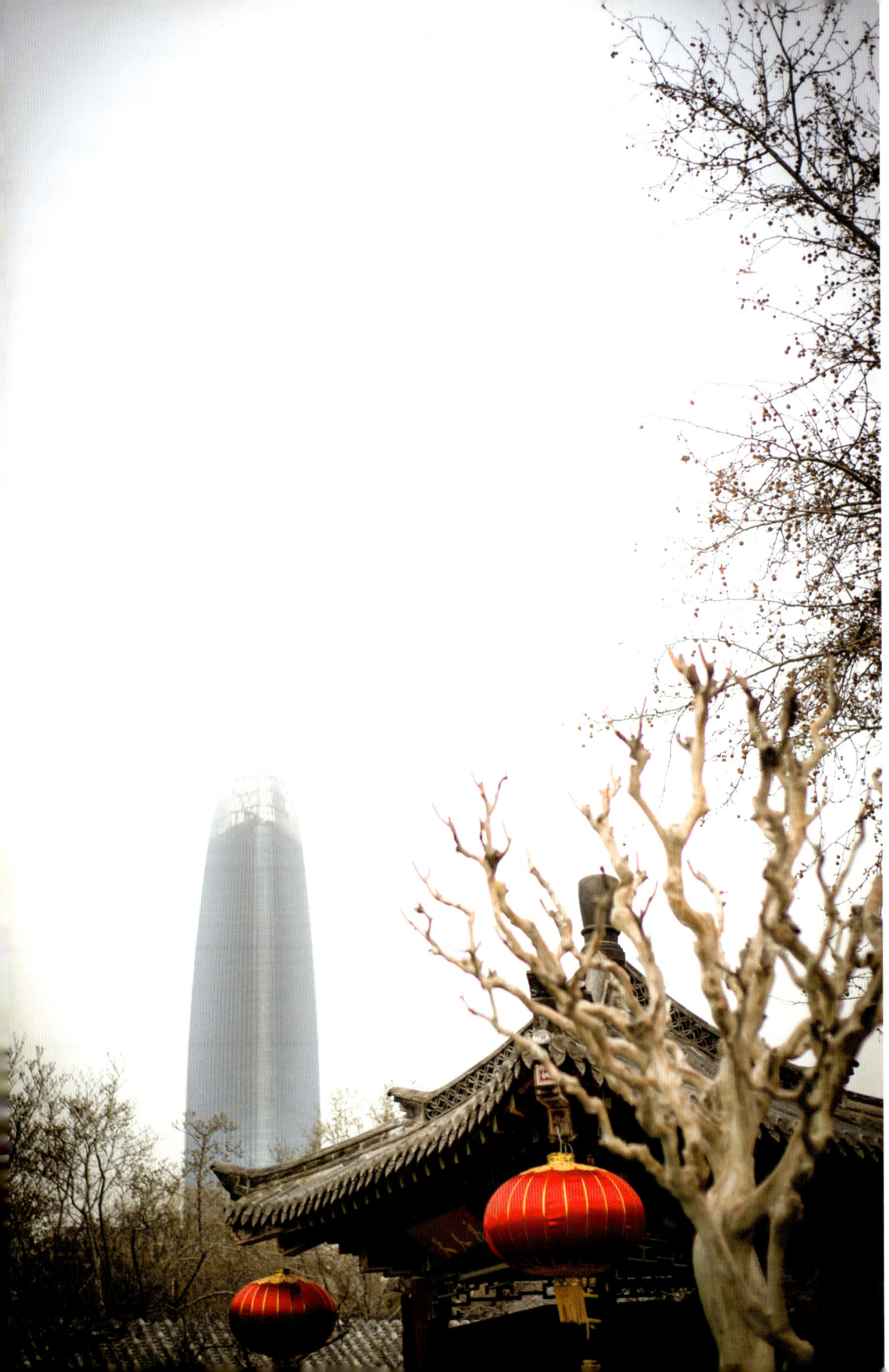

The ancient mingles with the modern everywhere you look in China. Here you see a traditional pagoda in the foreground, while a skyscraper looms in the background shrouded by thick smog.

Not as well preserved as the Imperial Palace, these structures at the Thousand Buddha Mountain in Jinan are open to visitors who wish to worship.

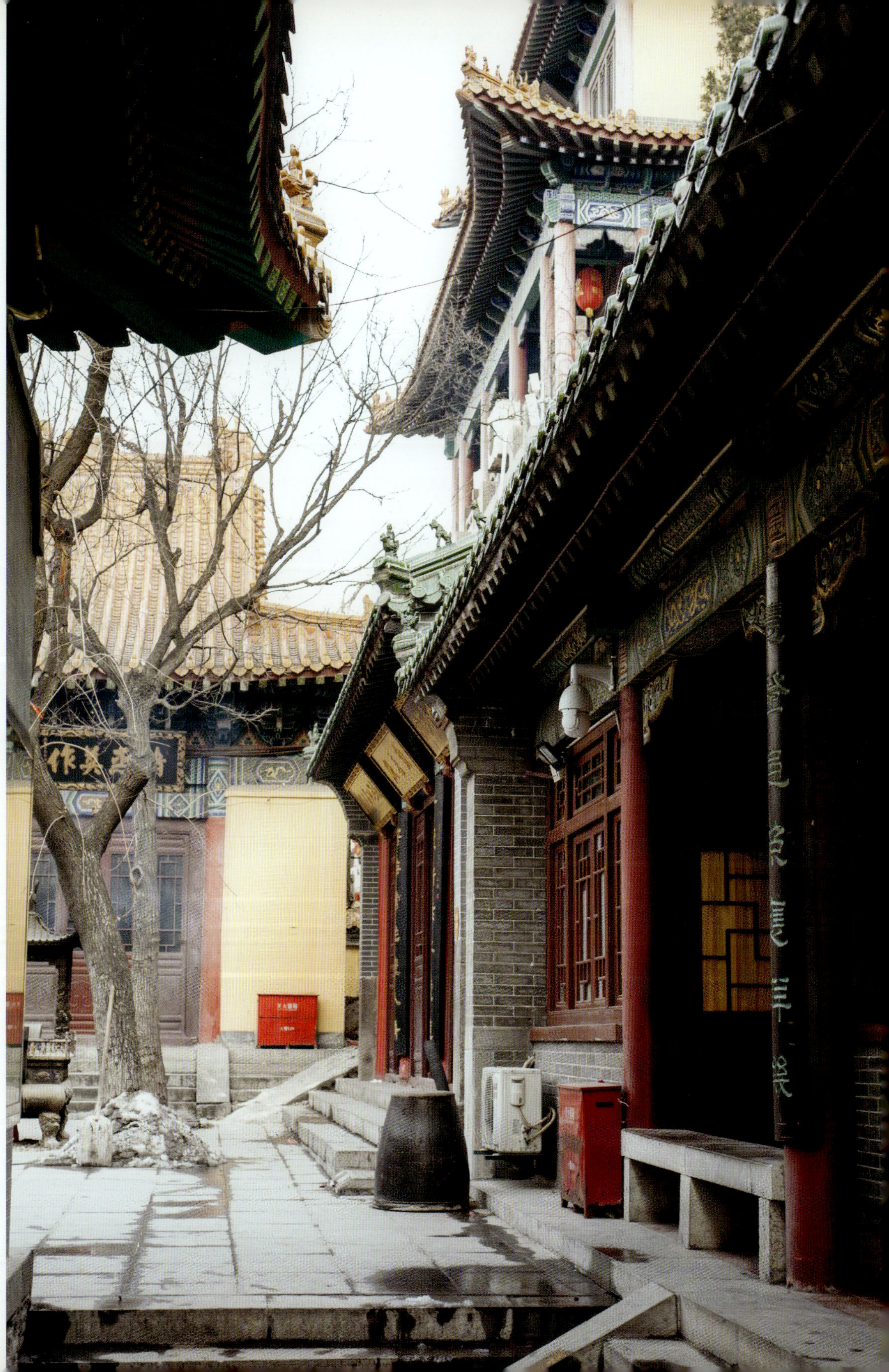

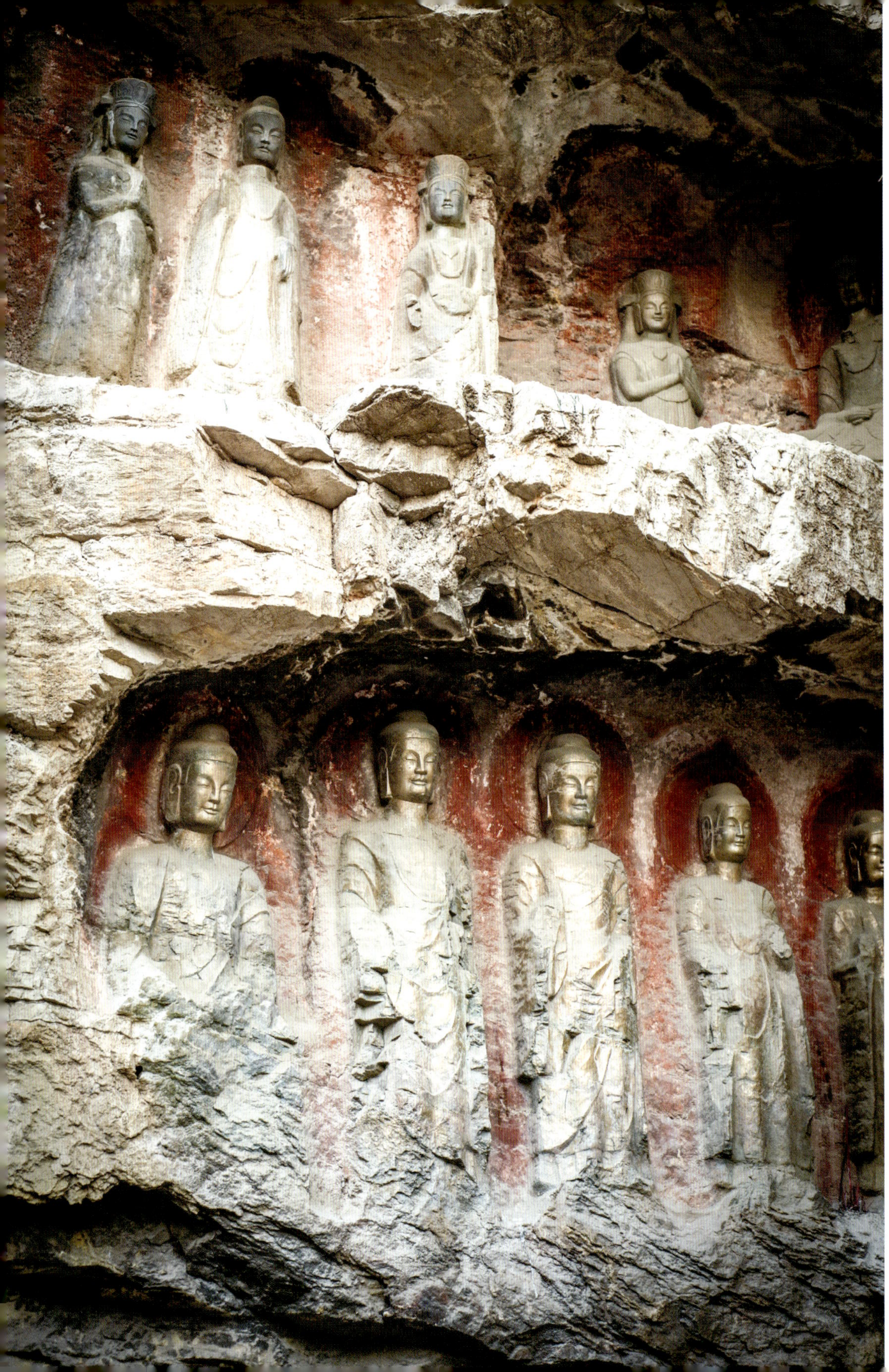

These Buddha statues are carved into a cliff located south of the Xingguochan Temple at the Thousand Buddha Mountain. Carved into the cliffside during the Sui period, there are about 130 of these statues standing today. The Jile Cave, one of five caves at the foot of the cliff, is among the most treasured places at the site and is home to sixteen Buddha statues.

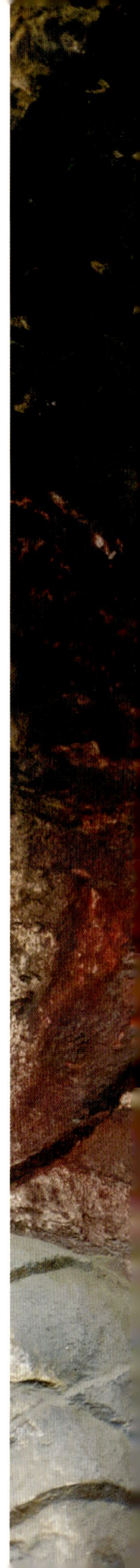

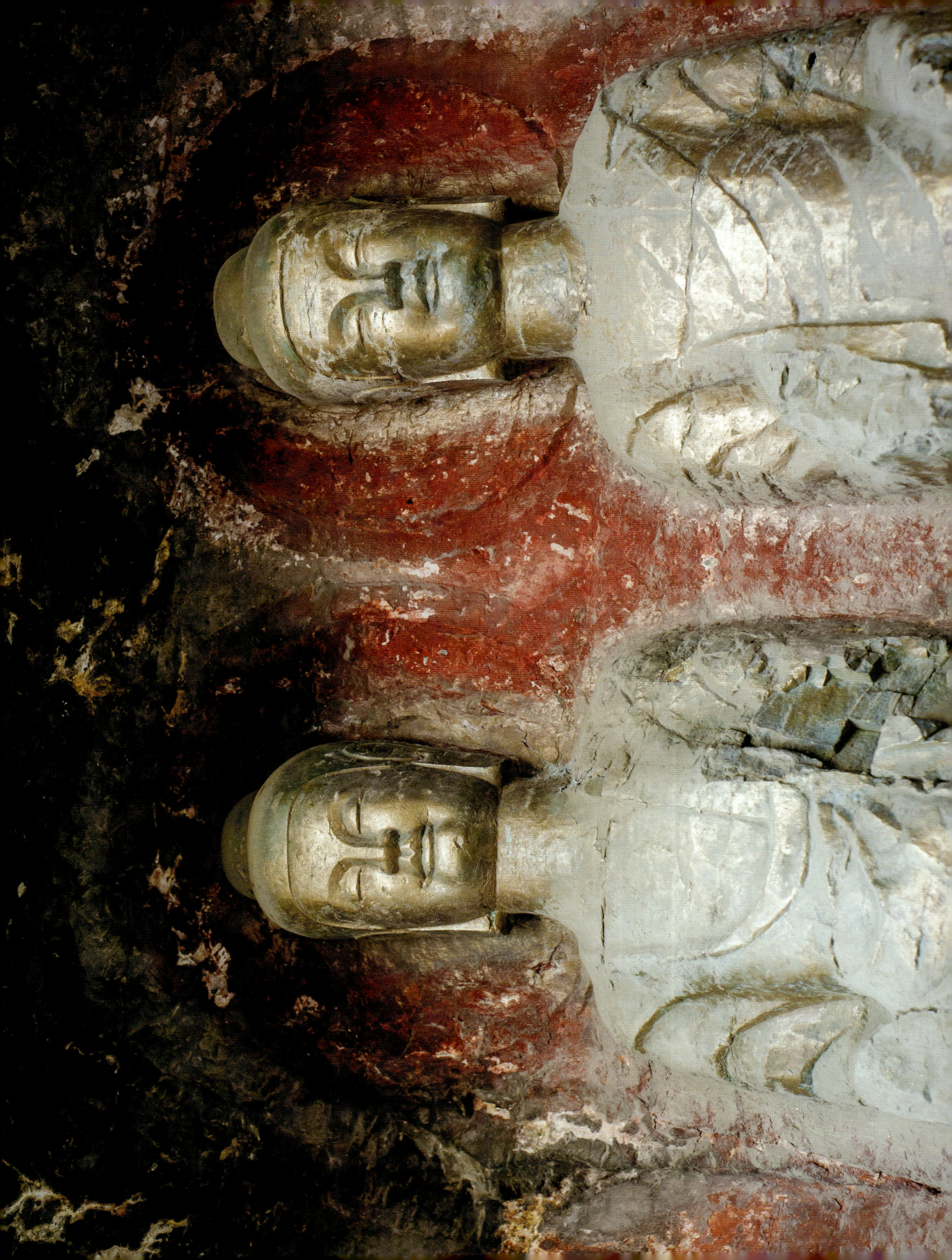

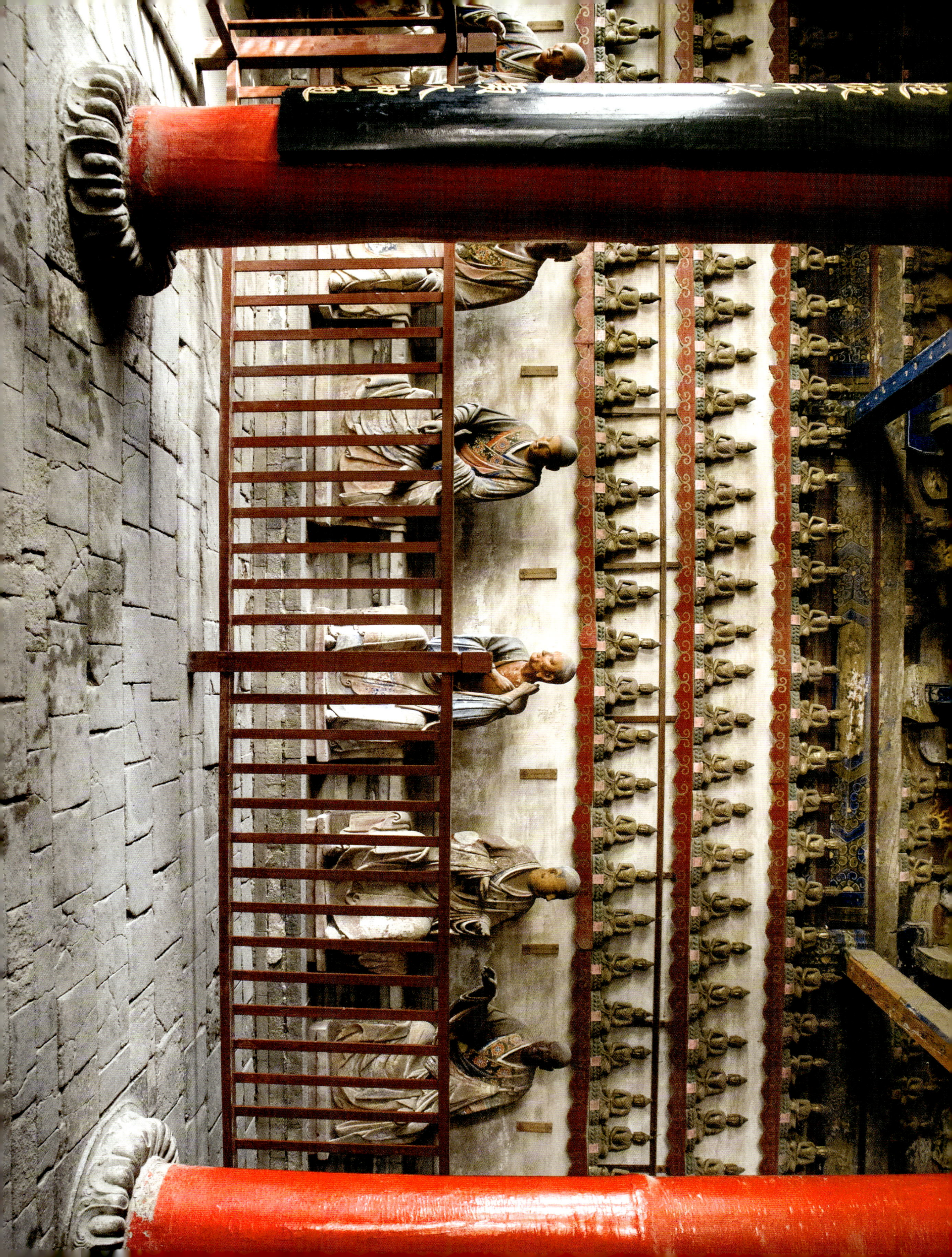

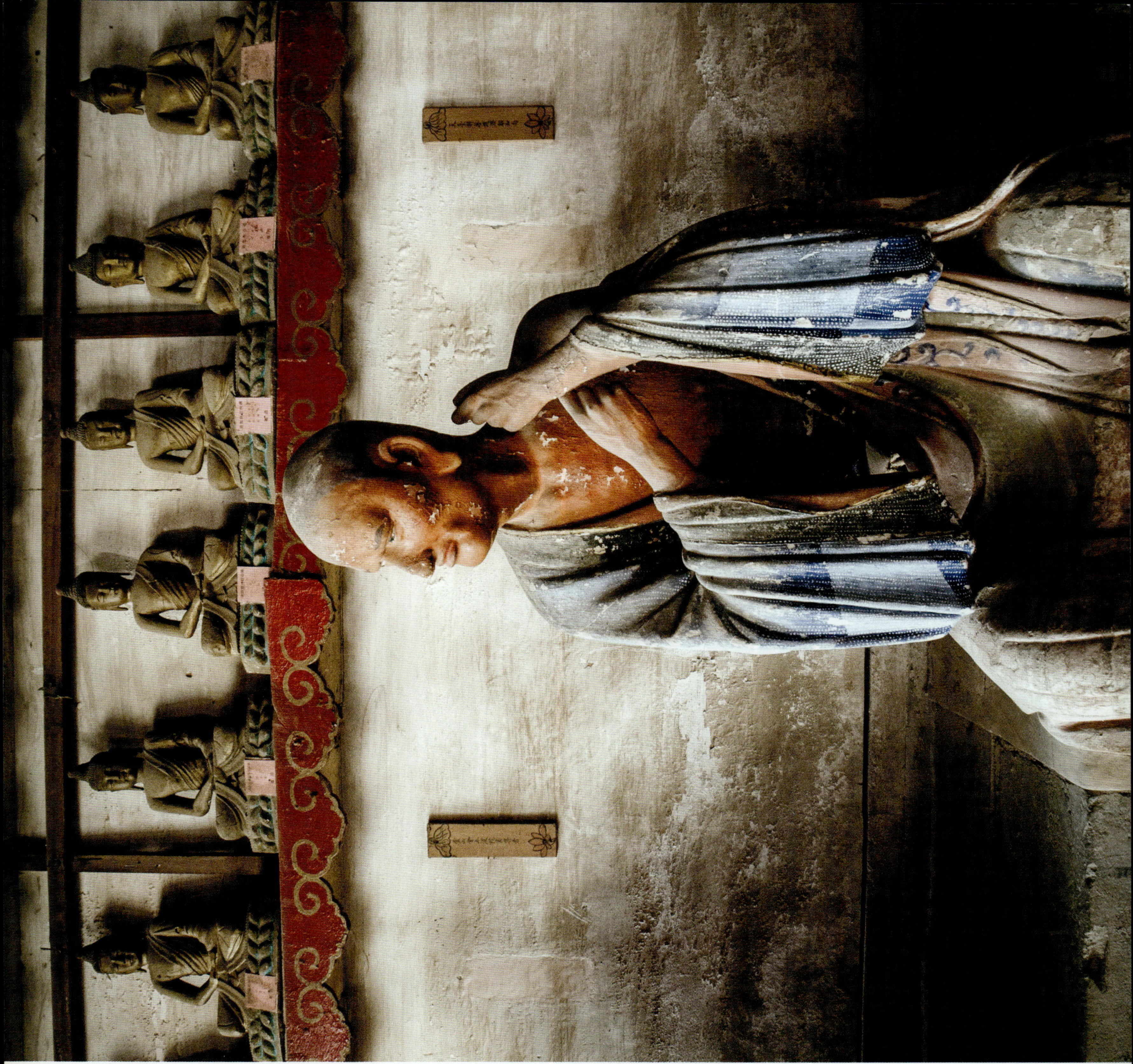

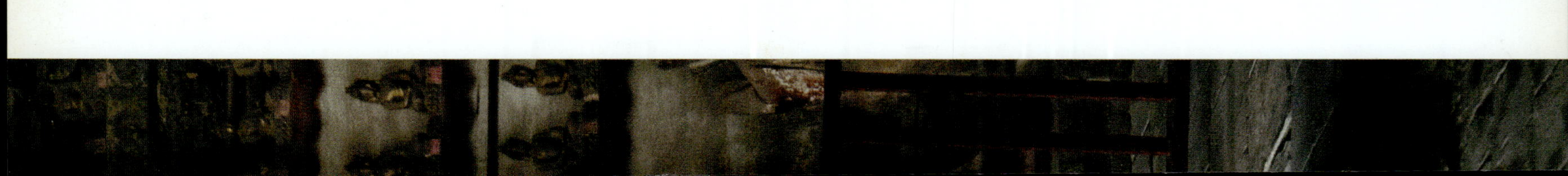

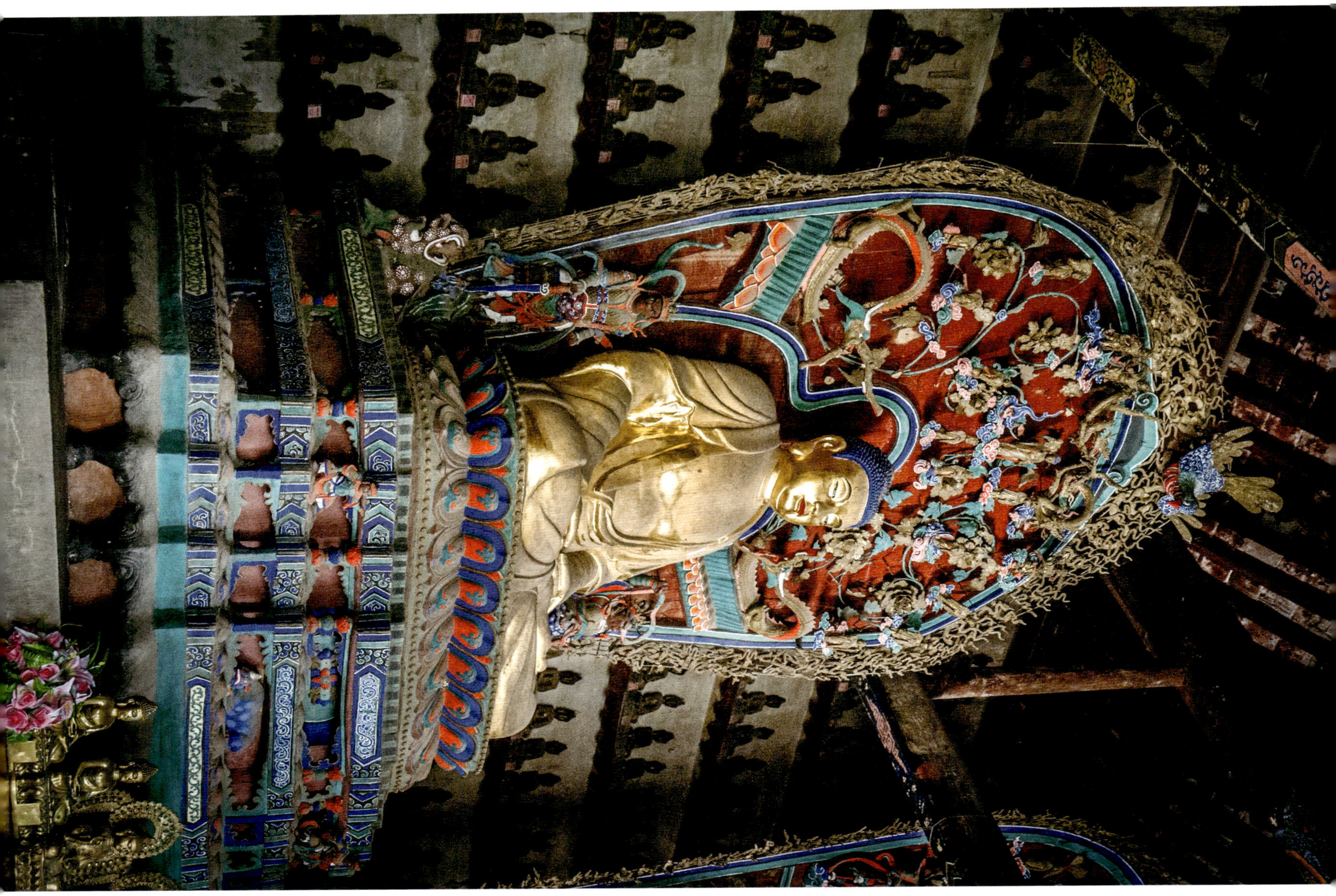

The insides of temples reveal intricate layers designed for worship. Buddhas are often decorated by worshipers with flowers and are surrounded with offerings like food, incense, and coins. These statues are thousands of years old and some have been better preserved than others. The most well-maintained of them all offer bright colors and even gold paint.

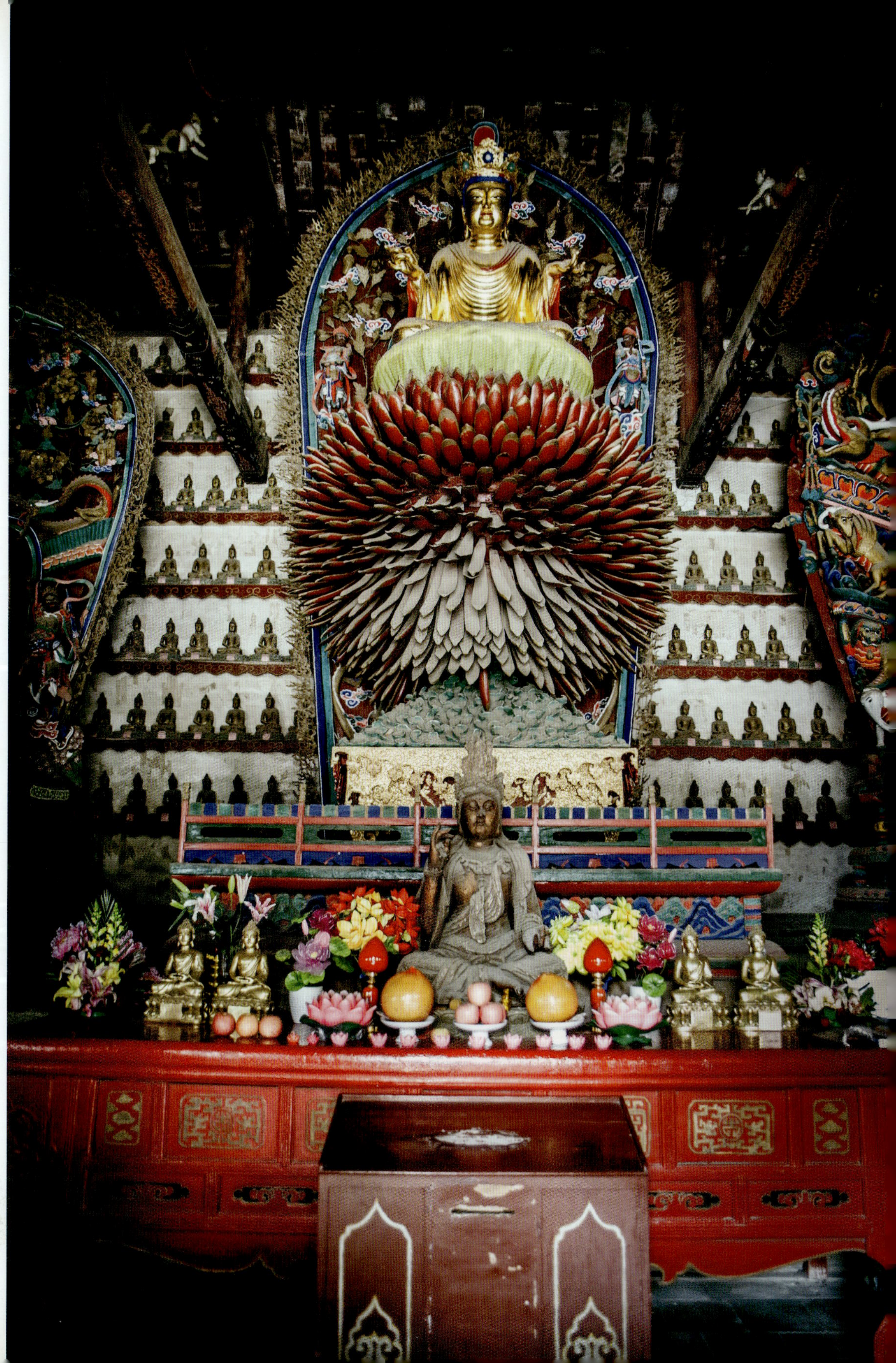

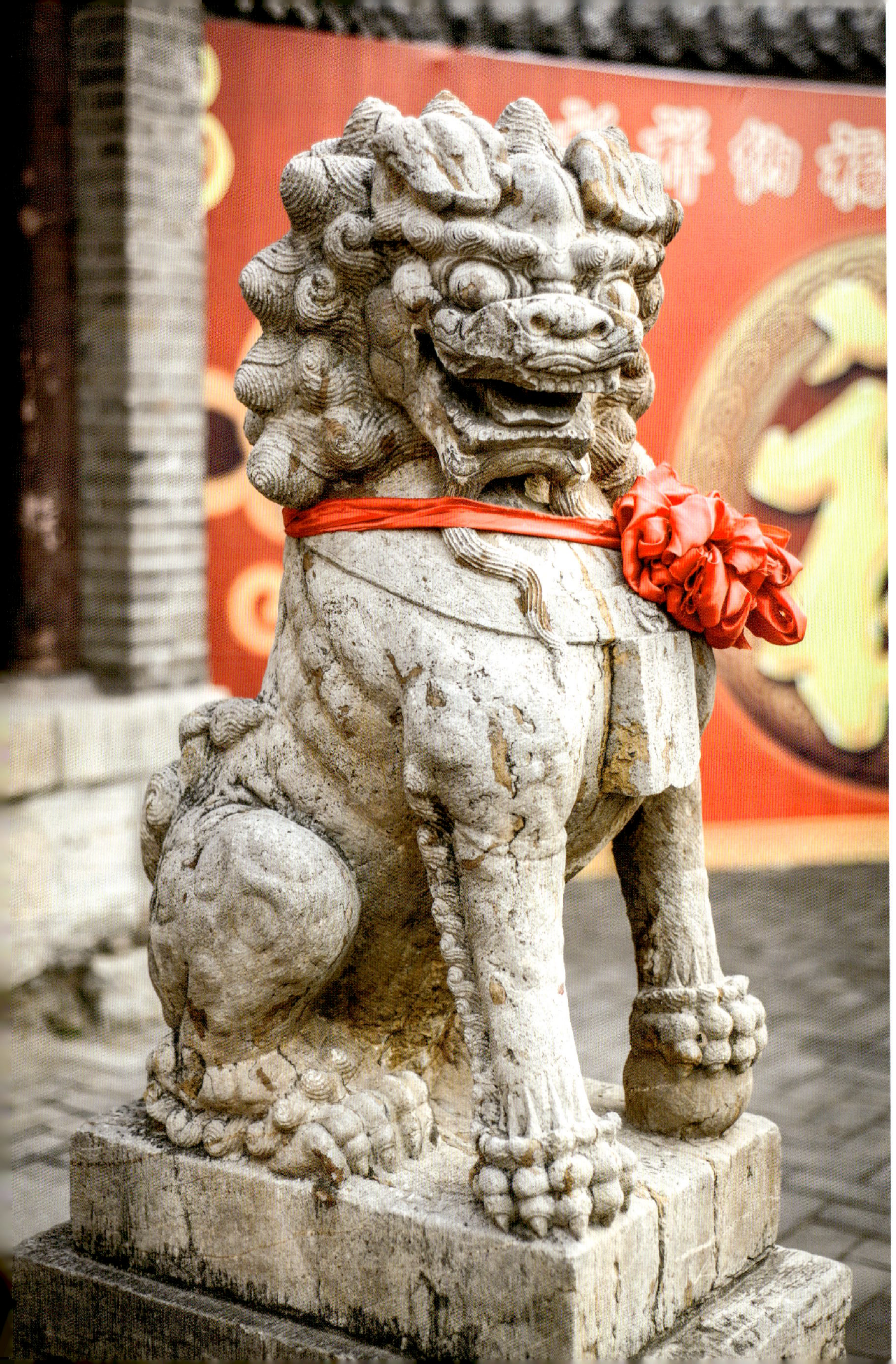

Foo Dogs, or Chinese Imperial guardian lions, are a symbol of mythic protection. Foo Dogs, which are believed to possess many powers, are often seen in pairs to provide protection for everything from palaces to restaurants and stores.

Here is a perfect example of traditional building material seen in many of the temple areas. Every rock has been placed with such careful detail that they are able to withstand thousands of years of weather and natural forces.

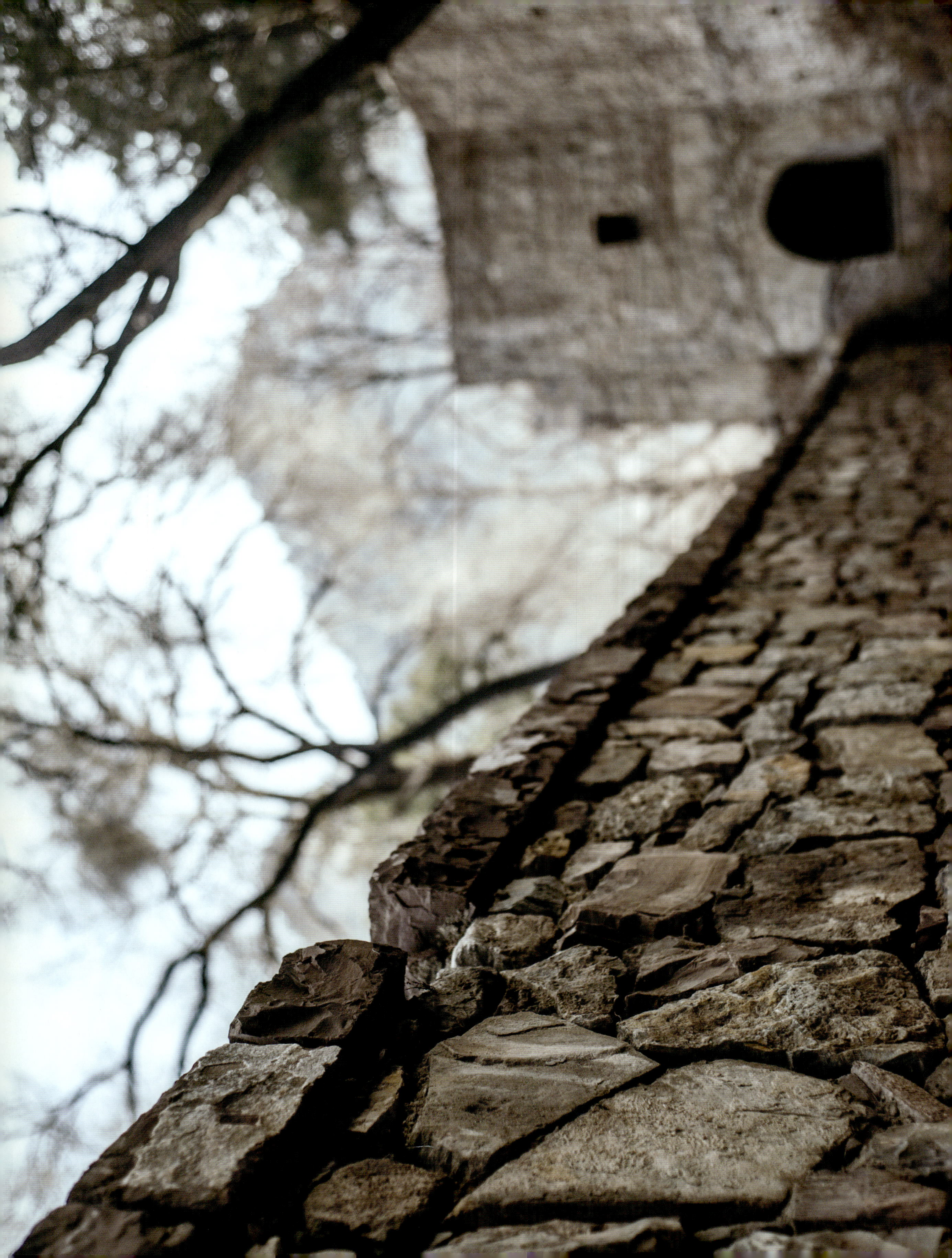

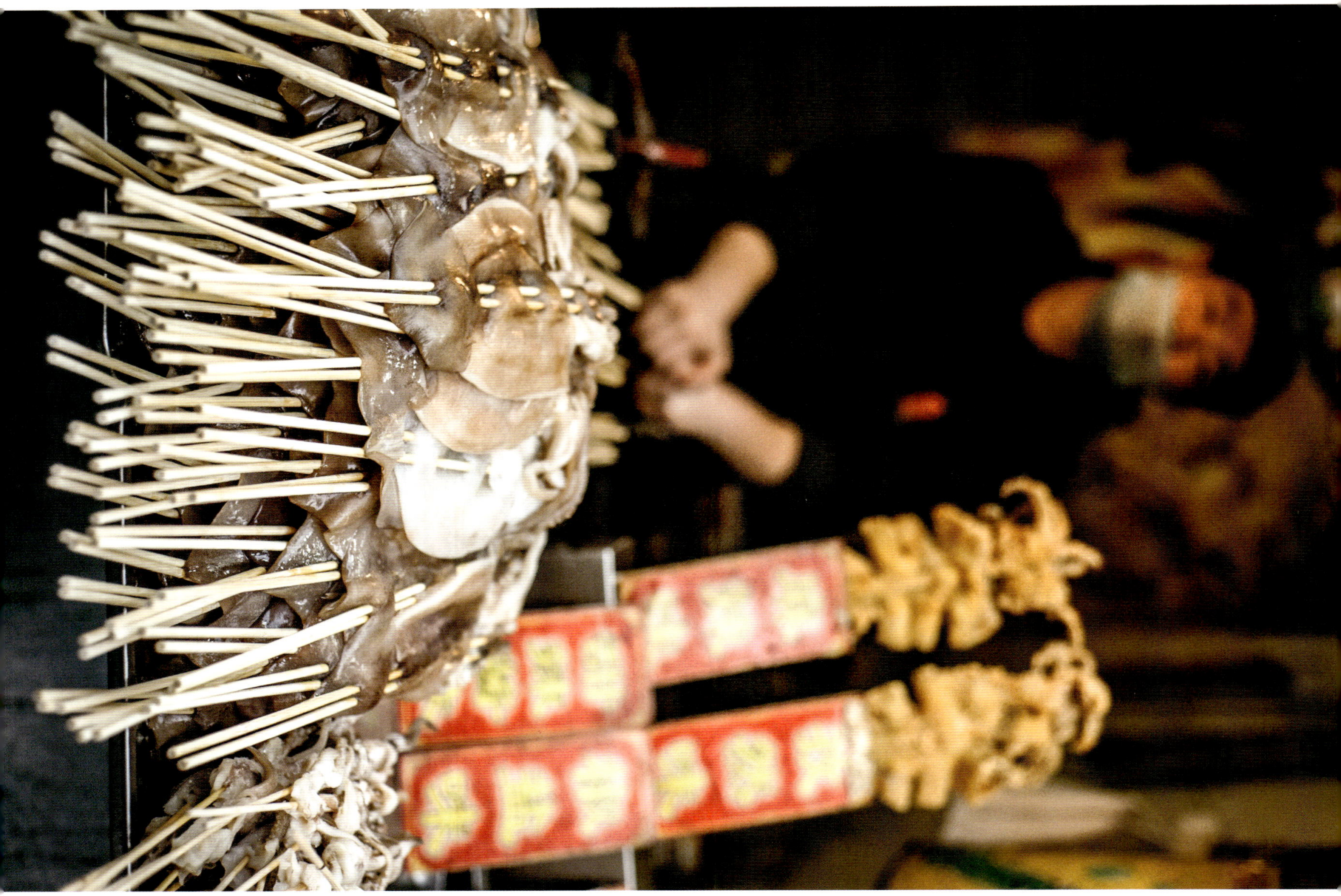

Tastes of the Silk Road

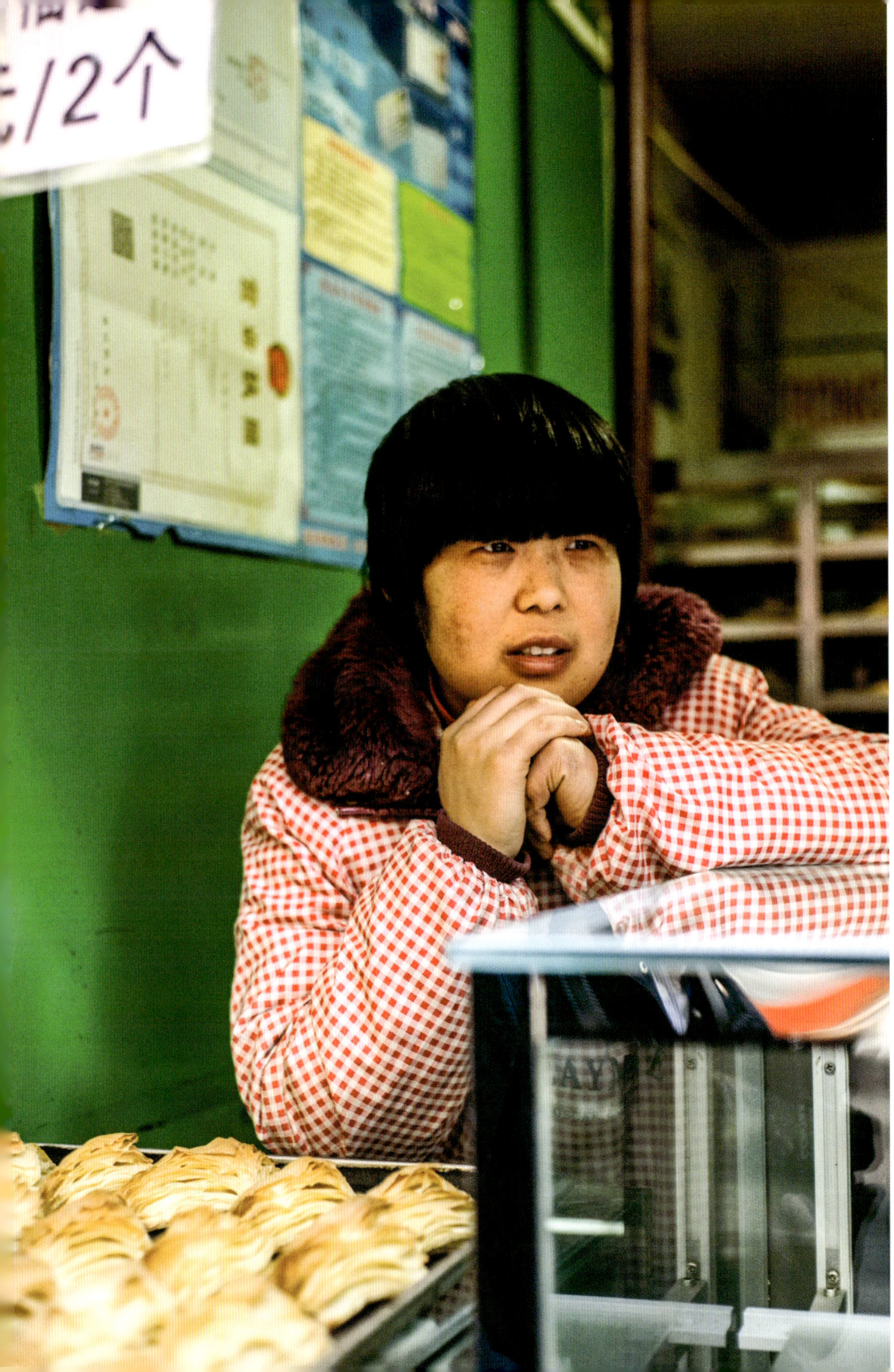

Street food is an important aspect of Chinese life. On the Silk Road, you can find delicacies like fried grasshoppers, silkworms roasted on a stick, quail eggs, fried octopus, sugar candy, and more.

This traditional Chinese snack is a New Year's delight and can be found at street fairs around the Shandong region. Children and adults alike enjoy the sticky, cotton candy–like texture of this delicious sweet treat.

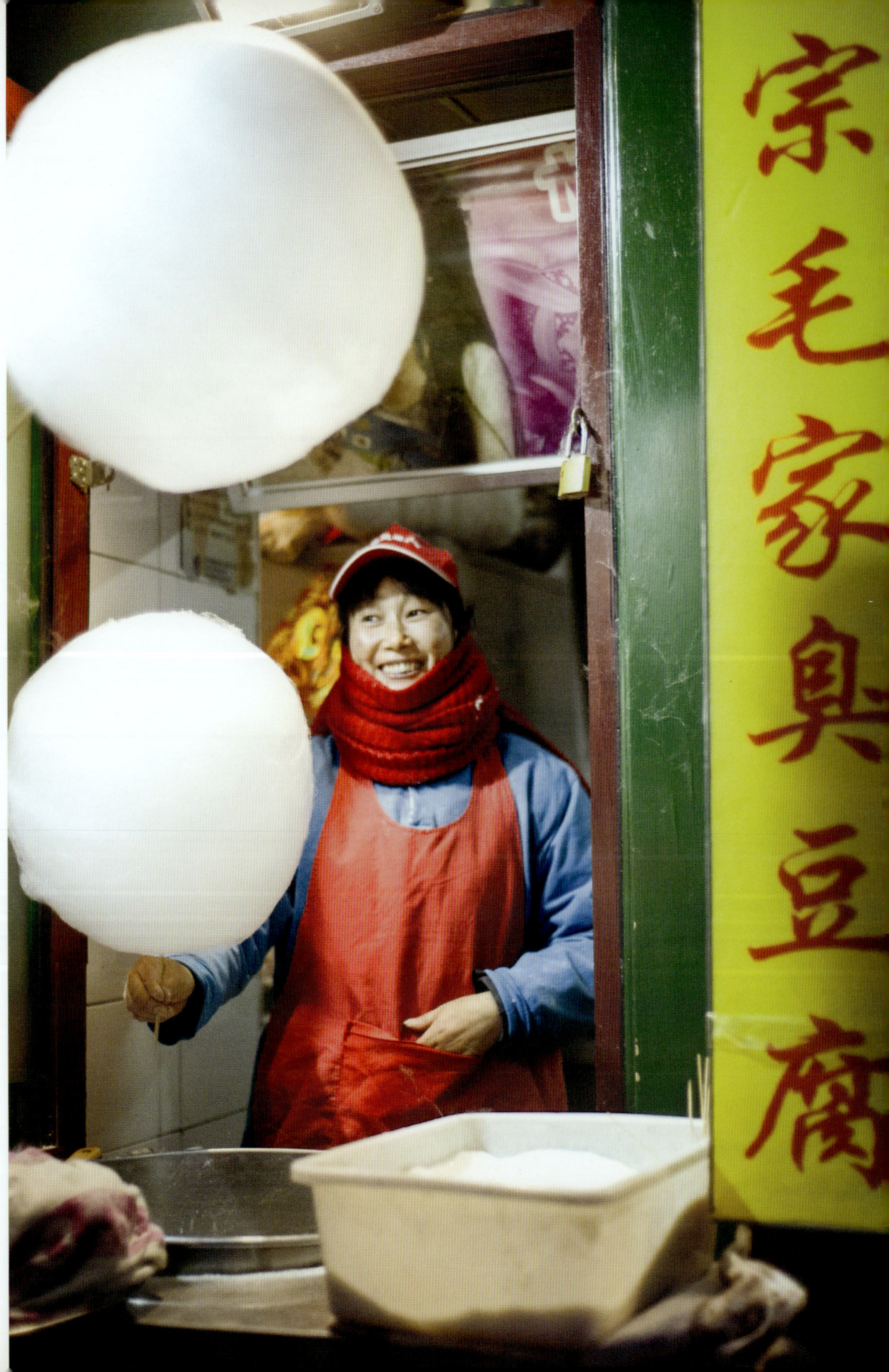

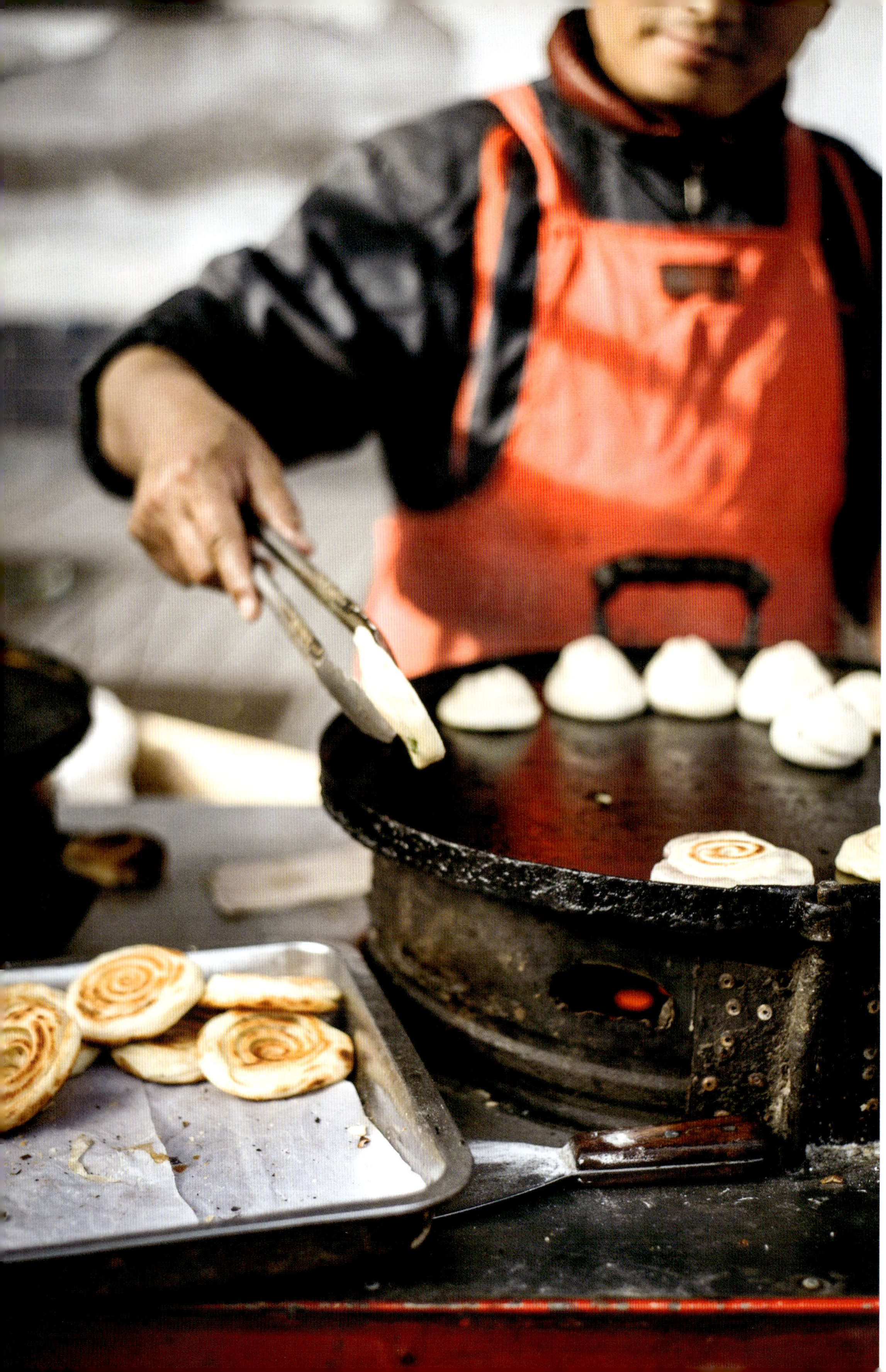

You xuan, a local food of Jinan City, is a savory doughy pancake made from flour, lard, and some spring onions. Street vendors sell these delights at outdoor markets and festivals throughout the year.

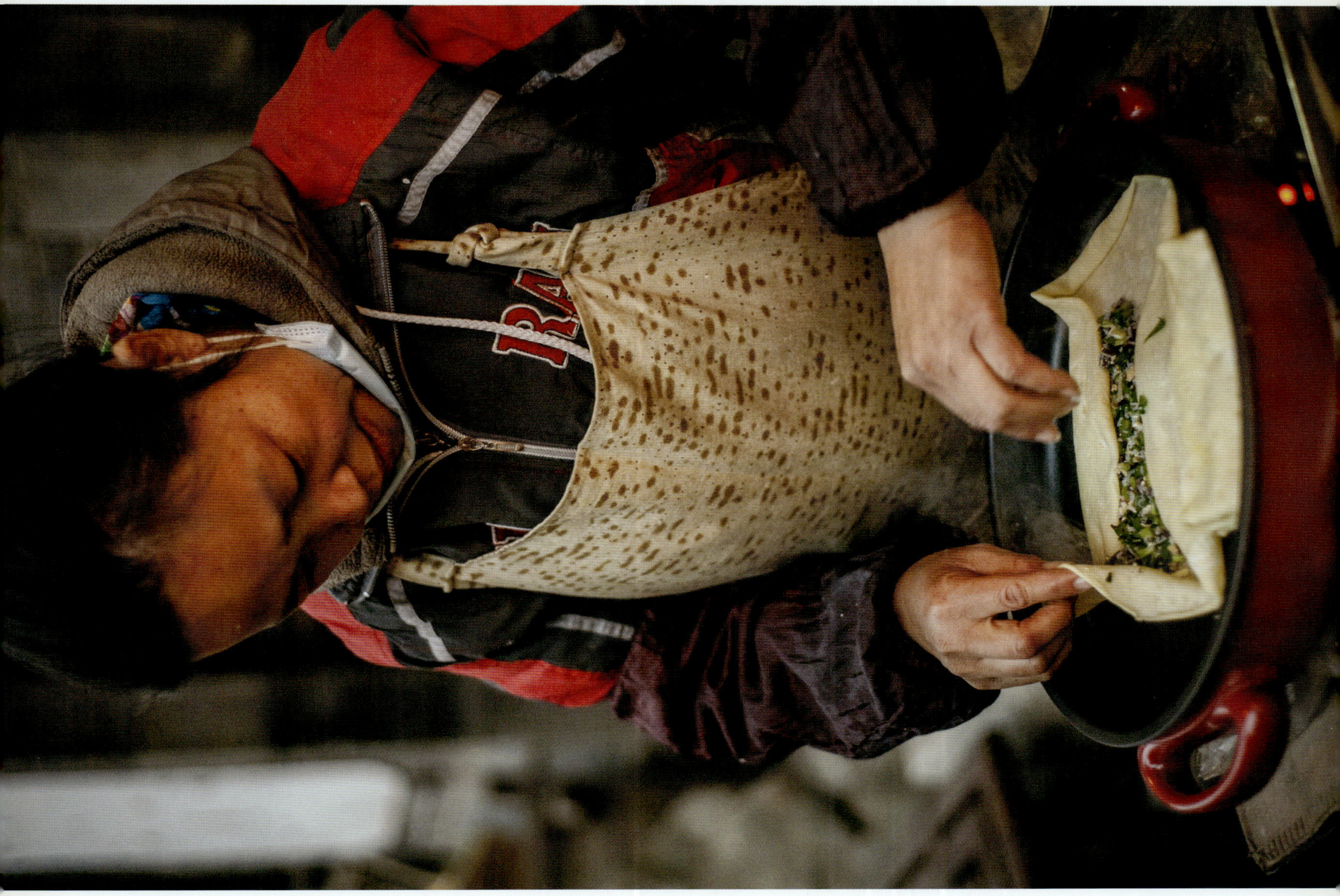

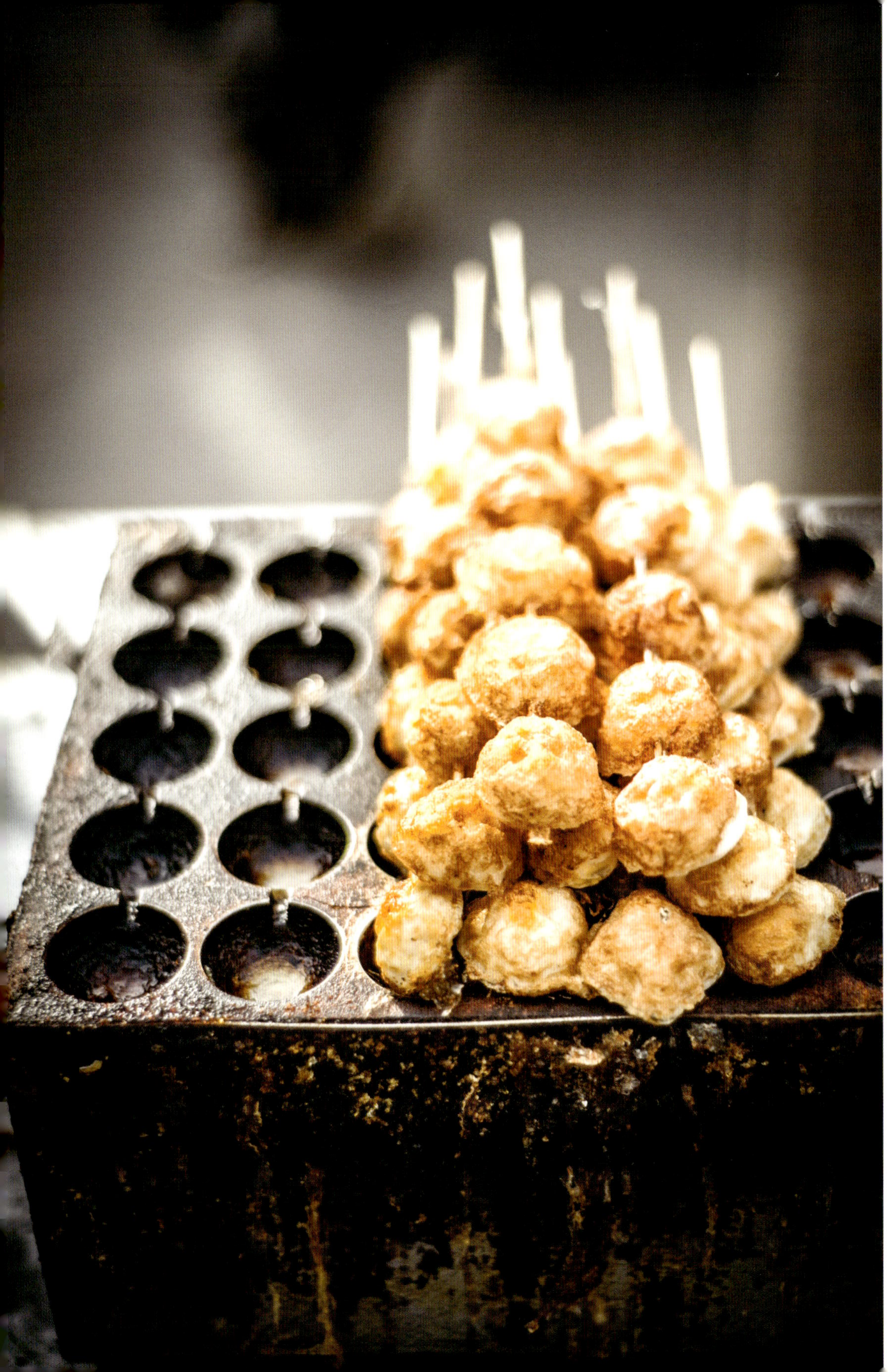

The sculptures on the right-hand page are made using a traditional Chinese folk art, sugar figure blowing, with the craftsman blowing air into the melted sugar and using his hands to help form various shapes. Although they are made from sugar, these works of art are inedible.

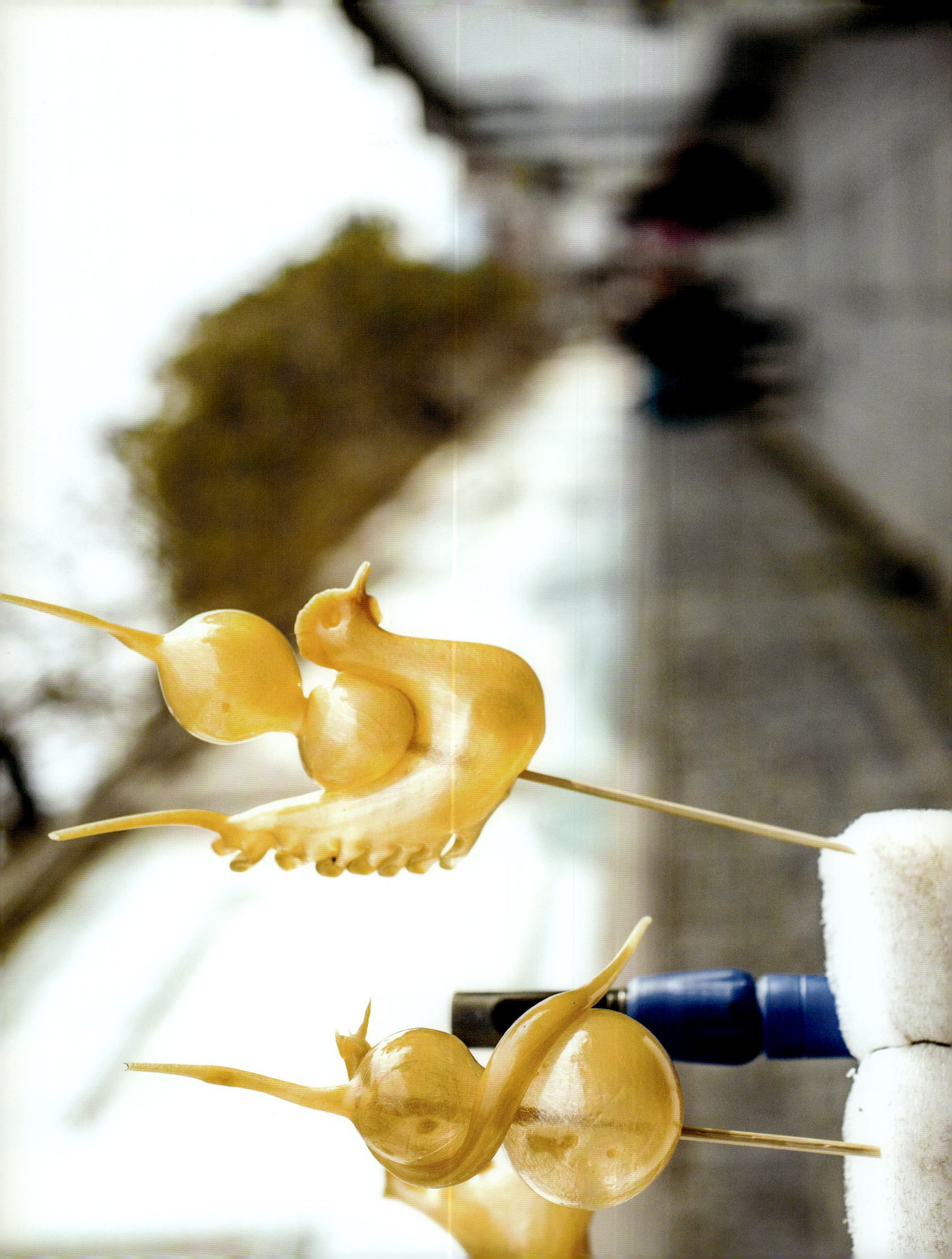

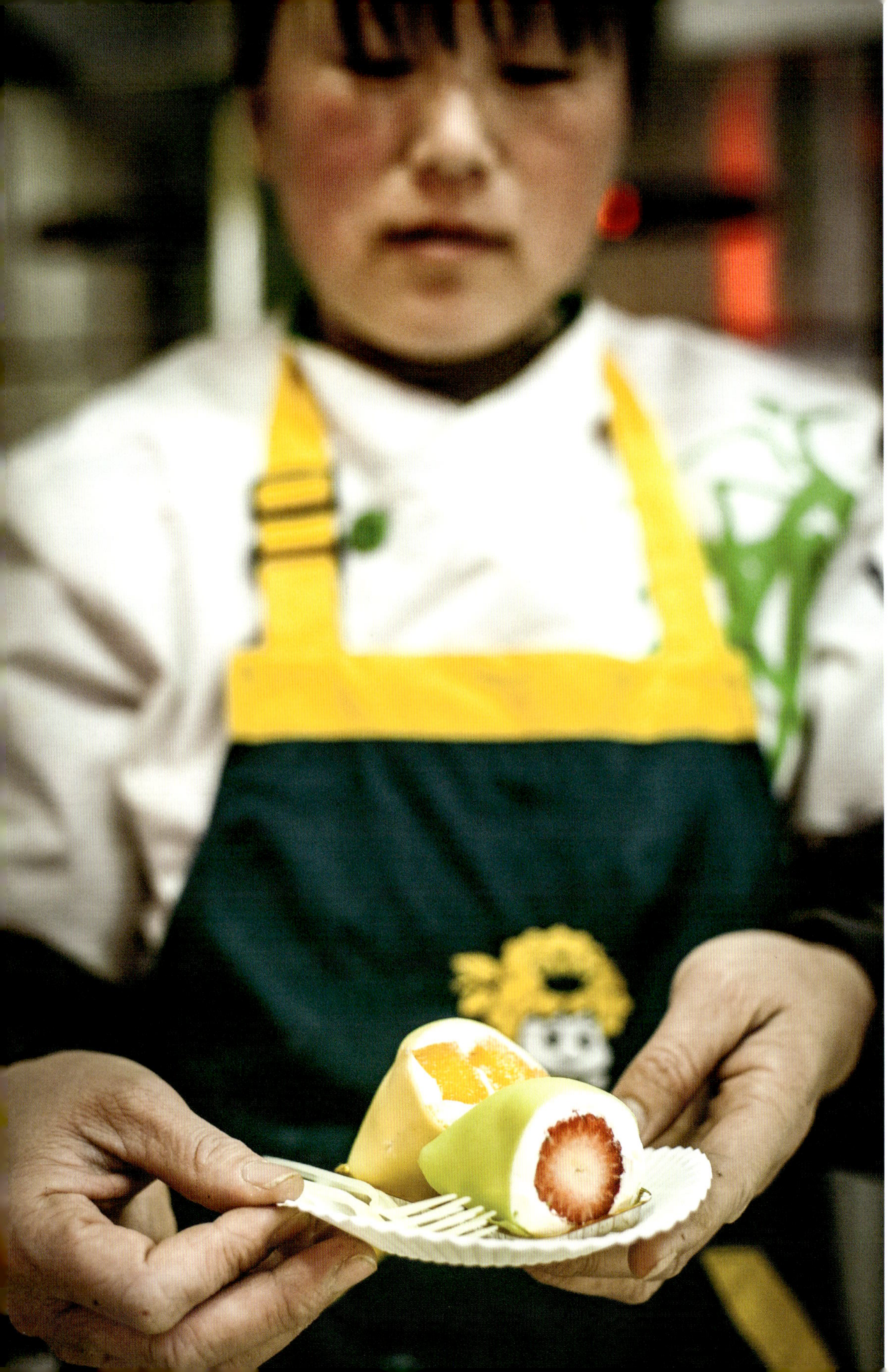

Similar to the exterior doughy texture of the Japanese treat mochi, this sweet fruit-filled treat has a cream filling and fresh strawberries or mango surrounded by a sweet dough.

Furong Street, known for both savory and sweet delicacies, is frequented by locals who relish tasting flavors from a wide variety of vendors. Items, which may include fried quail eggs, street barbecue, dumplings, soup, and fish dishes, cost very little, and crowds come in throngs during the Lantern Festival.

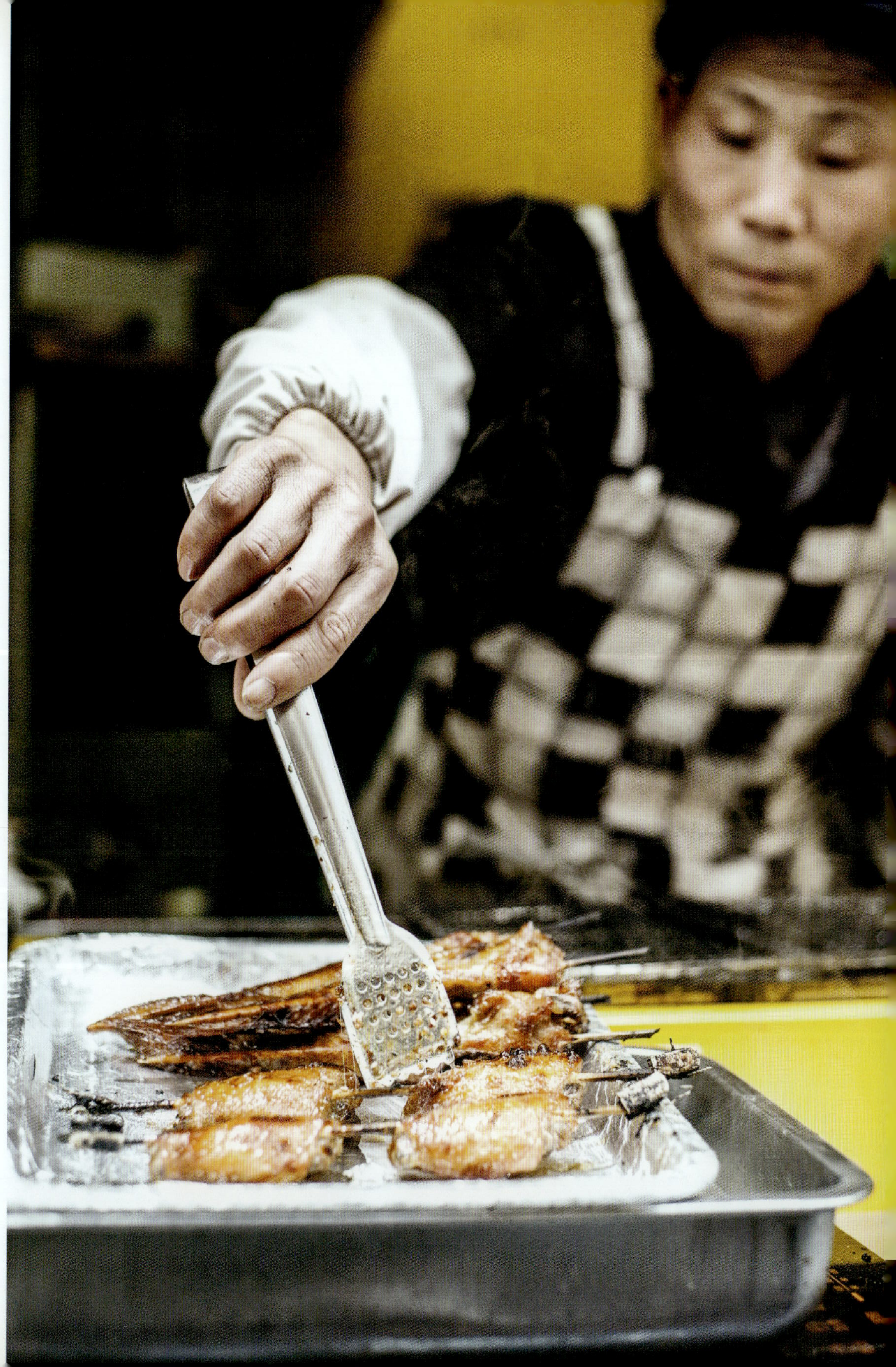

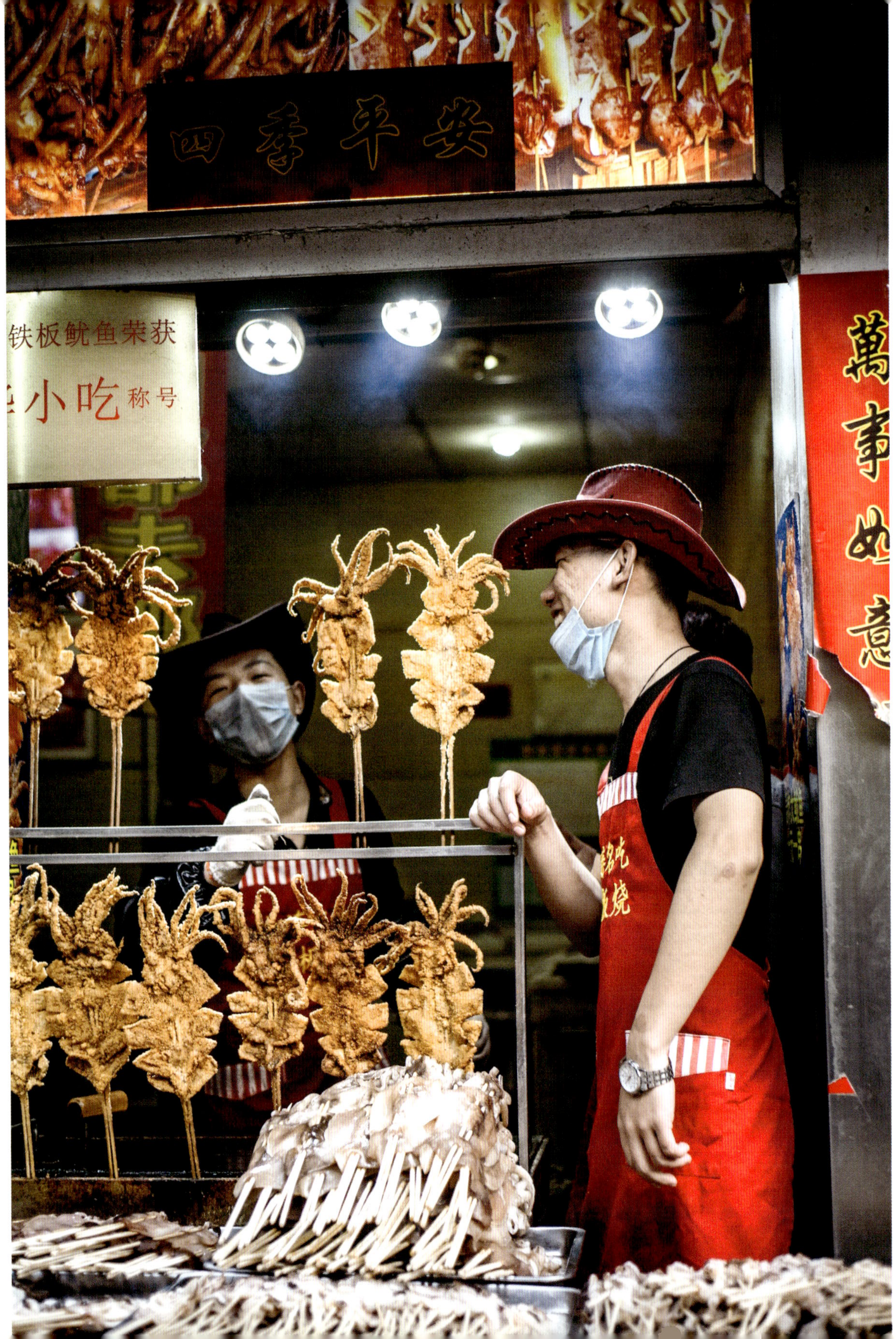
四季平安
铁板鱿鱼荣获
小吃 称号
萬事如意

Fried food is a staple of Silk Road street fare. Seafood is a local favorite and you can find many different options. Here squid is covered in flour, fried in oil, and served piping hot.

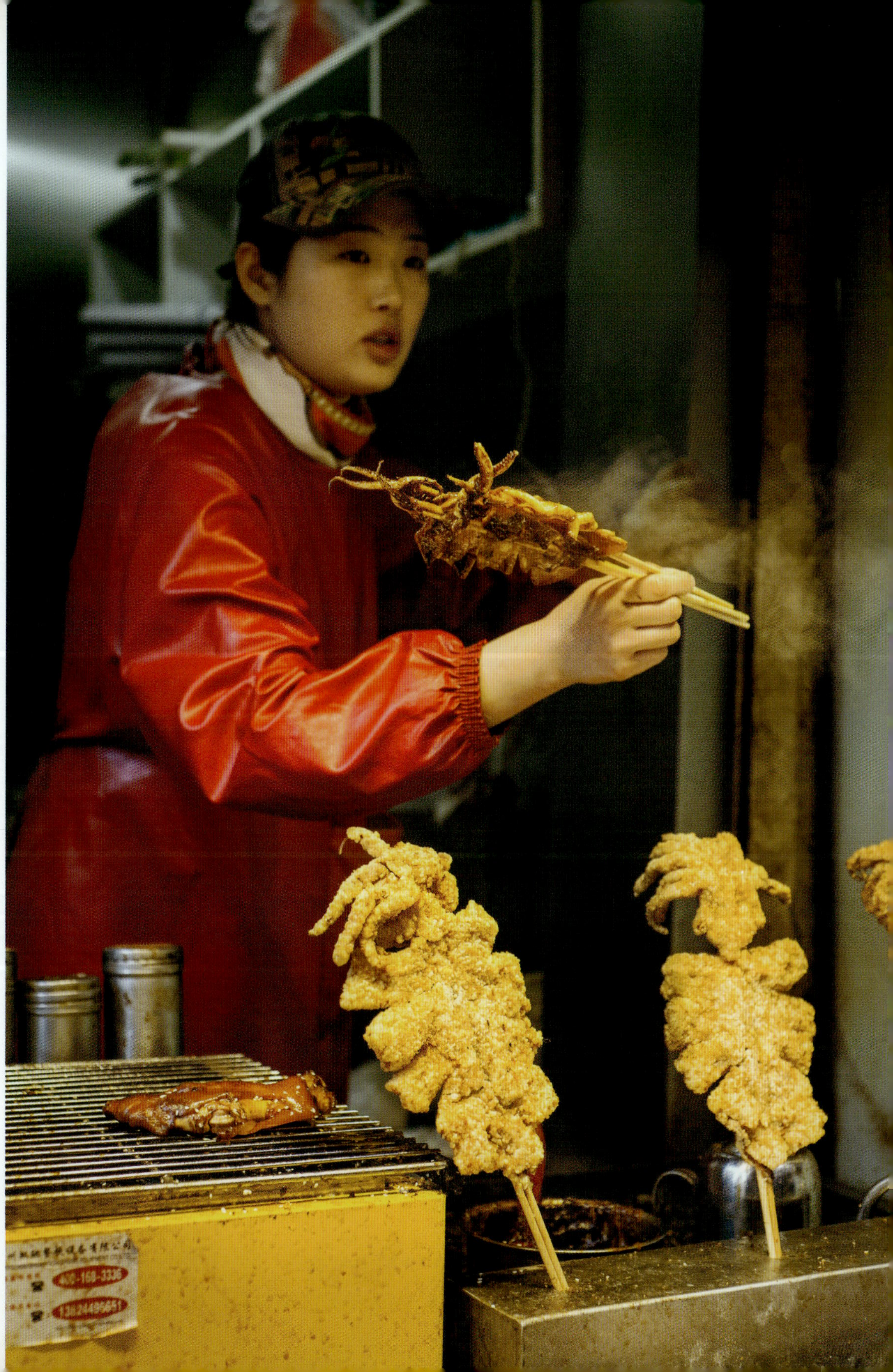

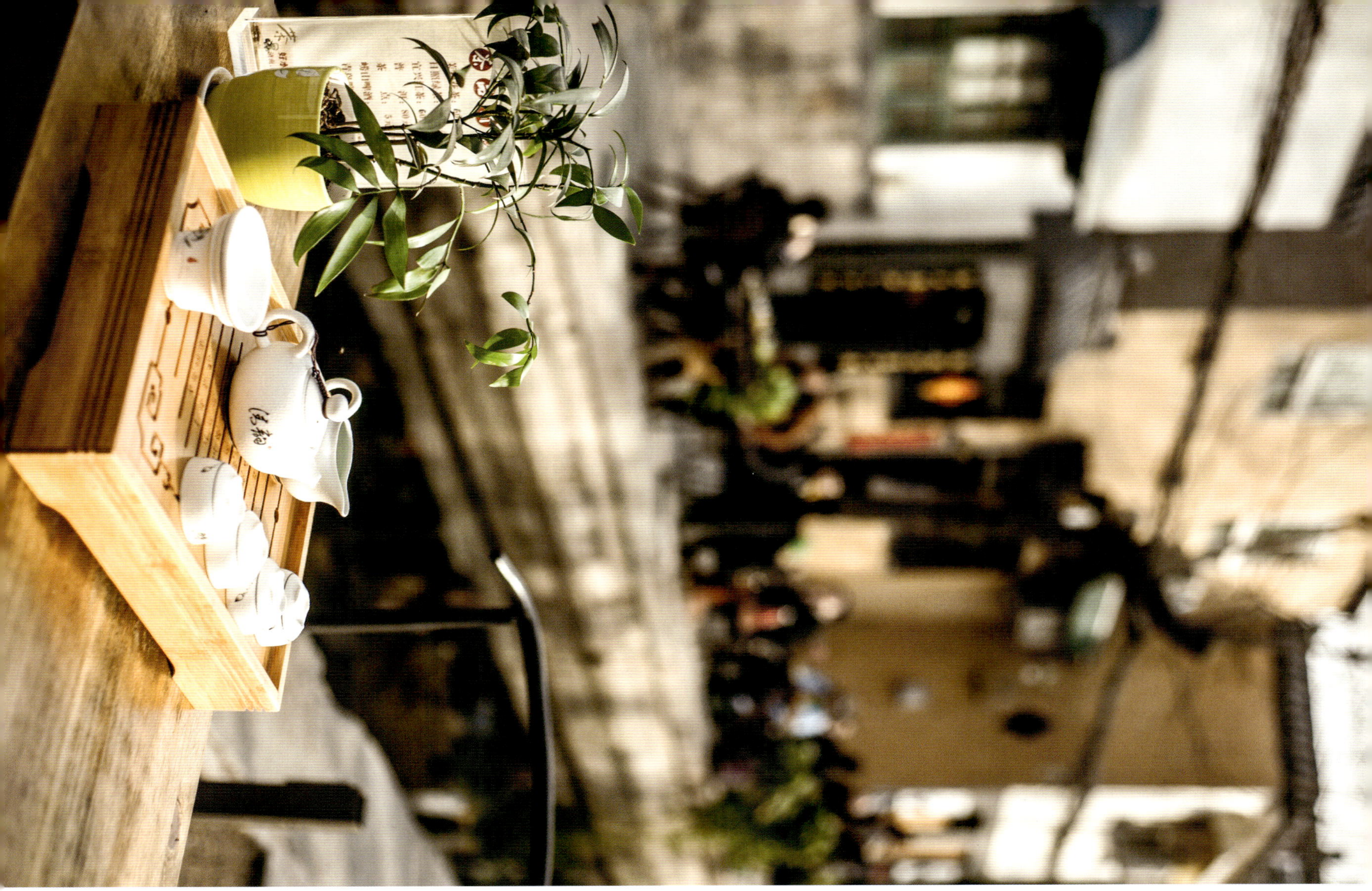

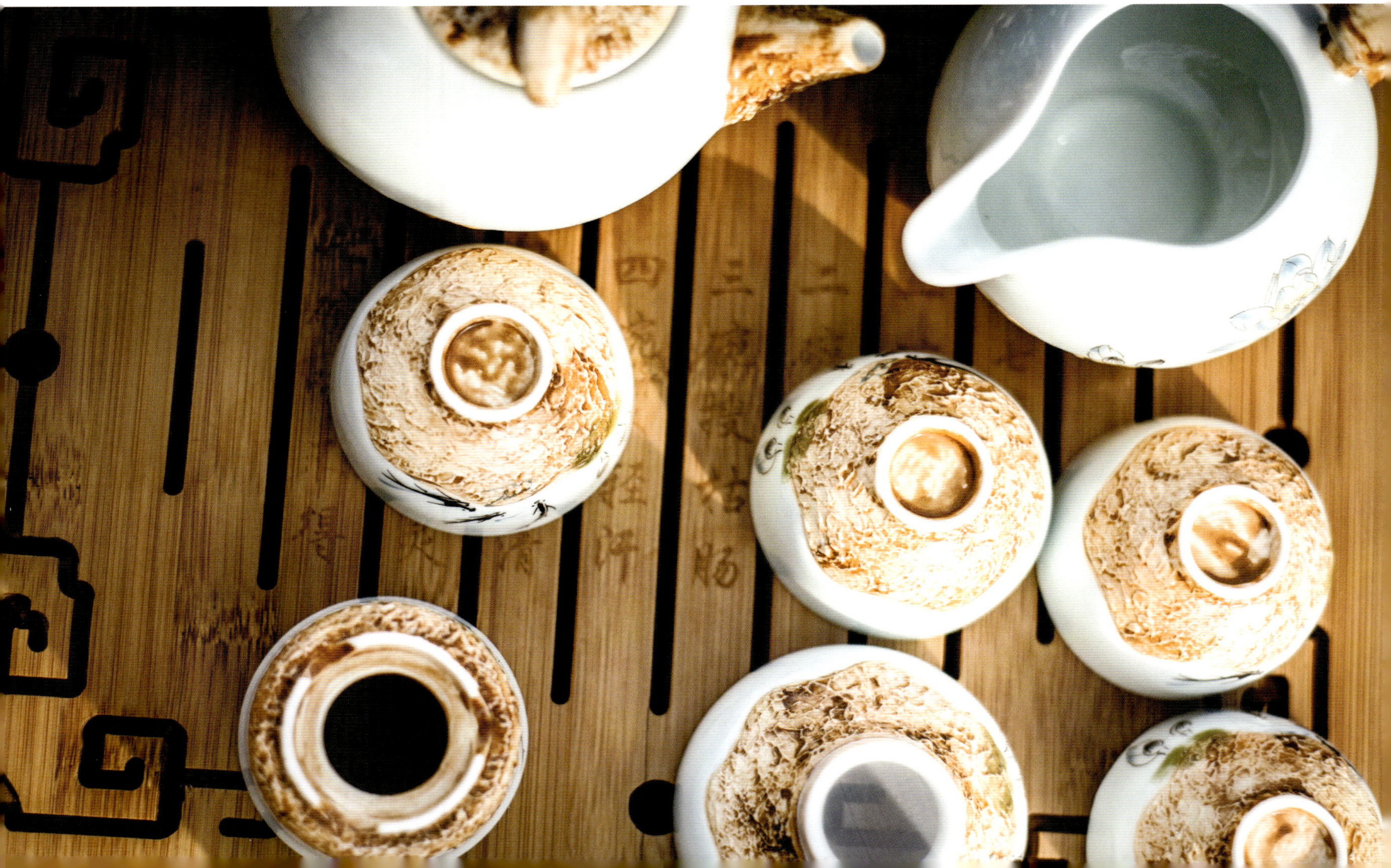

In traditional Chinese society, tea plays an essential part in cultural roles. Members of the younger generation show respect to their elders by offering a cup of tea. Historically, tea even played a role in the class system with people in lower social classes serving tea to the aristocracy. The pouring of tea continues to be a valued ritual, and a boss might pour tea for his subordinates while dining at restaurants to show appreciation.

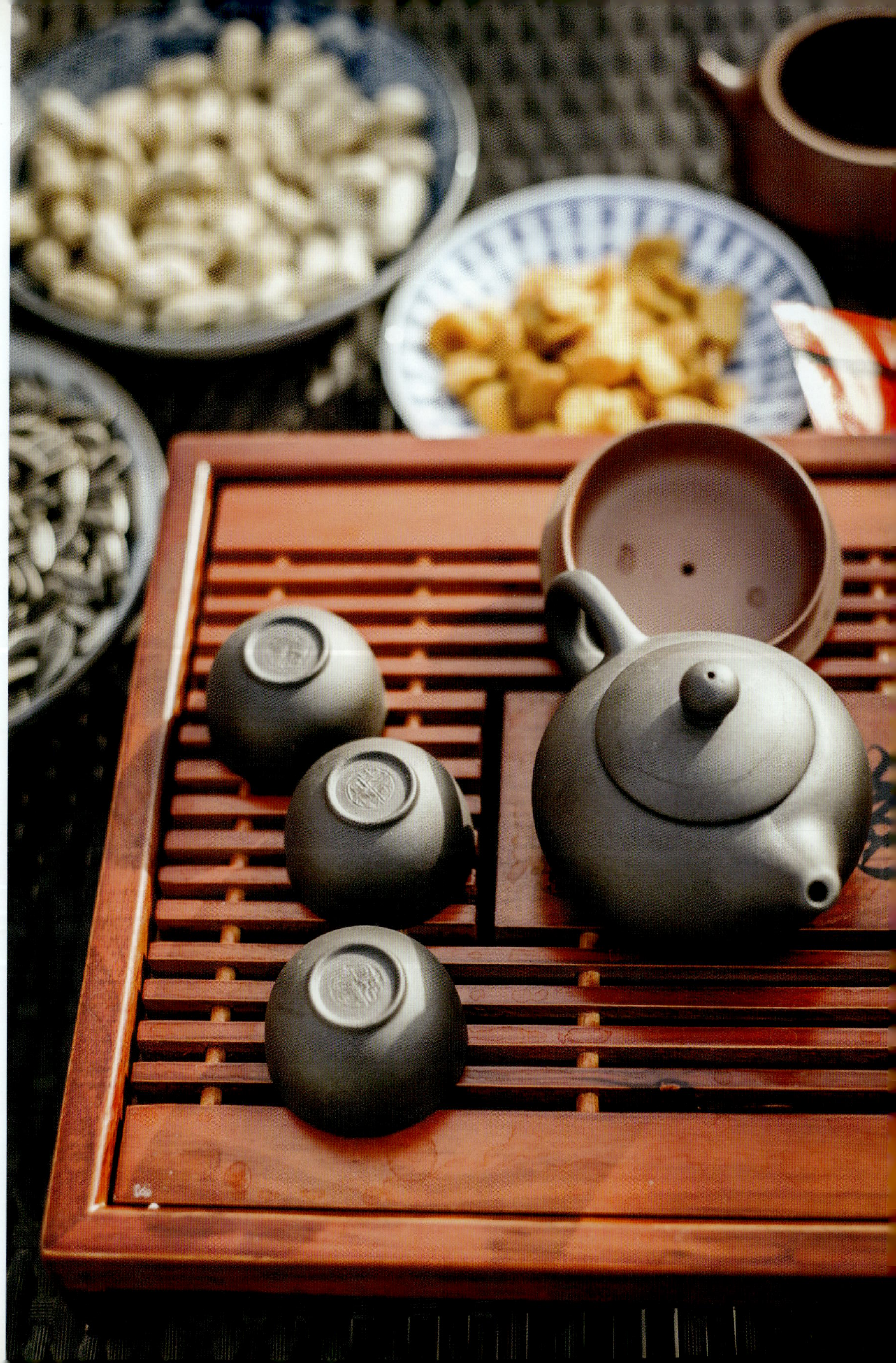

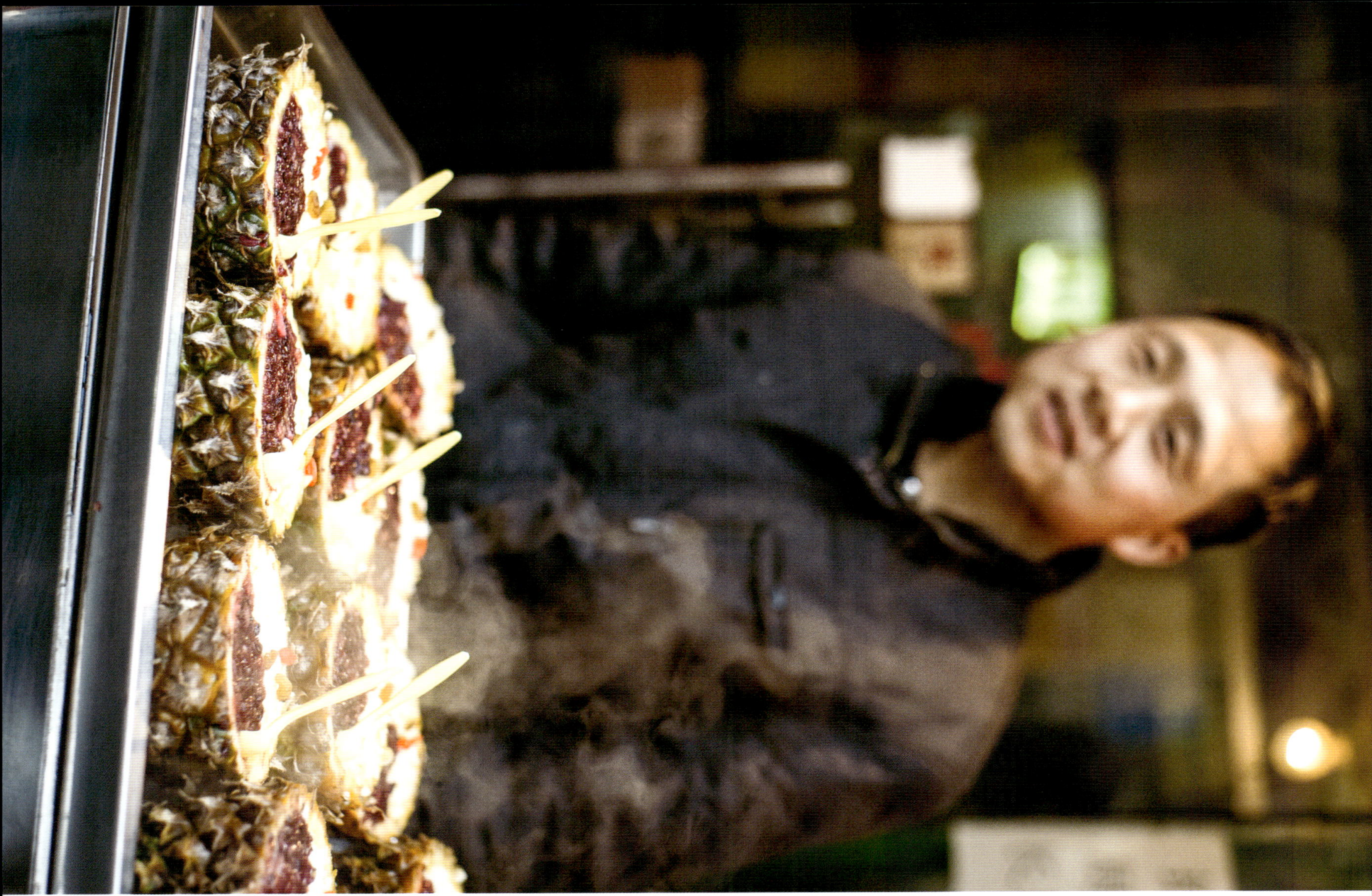

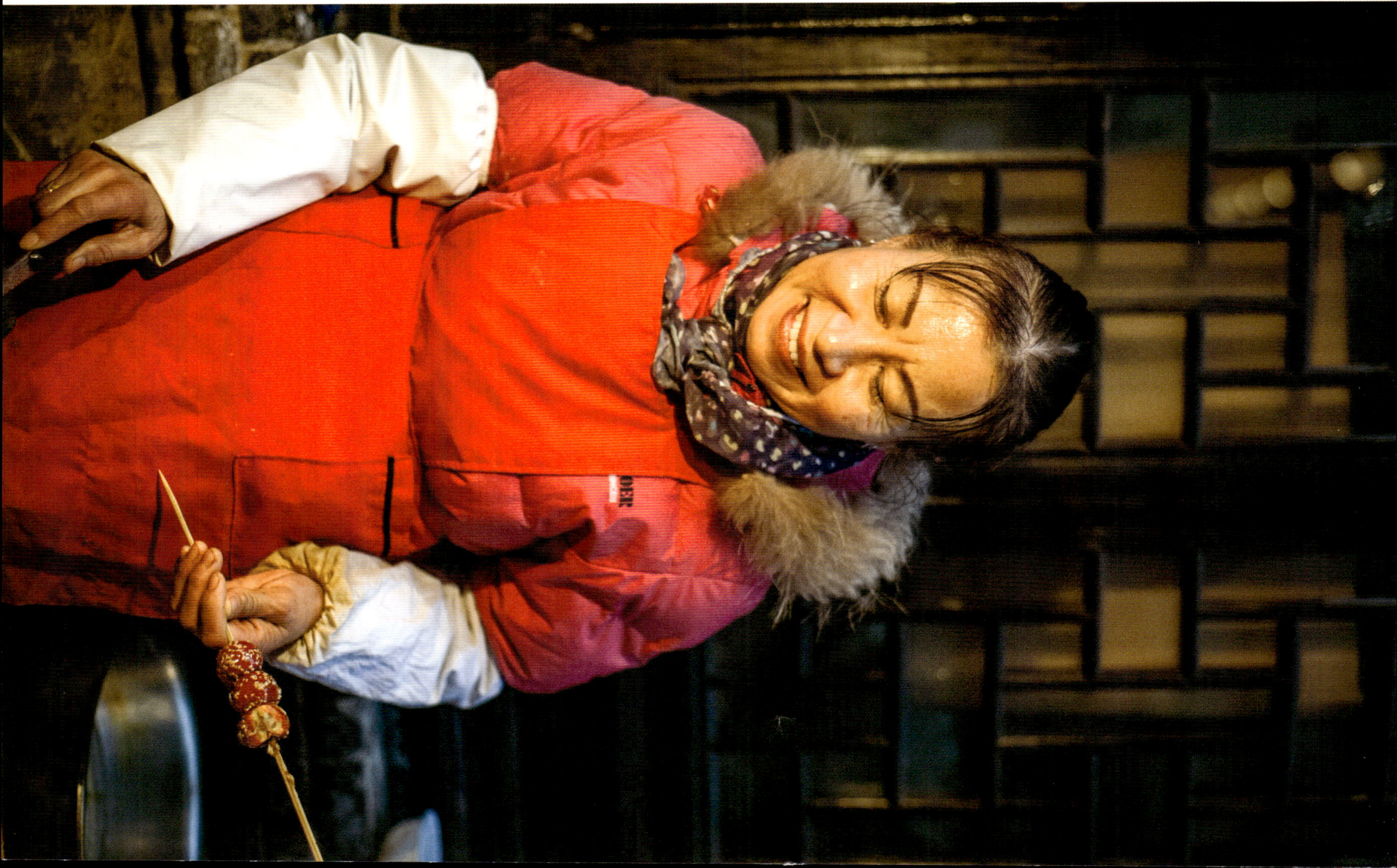

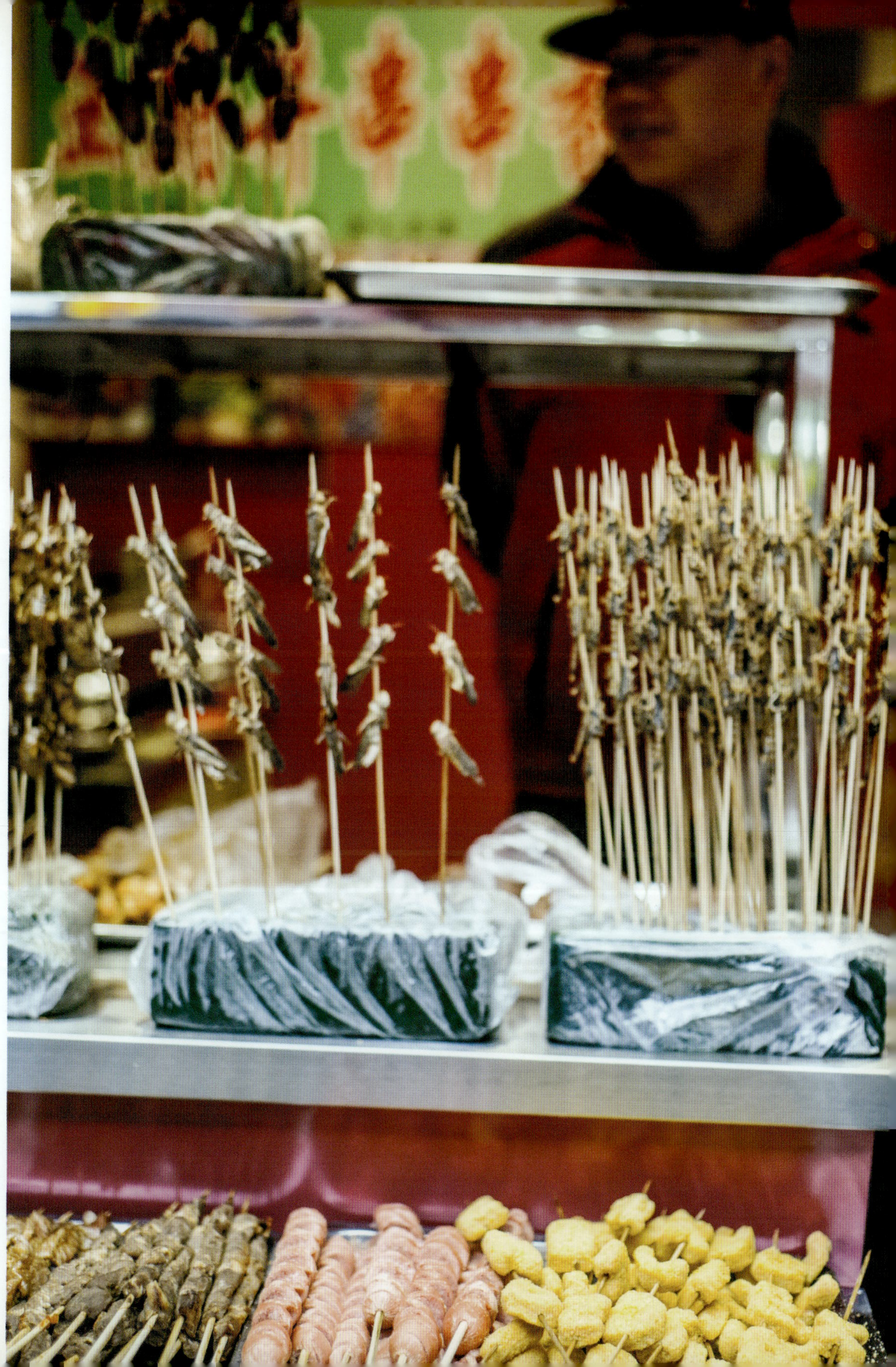

Grasshopper, anyone? Chinese delicacies are easy to come by "on a stick." You can find everything from silkworms to grasshoppers and more that you can easily eat on the go.

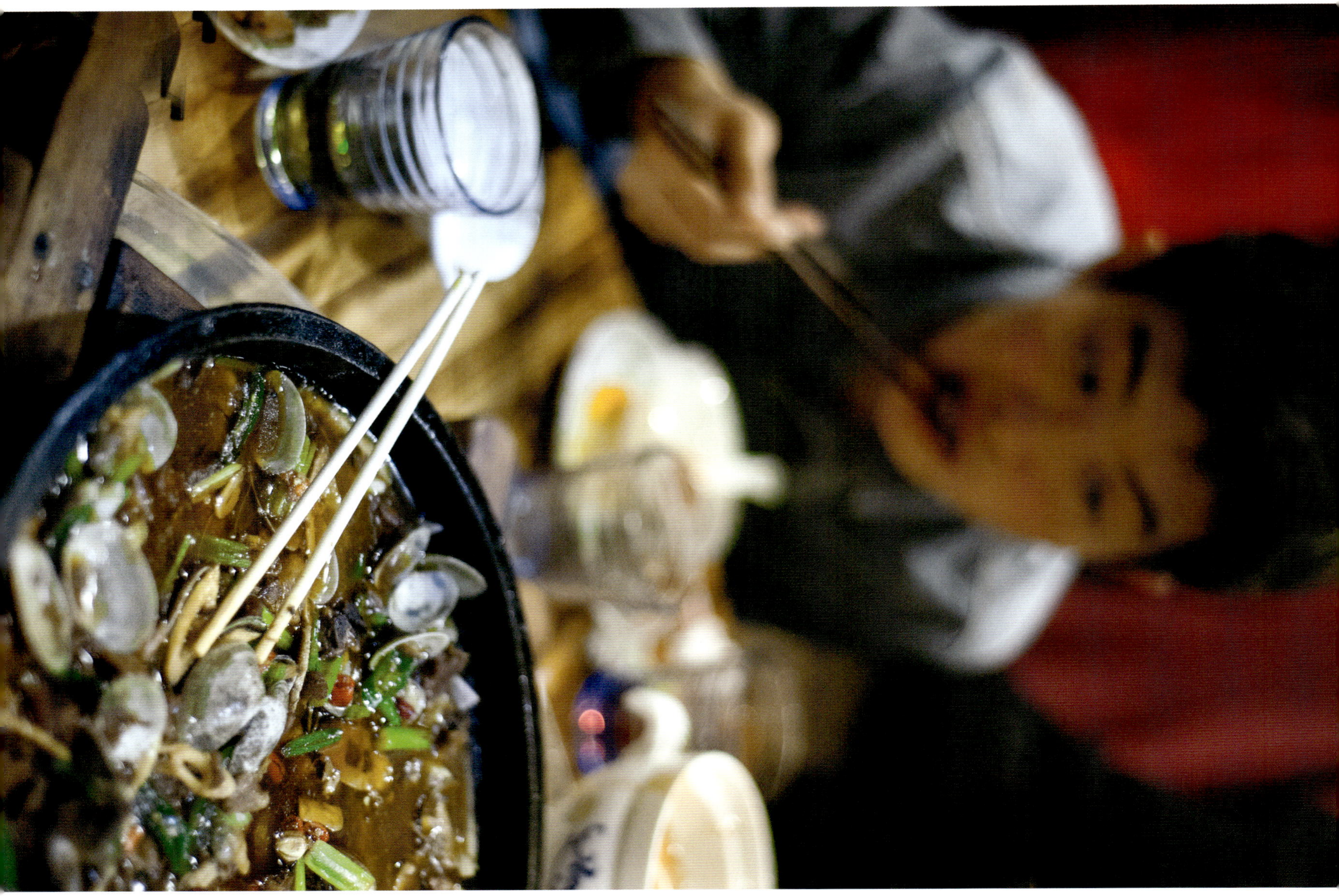

Fresh oysters are made to order right from the grill from one of the many street vendors that can be found here year-round on the famous Furong Street.

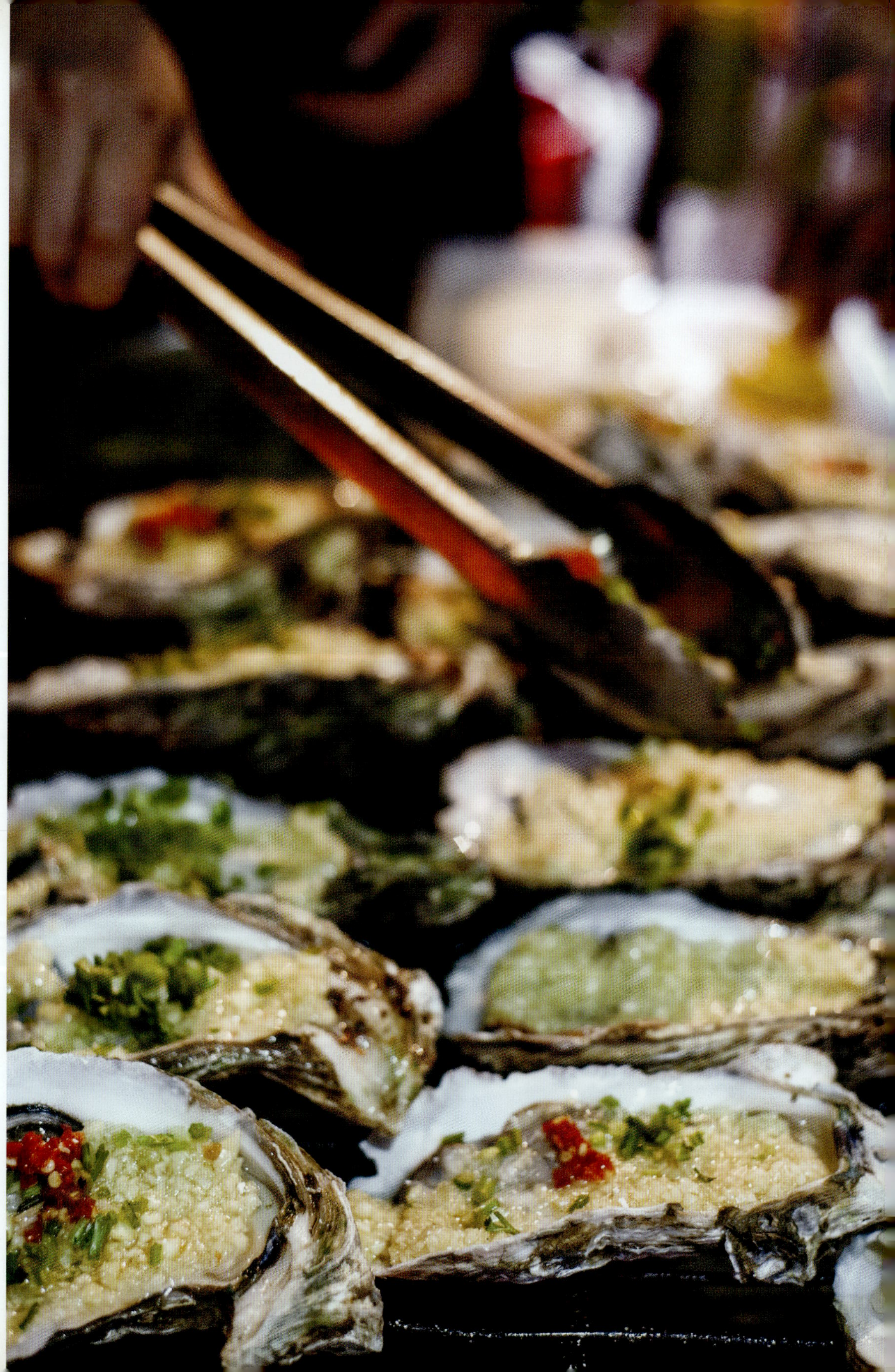

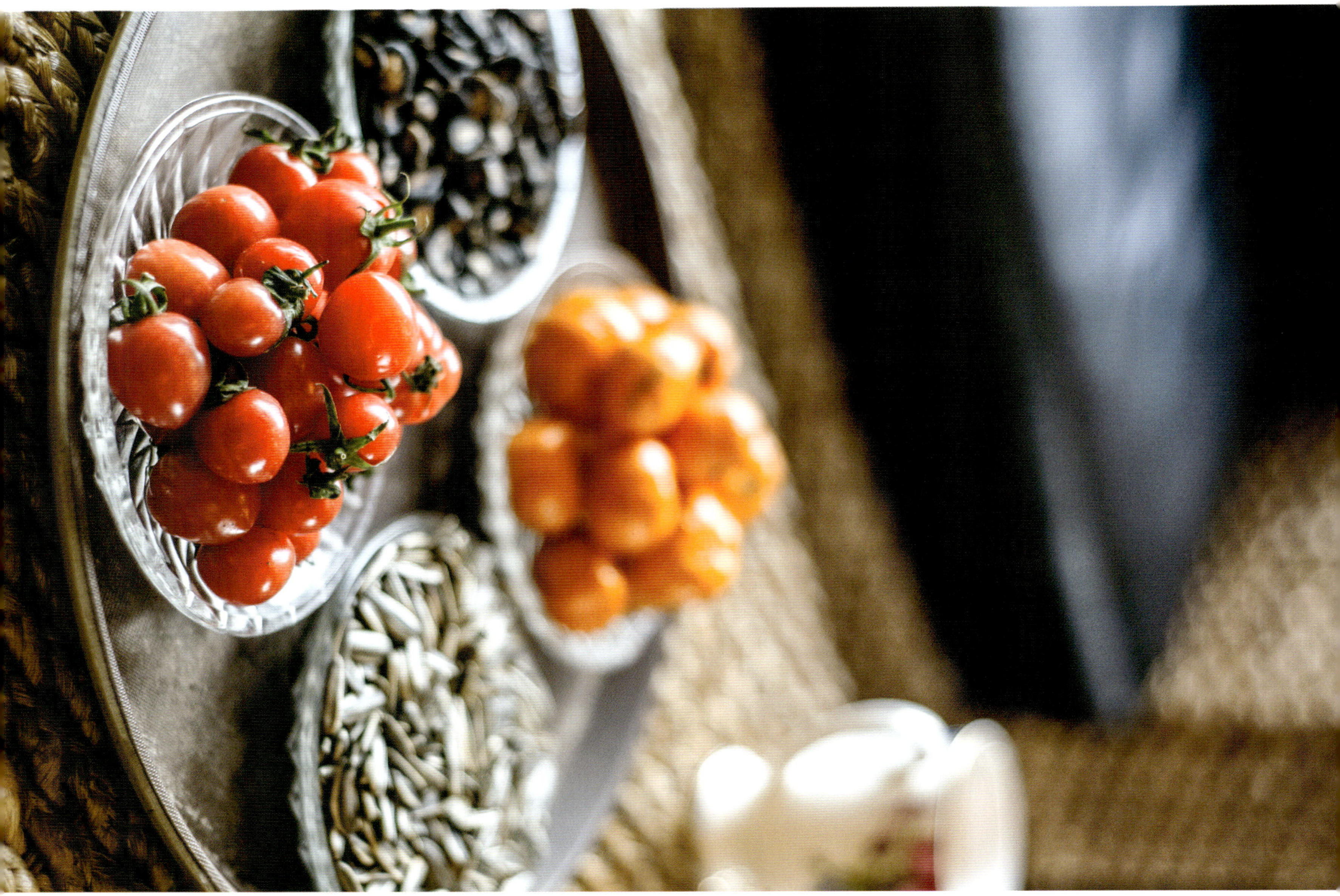

Giant, mouthwatering radishes are sold in diced sections. The "Beauty Heart" radish is very large, with four-inch round roots and white and green skin. It is often referred to as the "watermelon radish," due to its bright reddish-pink center, and has a sweeter taste than other radishes.

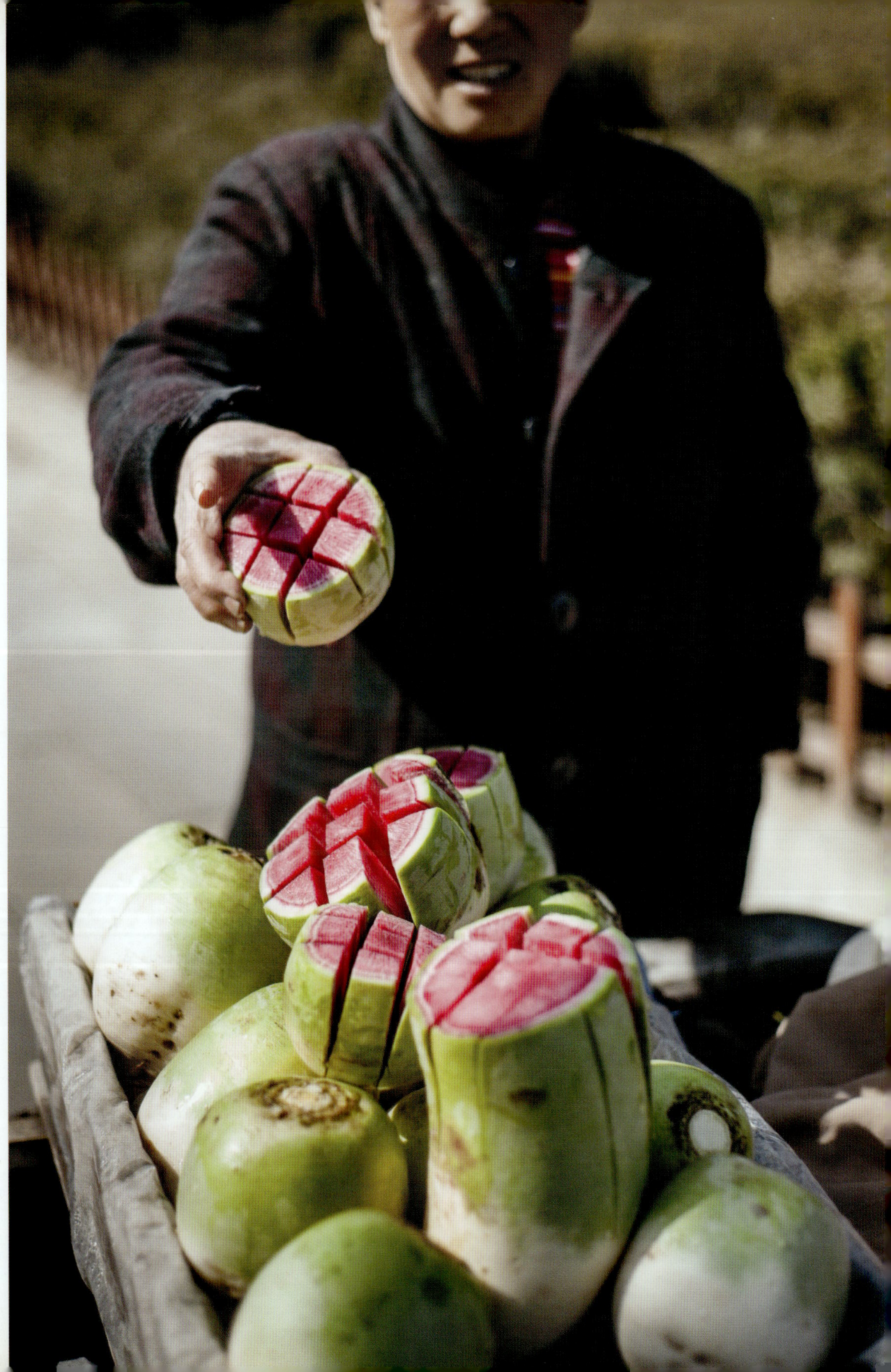

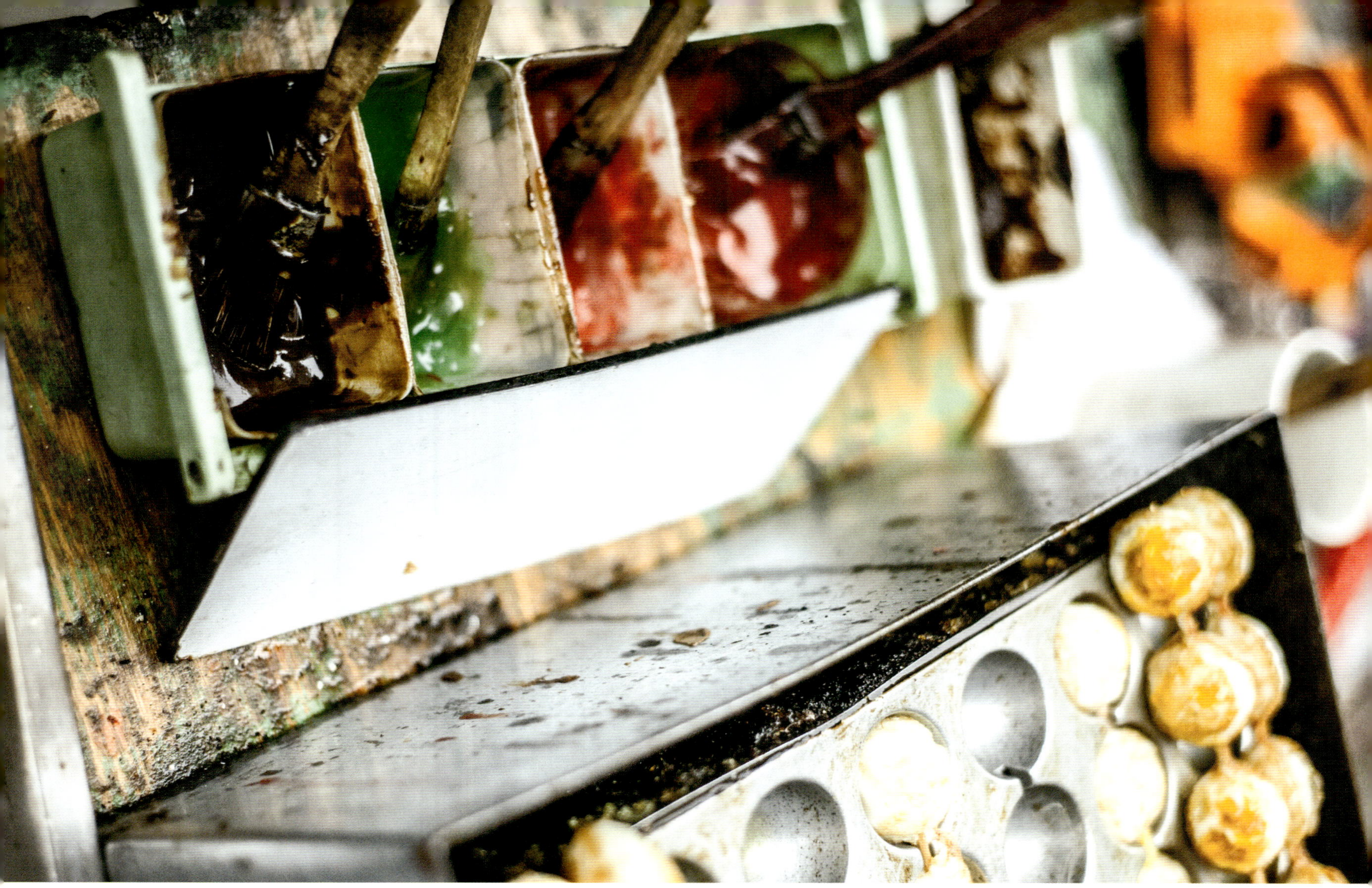

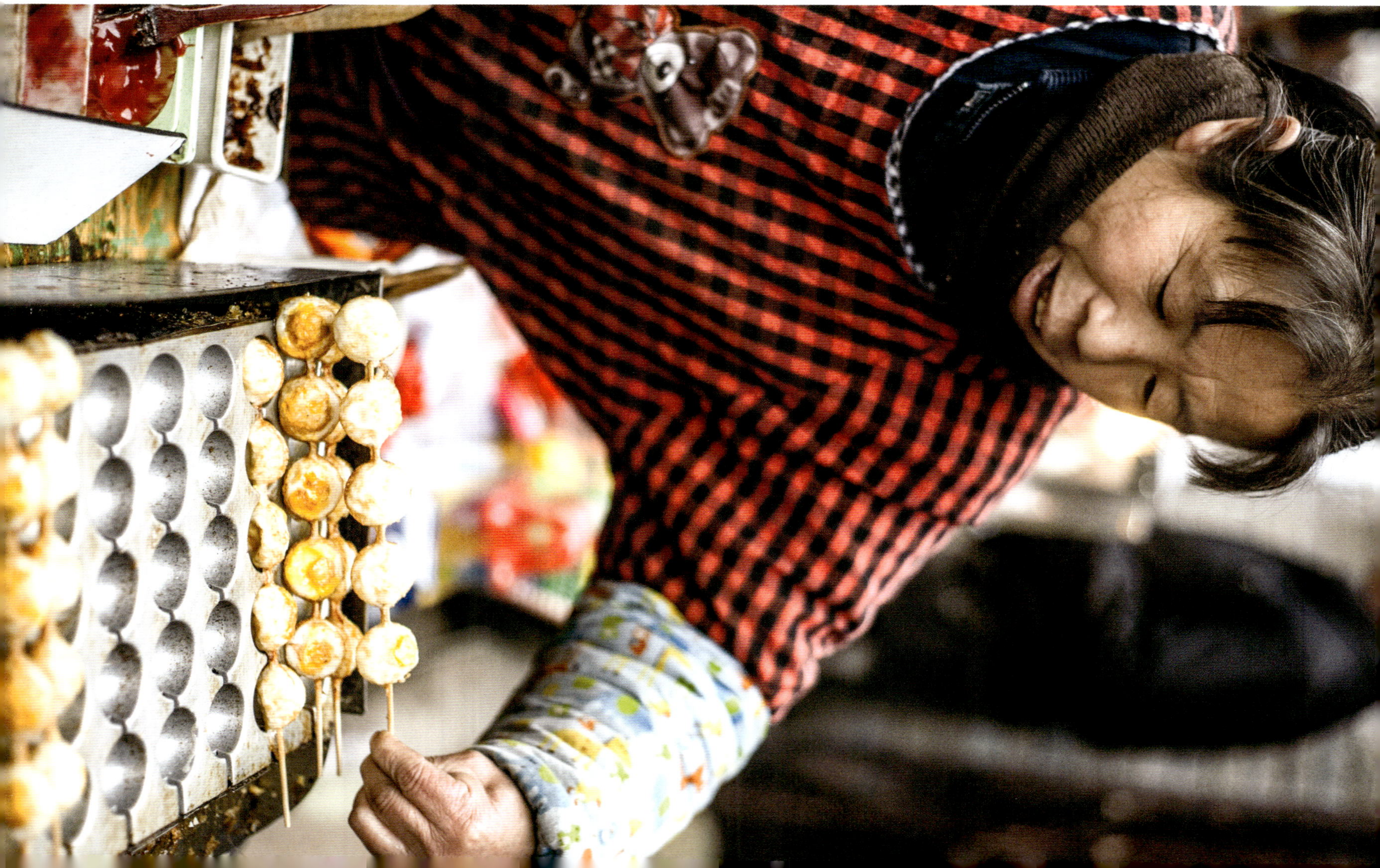

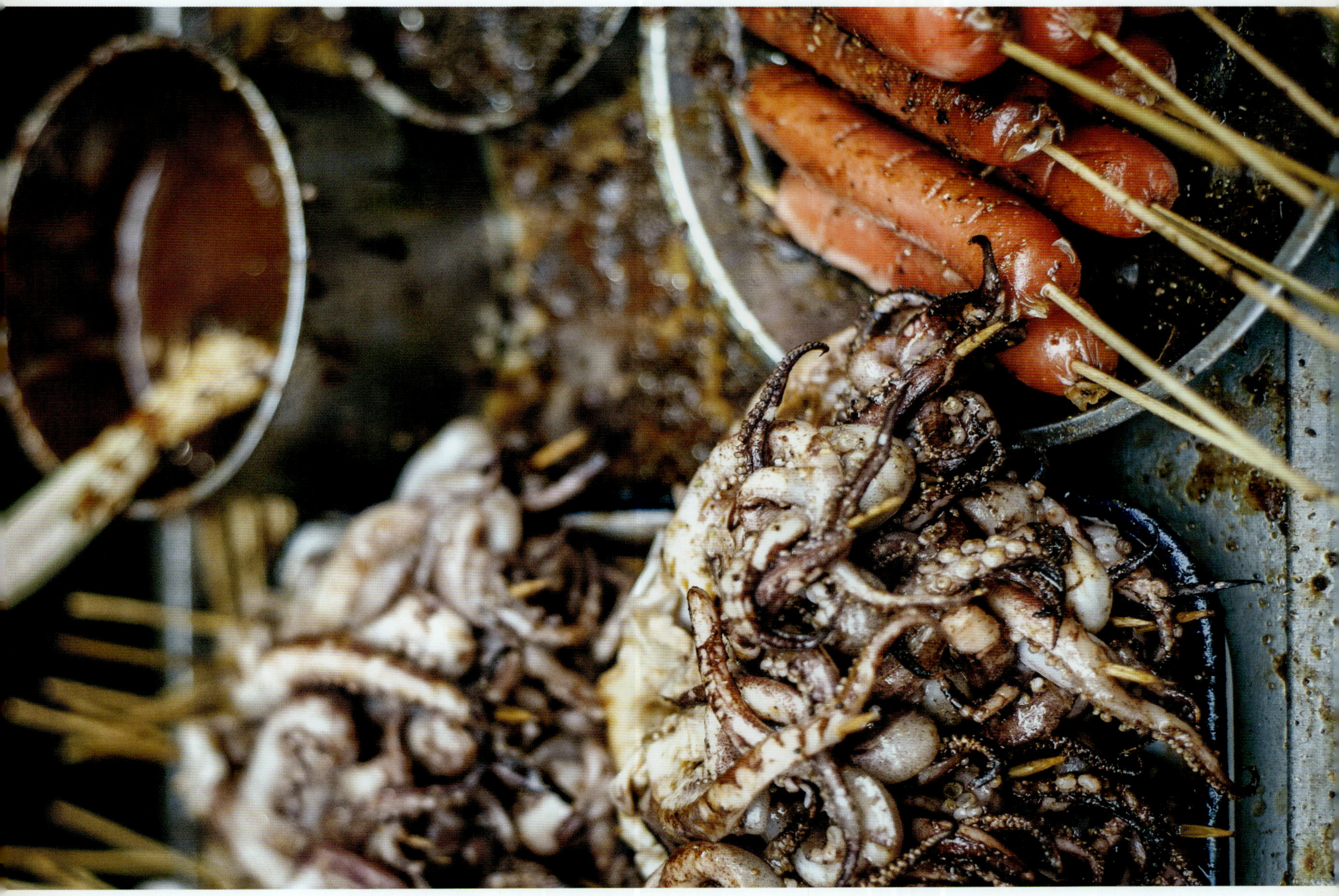

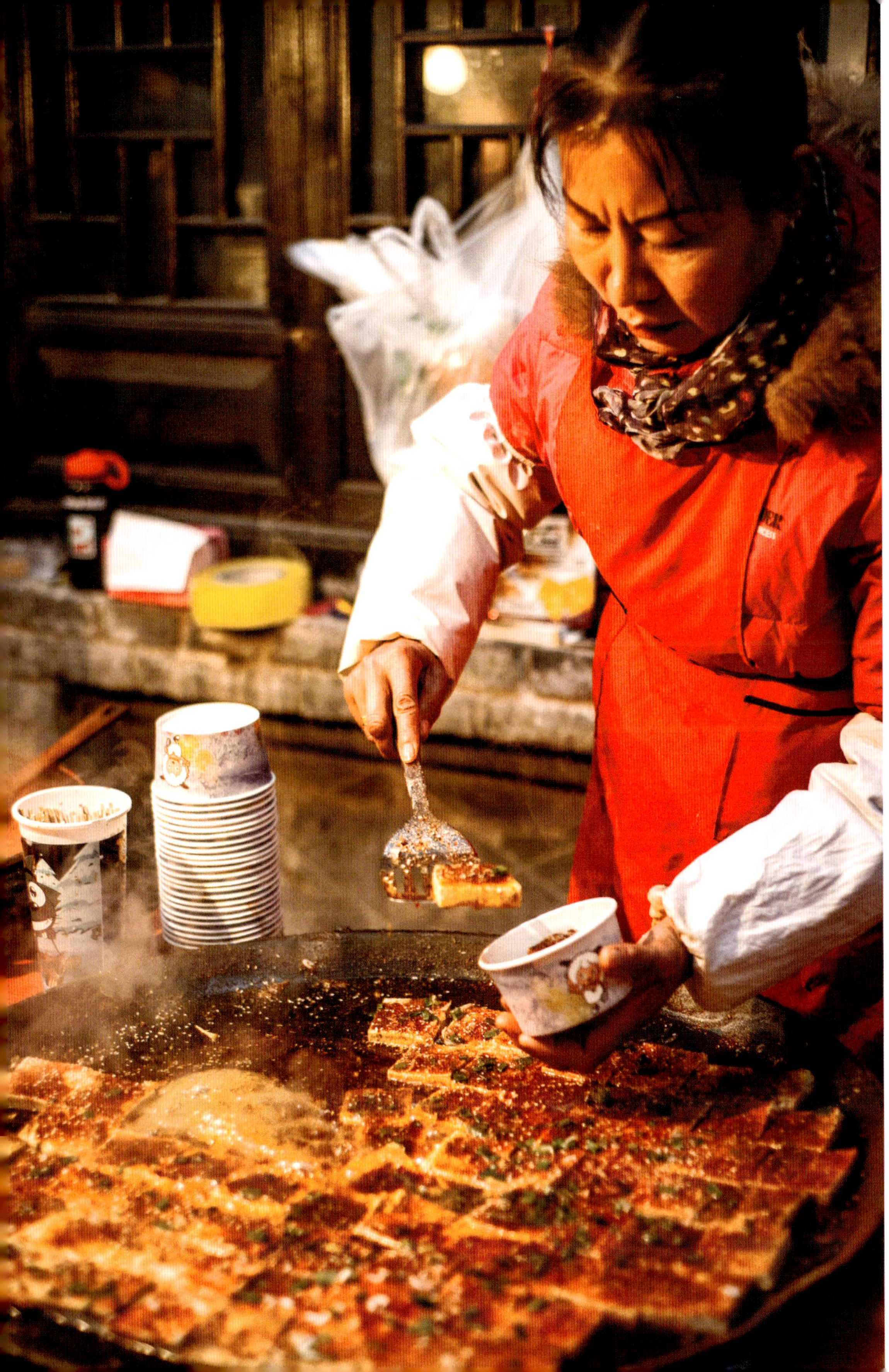

Fried tofu, a popular snack, is sold on the street by vendors.

Noodles are another popular snack sold on the street.

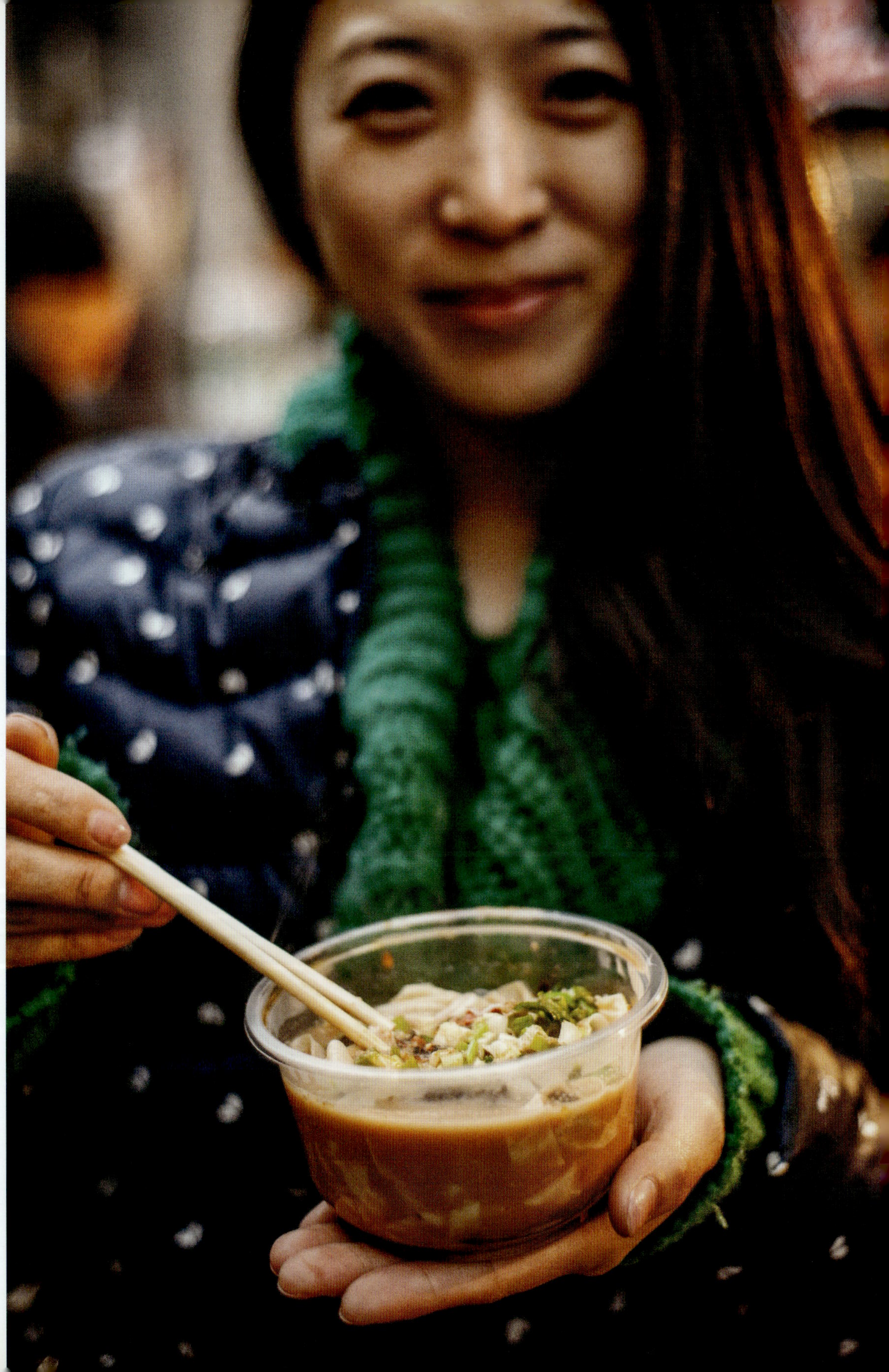

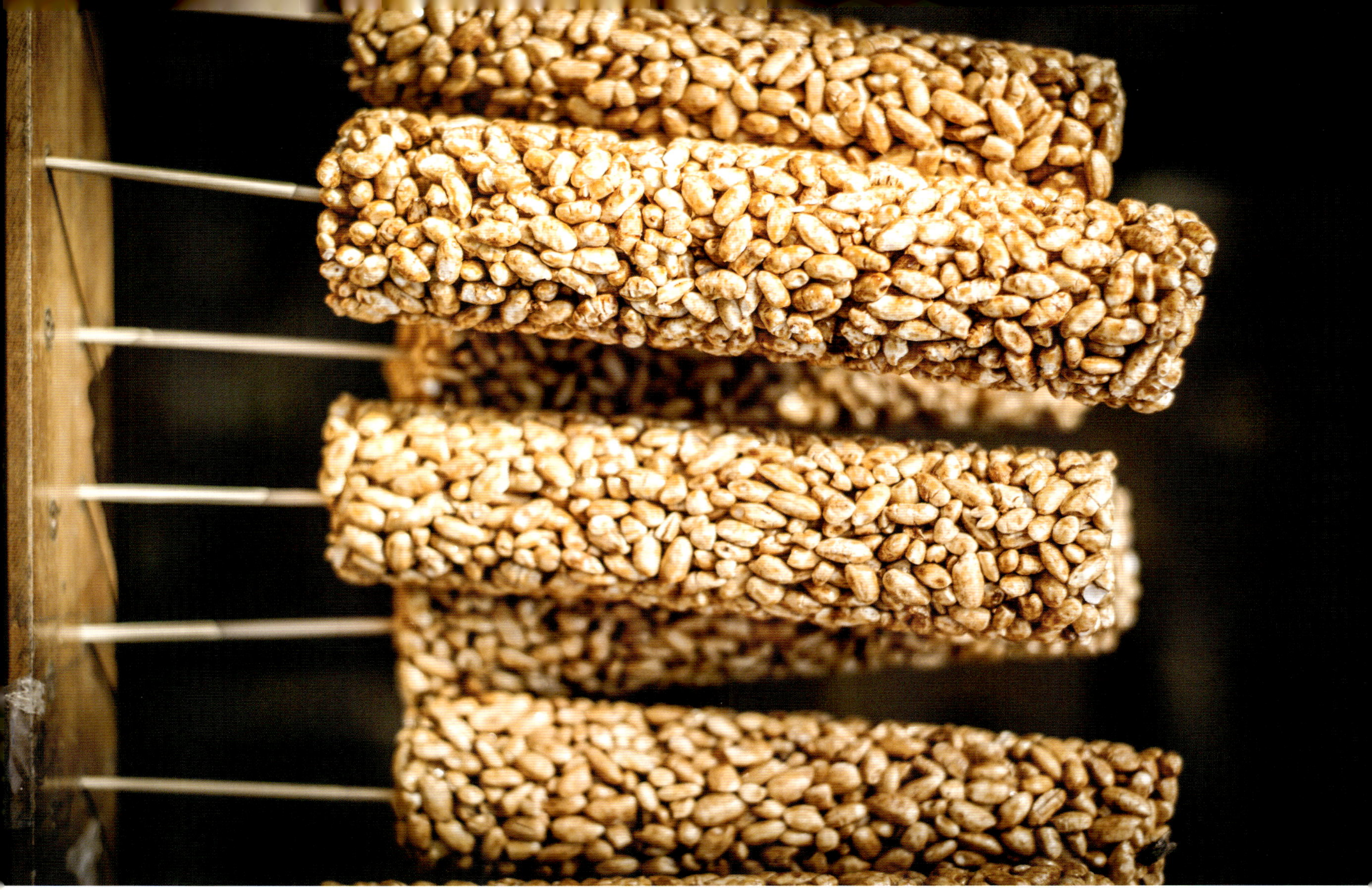

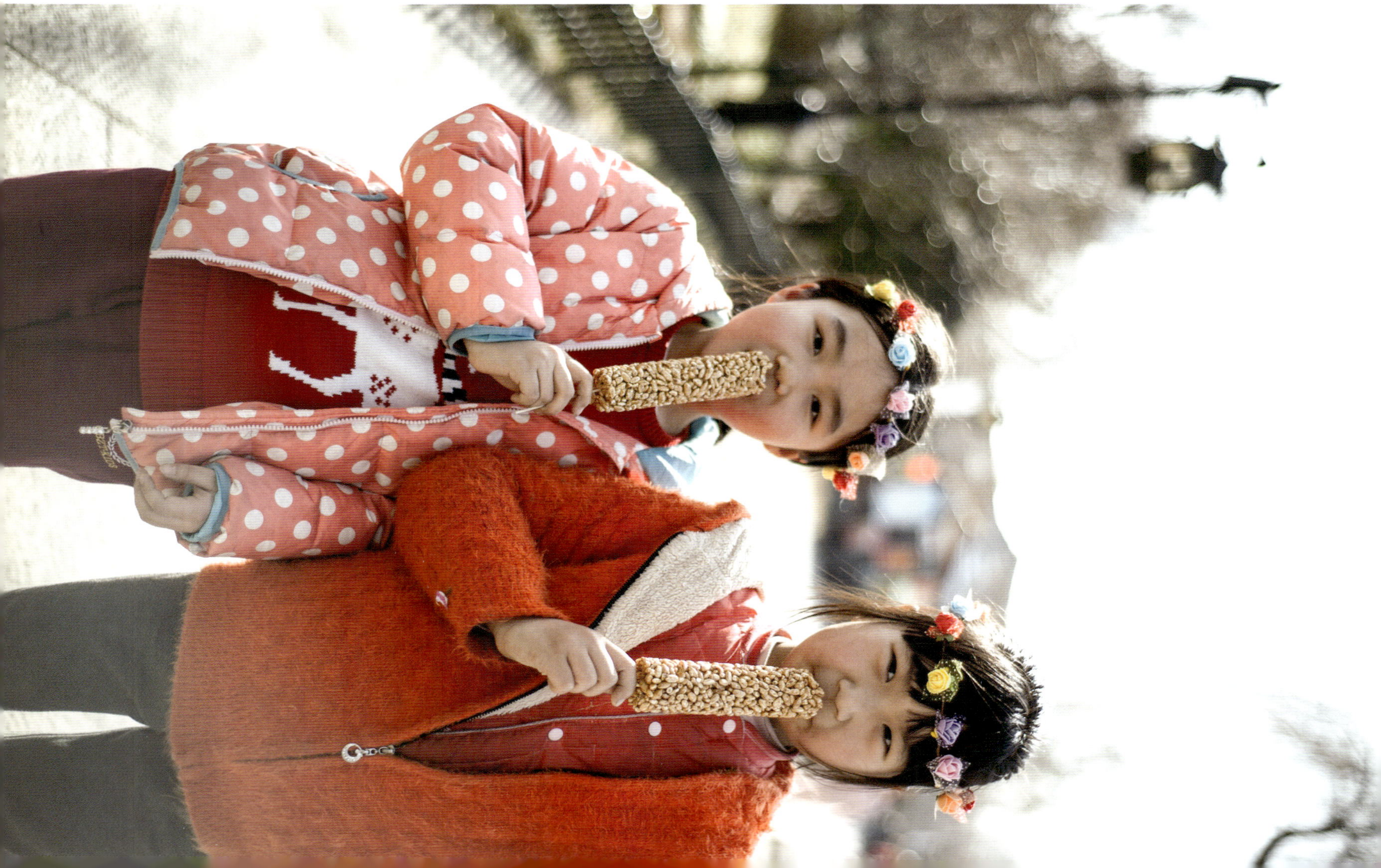

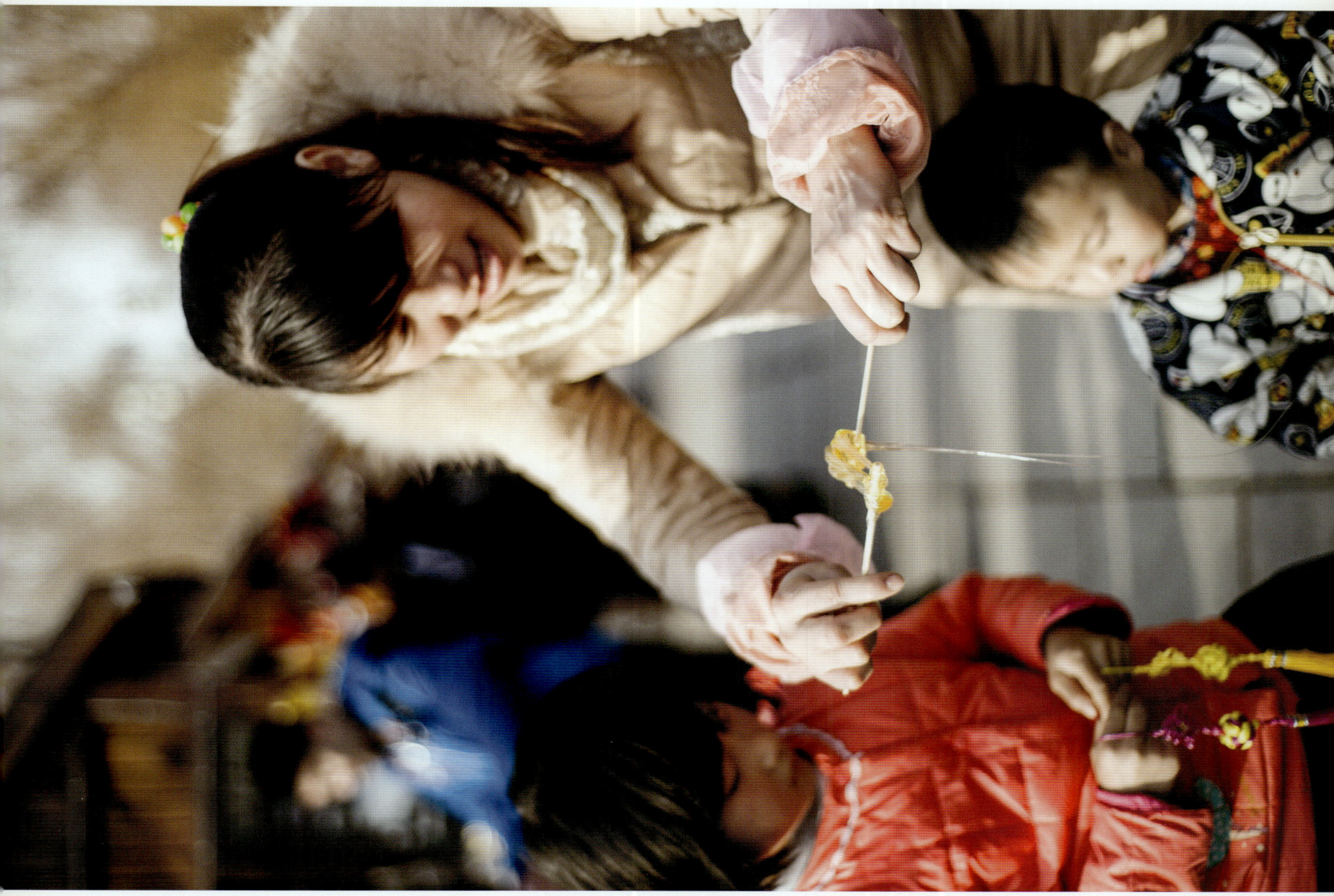

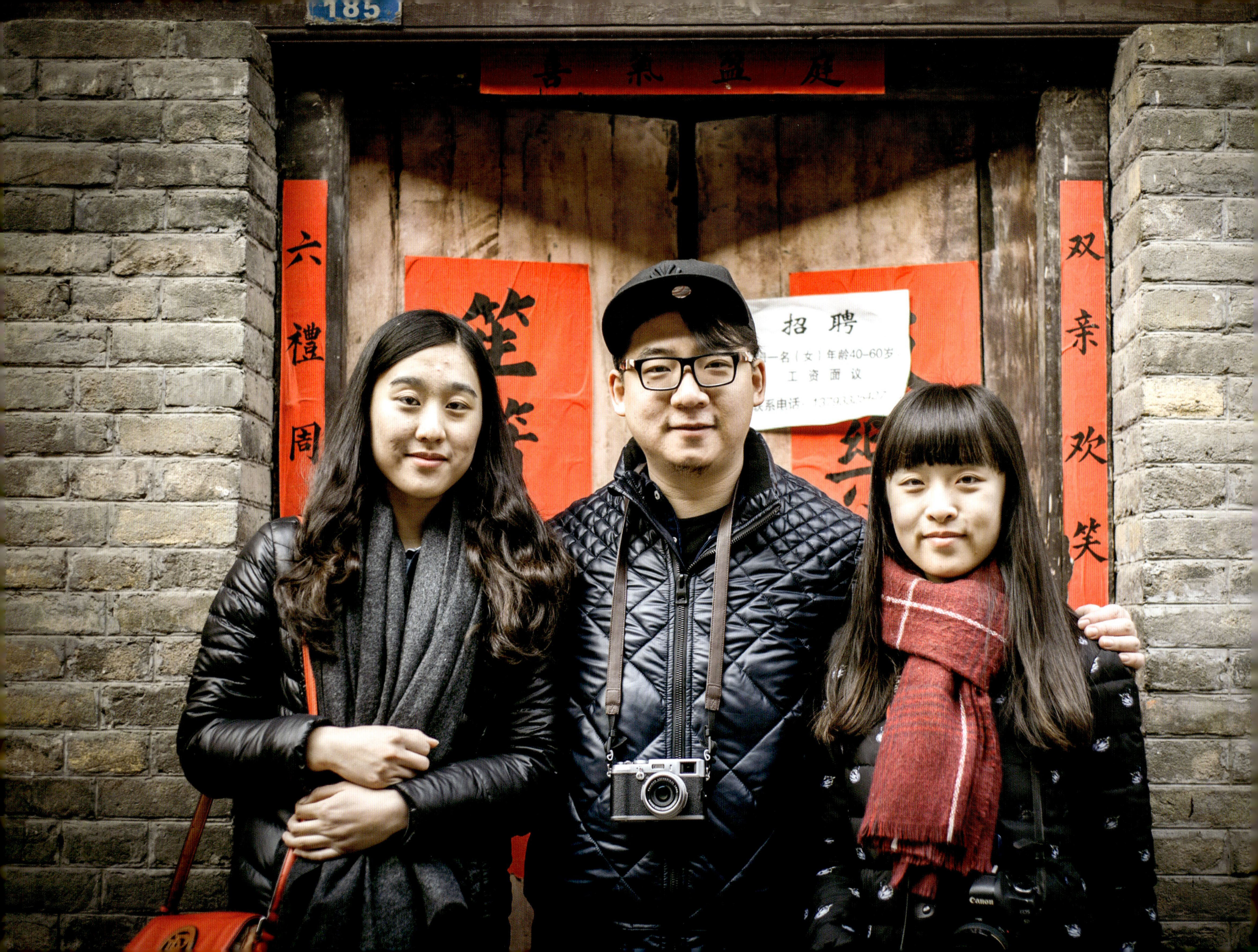
185
六禮周
双亲欢笑
招聘
工资面议

Faces of the Silk Road

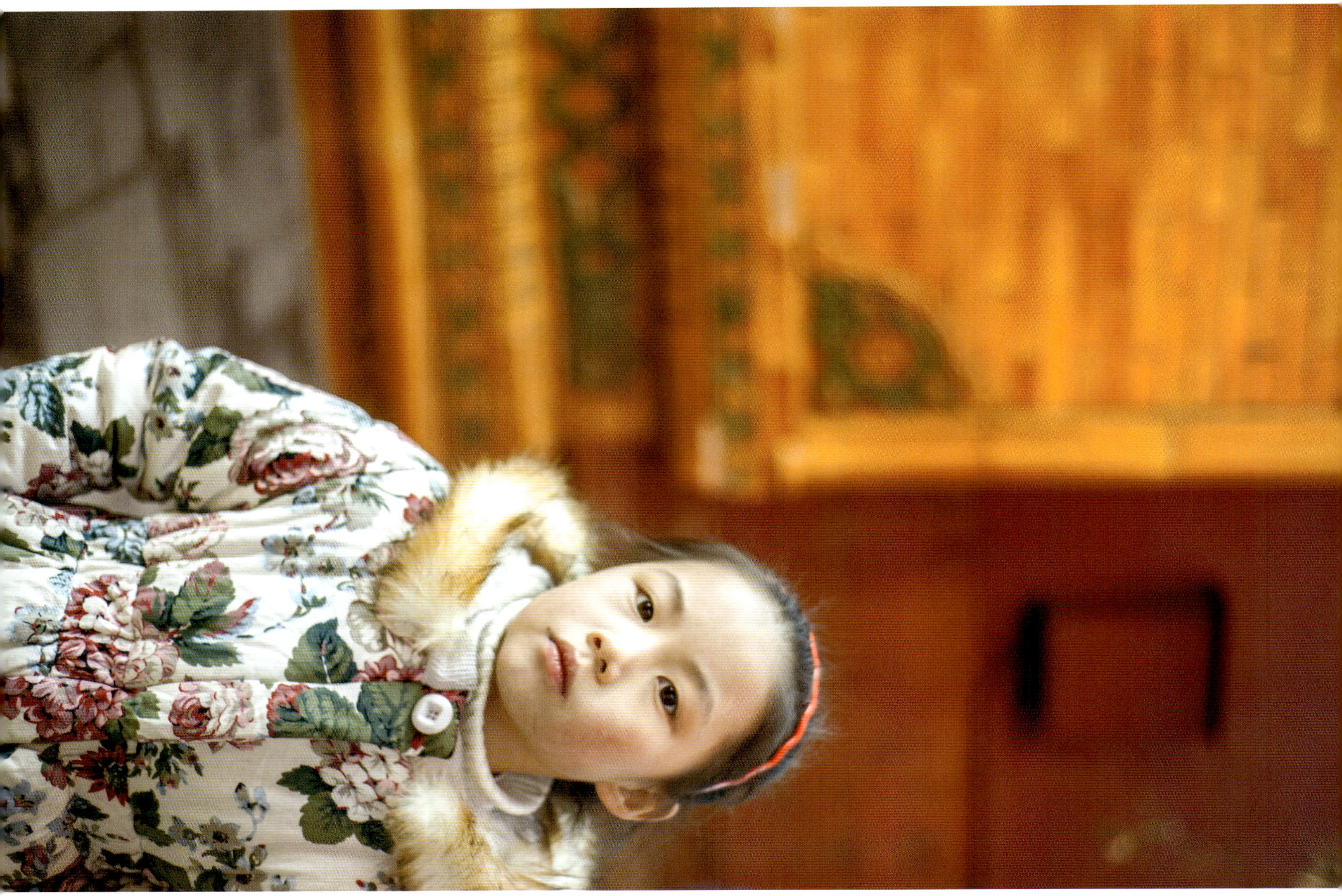

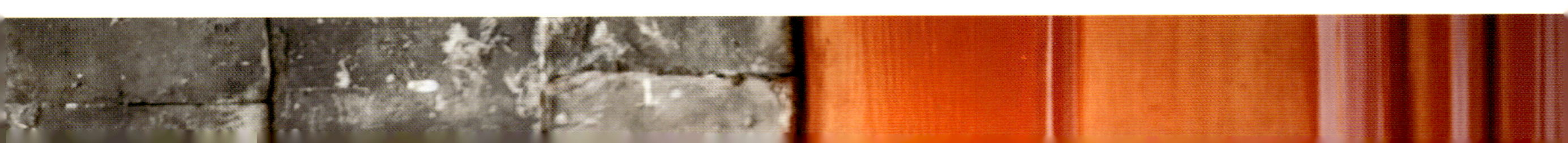

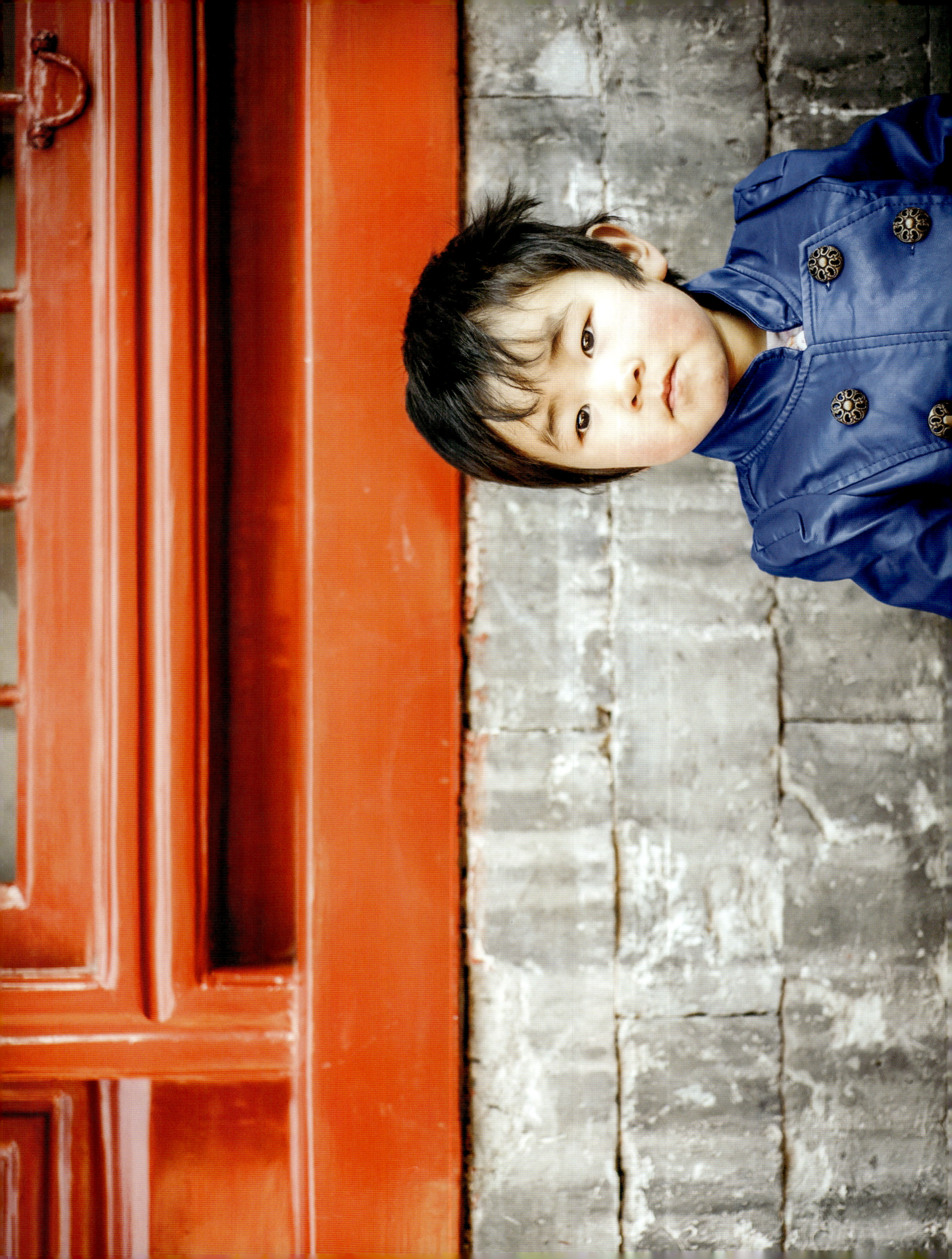

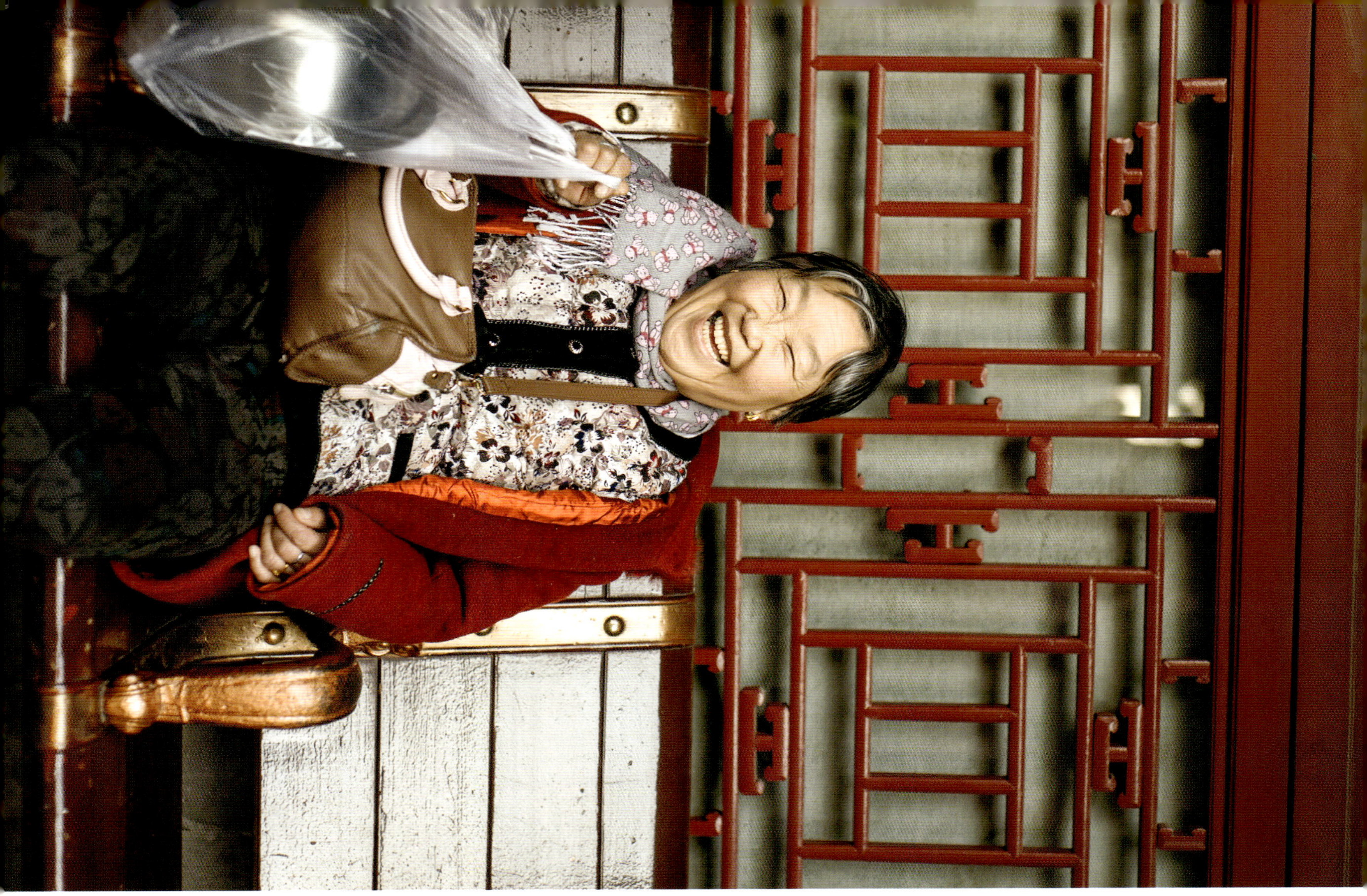

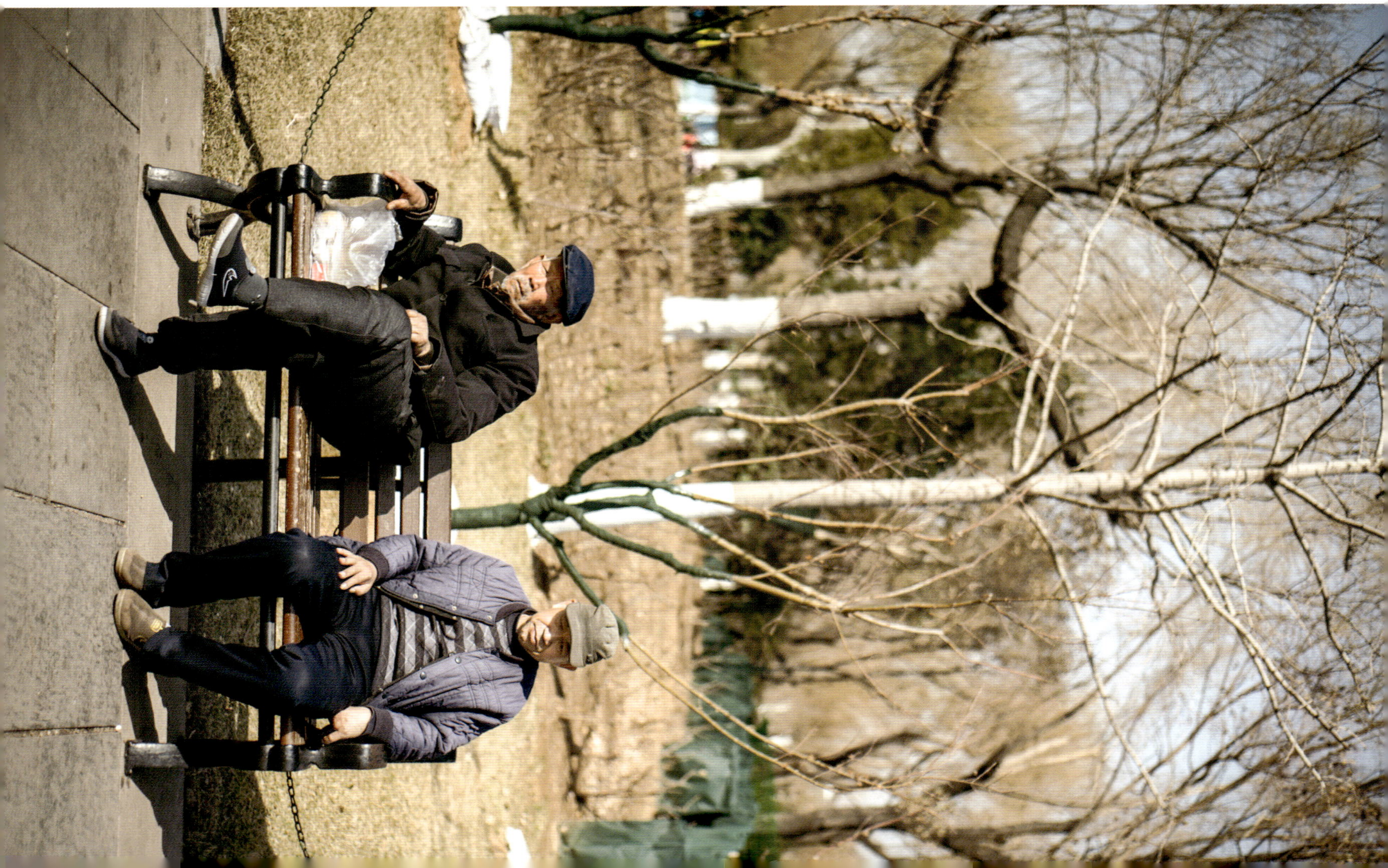

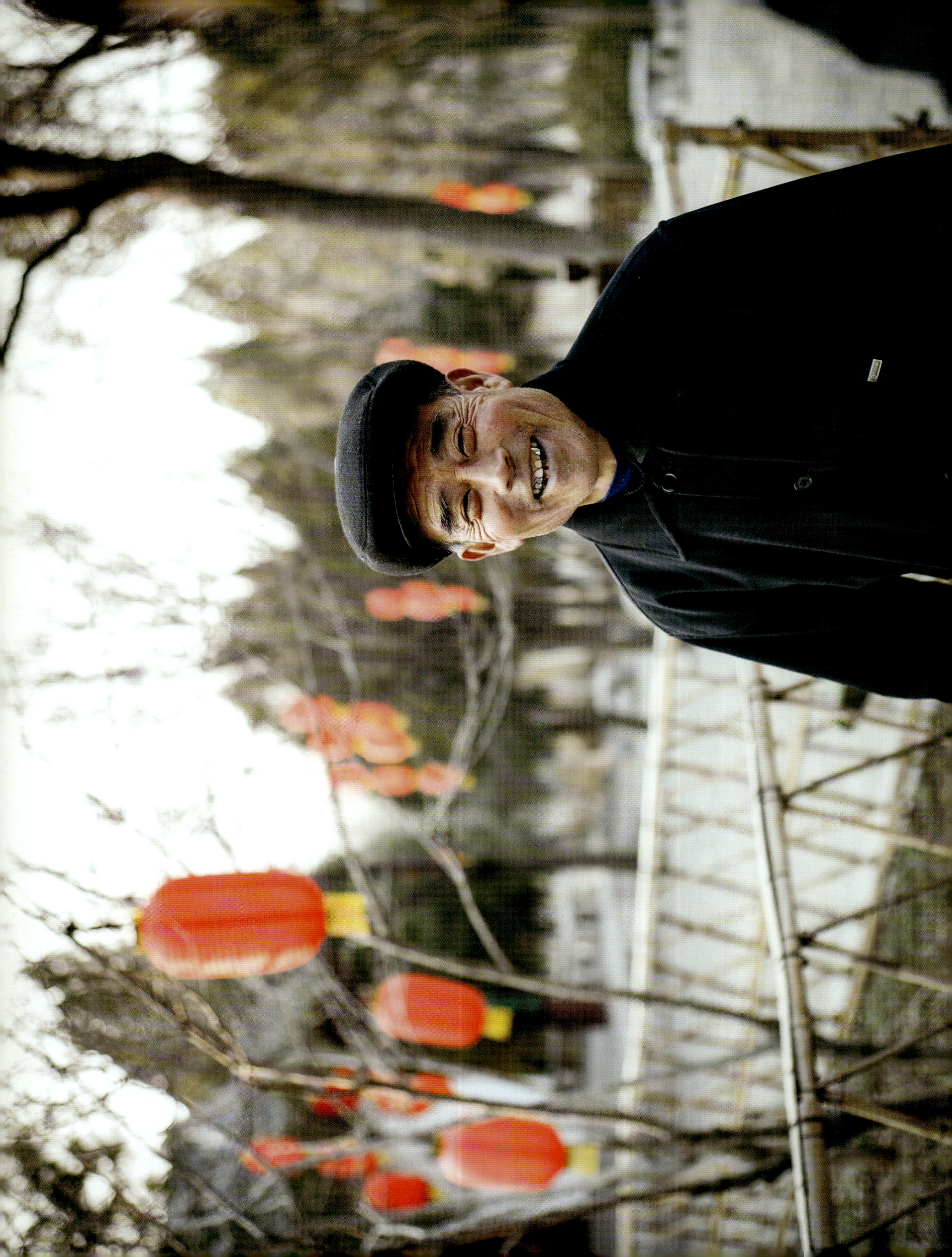

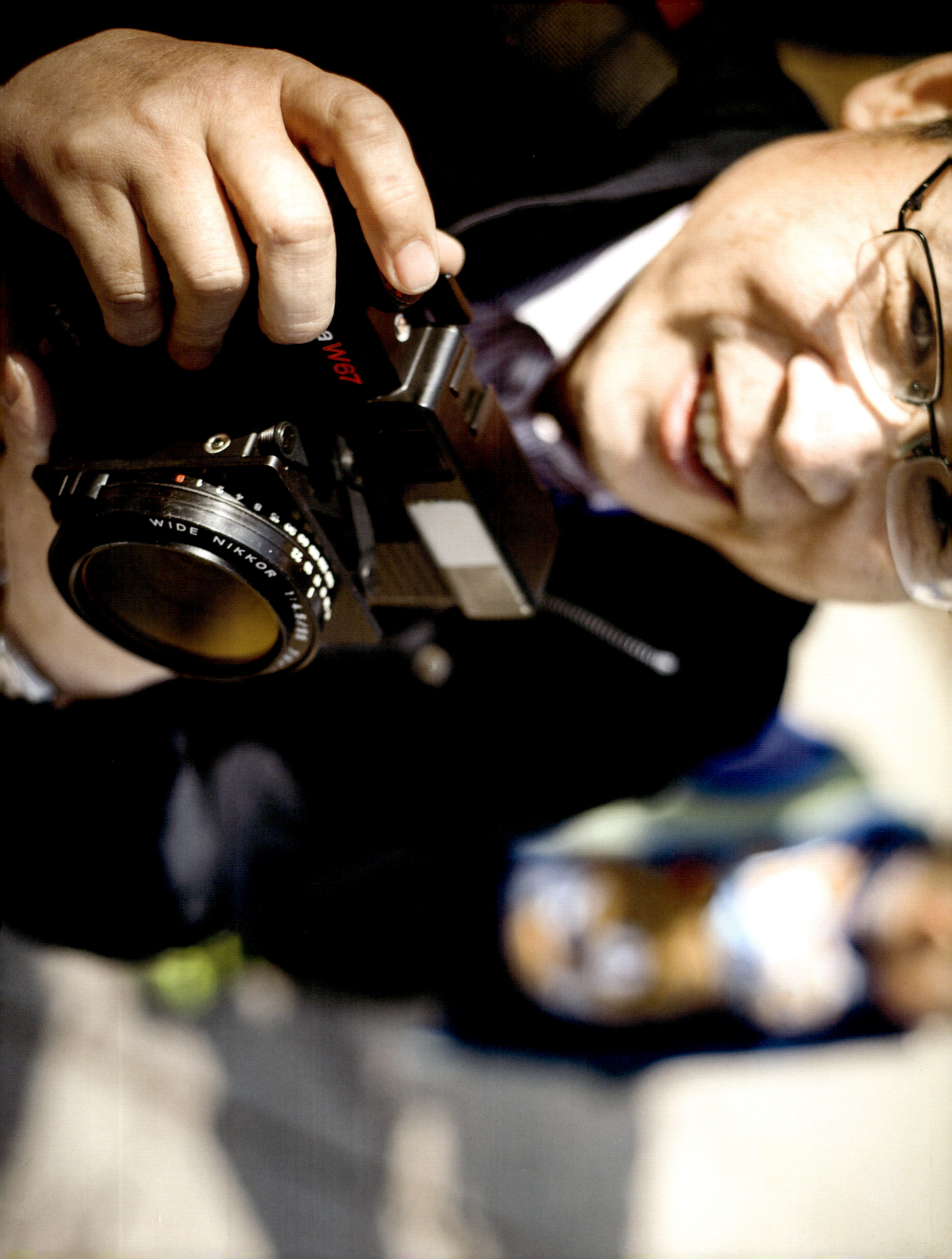
WIDE NIKKOR

Photography is very important in the Chinese culture. The gentleman on the left uses a Plaube IMakina W67 film camera.

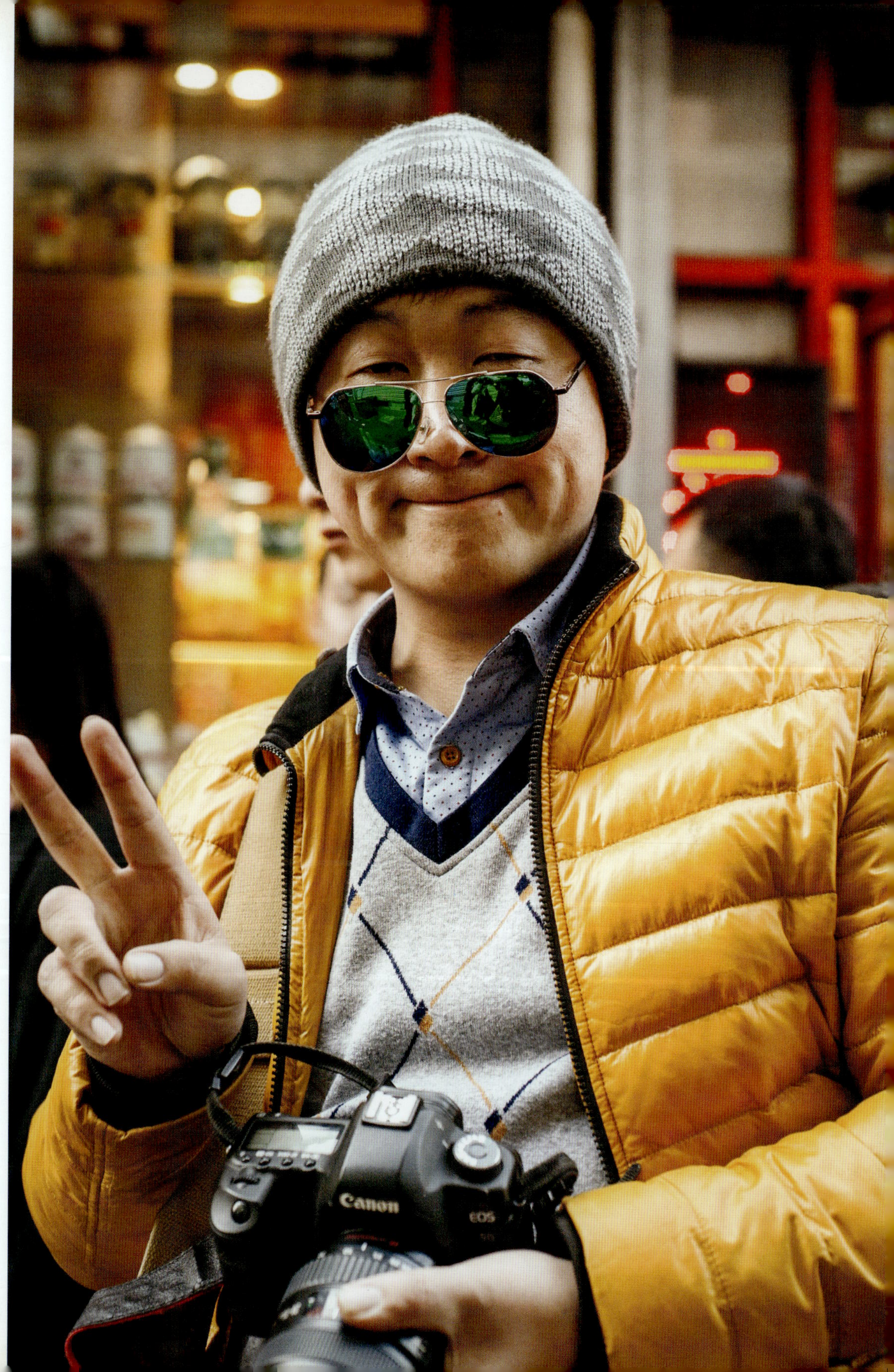

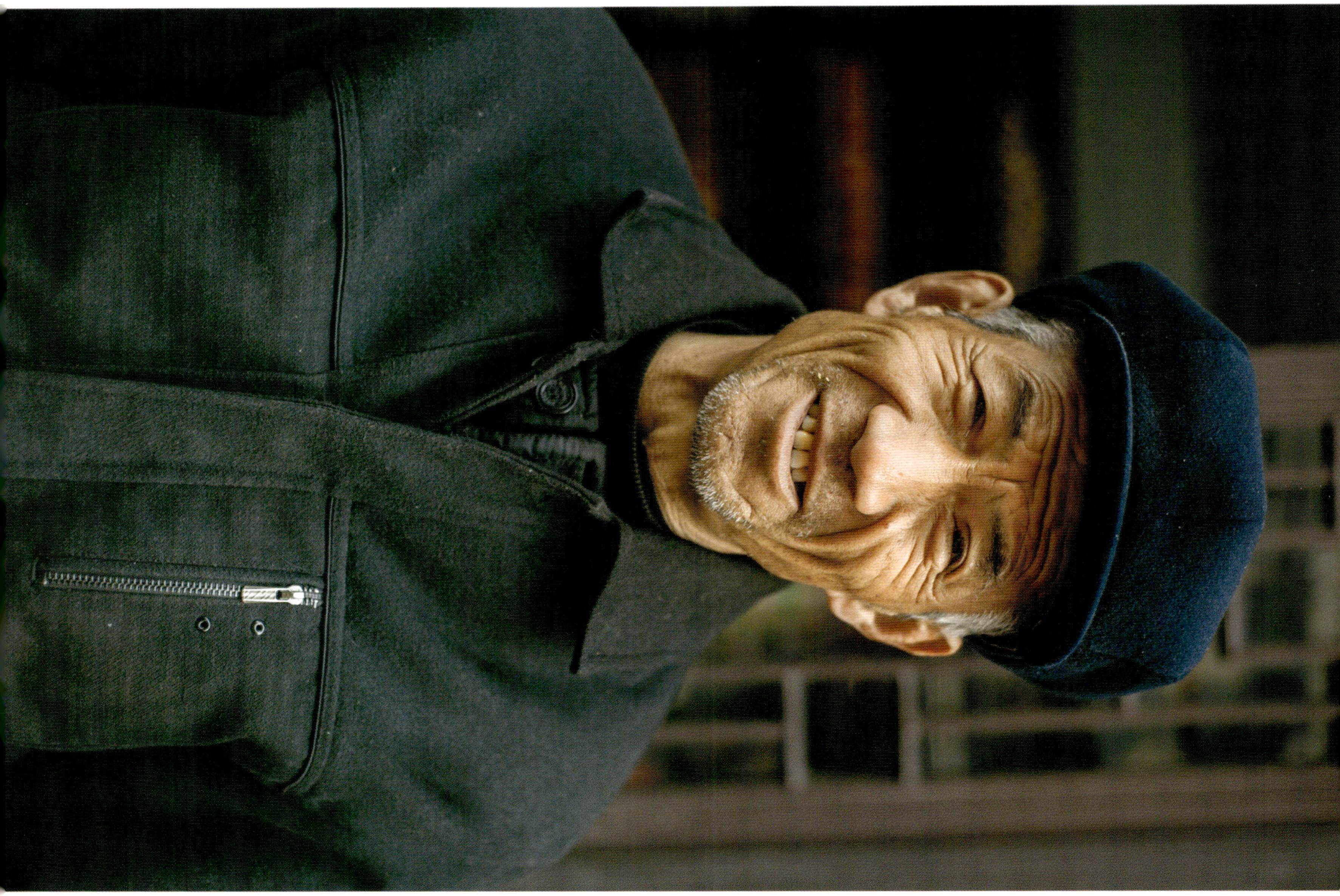

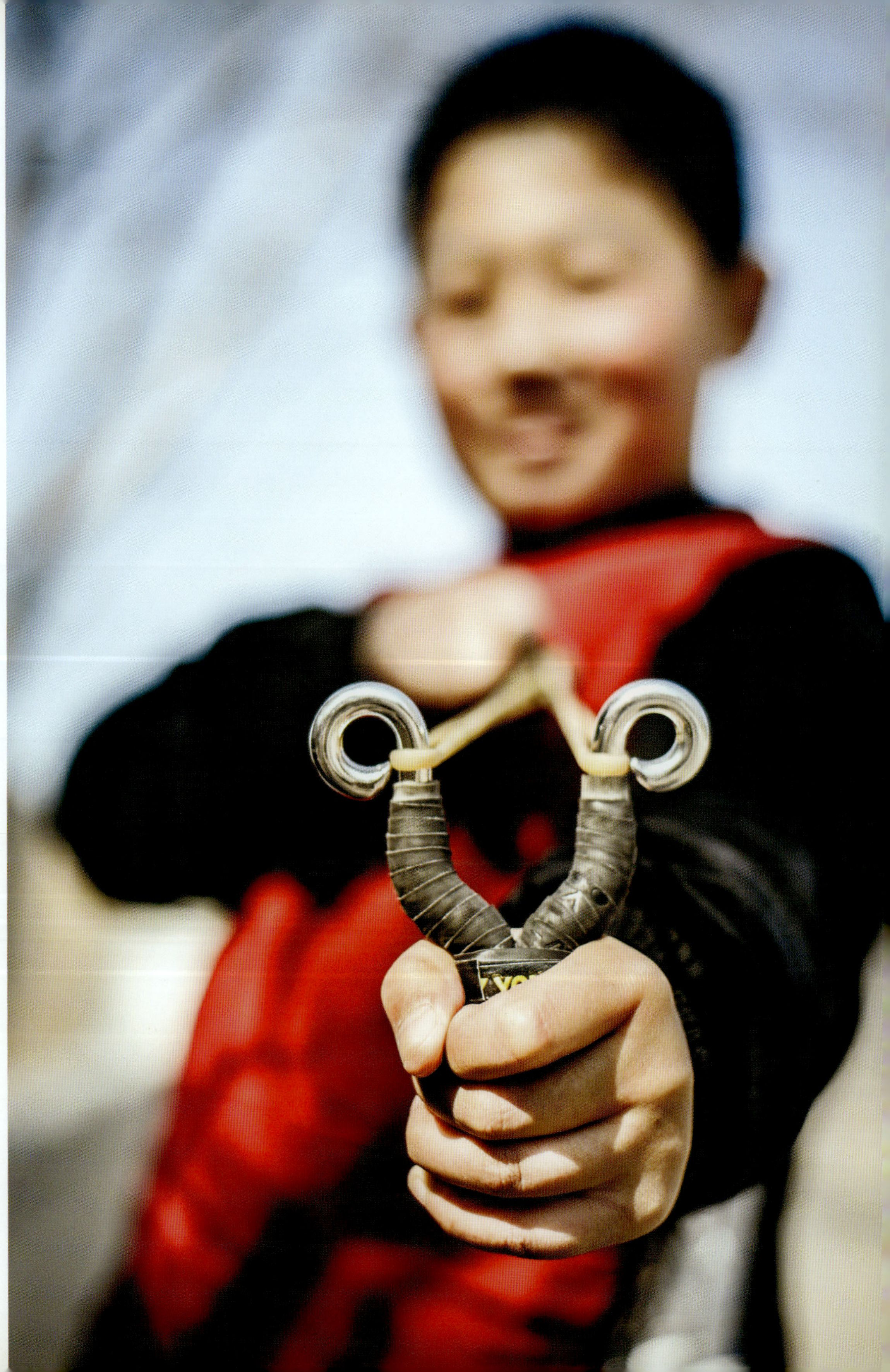

A young Chinese boy plays with his handmade slingshot and poses for the camera with a dangerous look.

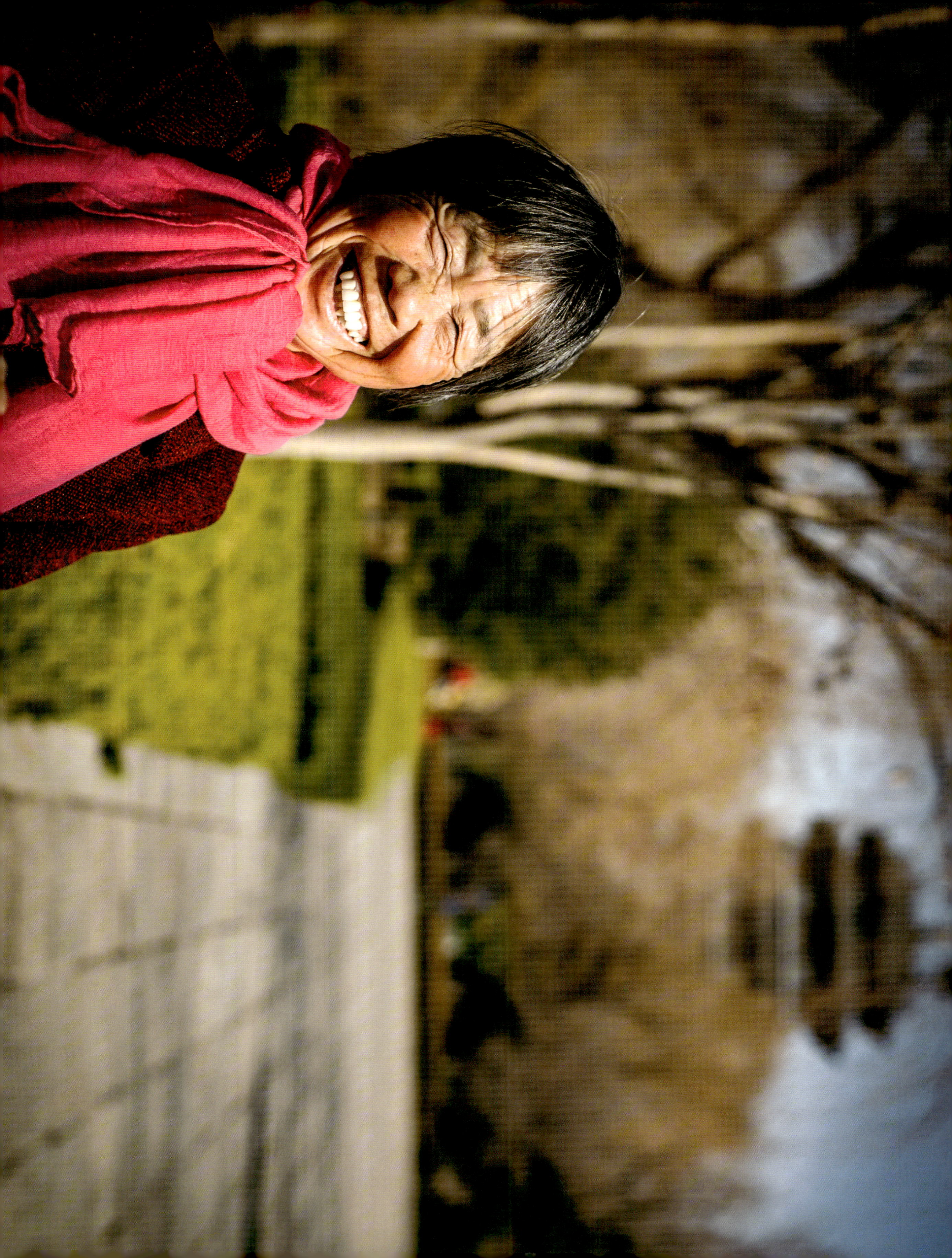

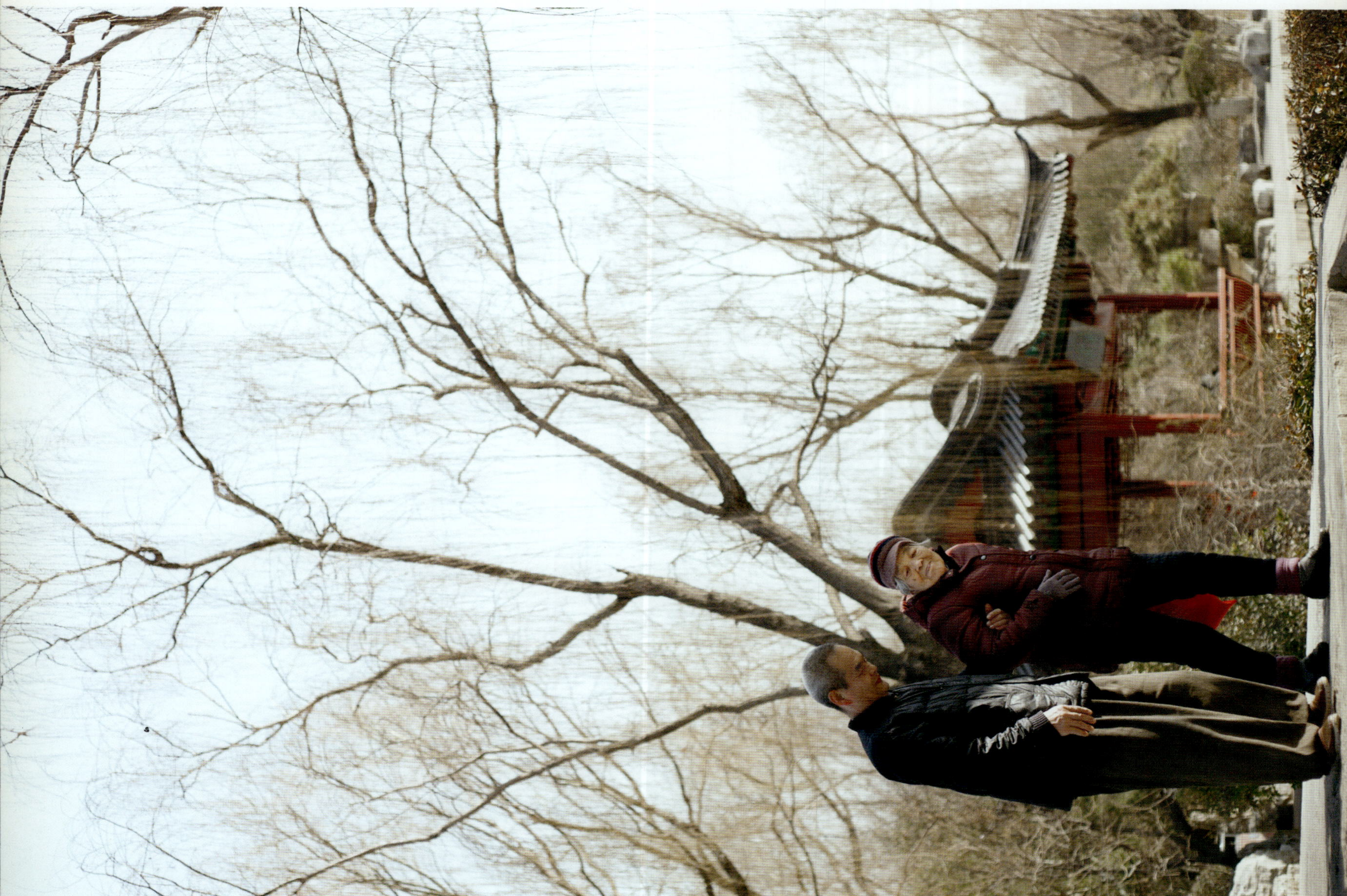

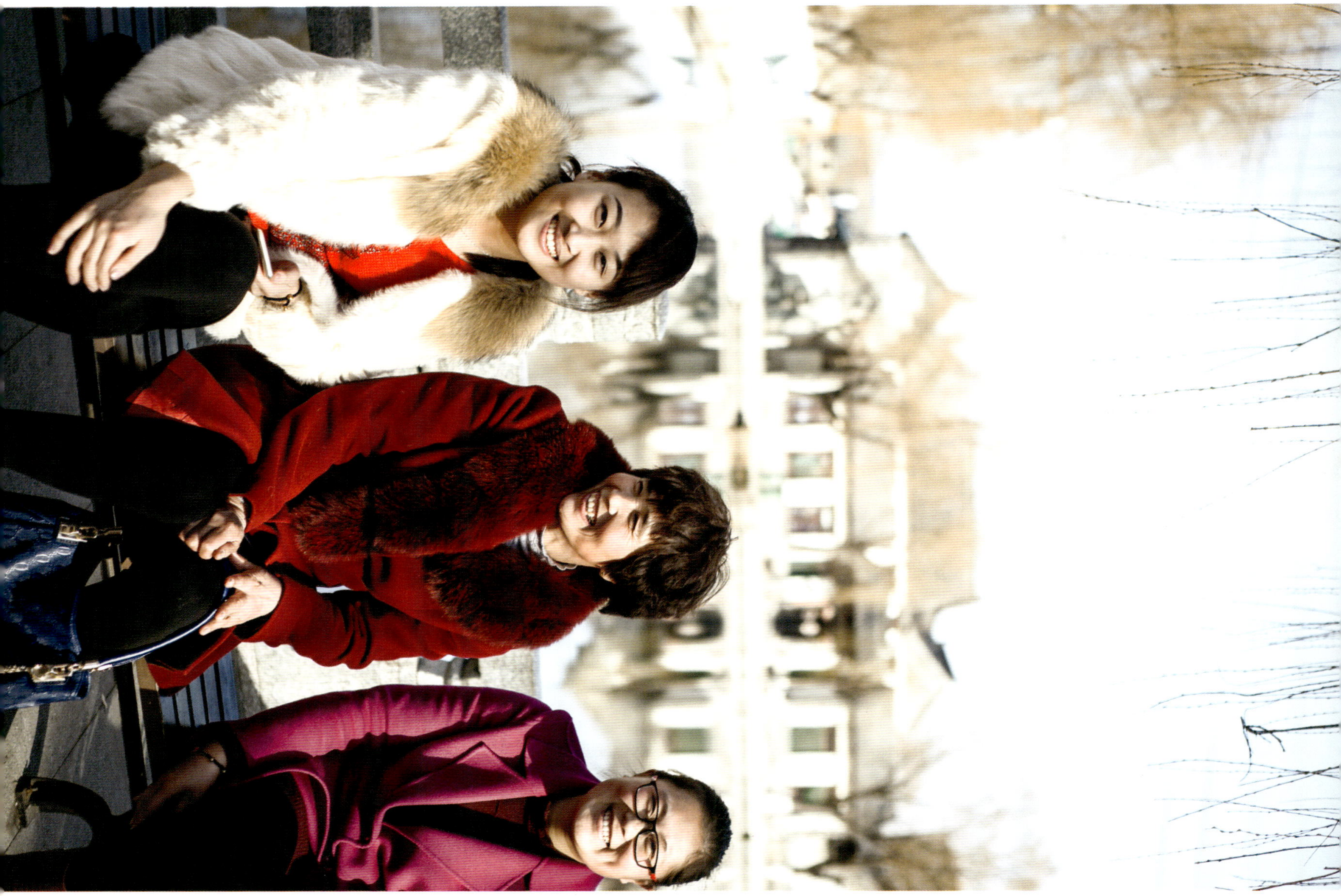

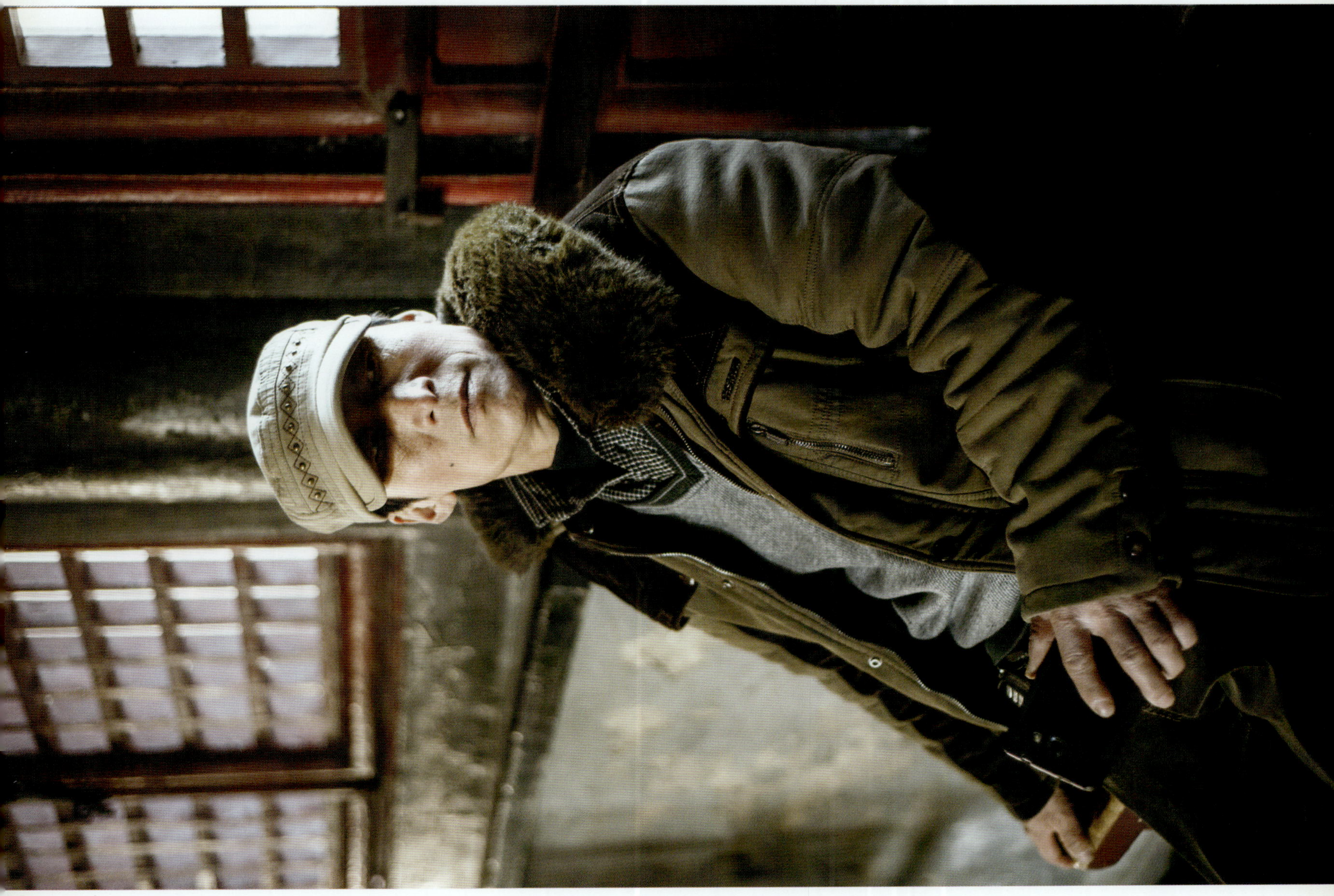

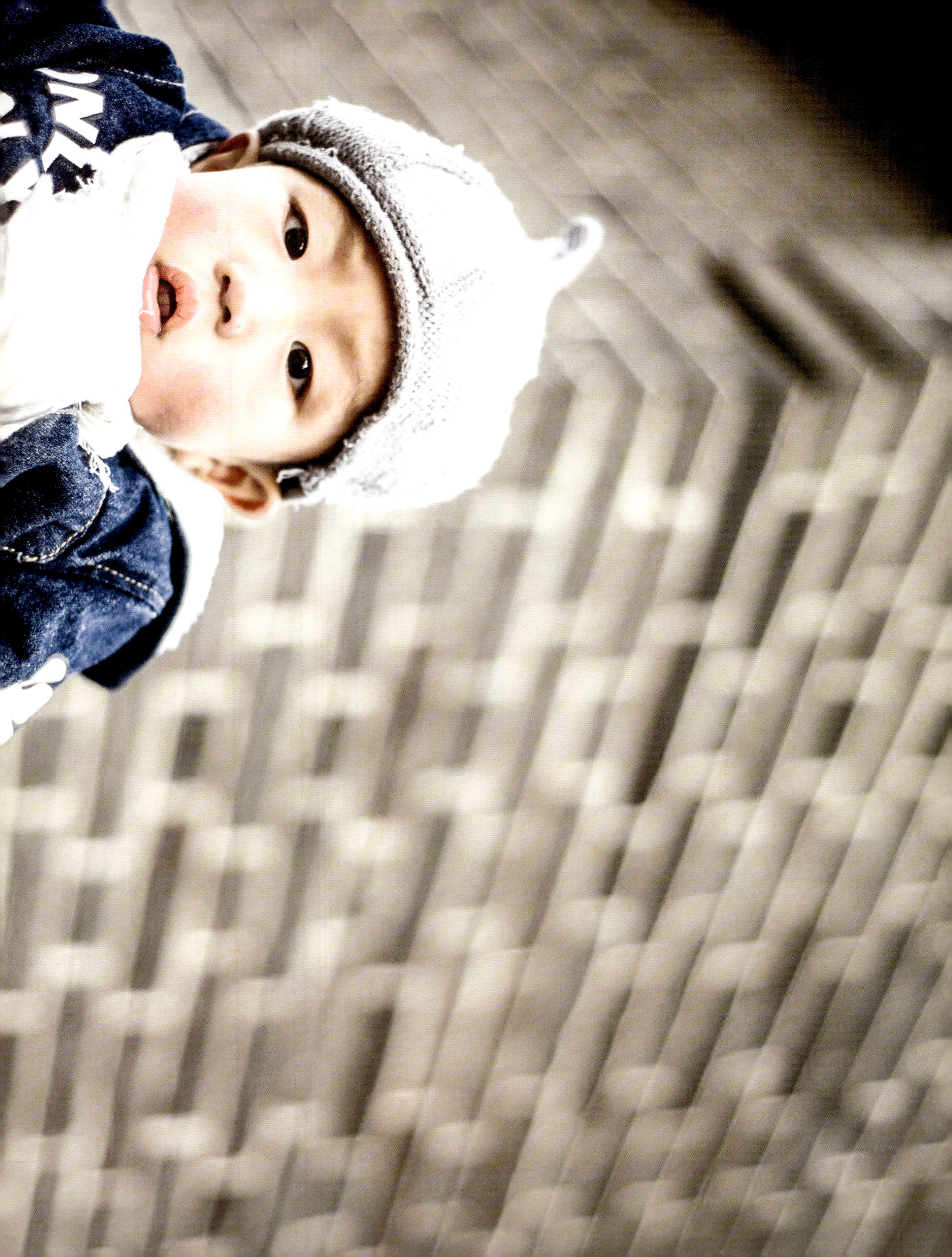

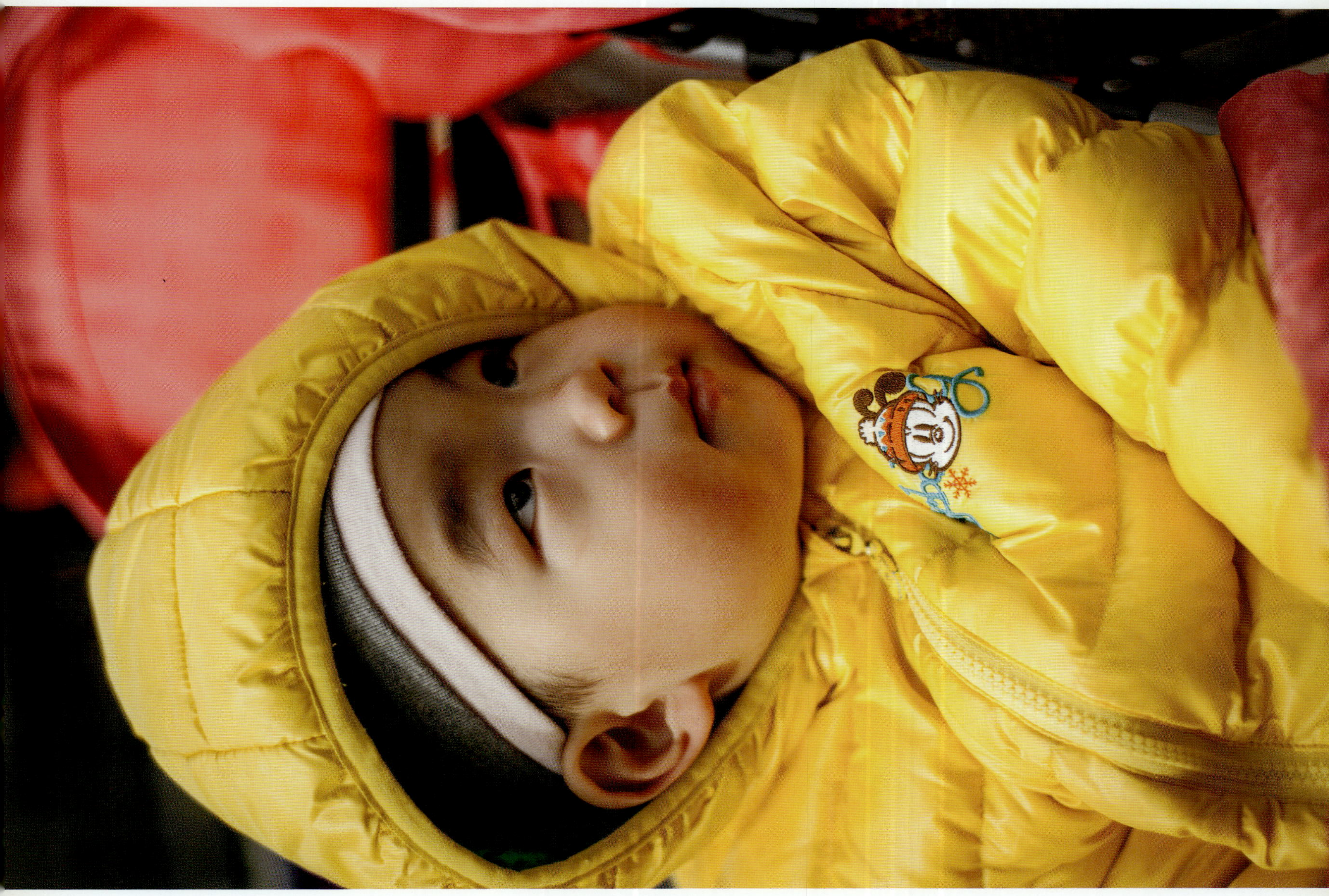

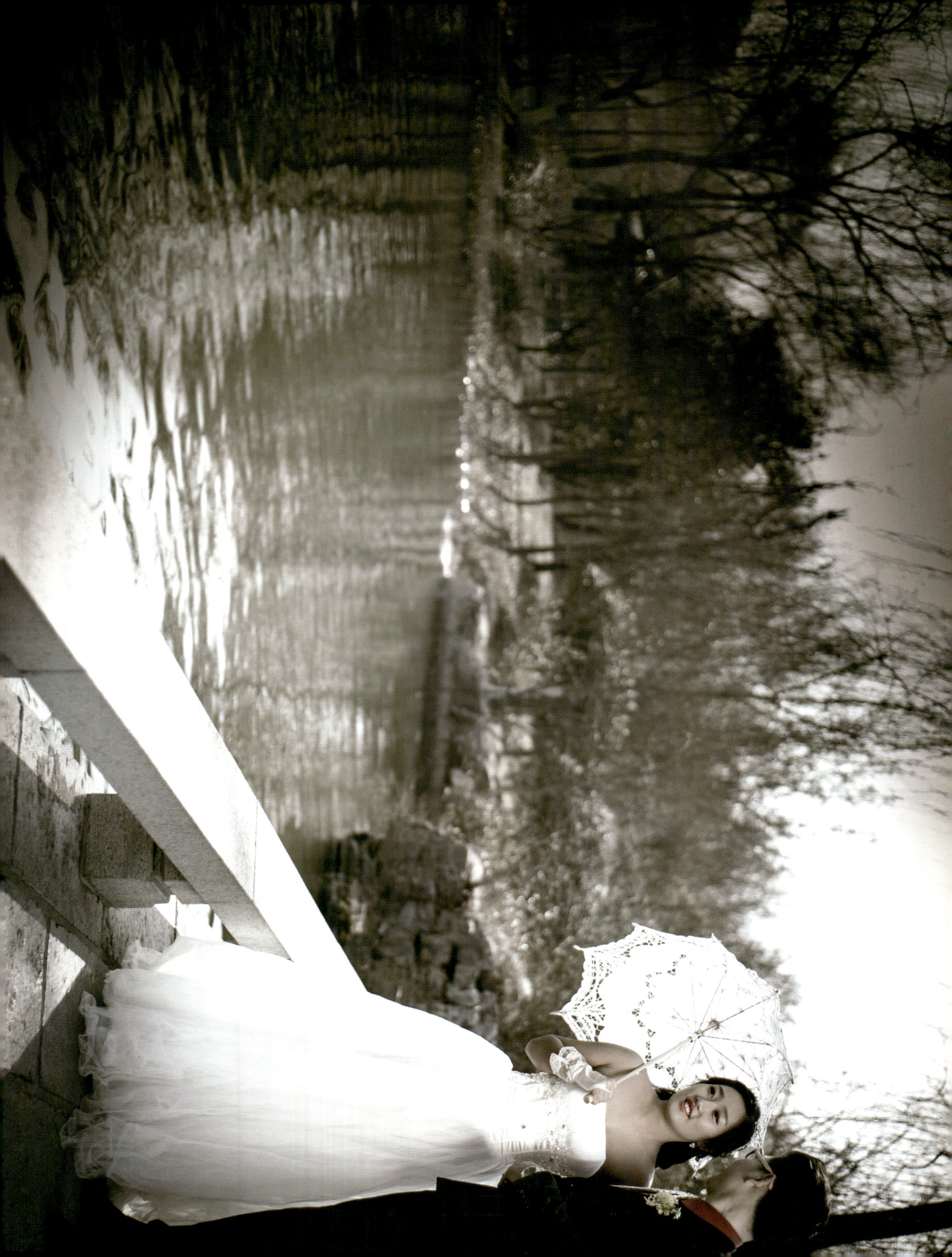

This lovely wedding couple was an unexpected surprise along the path inside one of Shandong's many parks. It is a common practice for young couples to hire professional photographers to take their wedding pictures before the ceremony. Wanting everything to look perfect, they will then post their wedding pictures on the invitation. Getting married during the Chinese New Year is very auspicious.

Couples will often visit astrologers, monks, and/or fortune-tellers to discover which day will be the most auspicious for their ceremony. These sources may also be consulted regarding the choice of gown, food, and number of guests and taken into consideration before making decisions. It is a culture of luck and superstition. In the traditional Chinese wedding, the bride will wear a red cheongsam, a form-fitting dress.

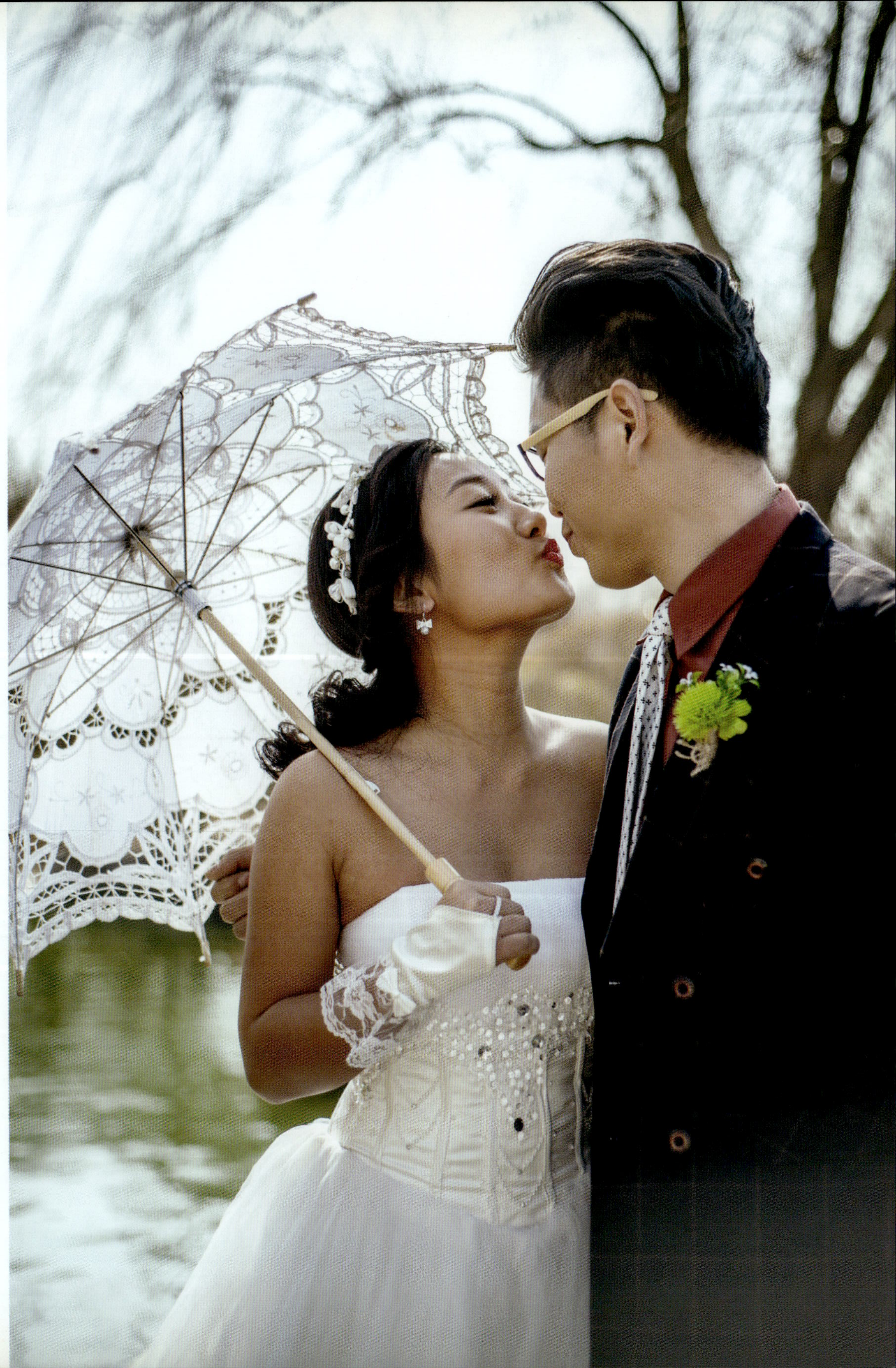

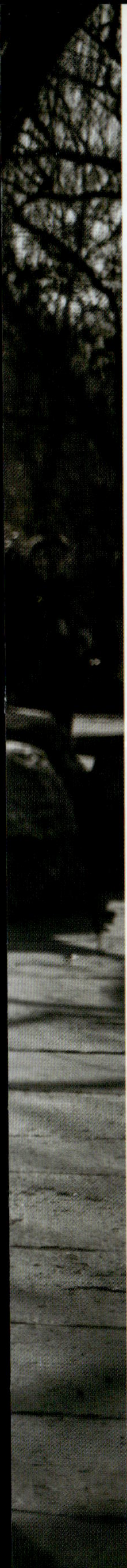

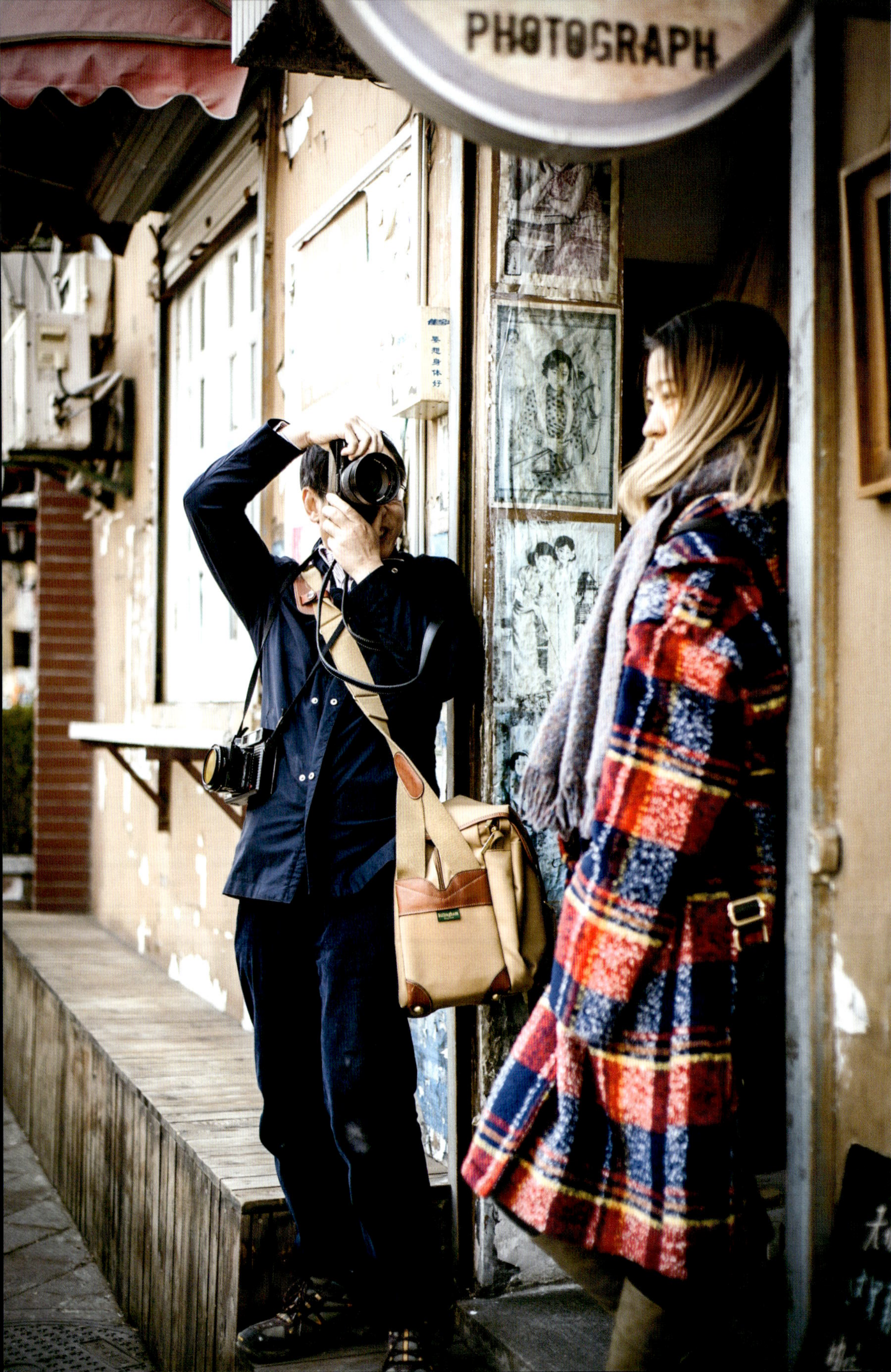

A Chinese photographer captures his subject in a fashion shoot on the well-visited Qu Shui Street, which has been preserved to depict what residences of the region looked like in the 1950s.

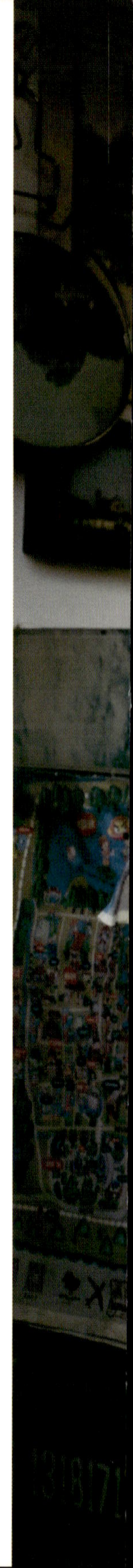

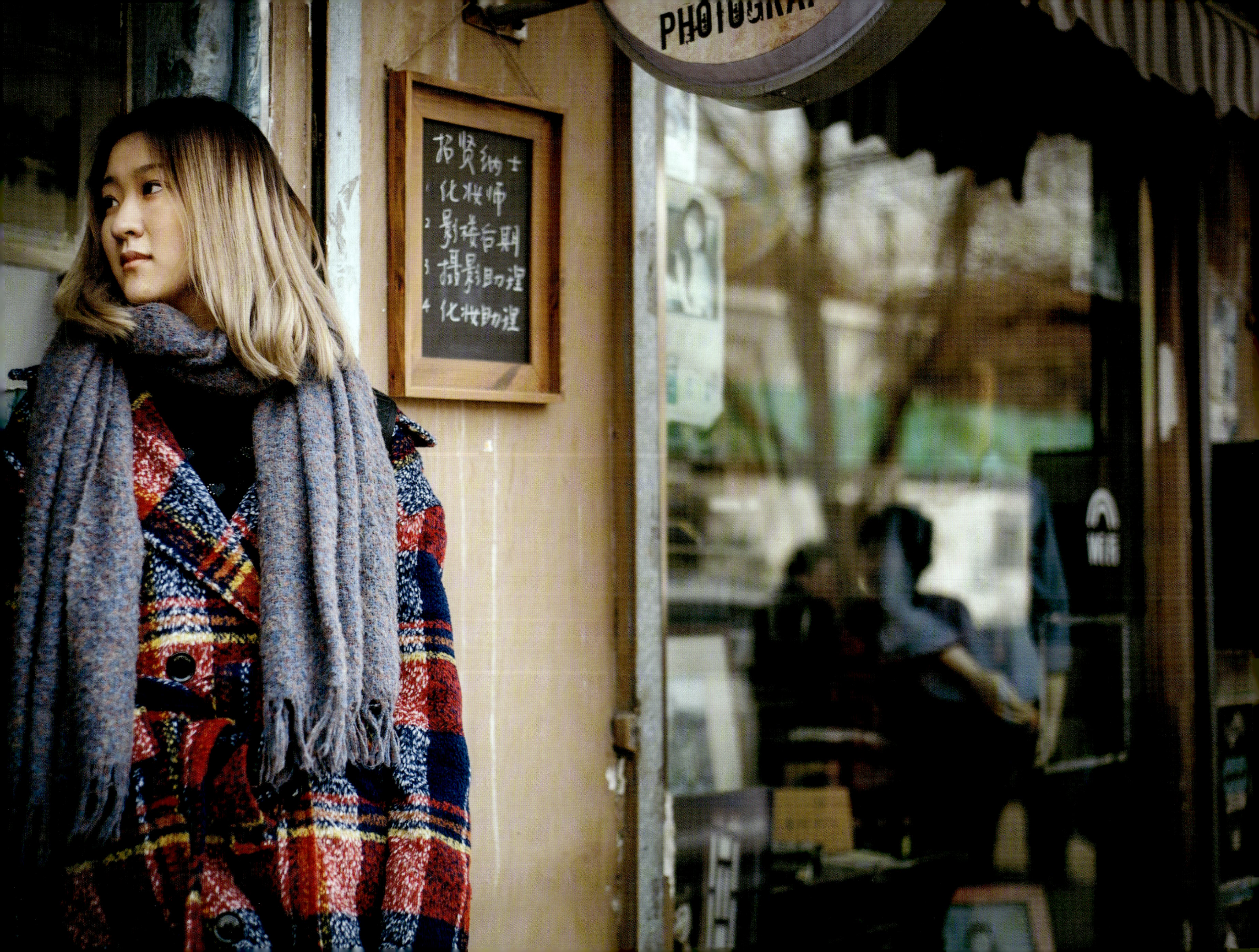
PHOTOGRA
招贤纳士
1 化妆师
2 影楼后期
3 摄影助理
4 化妆助理

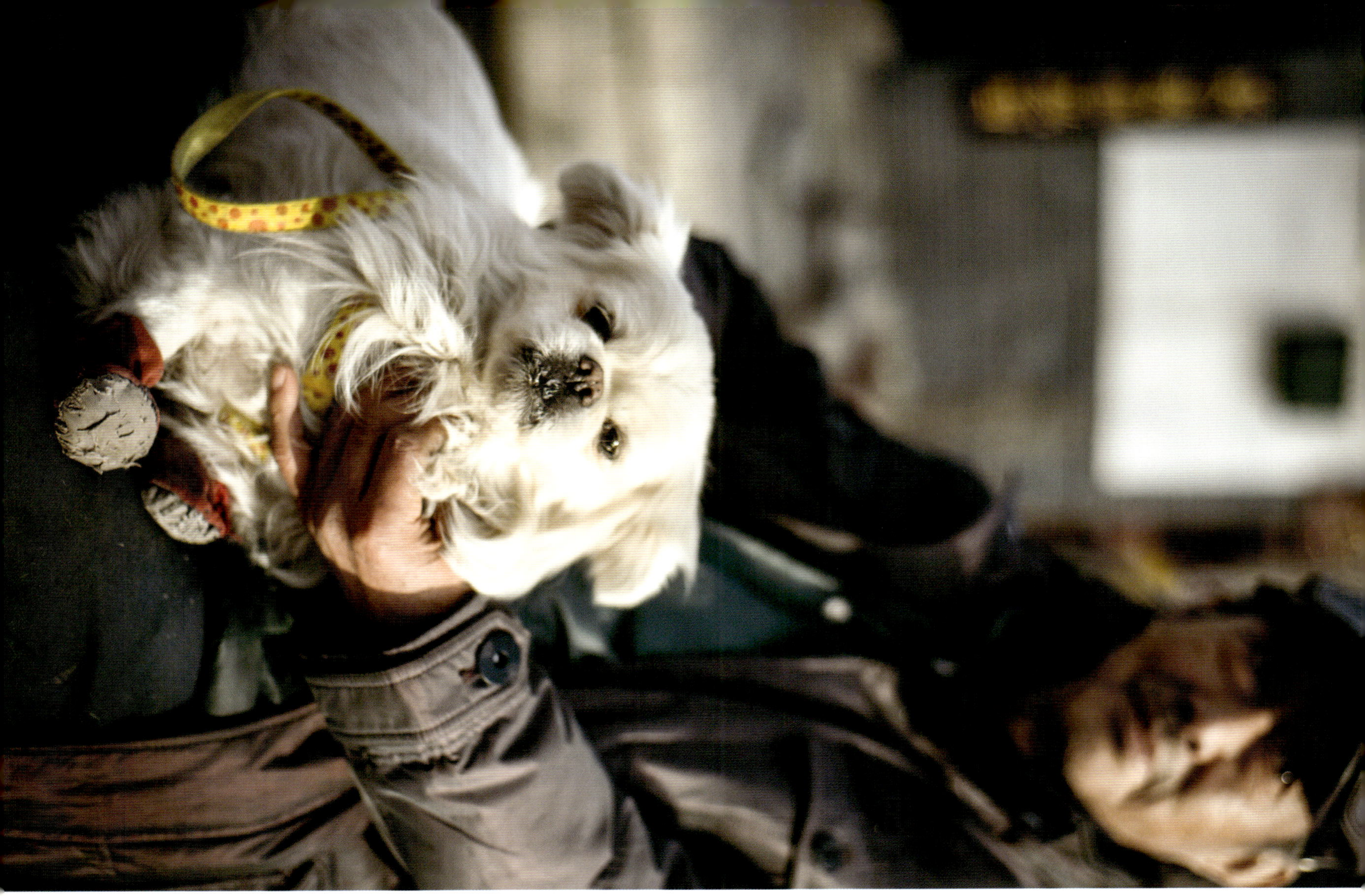

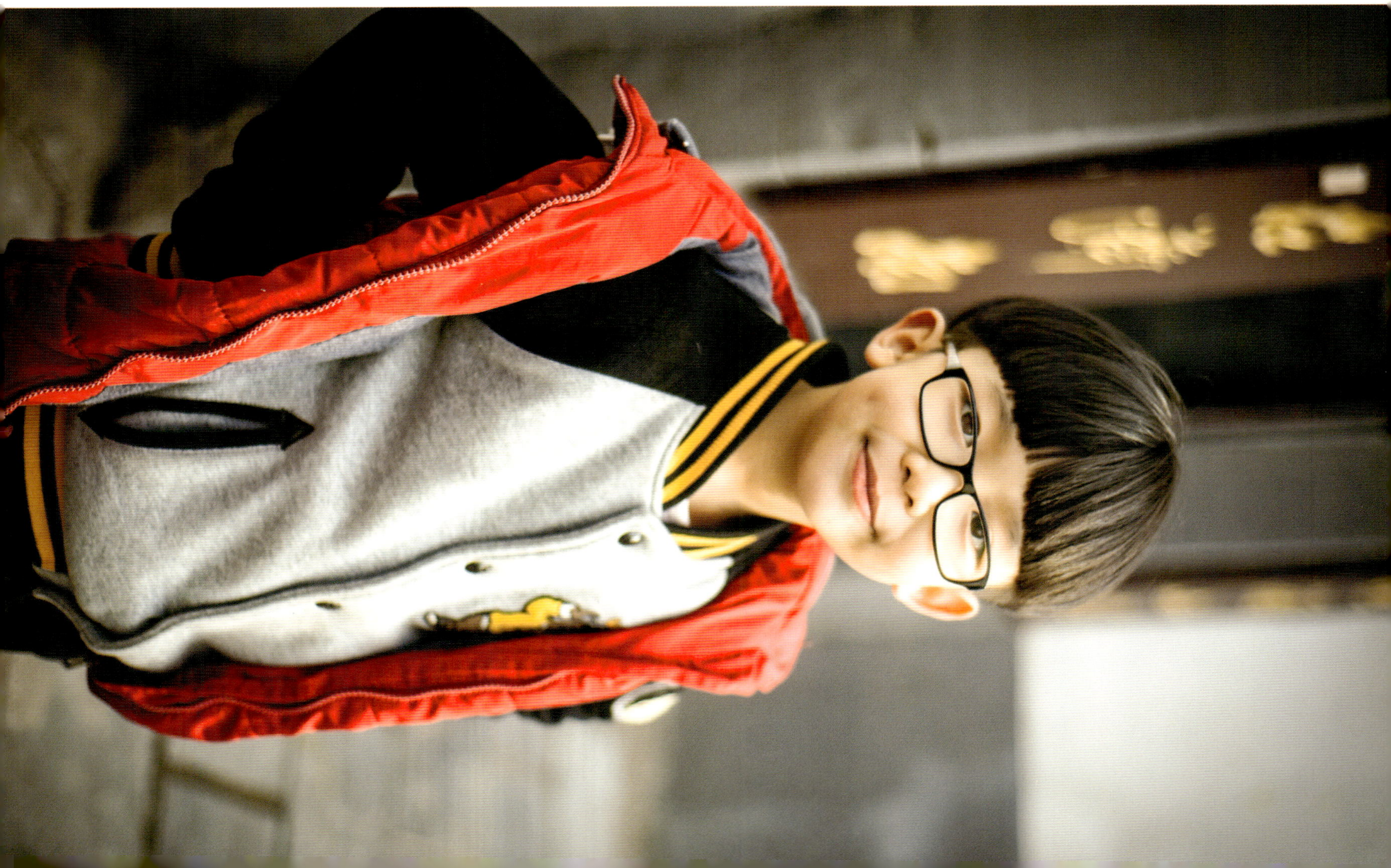

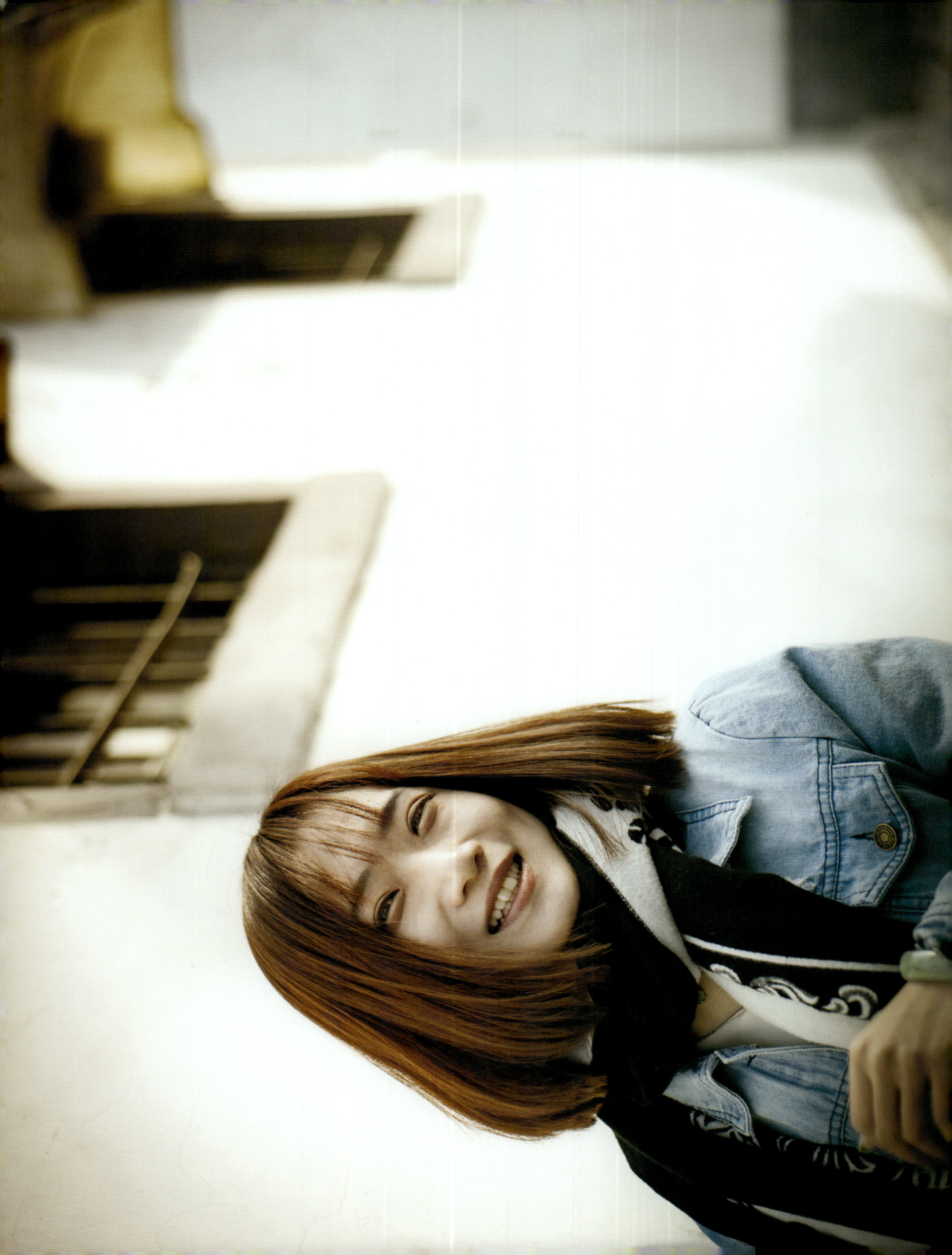

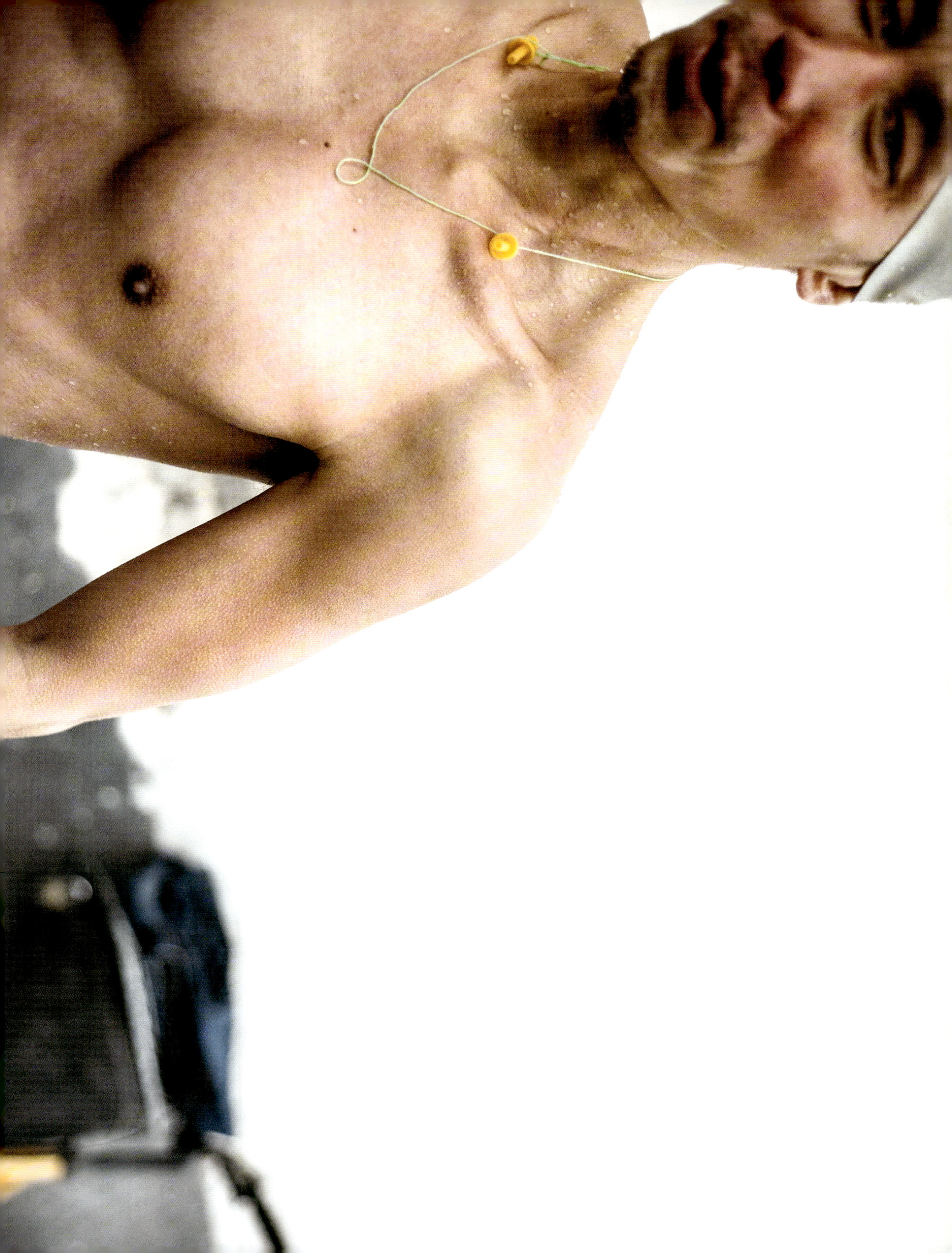

A man poses for the camera after a swim in a city pond.

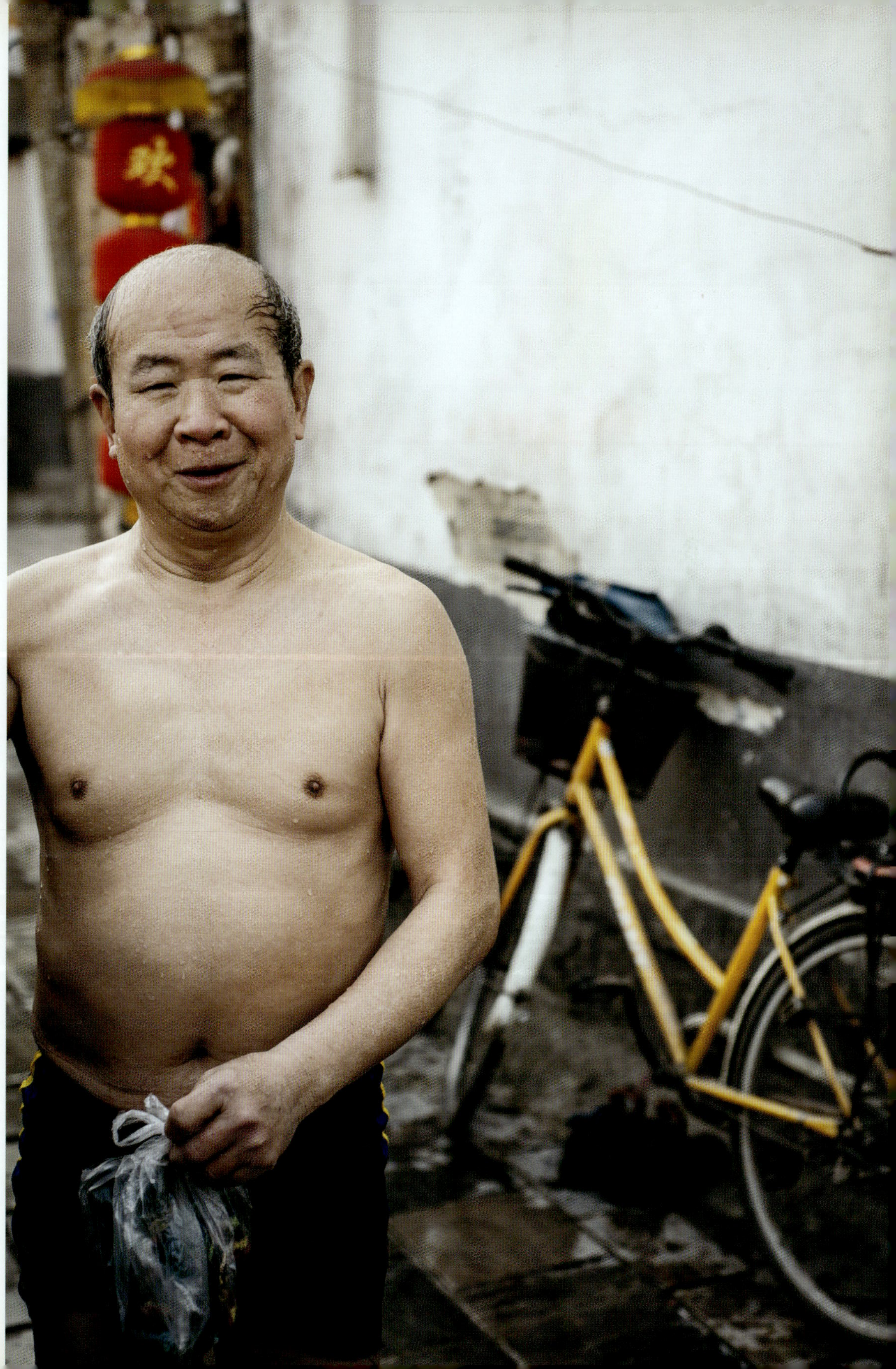

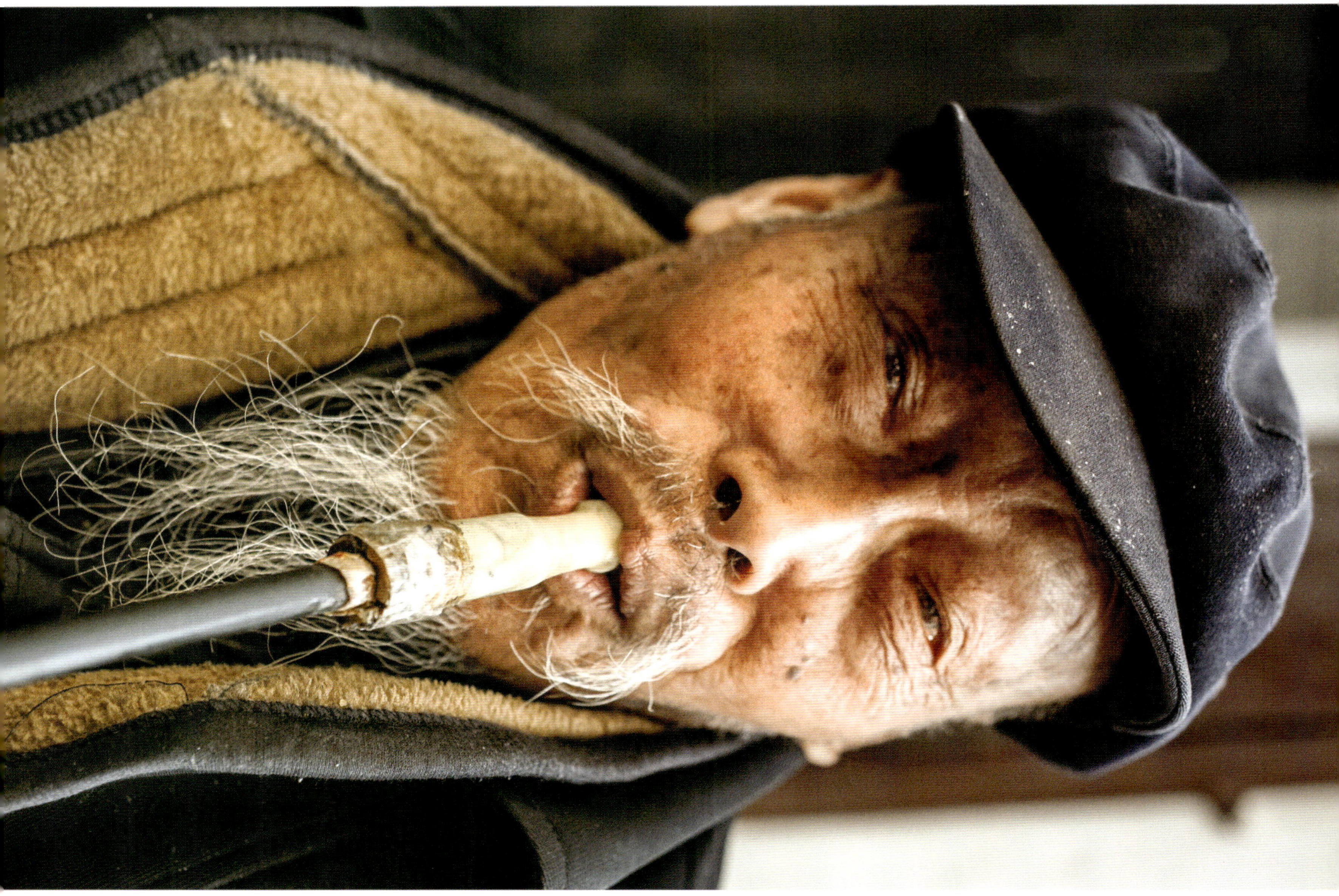

What is this man smoking? It's difficult to say, but this elderly man's hands and long whiskers certainly have many stories to tell.

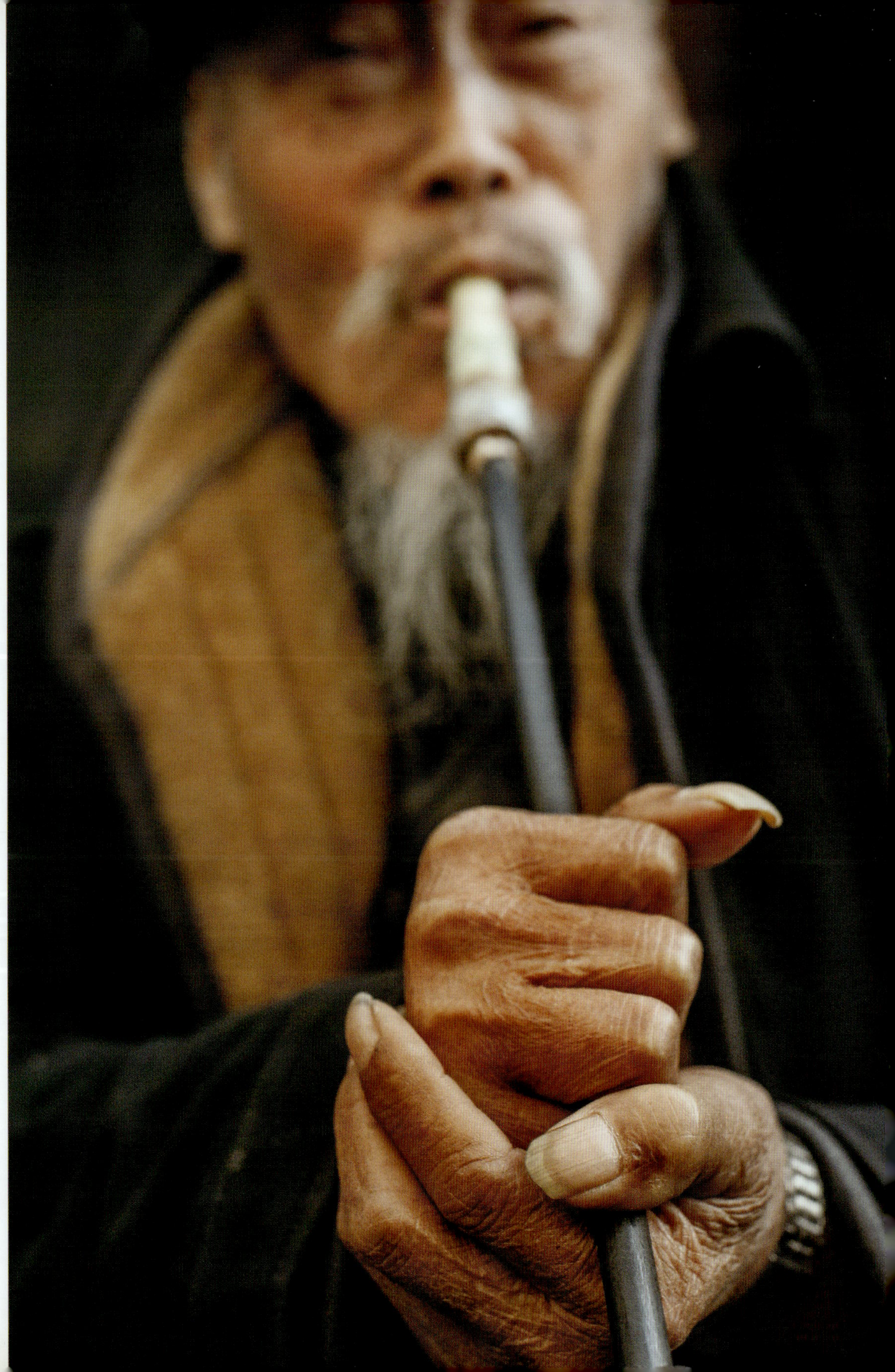

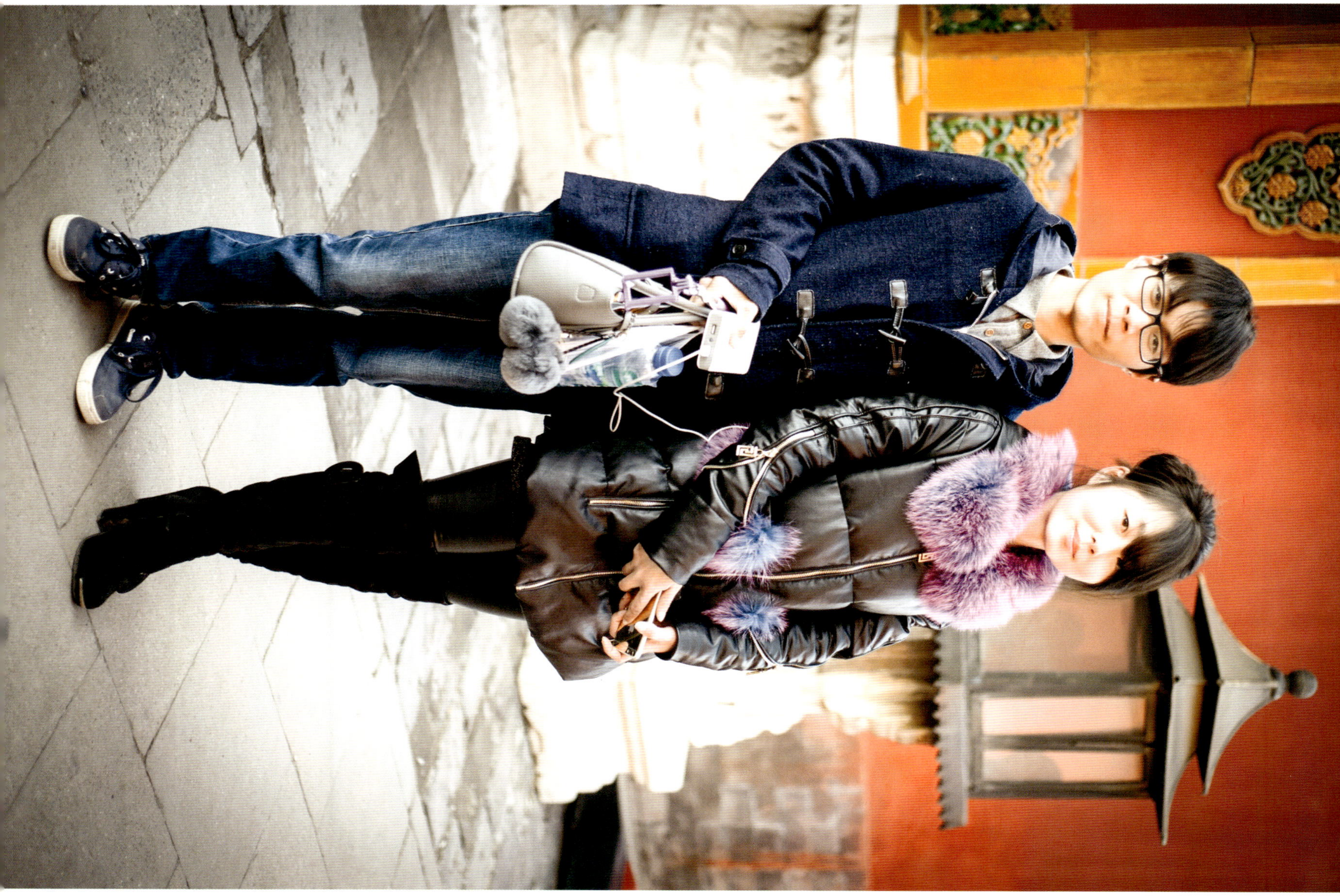

This is a typical street scene during the Chinese Lantern Festival. People of all ages come to see, be seen, and taste the offerings of the New Year.

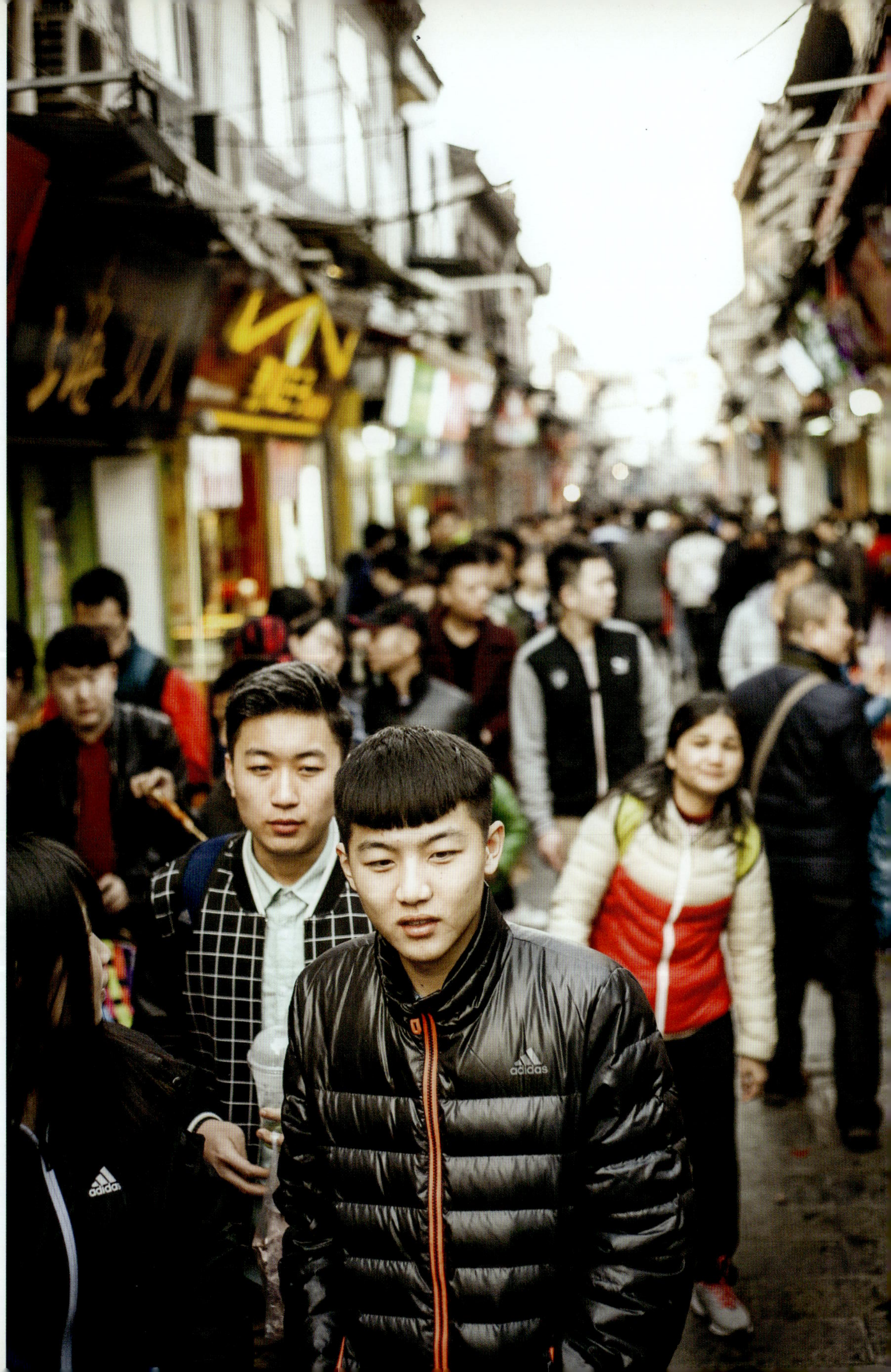

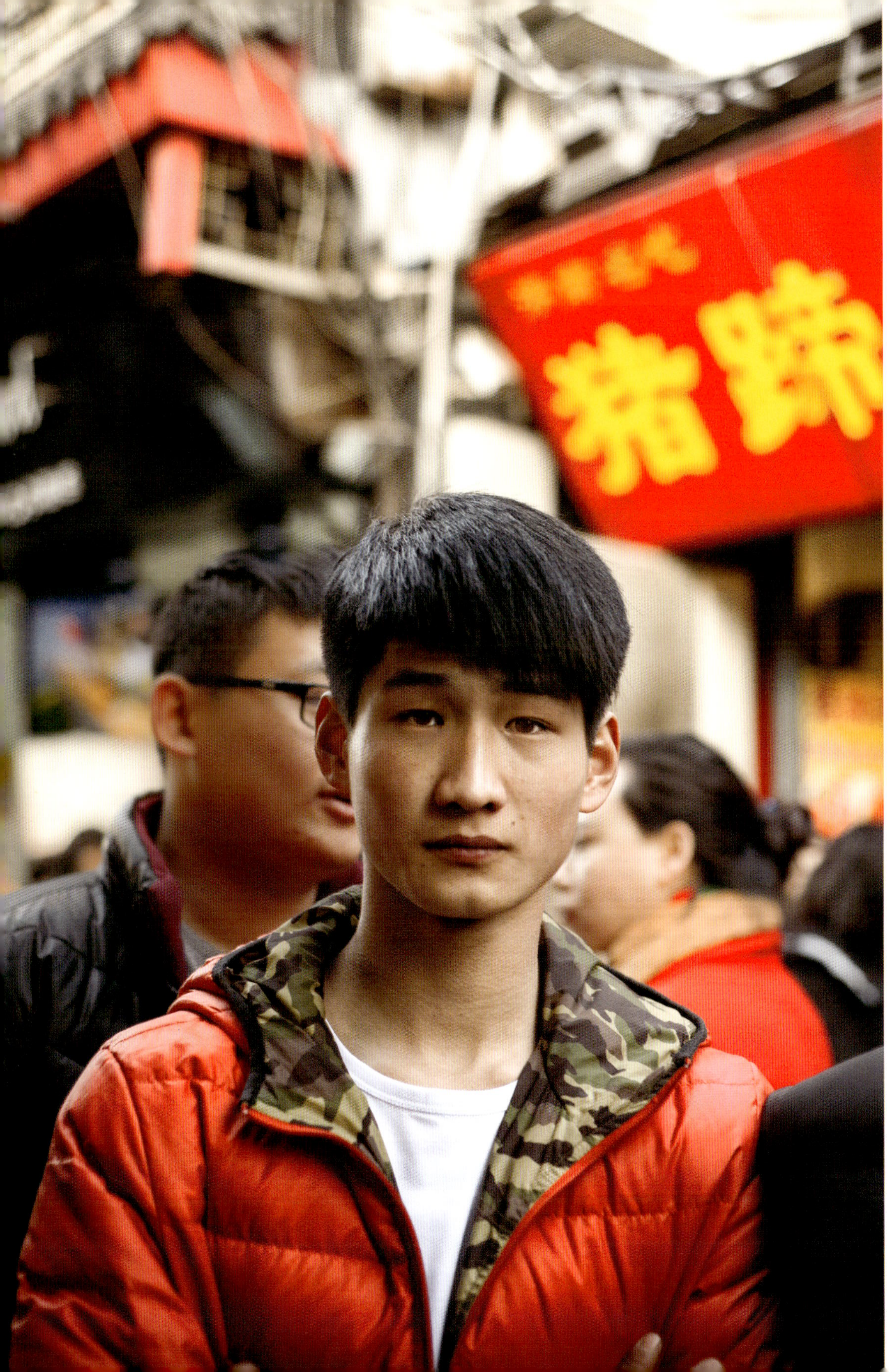
猪蹄

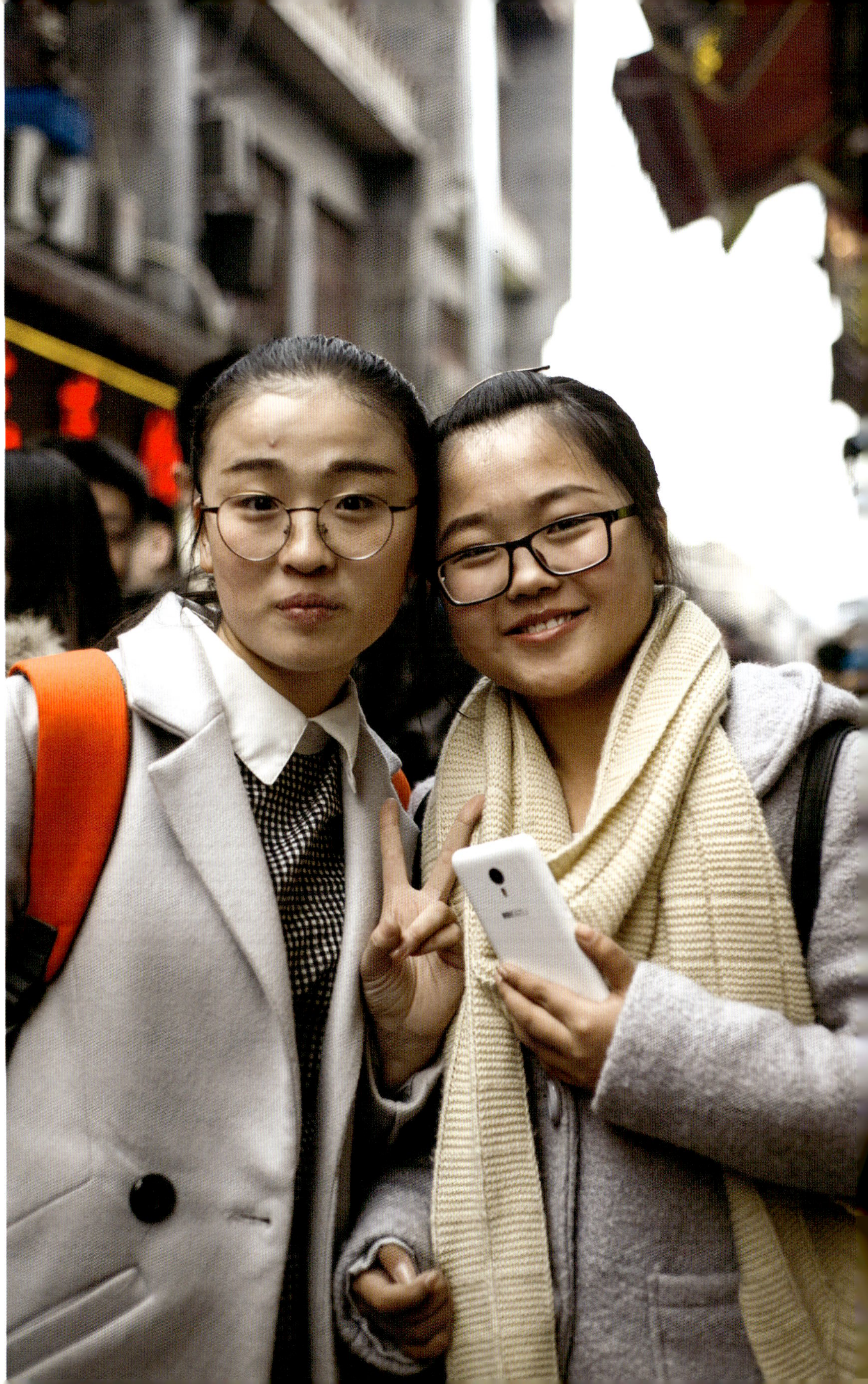

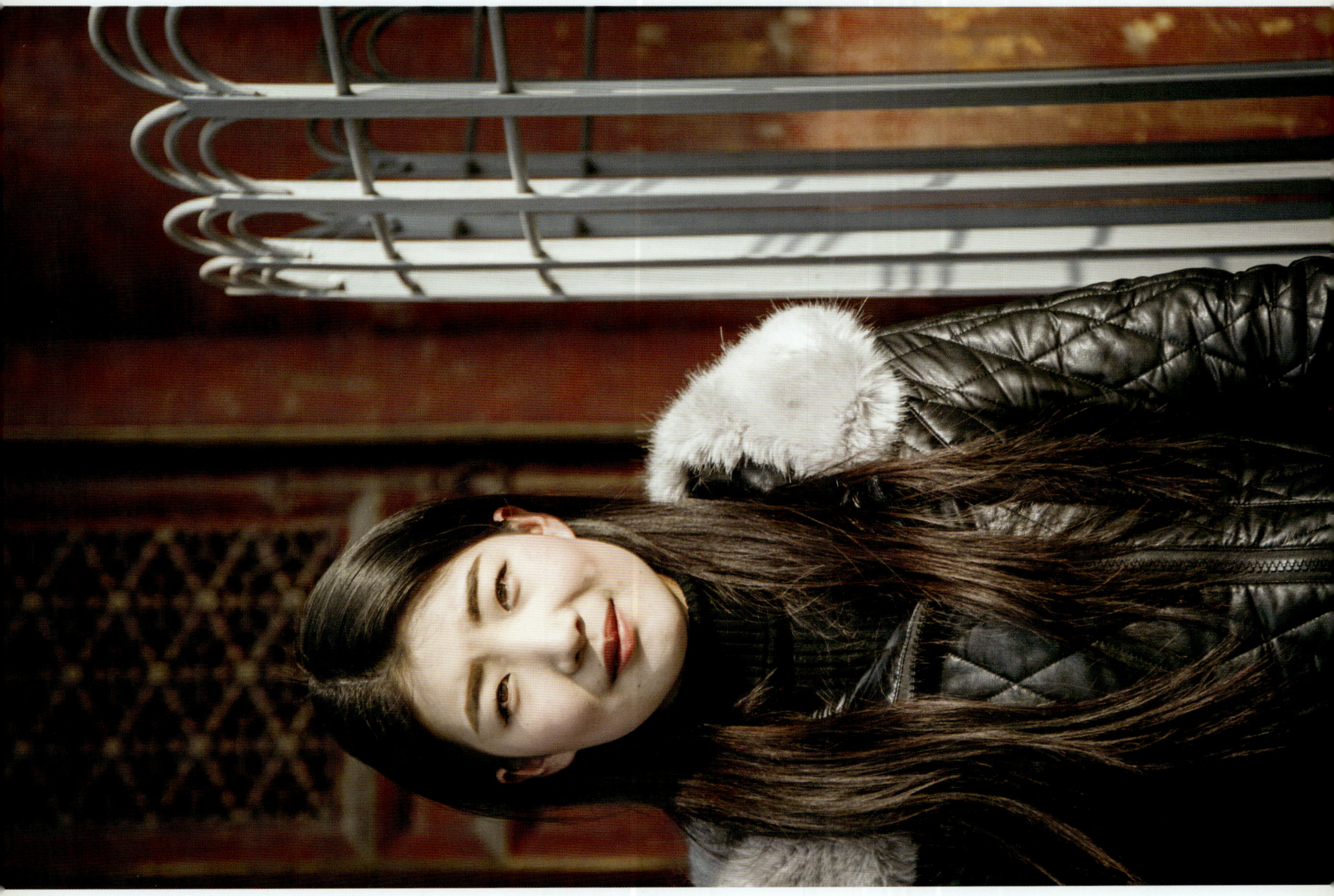

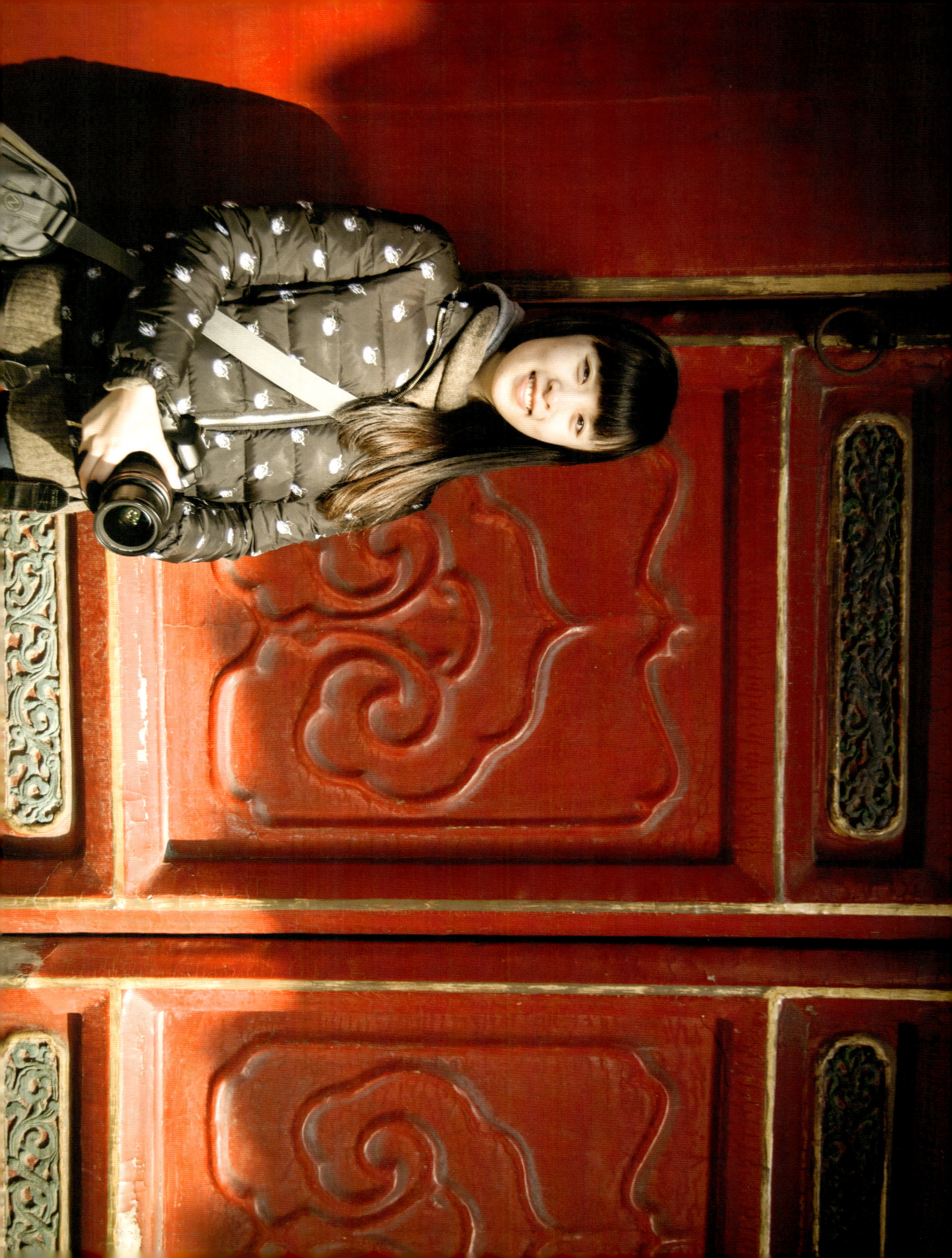

Coats are a primary facet of winter fashion in this cool climate. Beijing has four seasons, with temperatures in the warmer months averaging 81 degrees Fahrenheit, but in the height of summer (July and August) they can reach 99 degrees Fahrenheit. In the winter months, the average temperature is 25 degrees Fahrenheit, but in January, the coldest month, temperatures can drop to as low as 5 degrees Fahrenheit.

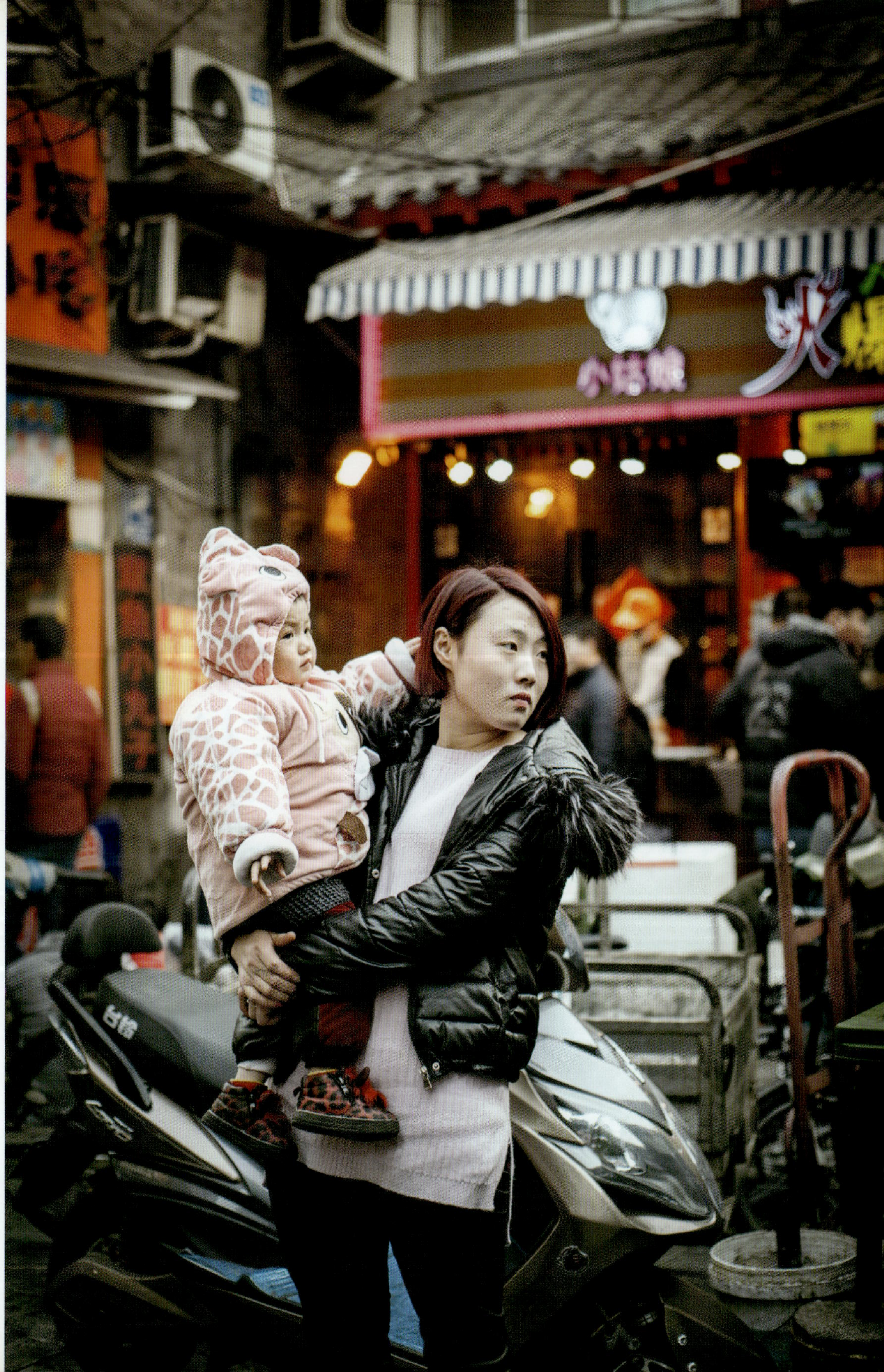

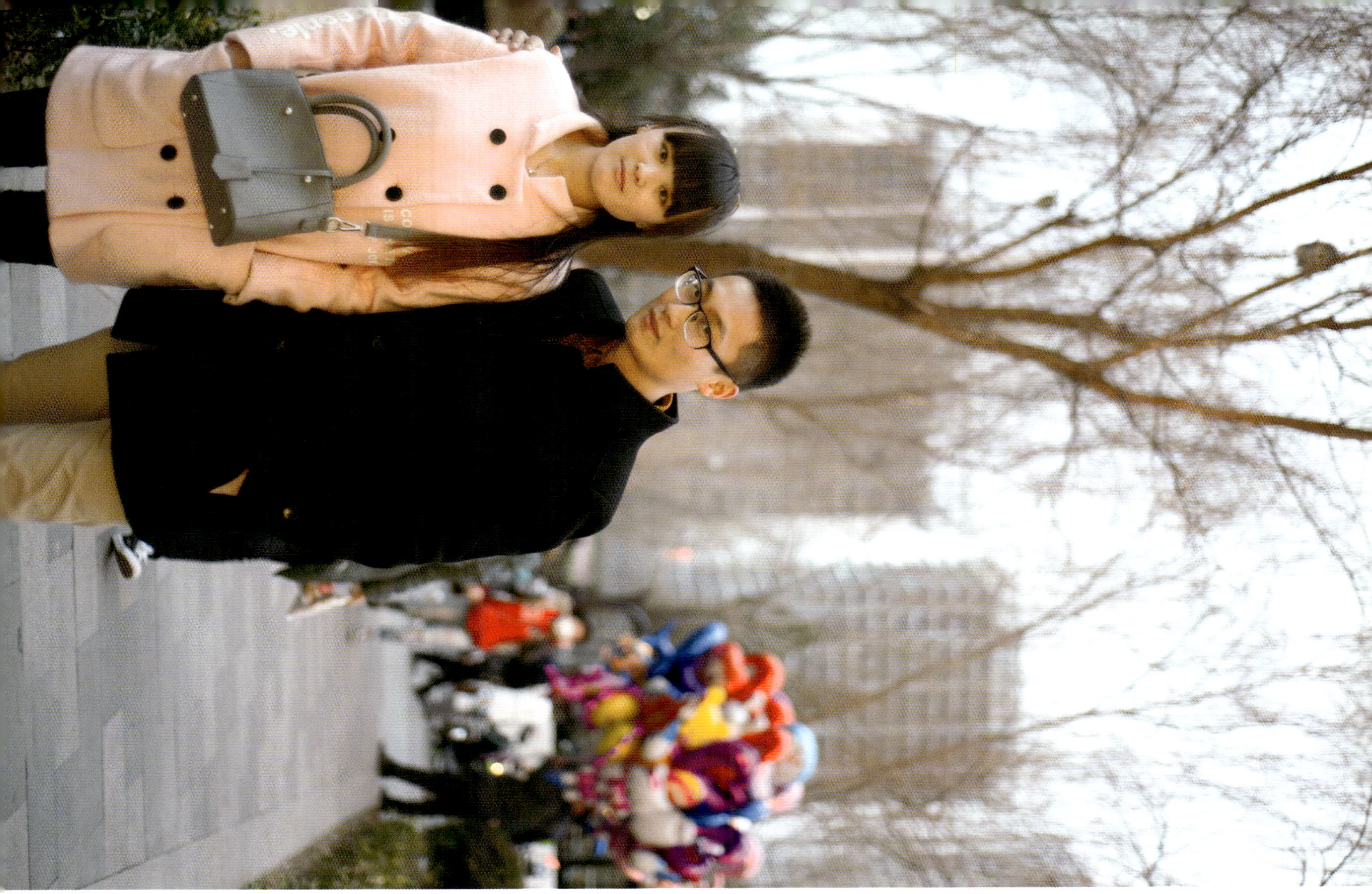

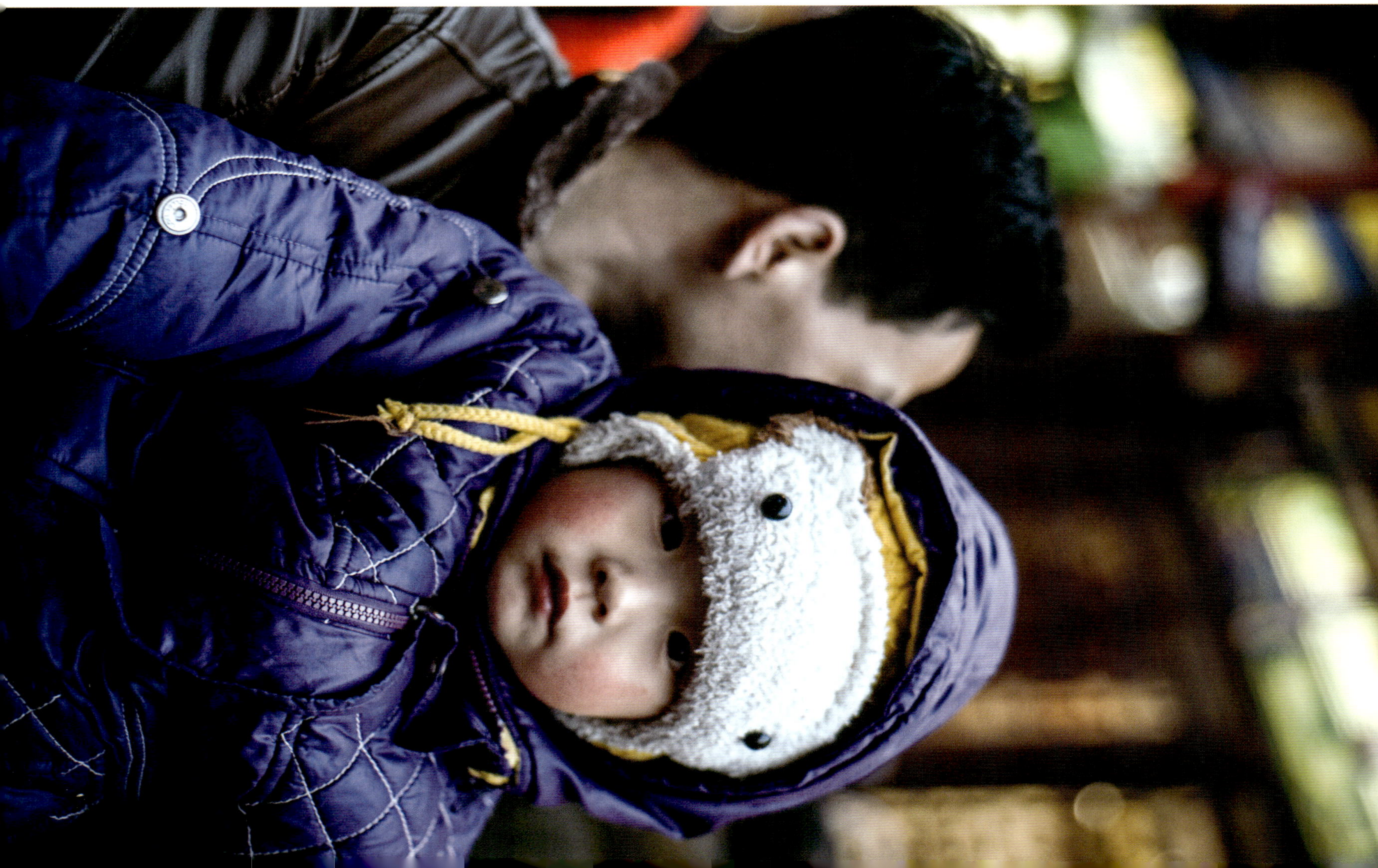

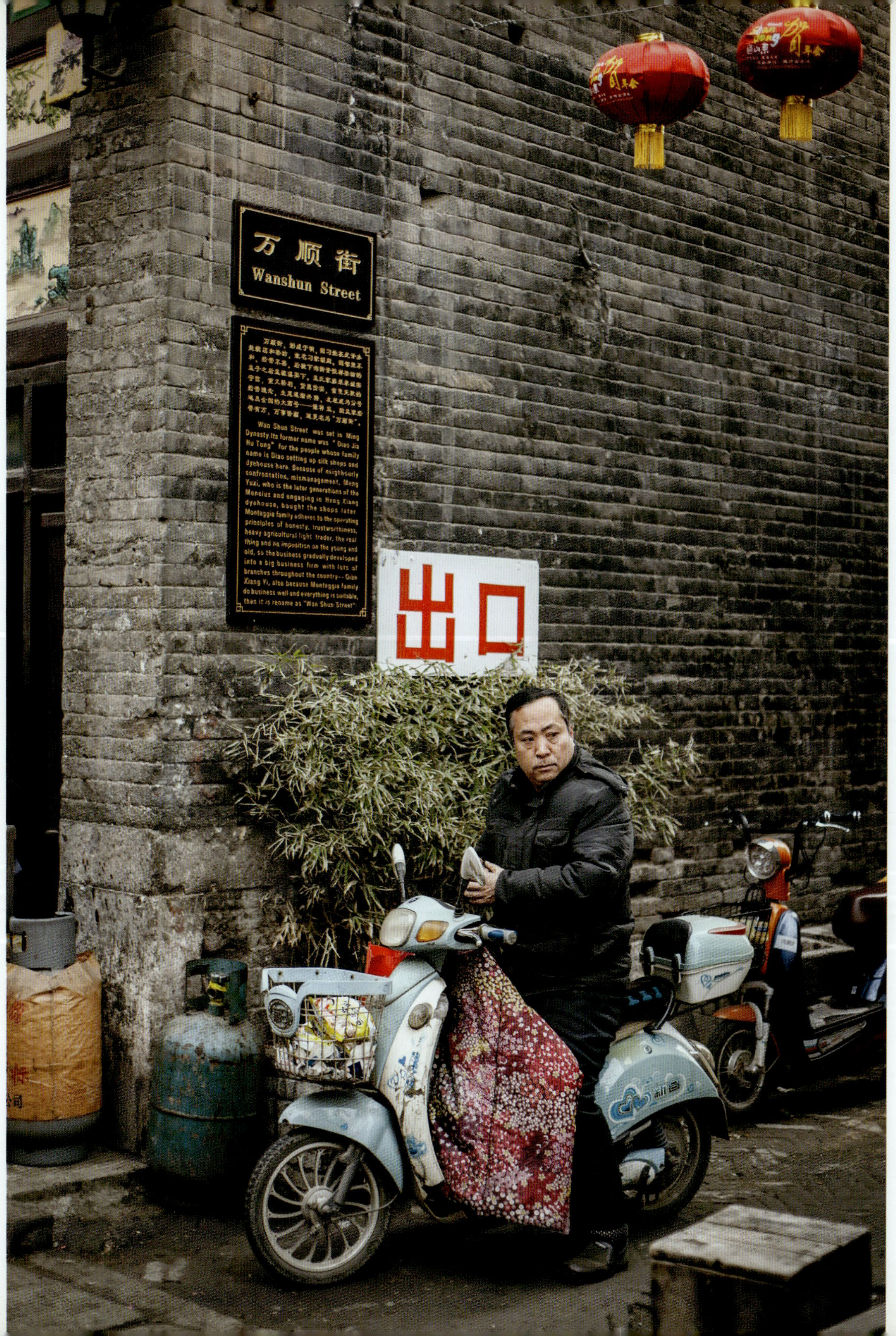
万顺街
Wanshun Street
Wan Shun Street was set in Ming Dynasty.Its former name was " Diao Jia Hu Tong" for the people whose family name is Diao setting up silk shops and dyehouse here. Because of neighbourly confrontation, mismanagement, Meng Yuxi, who is the later generations of the Mencius and engaging in Hang Xiang dyehouse, bought the shops later. Monteggia family adheres to the operating principles of honesty, trustworthiness, heavy agricultural light trader, the real thing and no imposition on the young and old, so the business gradually developed into a big business firm with lots of branches throughout the country--Gian Xiang Yi, also because Monteggia family do business well and everything is suitable, then it is rename as "Wan Shun Street".
出口

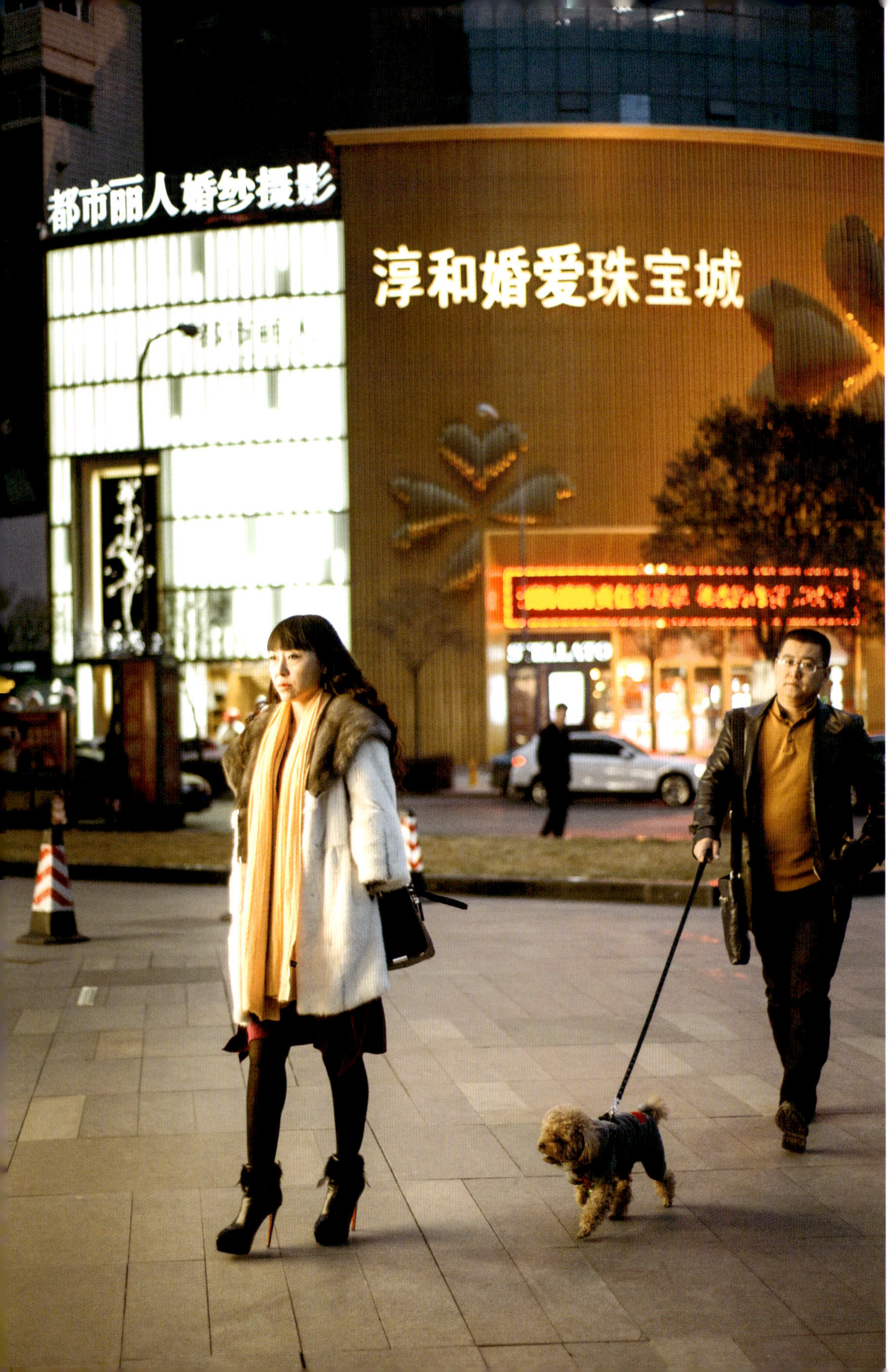
都市丽人婚纱摄影
淳和婚爱珠宝城

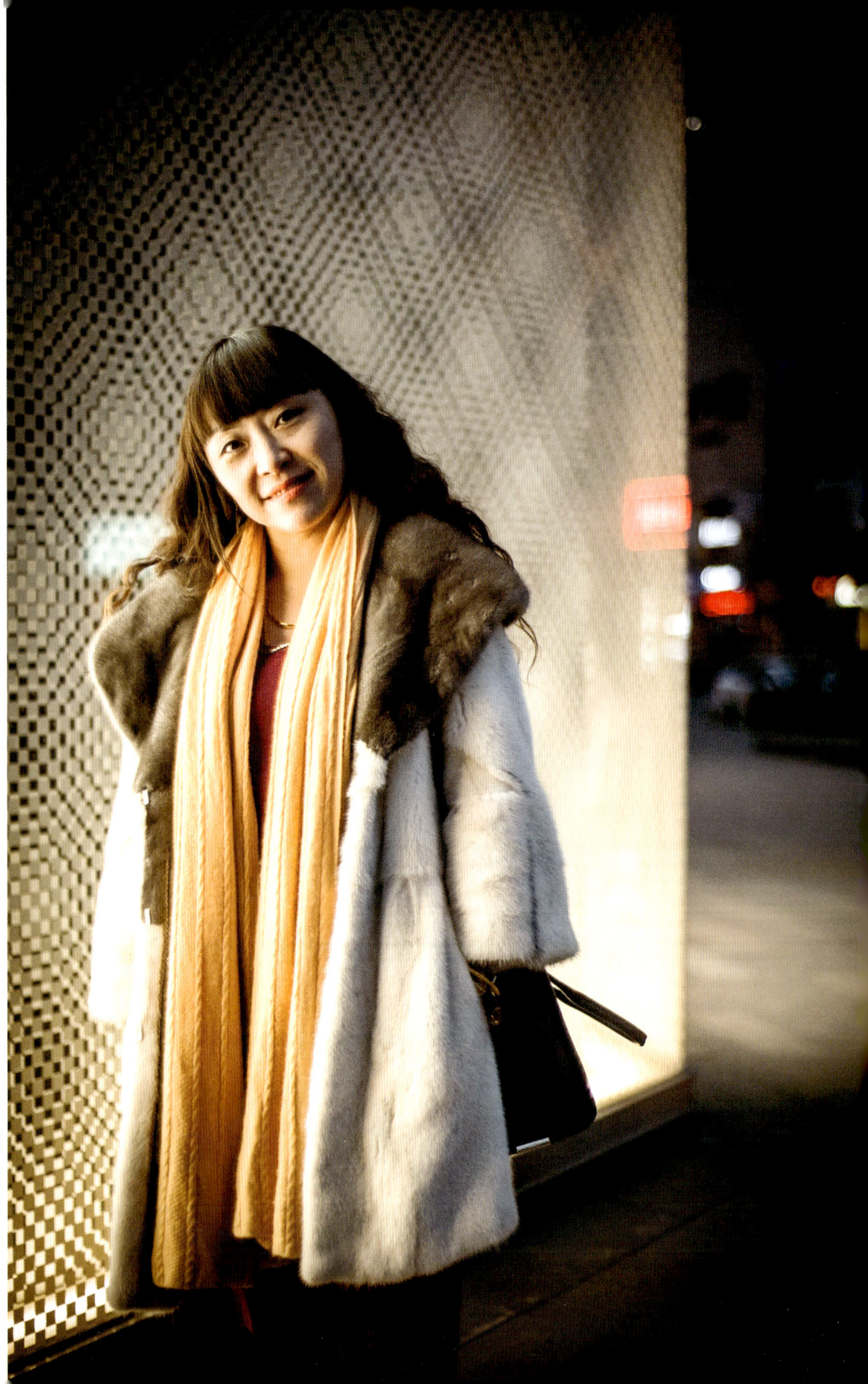

Always fashionable, Chinese women are on the forefront of cutting-edge style. Coats are particularly interesting, and most are made from leathers and fur.

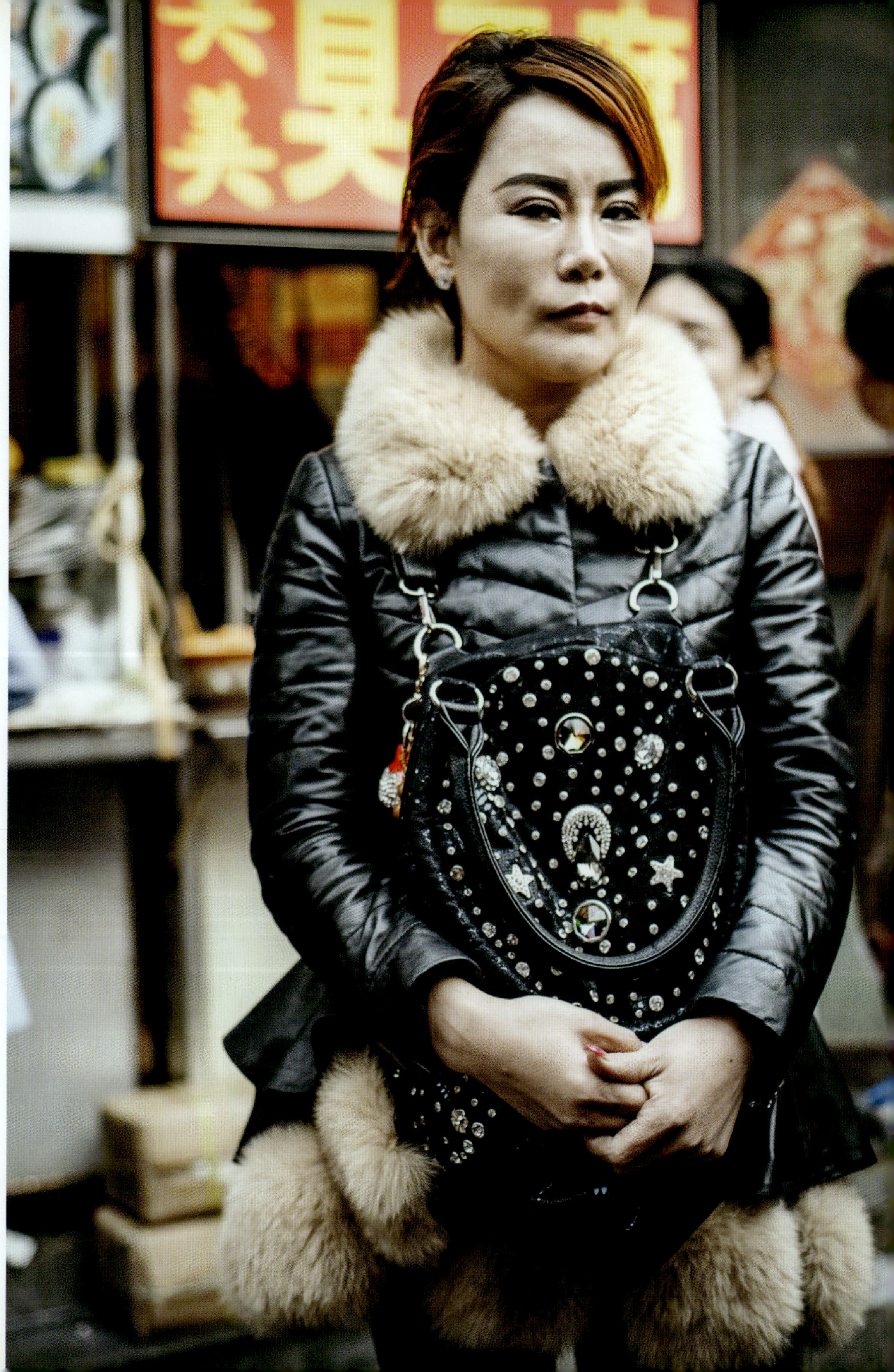

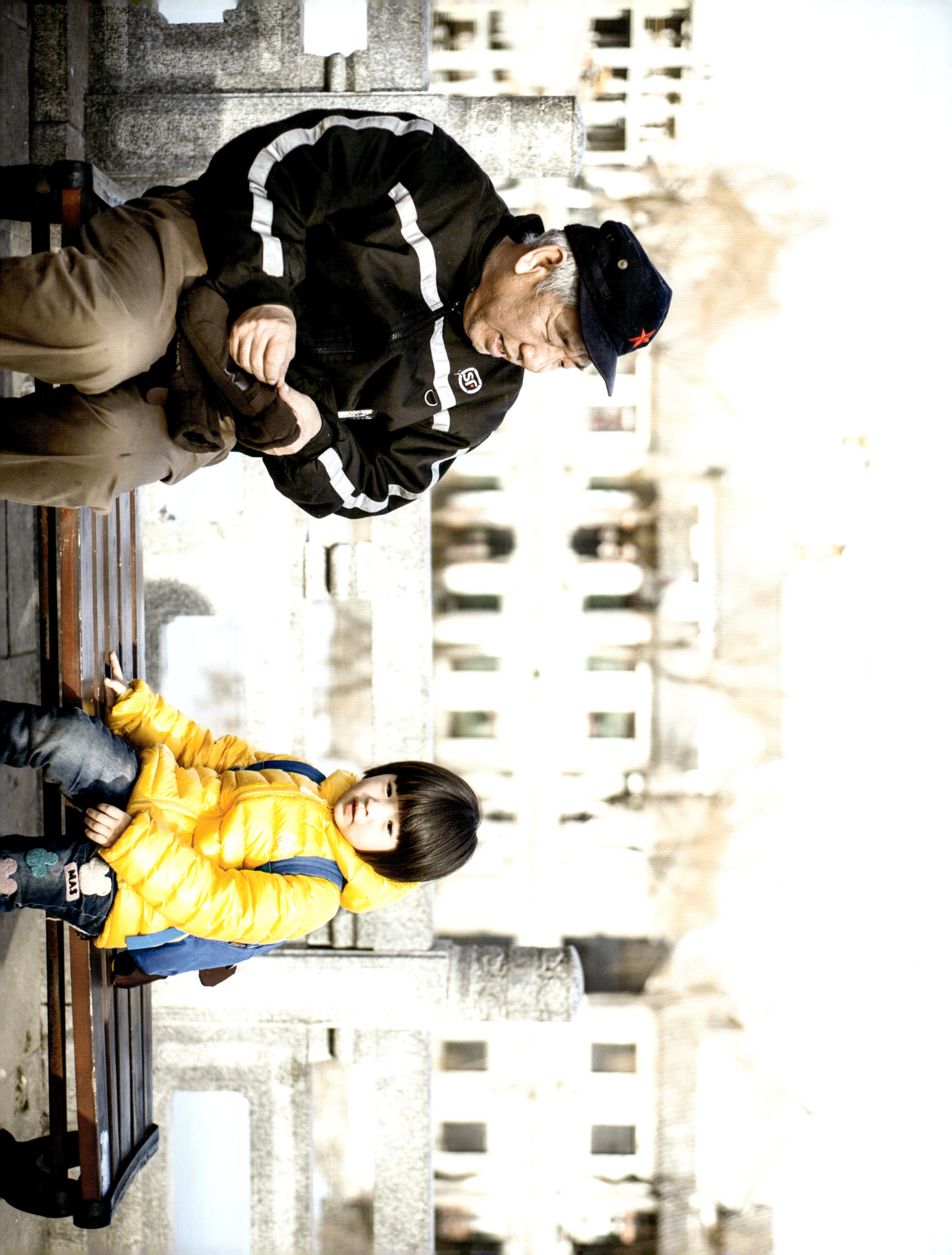

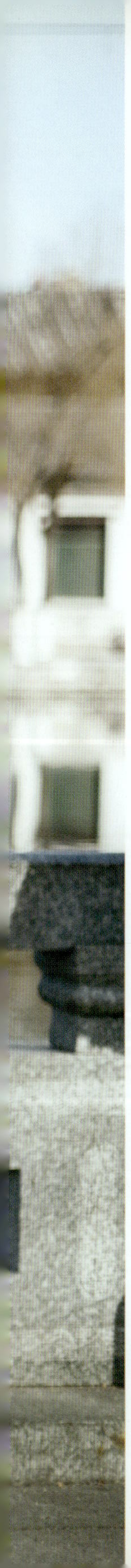

Red and pink signify the New Year, and many people wear the colors (even at the same time) to symbolize luck and prosperity for the upcoming year.

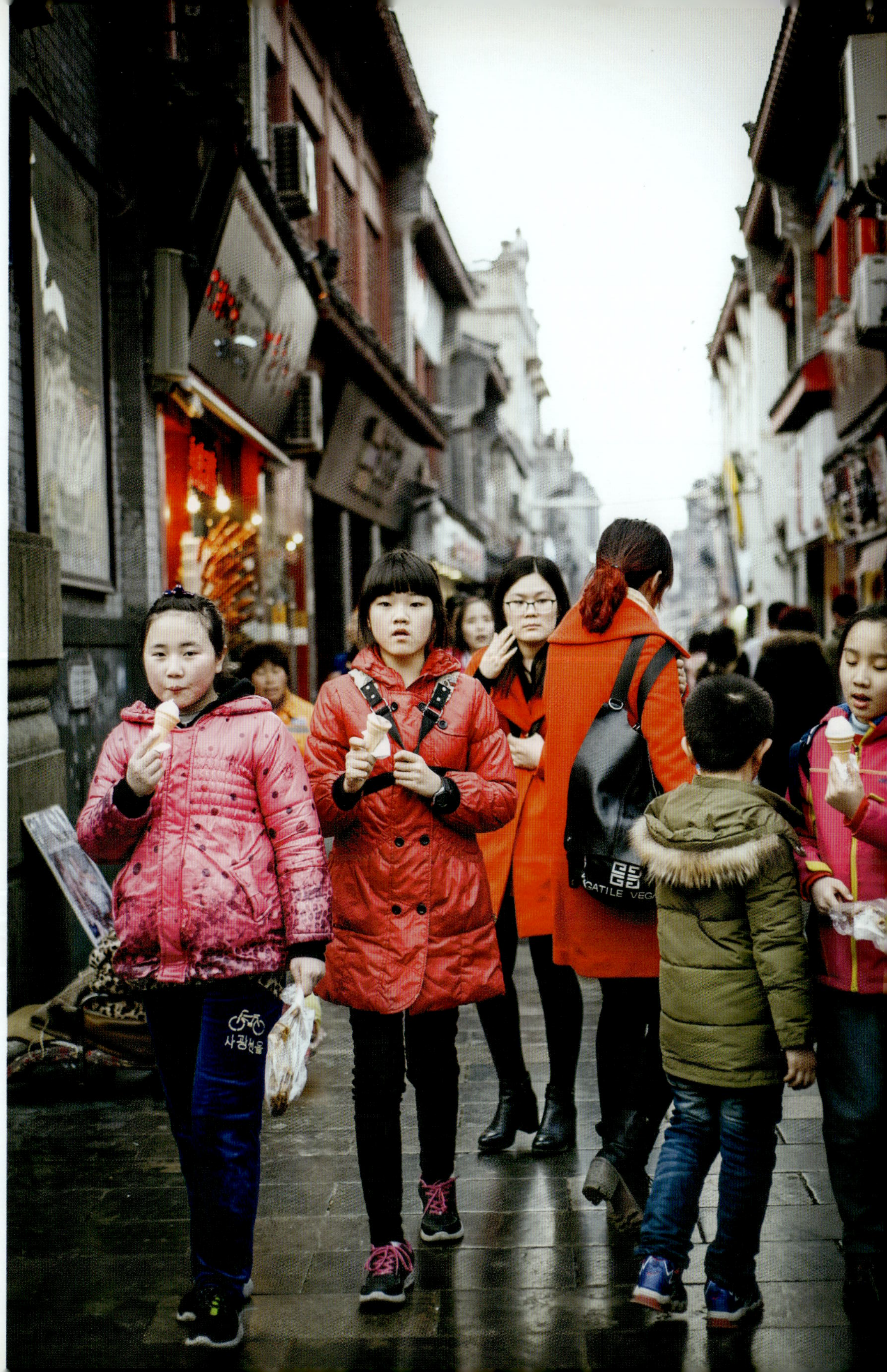

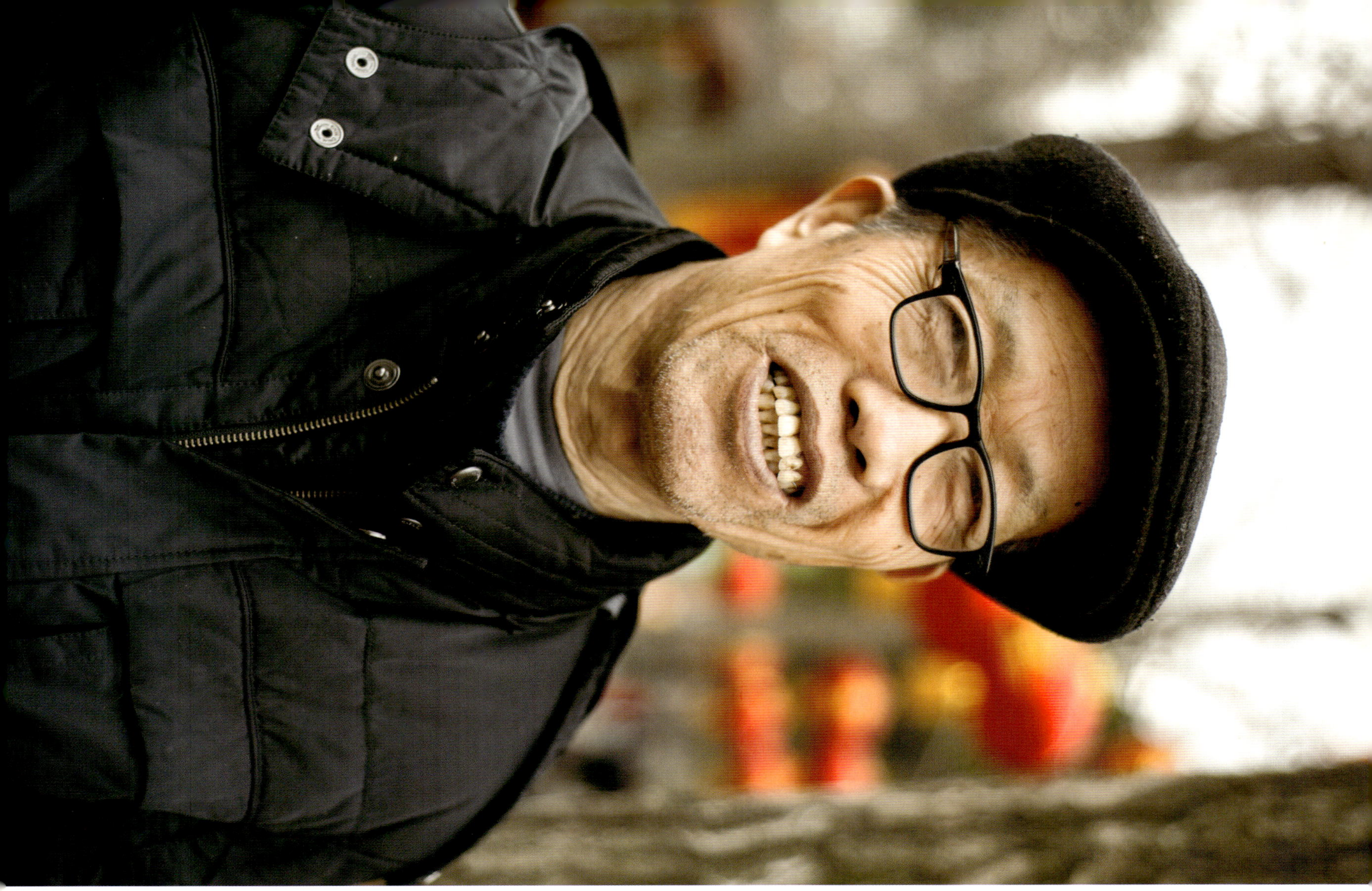

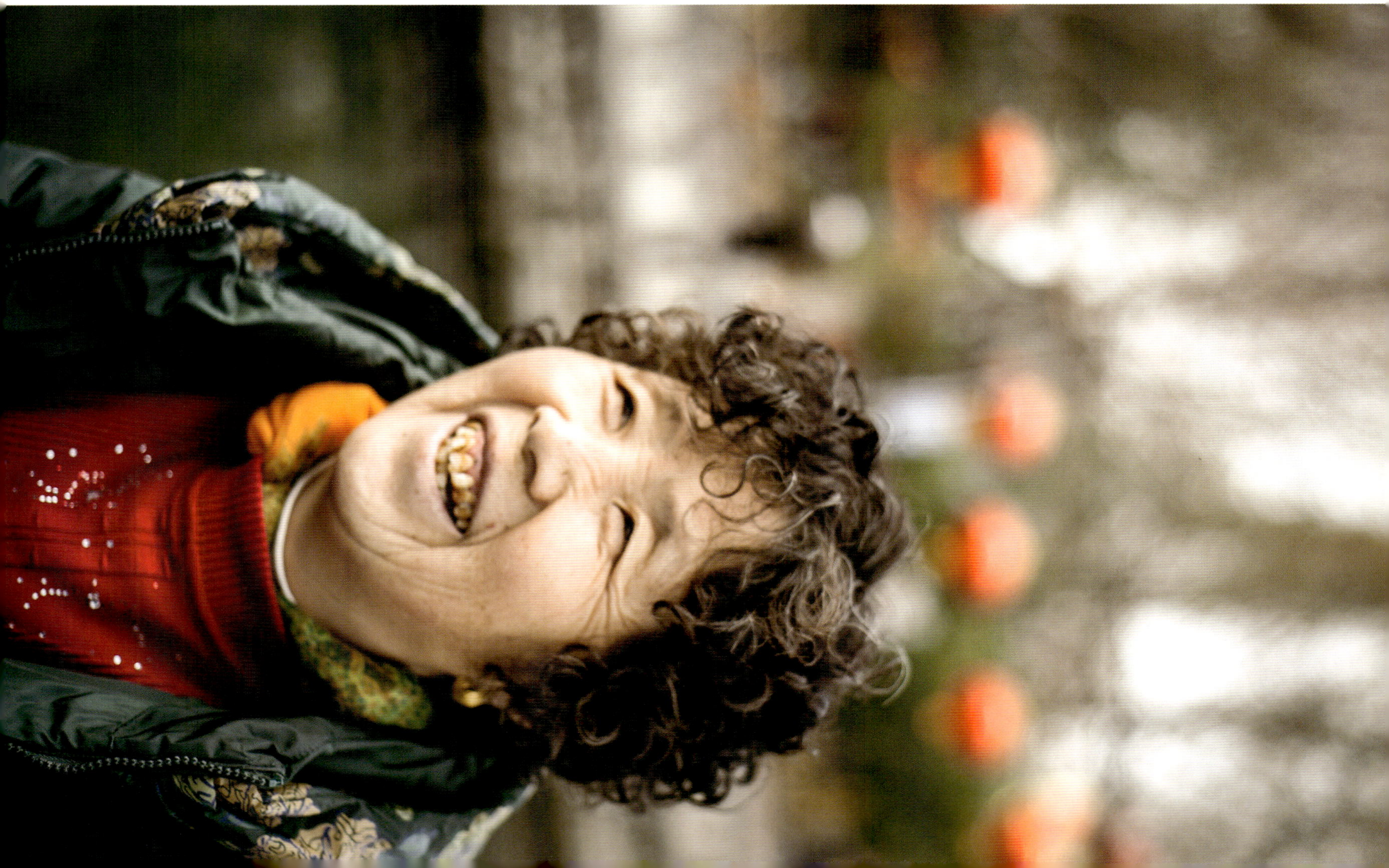

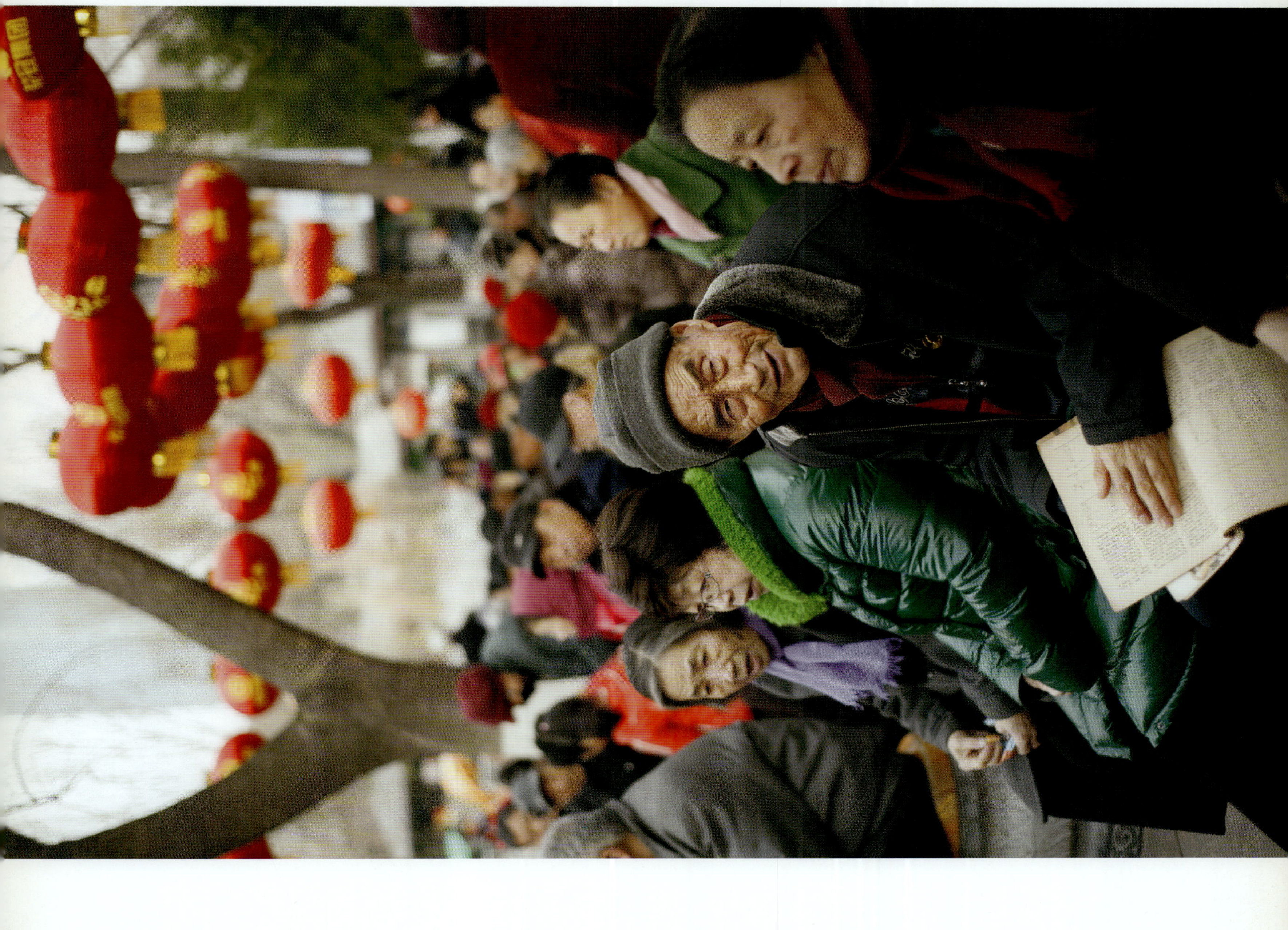

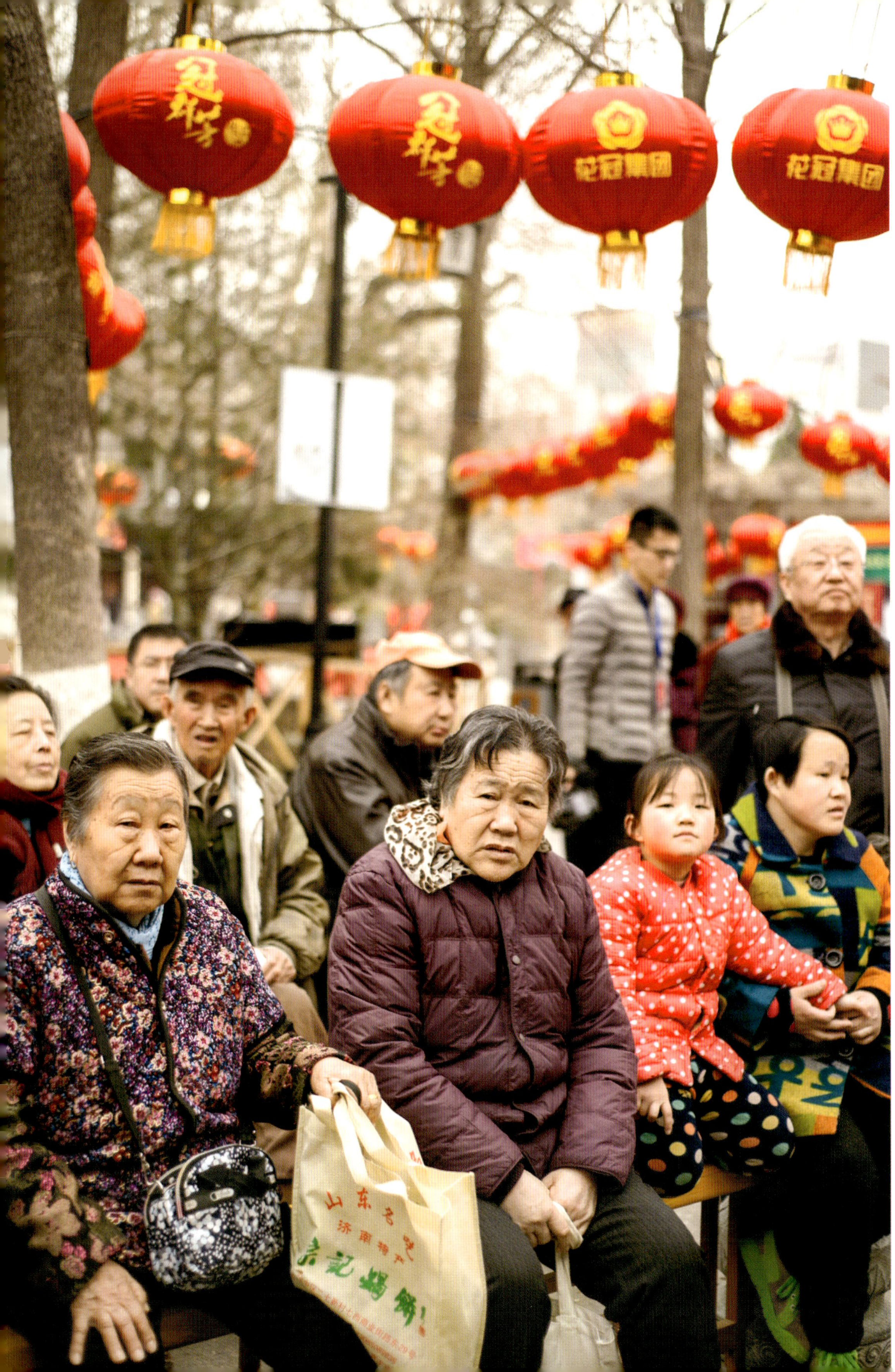

Many parks are free to grandparents who look after their grandchildren while the parents are at work. In this park the crowd enjoyed an outdoor performance of a traditional Chinese musical play. During the New Year Lantern Festival, traditional Peking Operat is performed for all to enjoy.

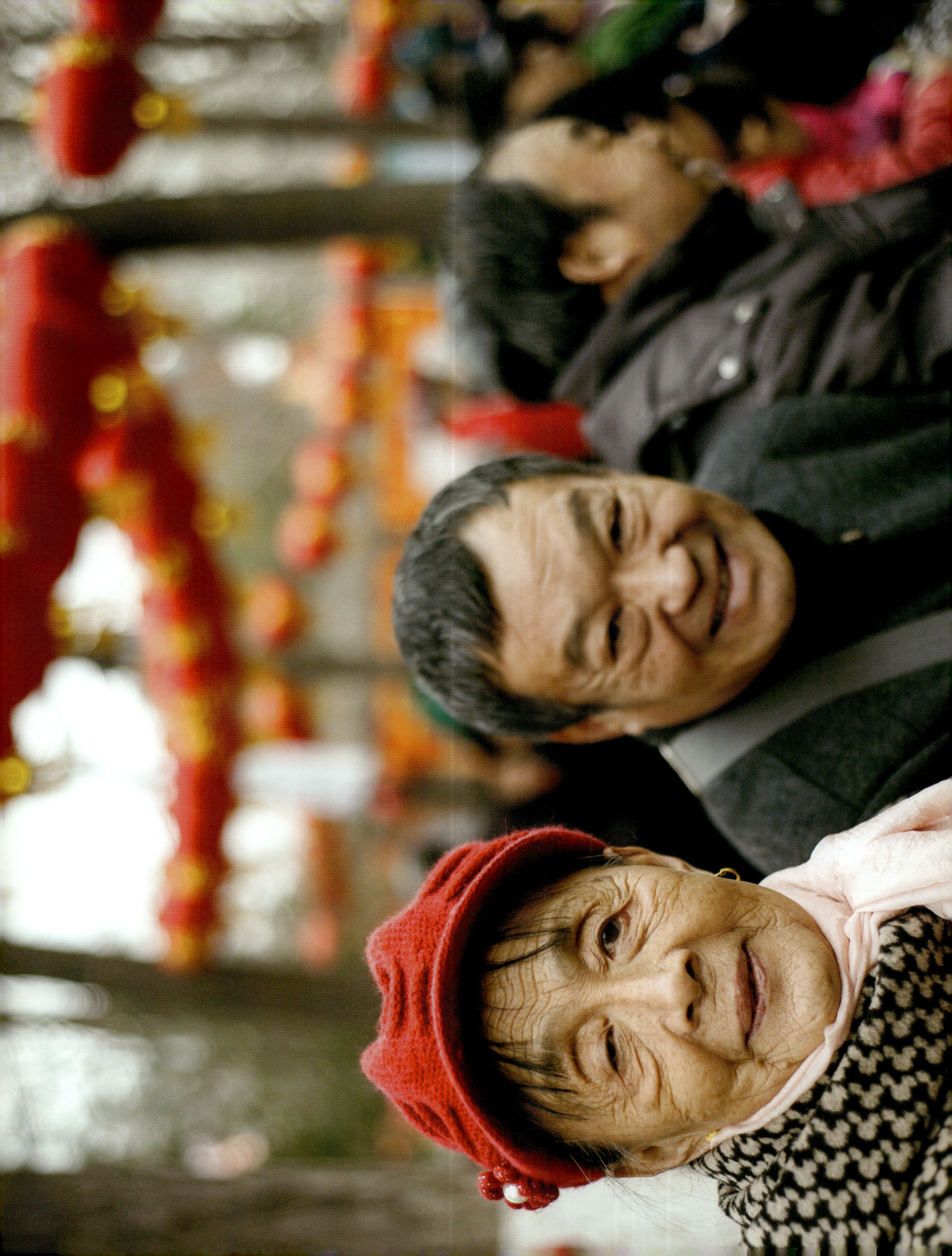

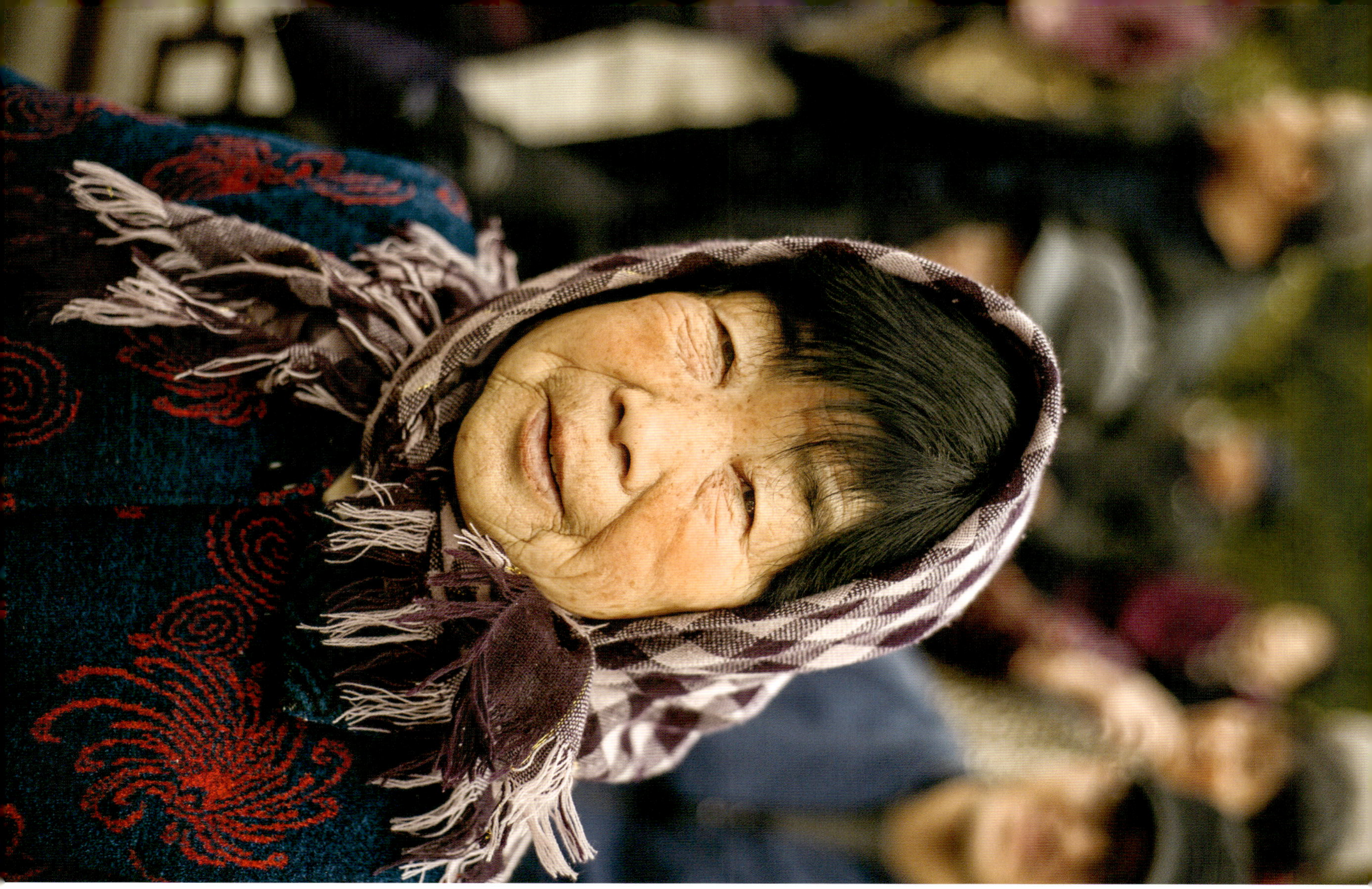

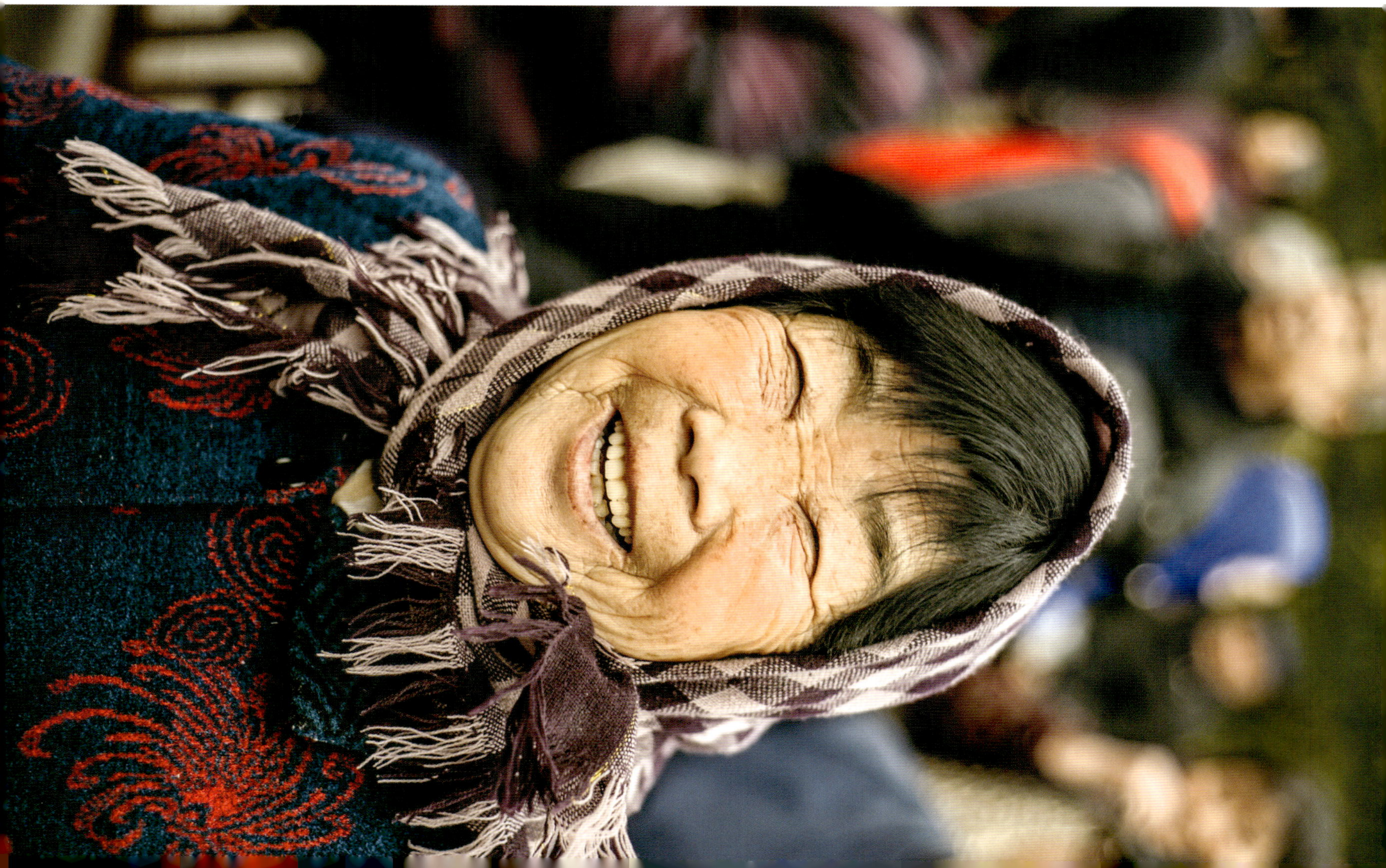

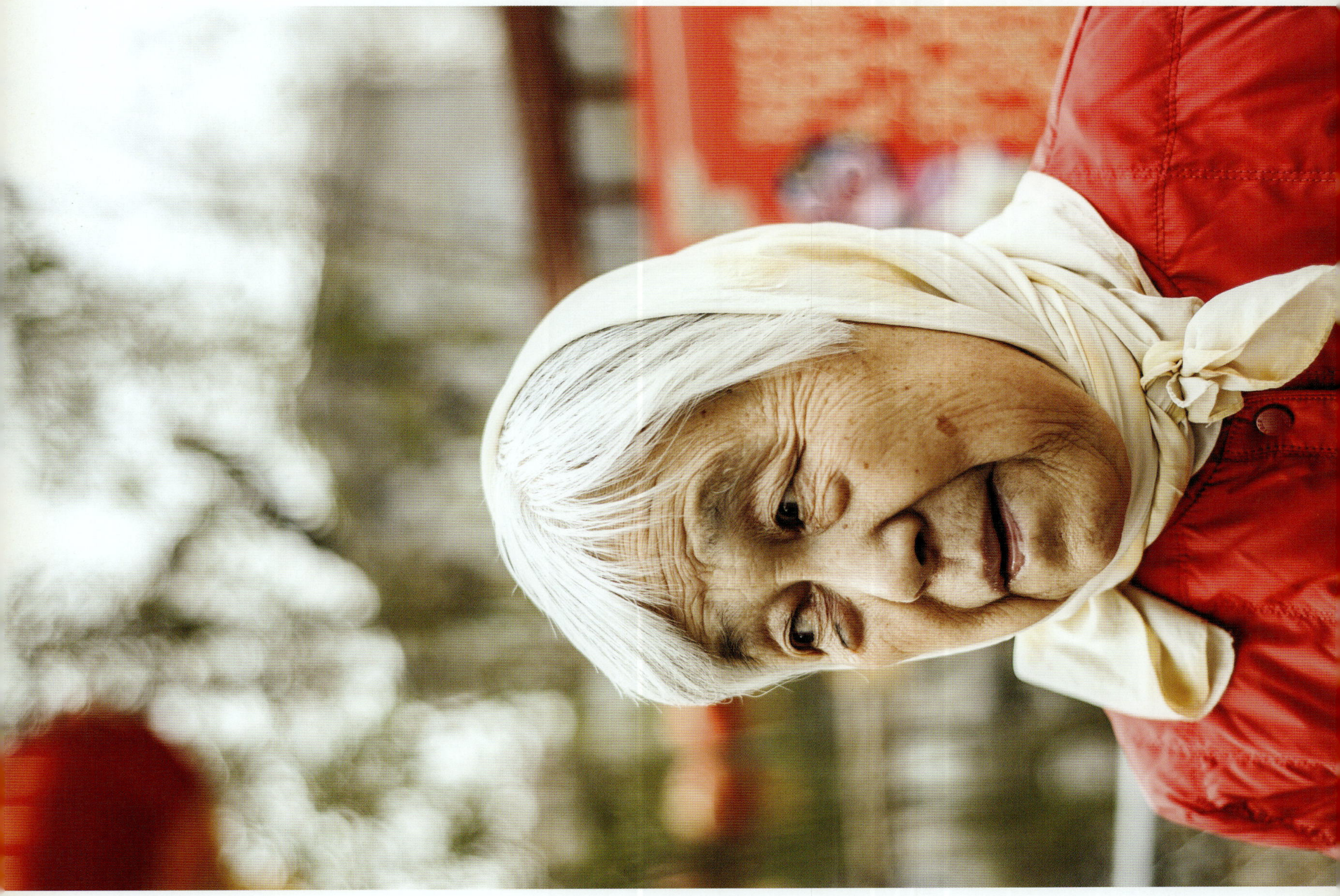

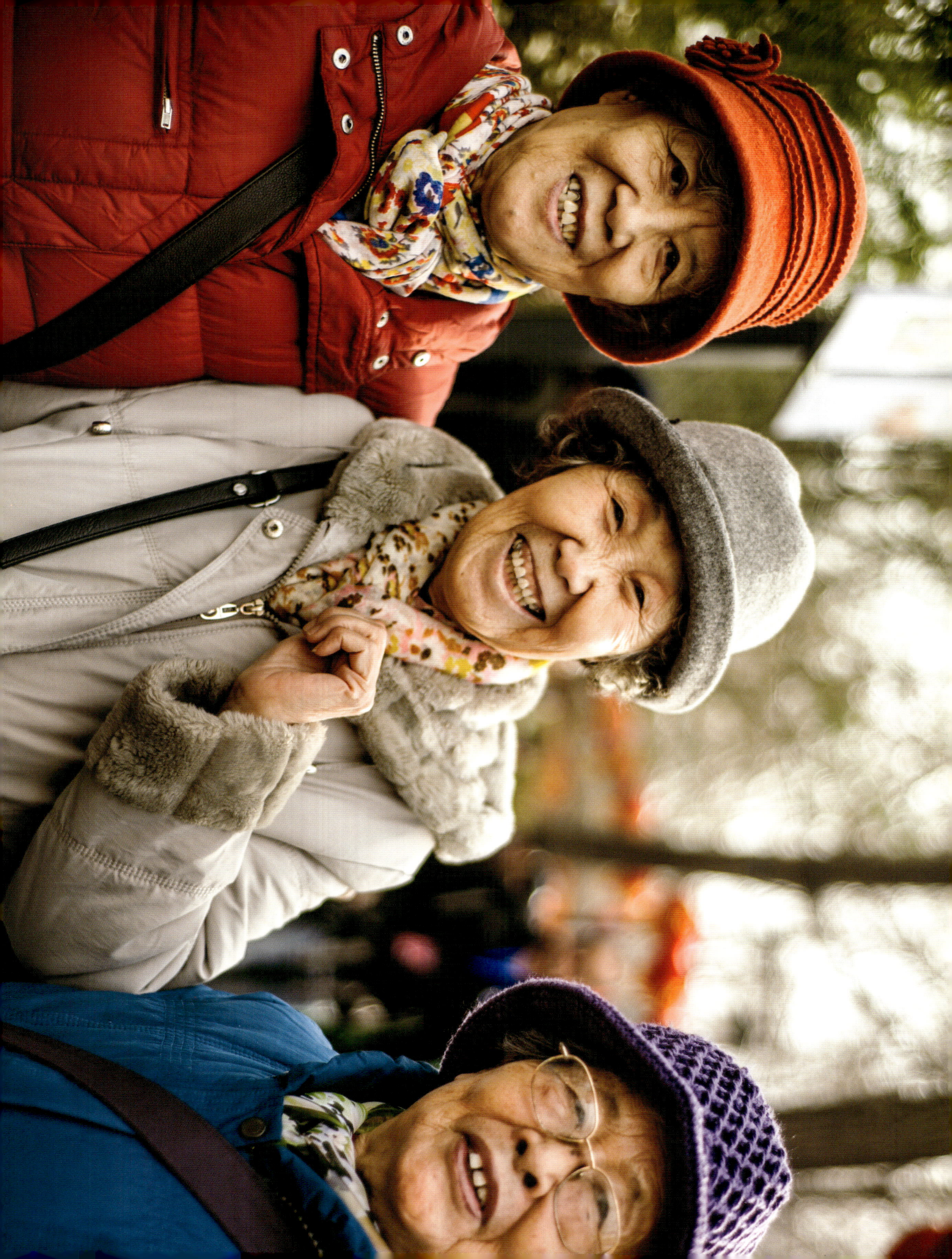

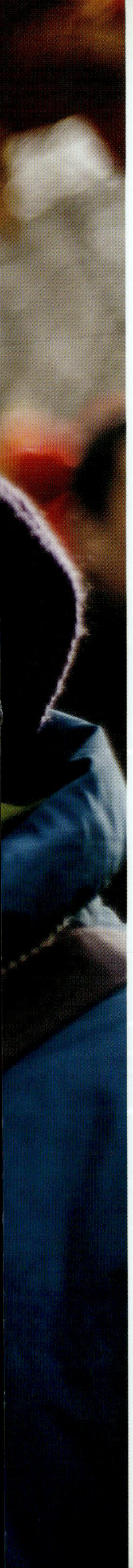

Baotu Spring, which translates to Jet Spring or Spurting Spring, is the most famous spring in China. An artesian karst spring, it is located within Baotu Spring Cultural Park and is one of the three major attractions in Jinan. The water originates from an Ordovician karst aquifer that sits under the city. The water, which travels through underground limestone caves, stays about 65 degrees Fahrenheit year-round.

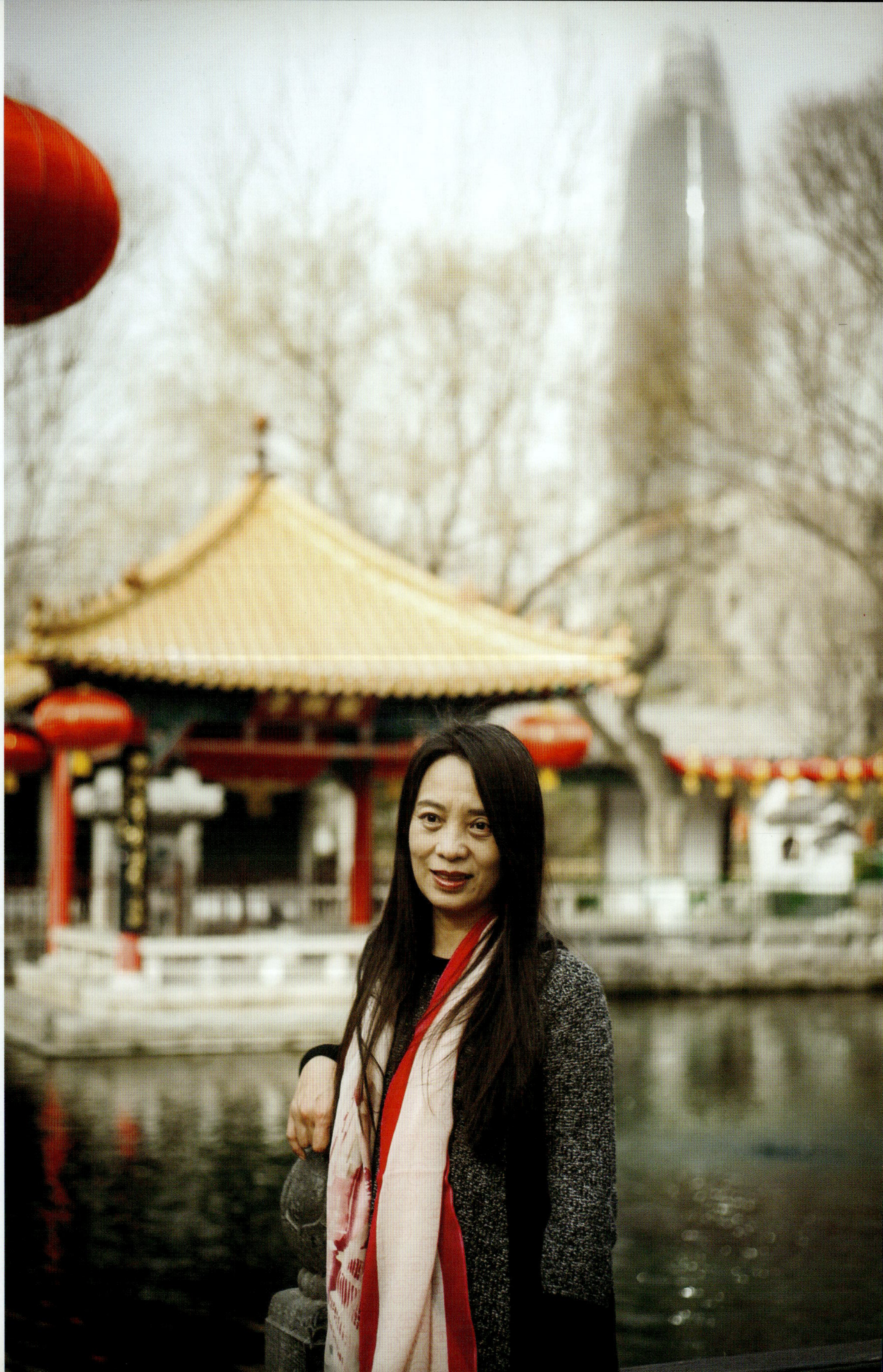

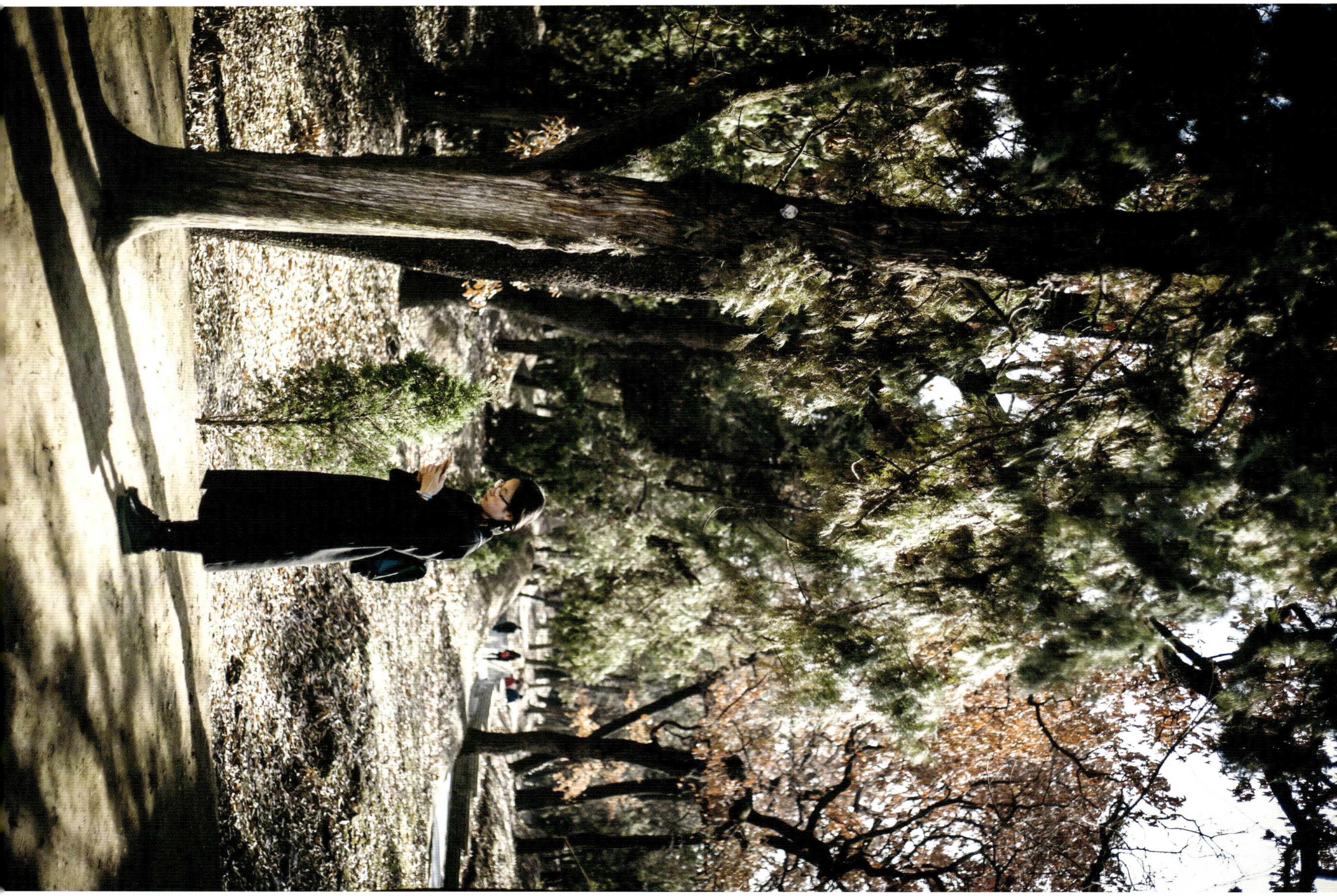

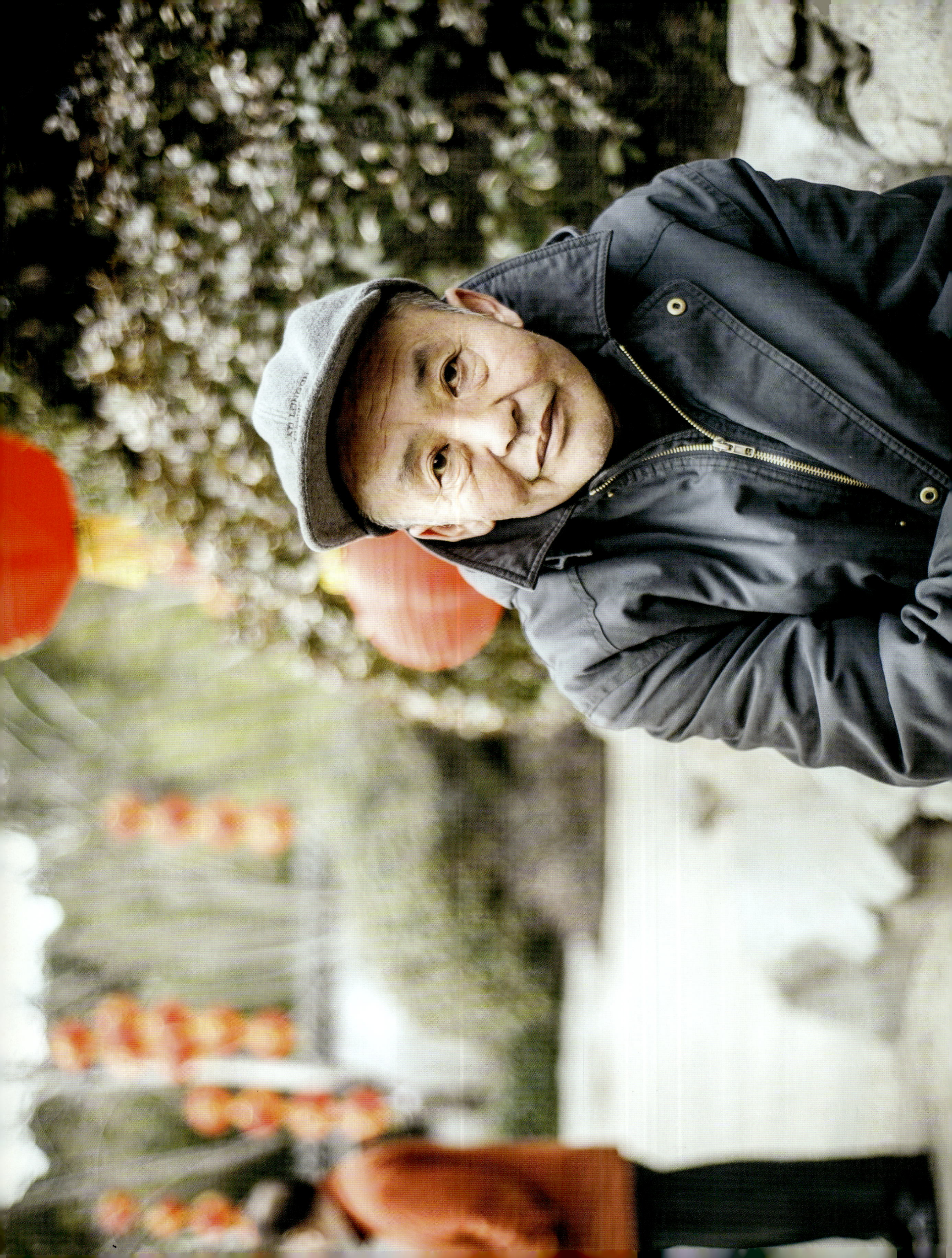

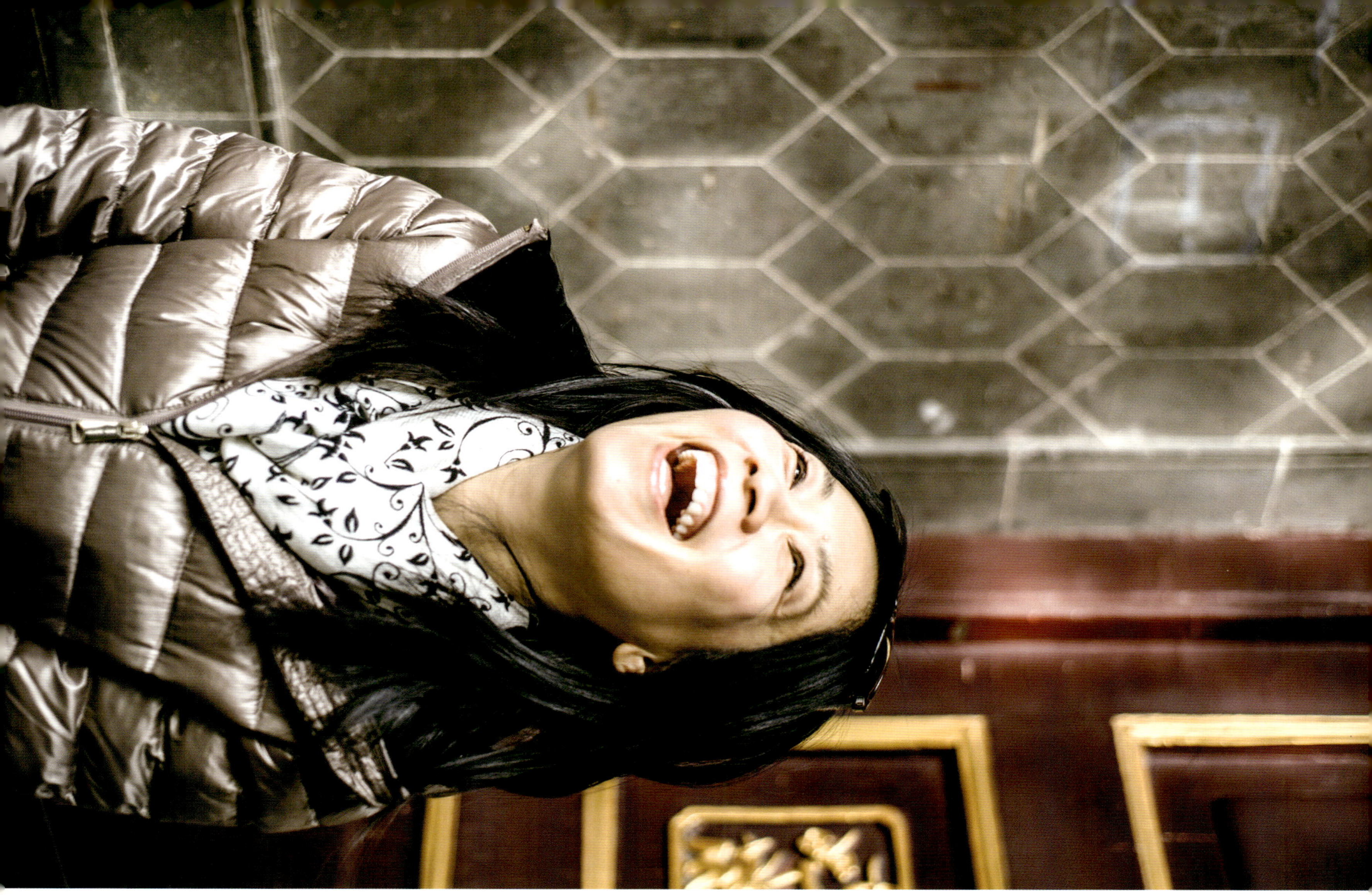

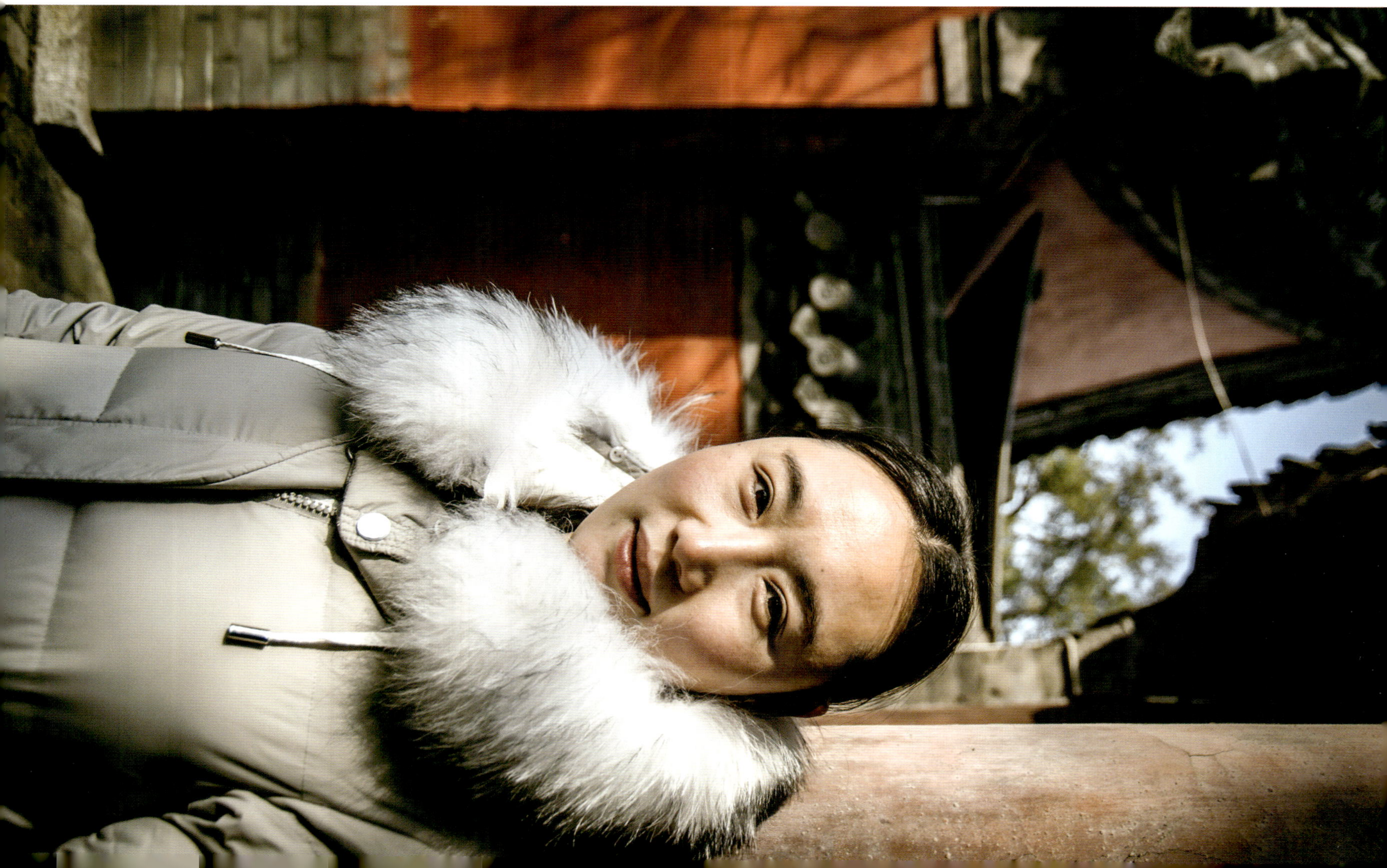

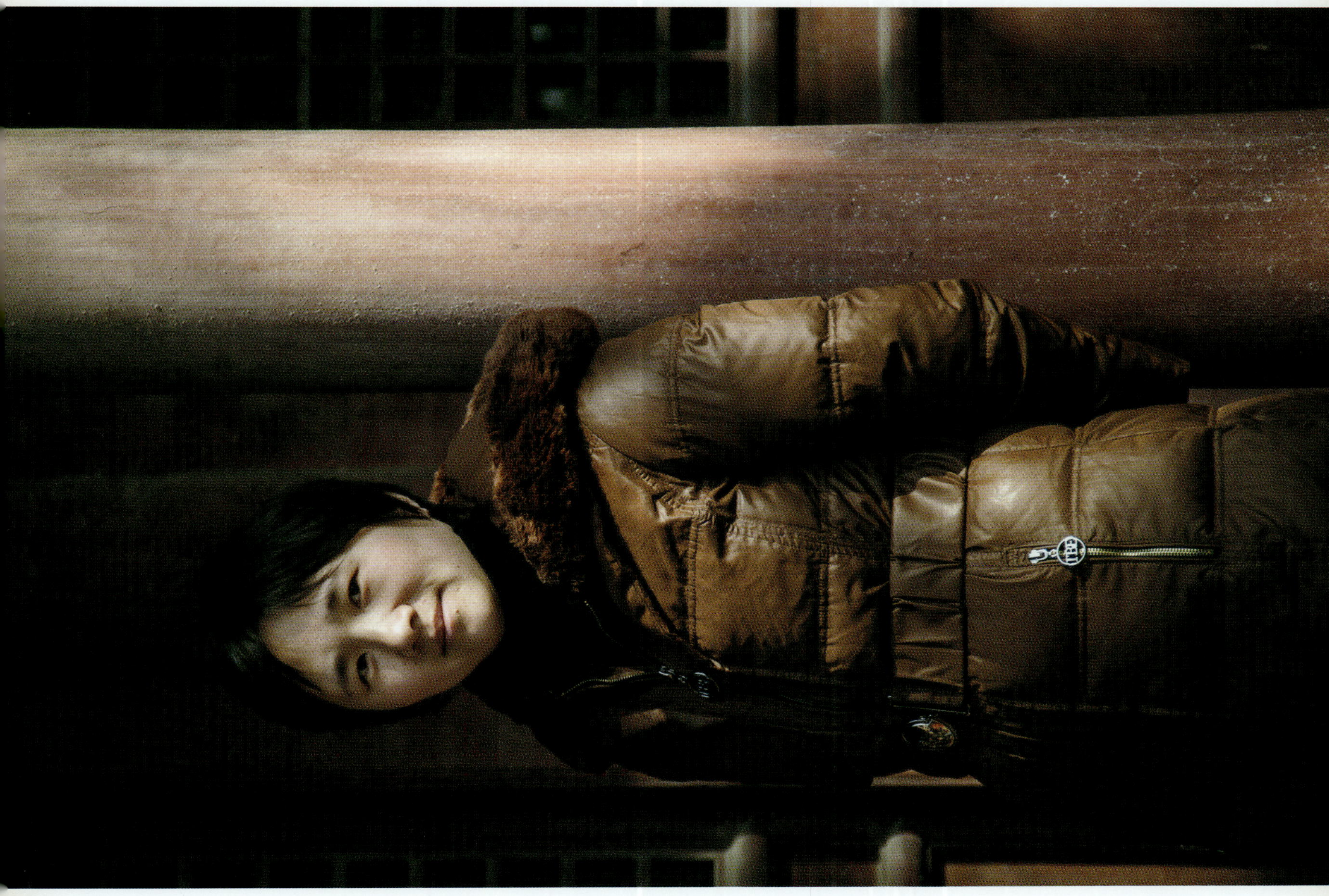

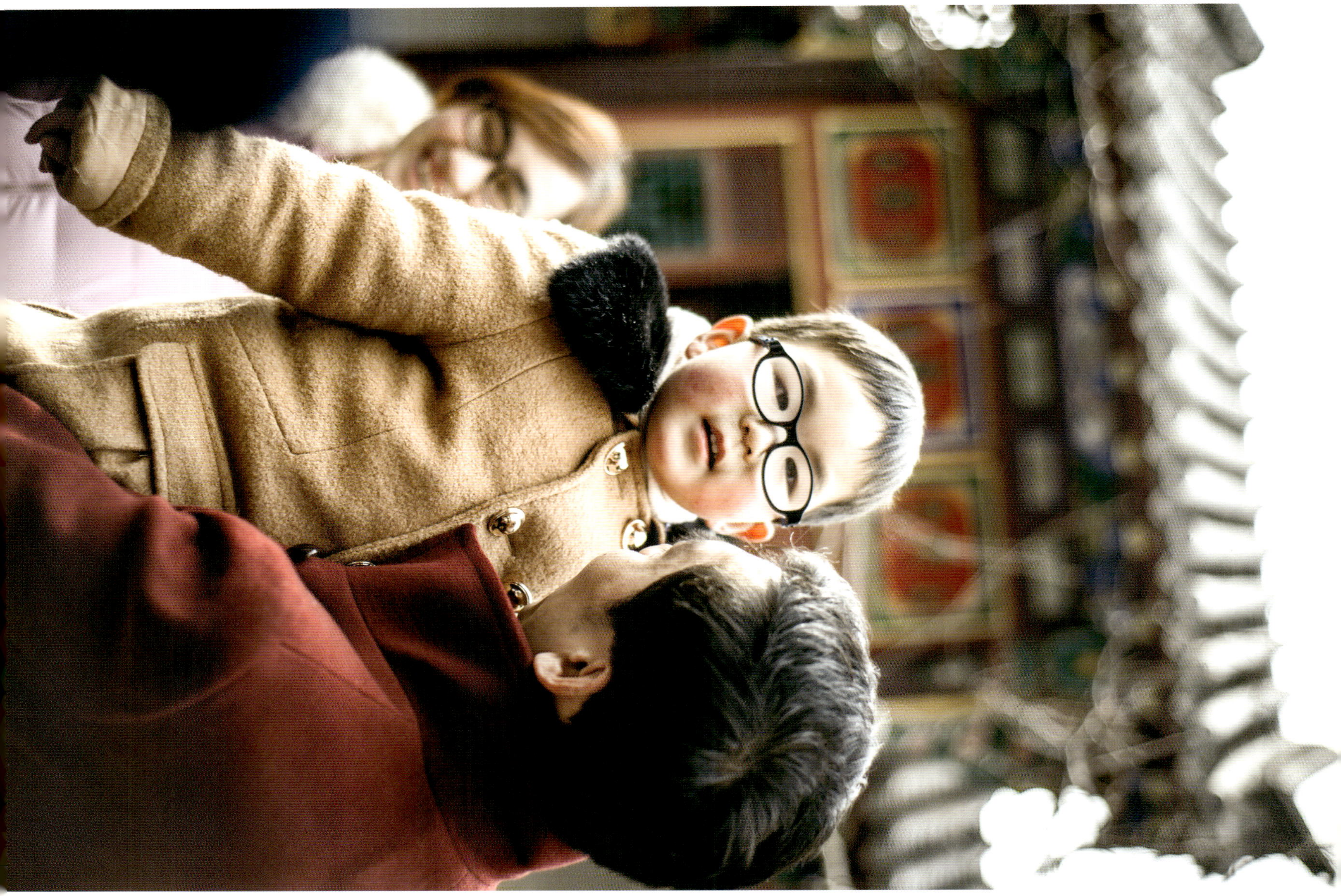

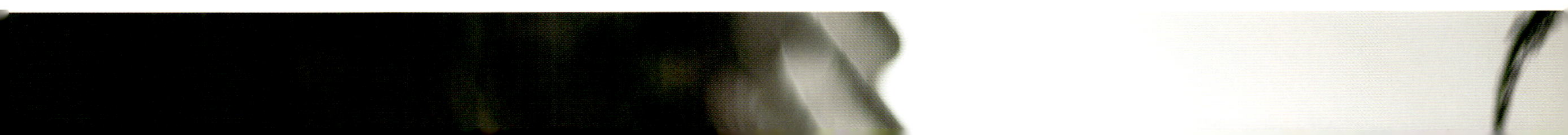

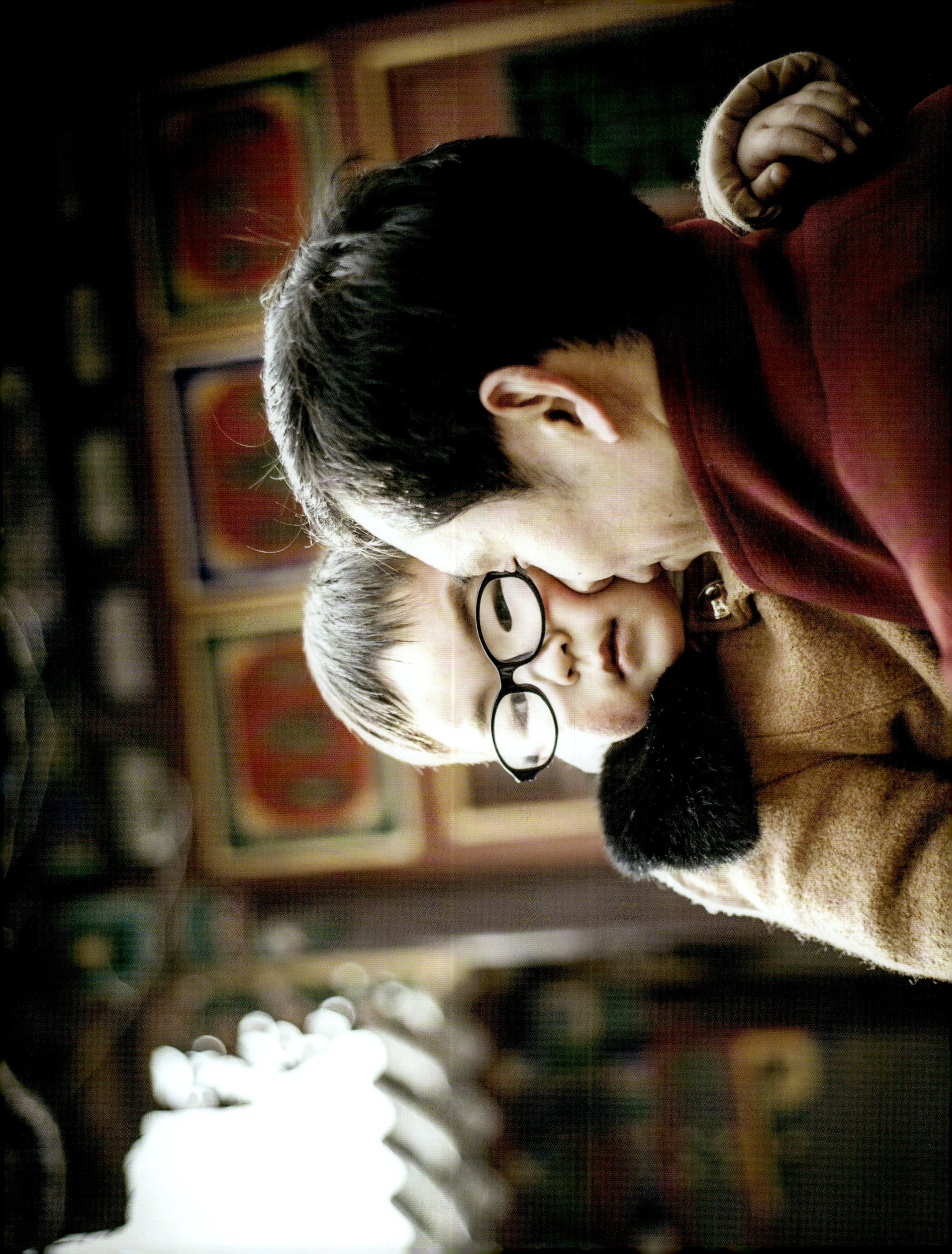

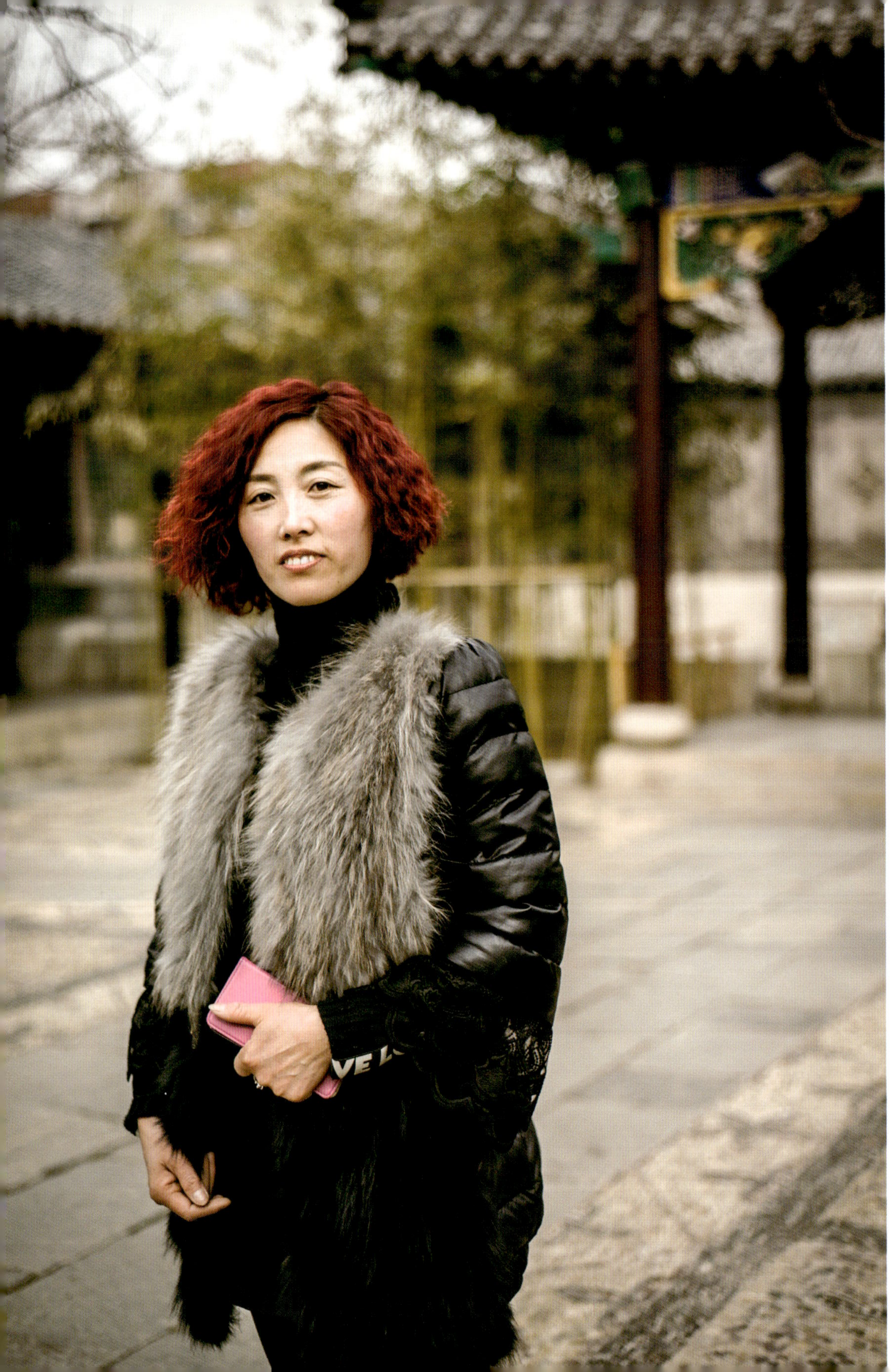

Daring colored hair isn't all that uncommon in China, where women push fashion to the edge.

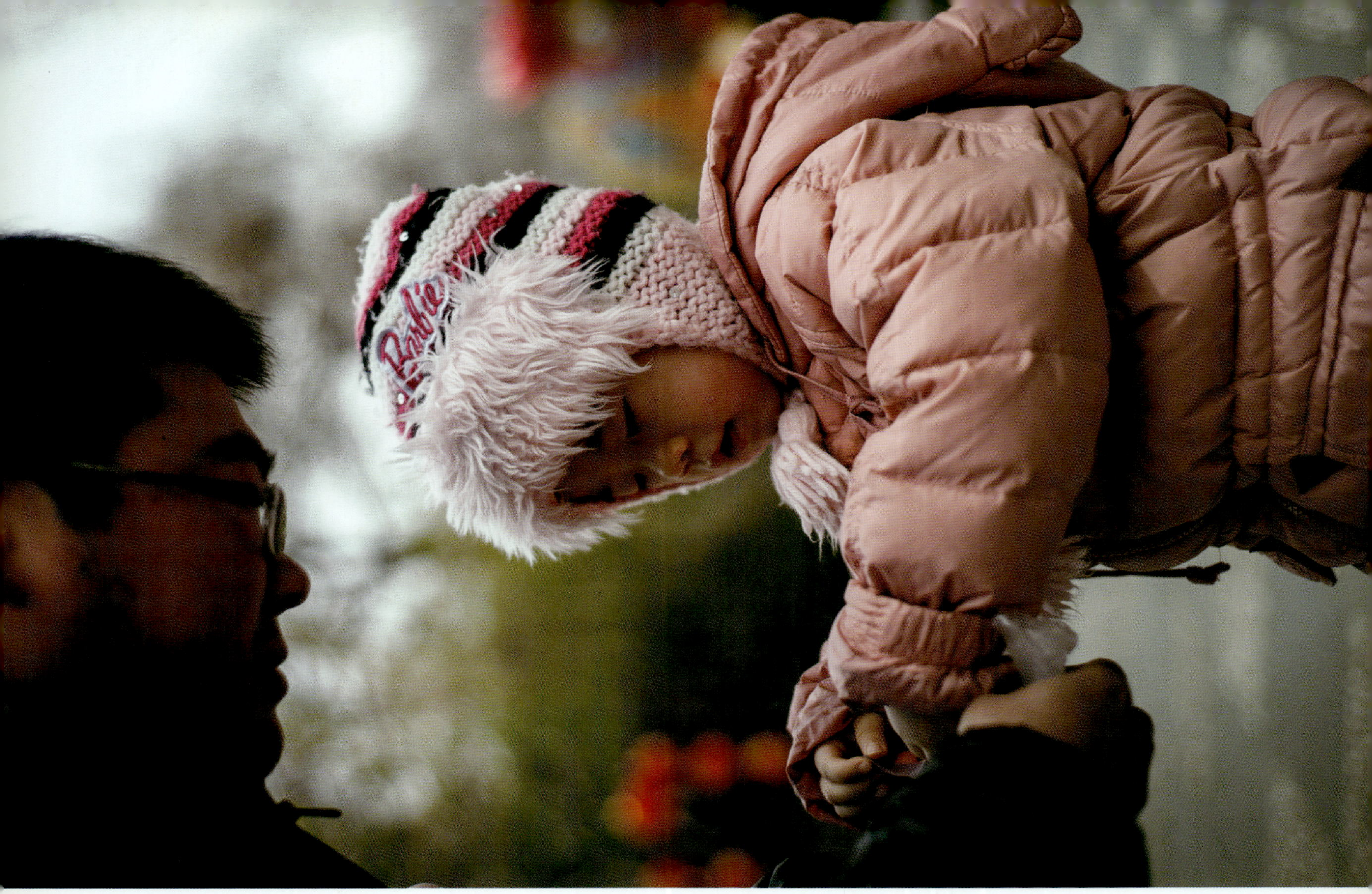
Barbie

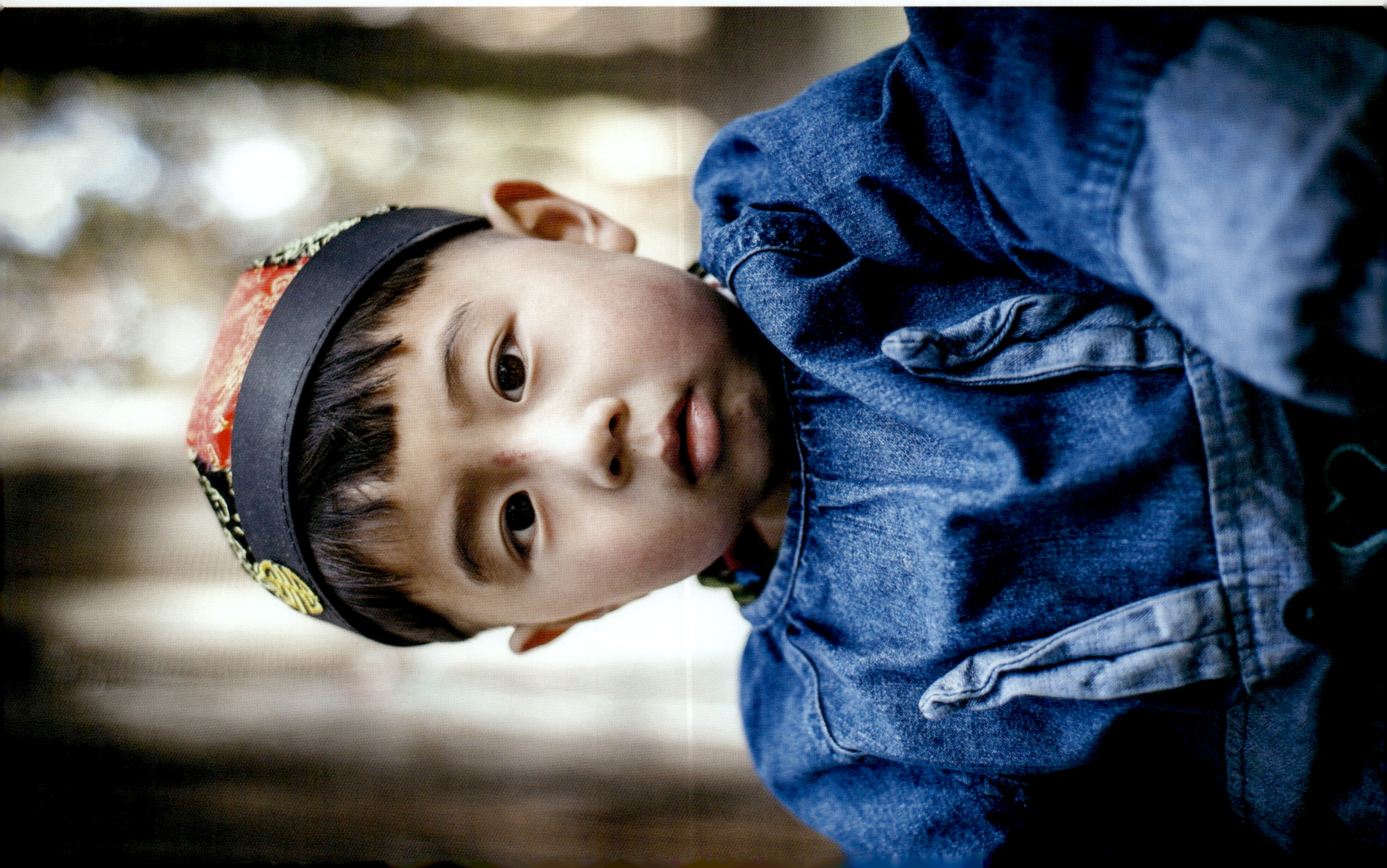

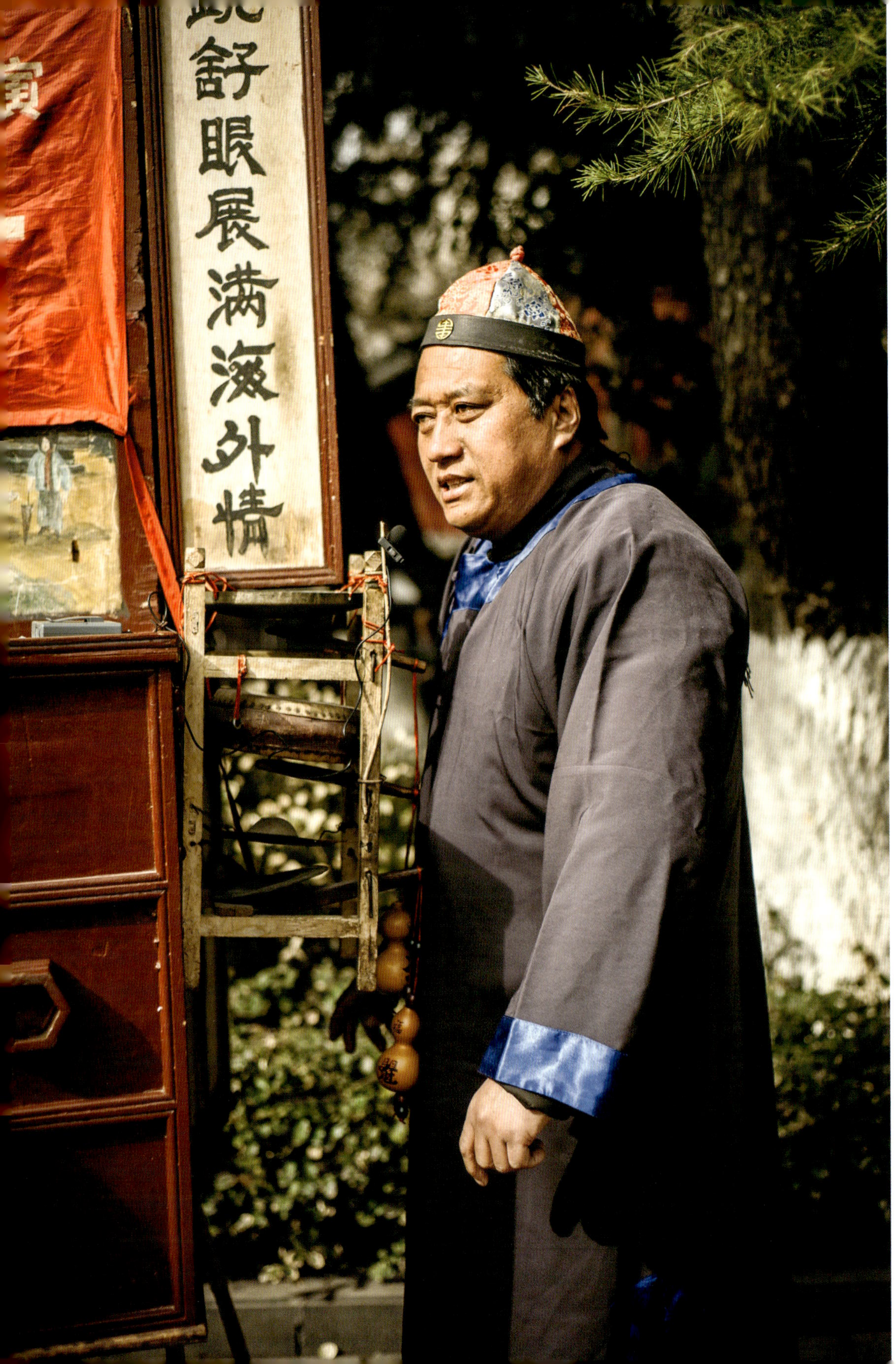

In Jinan, street vendors of all sorts demonstrate tricks and play music for their peers during the Lantern Festival. This local businessman, dressed in traditional Chinese clothing, uses a device showing the prototype of motion pictures to entertain his audience. His traditional attire draws in his street audience, much like street performers do in the US.

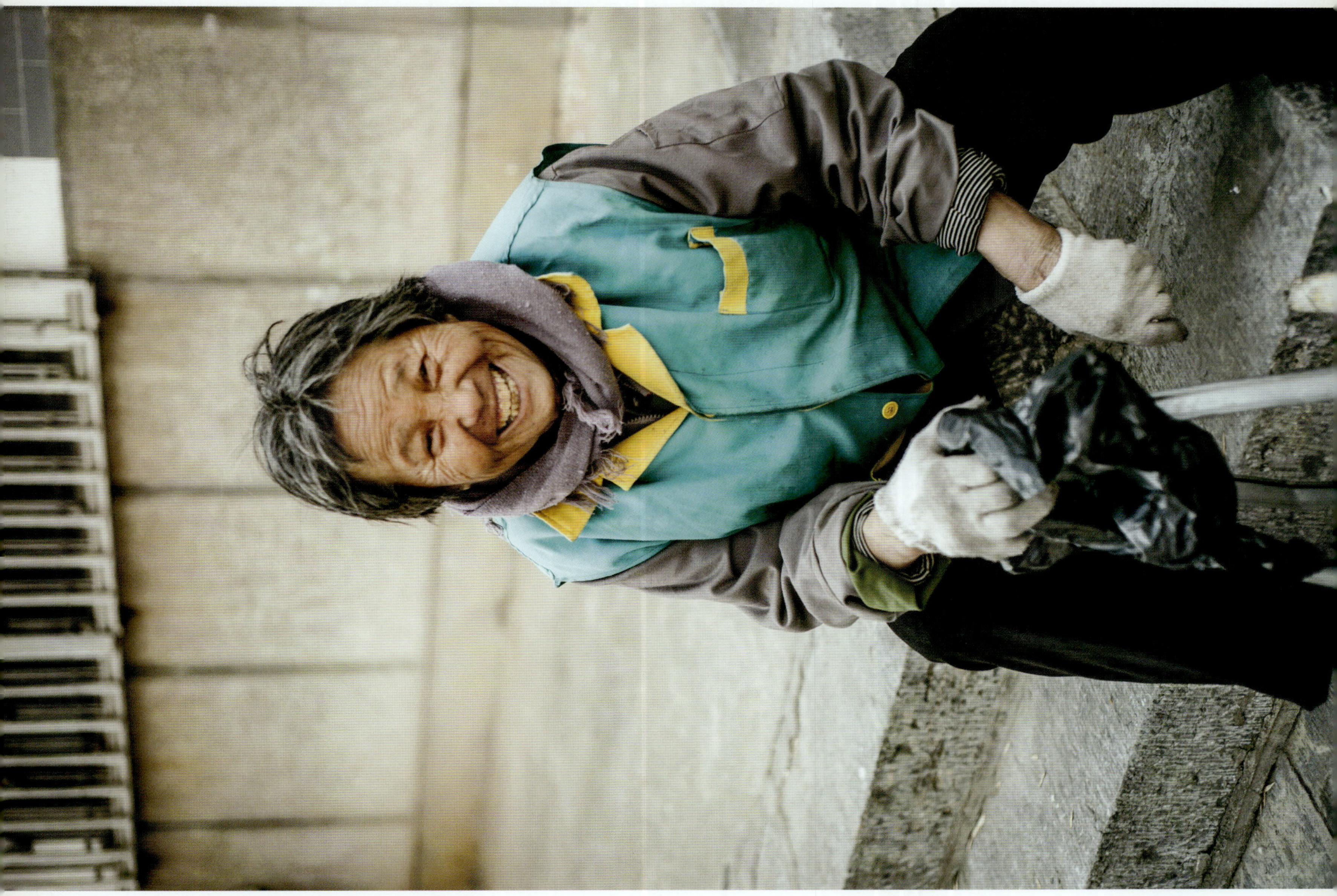

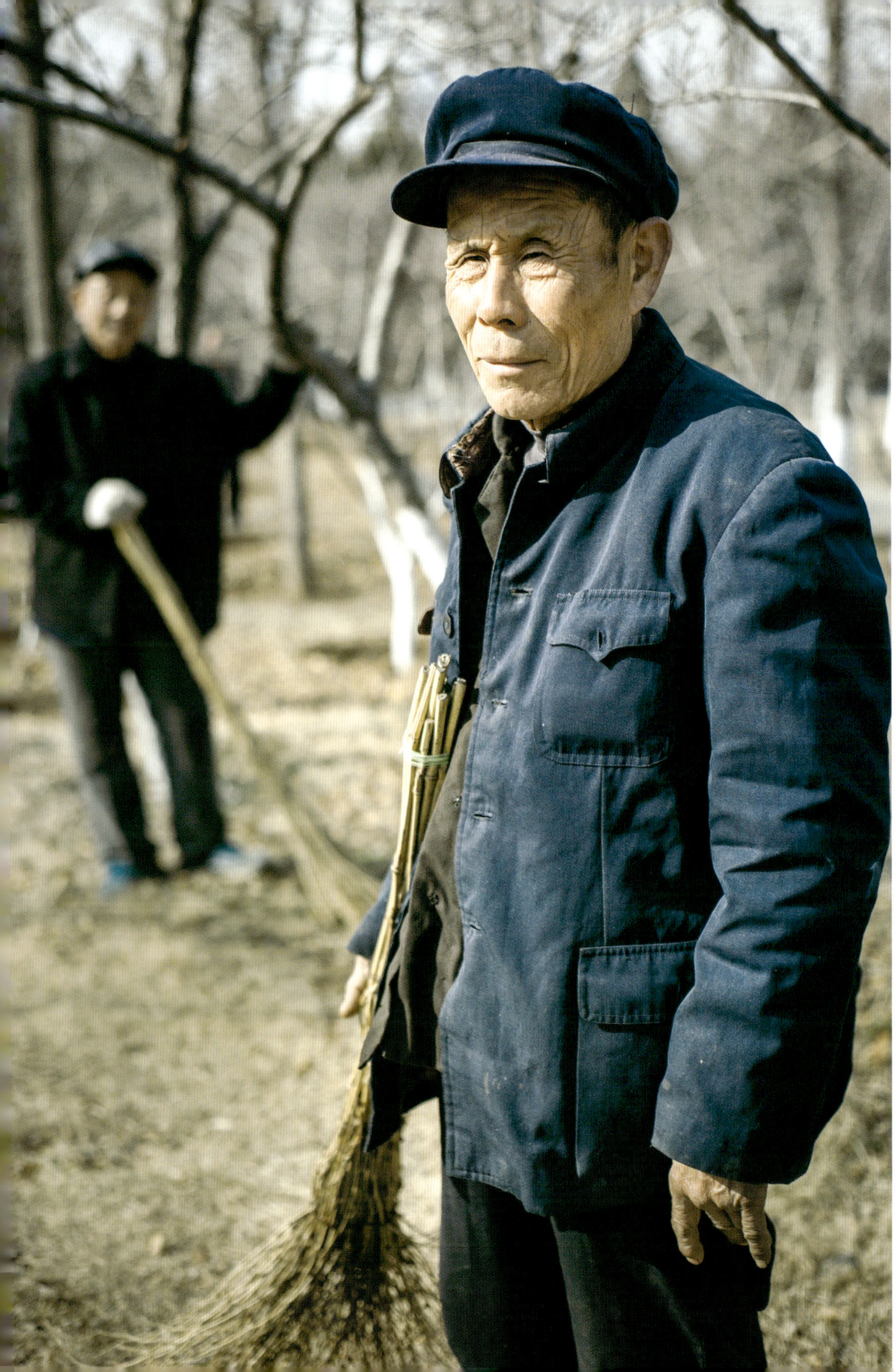

Landscapers at the Thousand Buddha Mountain work to maintain a perfect balance of natural and sculpted landscape.

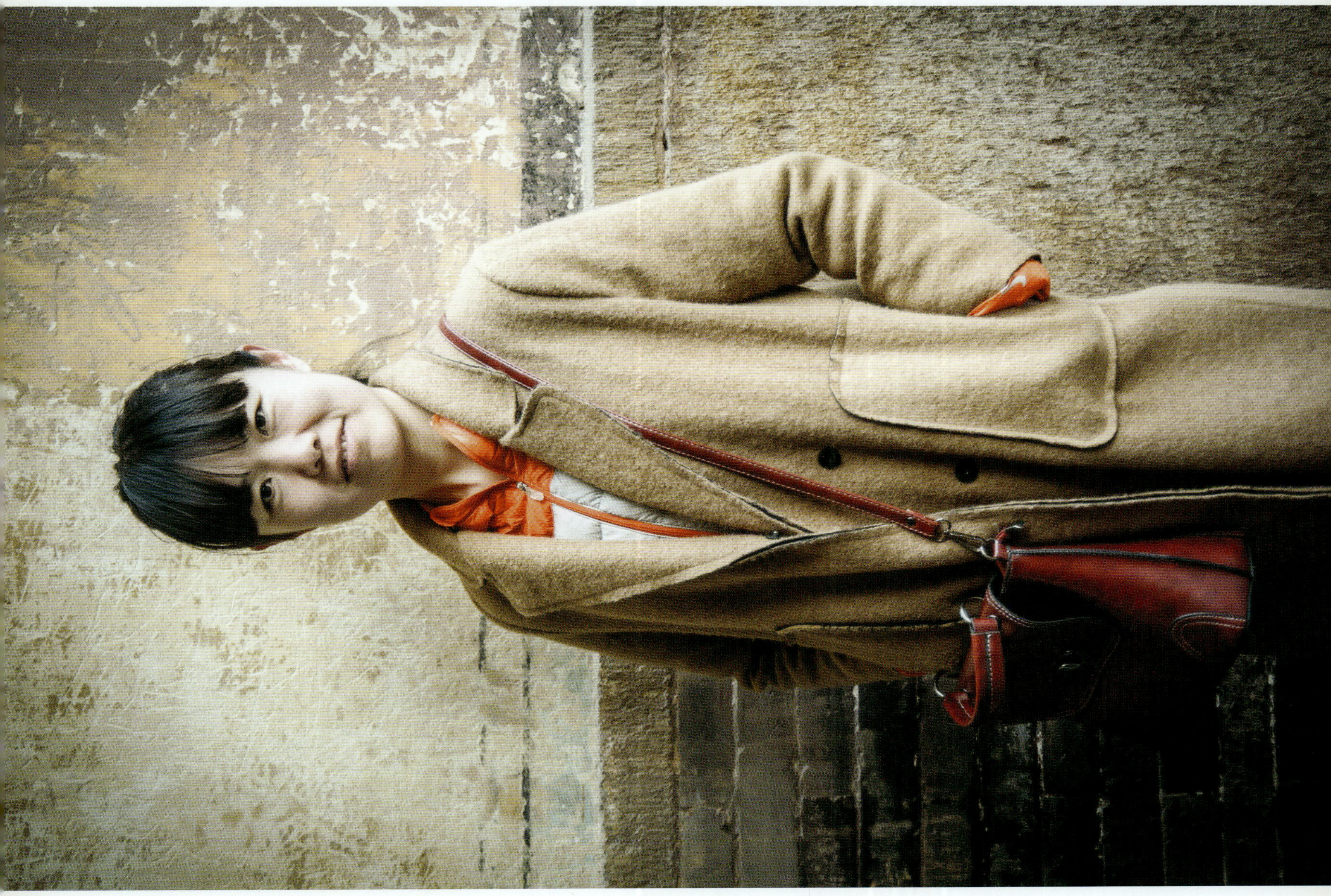

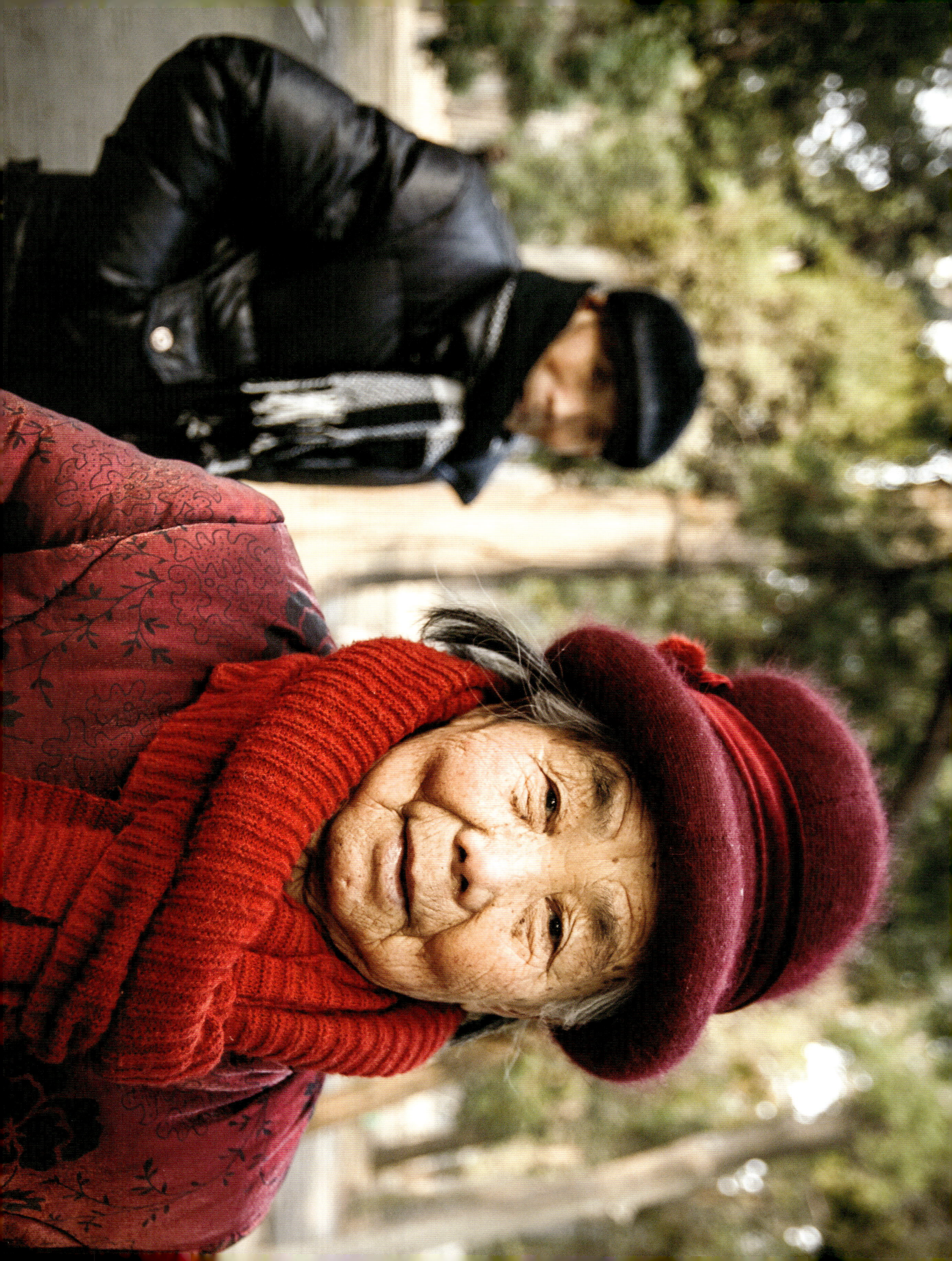

The military commander of the Chinese Army in Kashgar, an appointed military official, loves photography and was one of my many very gracious hosts. A region of China that has its own cultural, political, and religious systems, Kashgar has been historically considered the convergence point of widely varying cultures and empires. A strategically important city on the Silk Road, it served as a trading post.

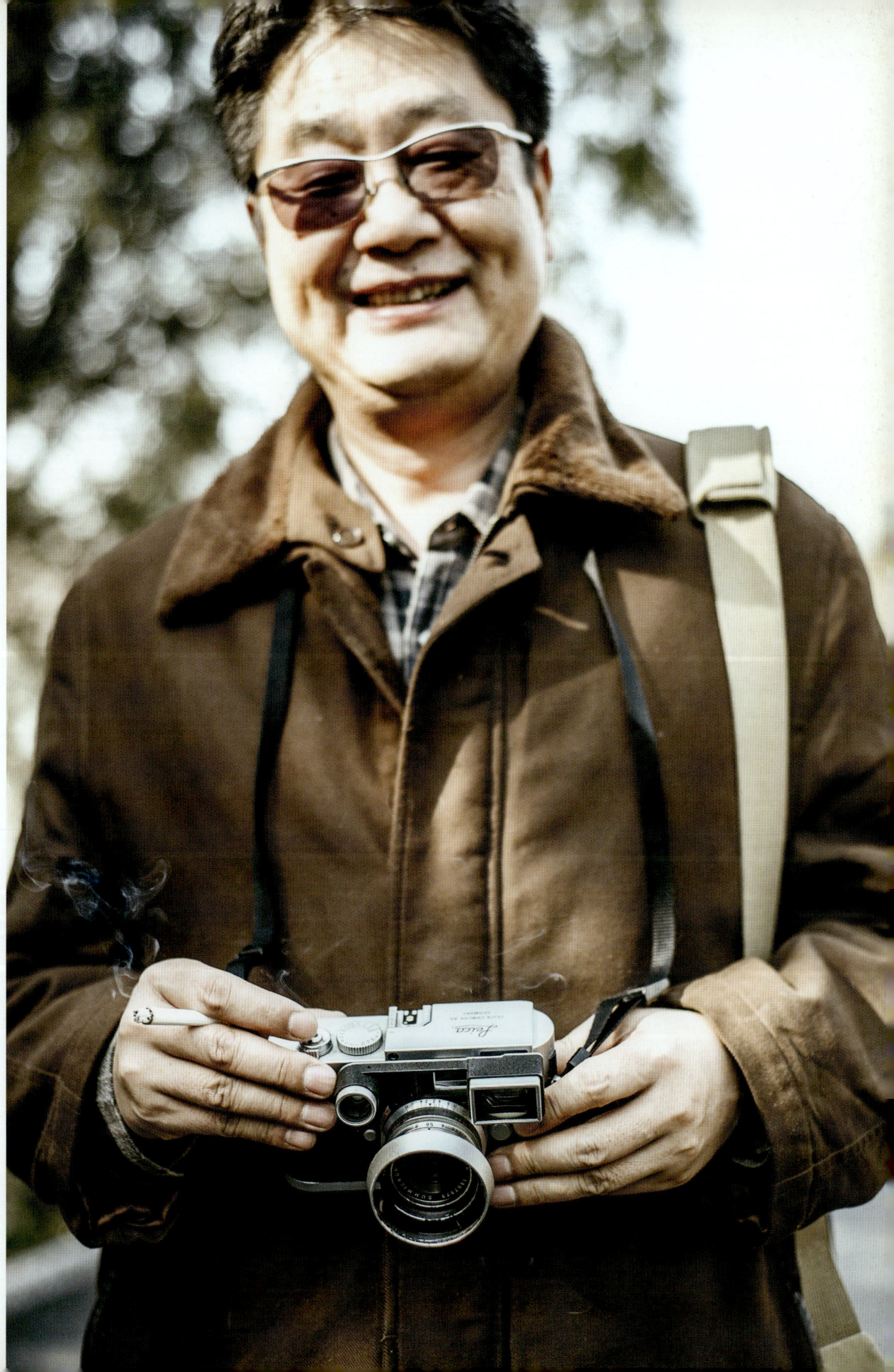

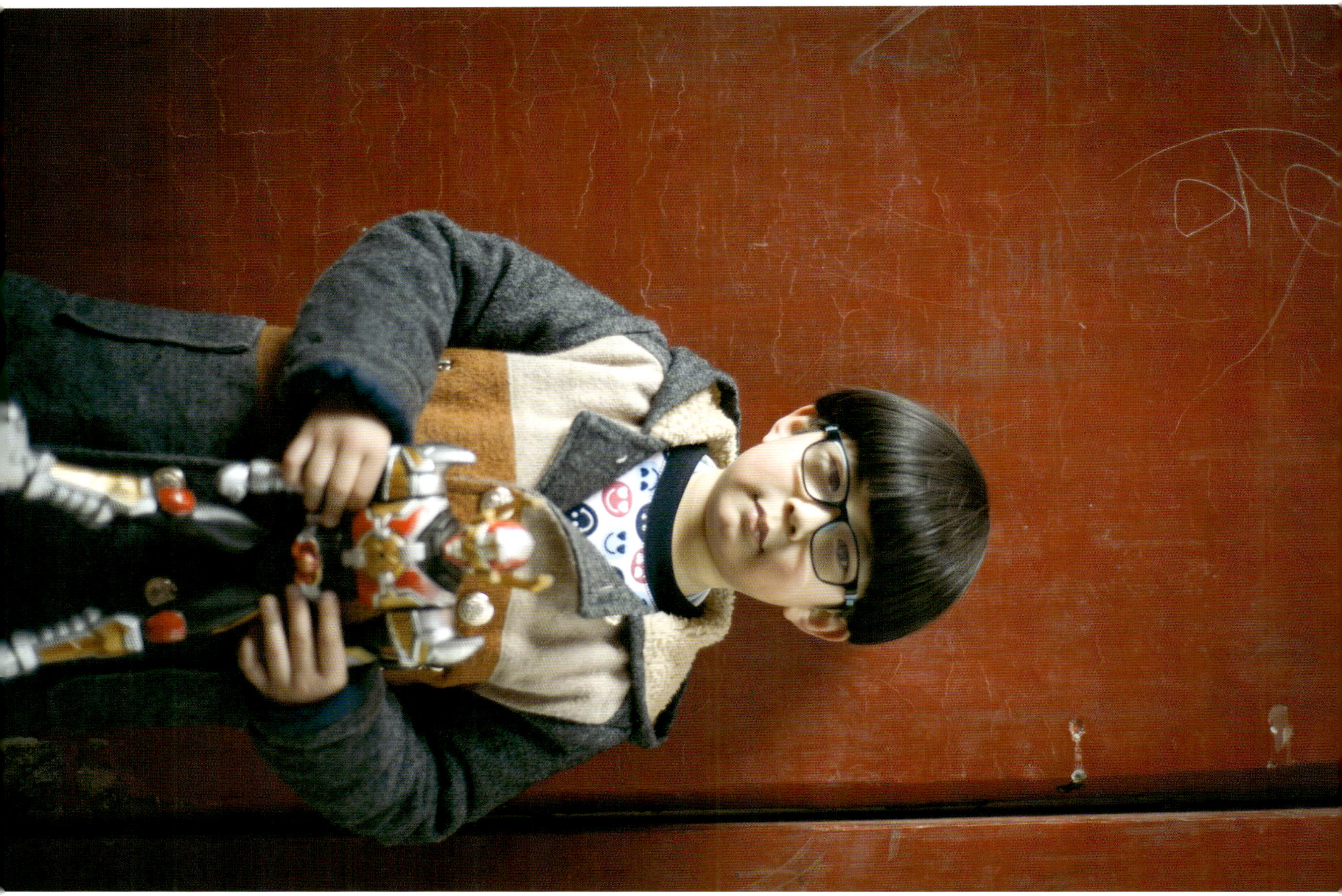

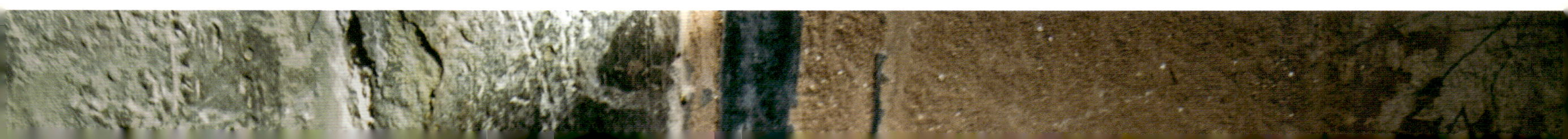

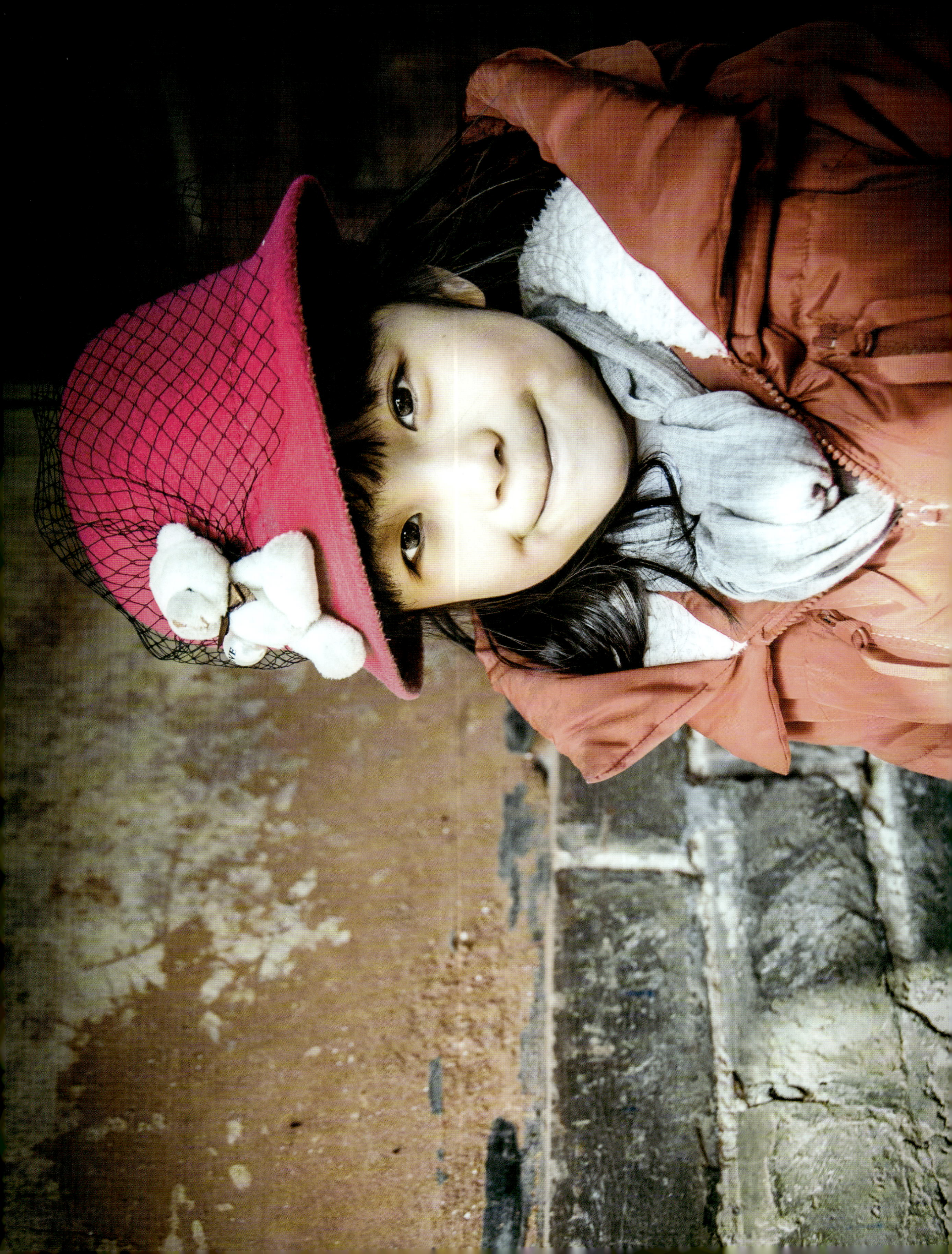

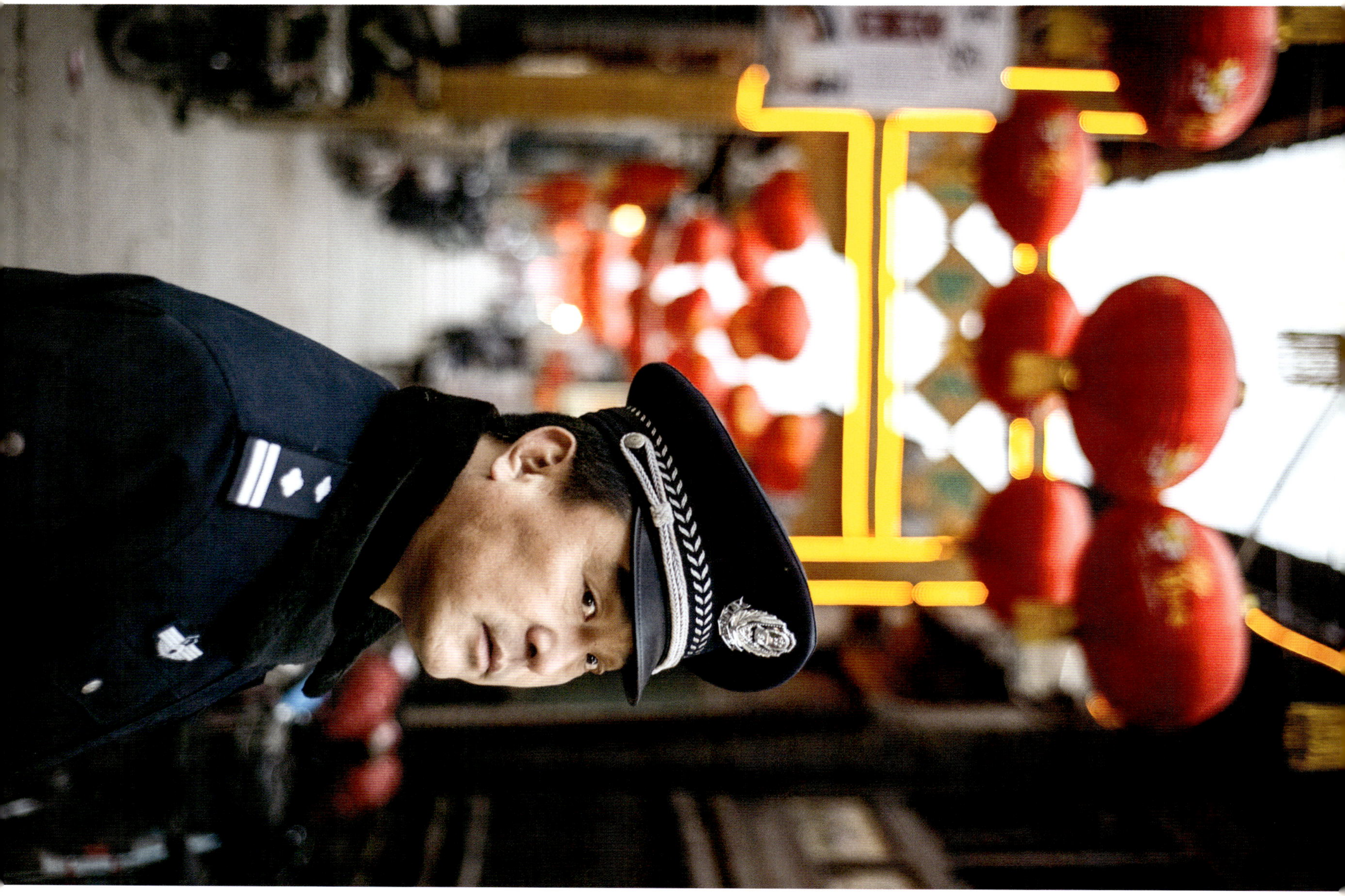

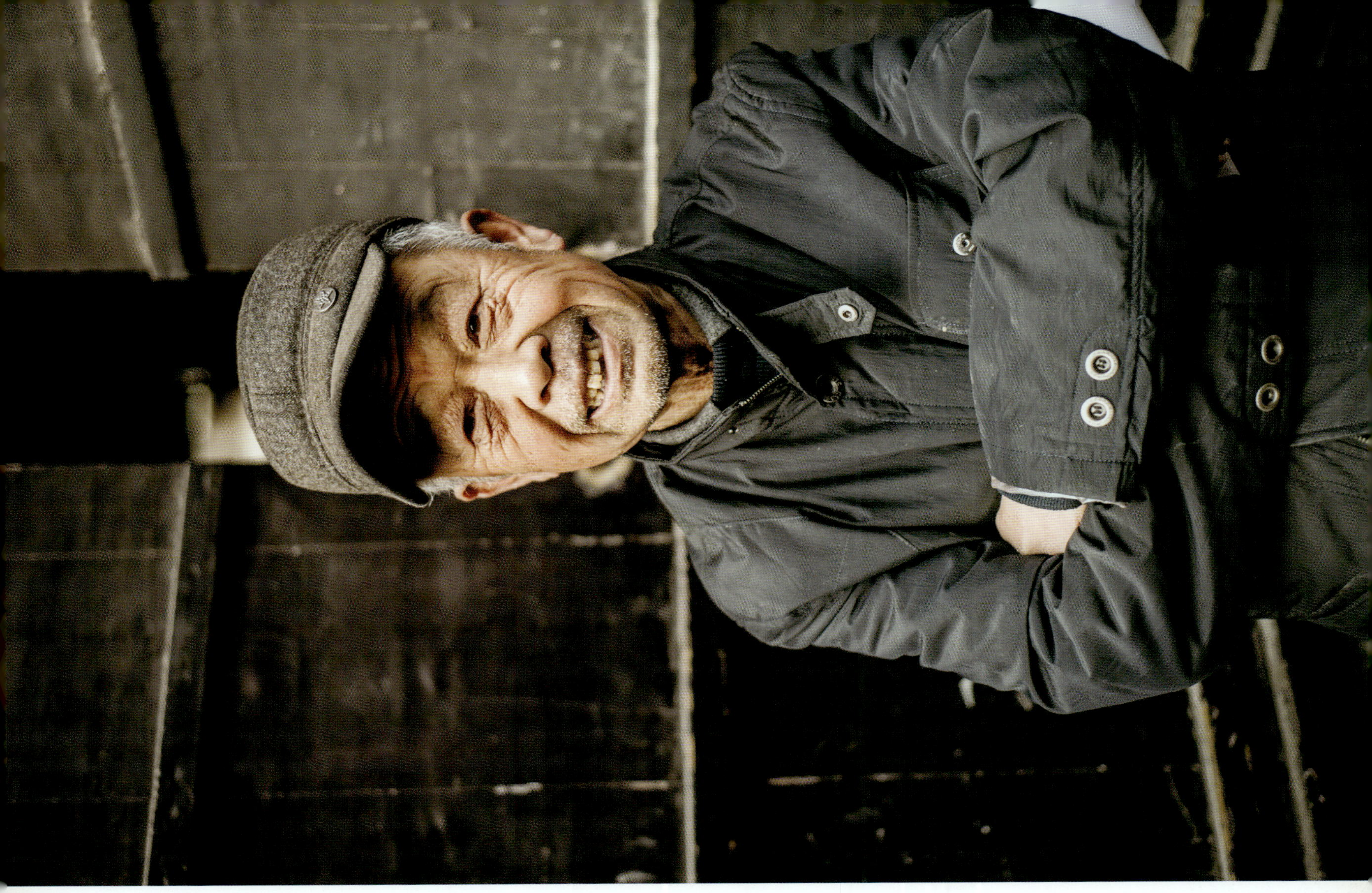

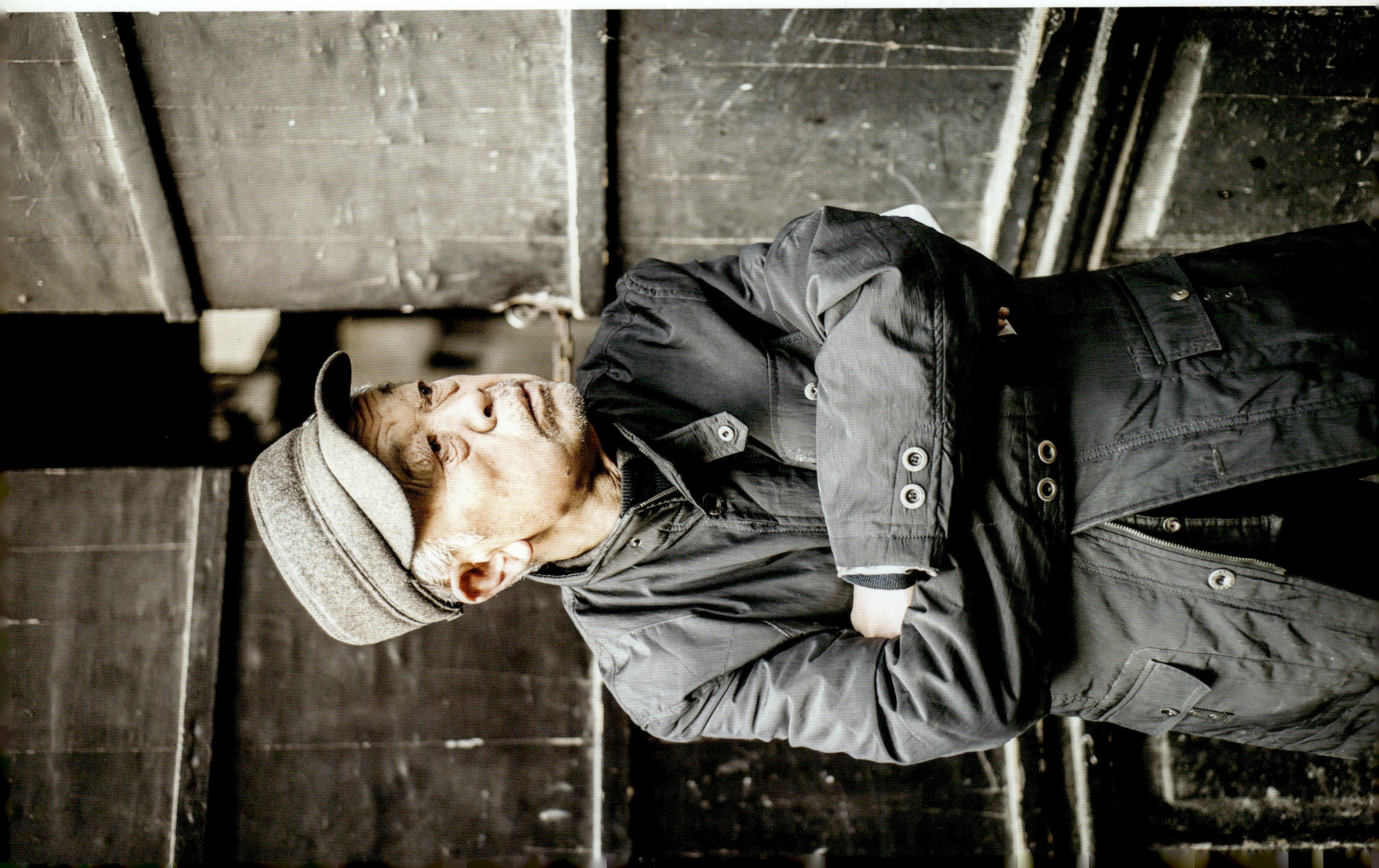

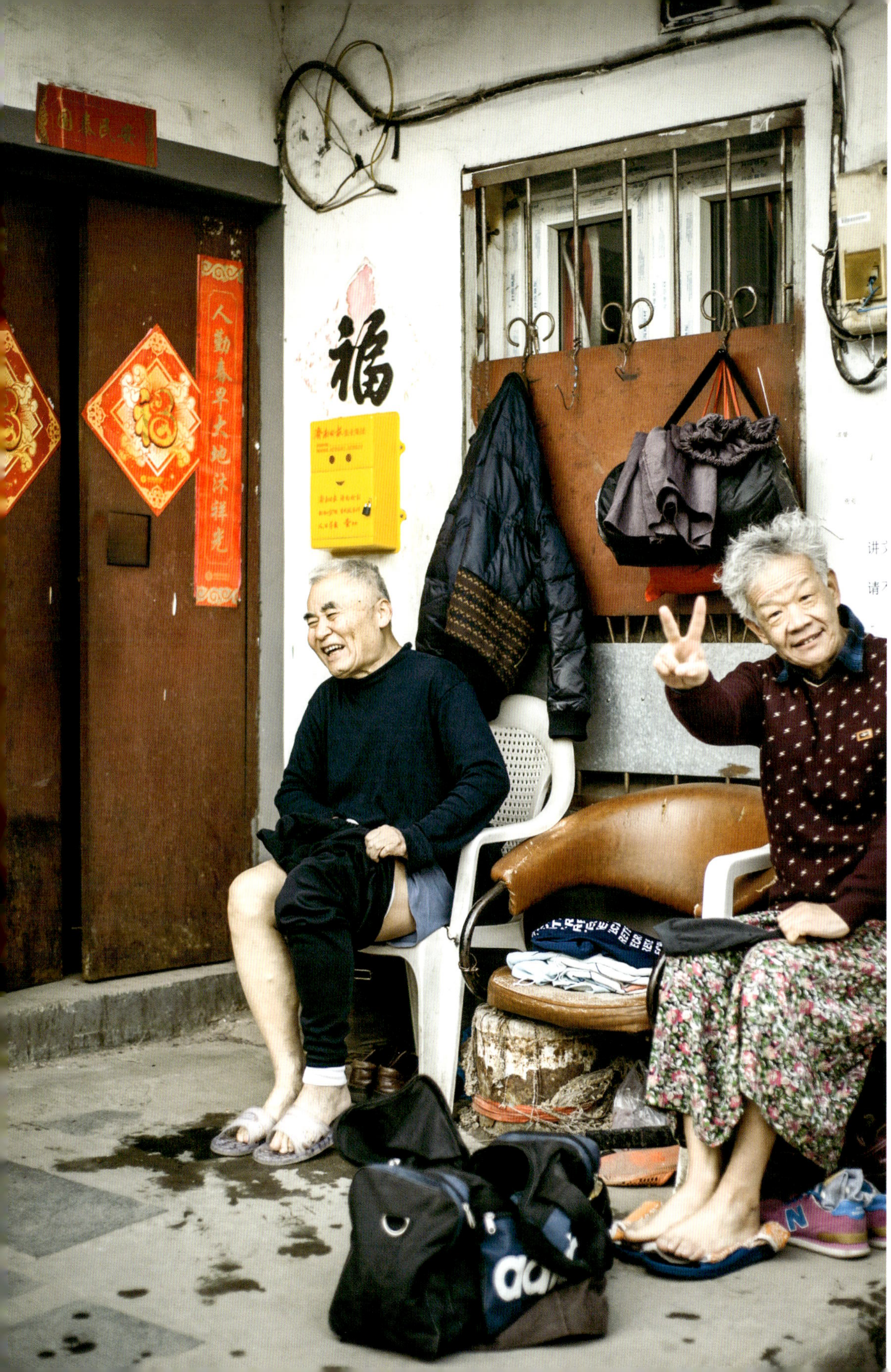

At right, cleaners at the Imperial Palace have the highly specialized and significant role of protecting one of China's most treasured landmarks. Although they seem relatively relaxed, it is their job to stop tourists from doing any damage to the grounds.

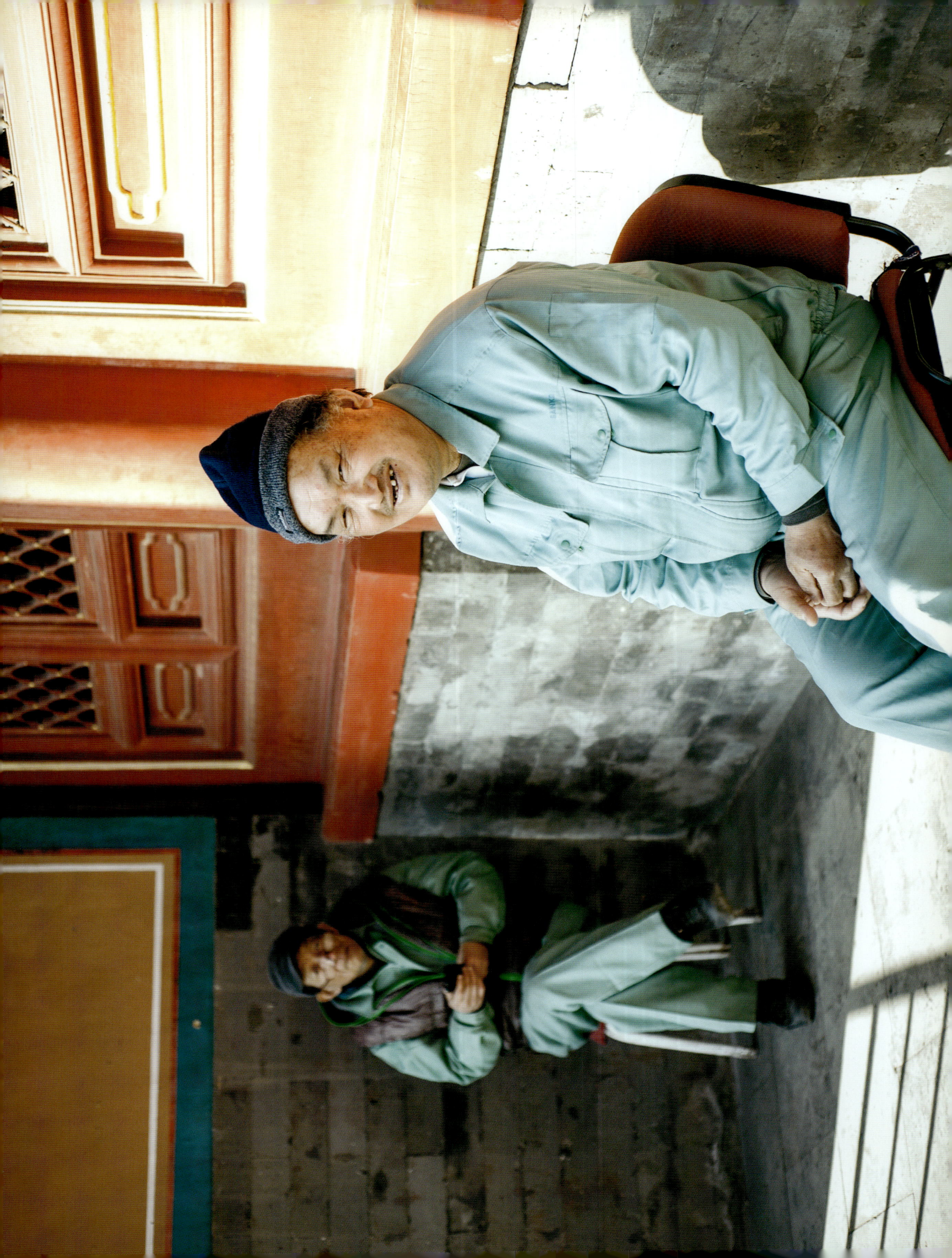

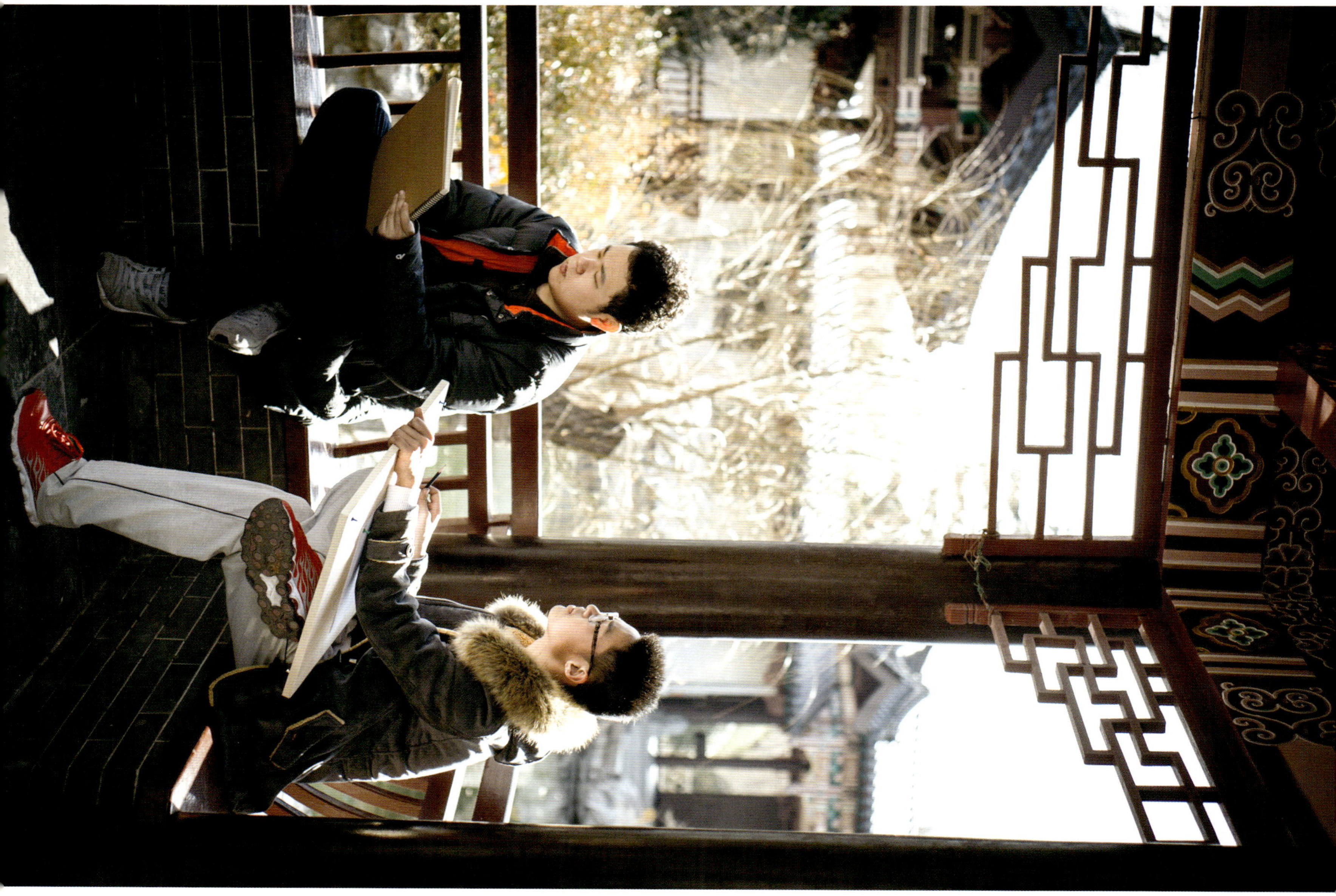

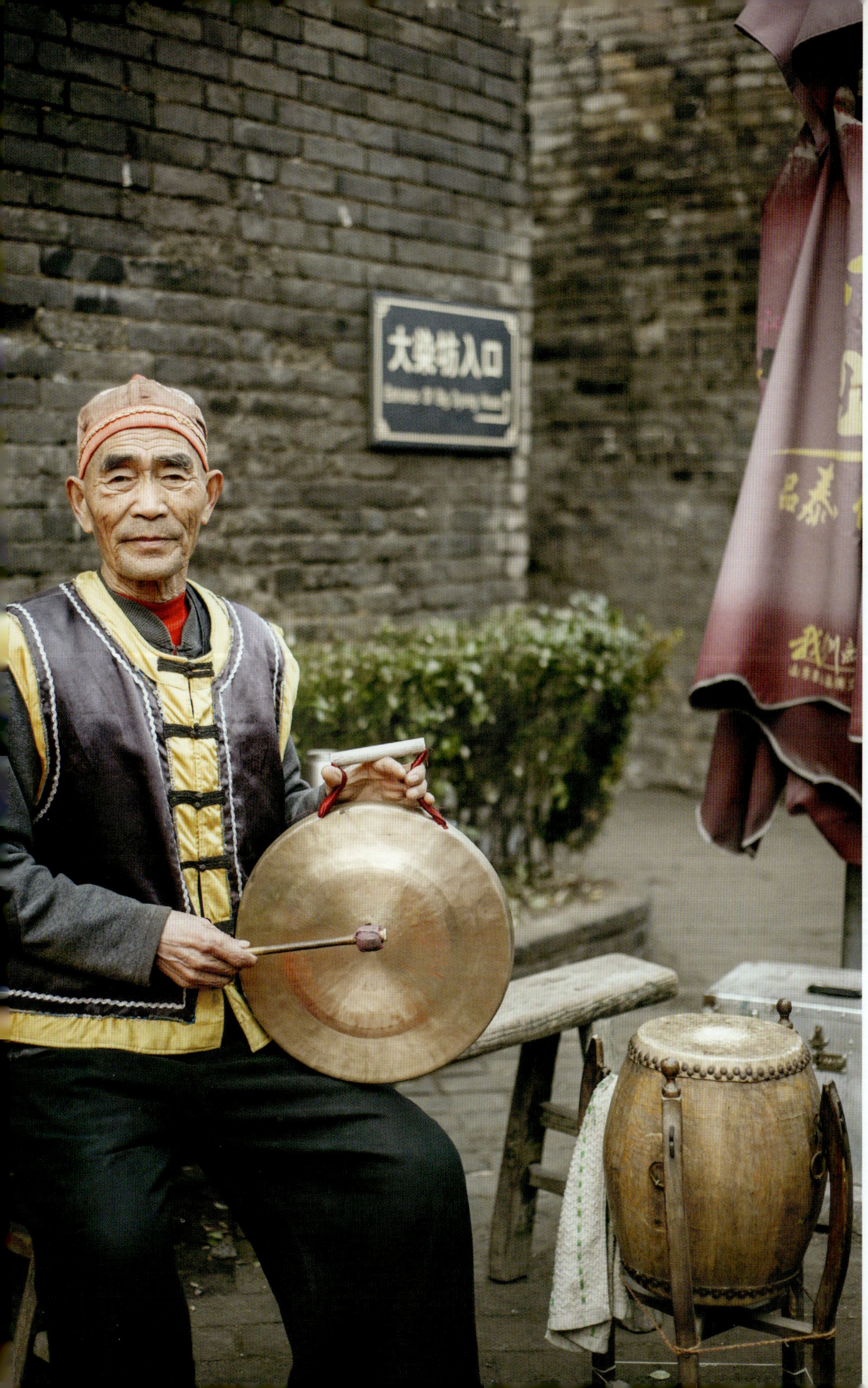
大梁街入口
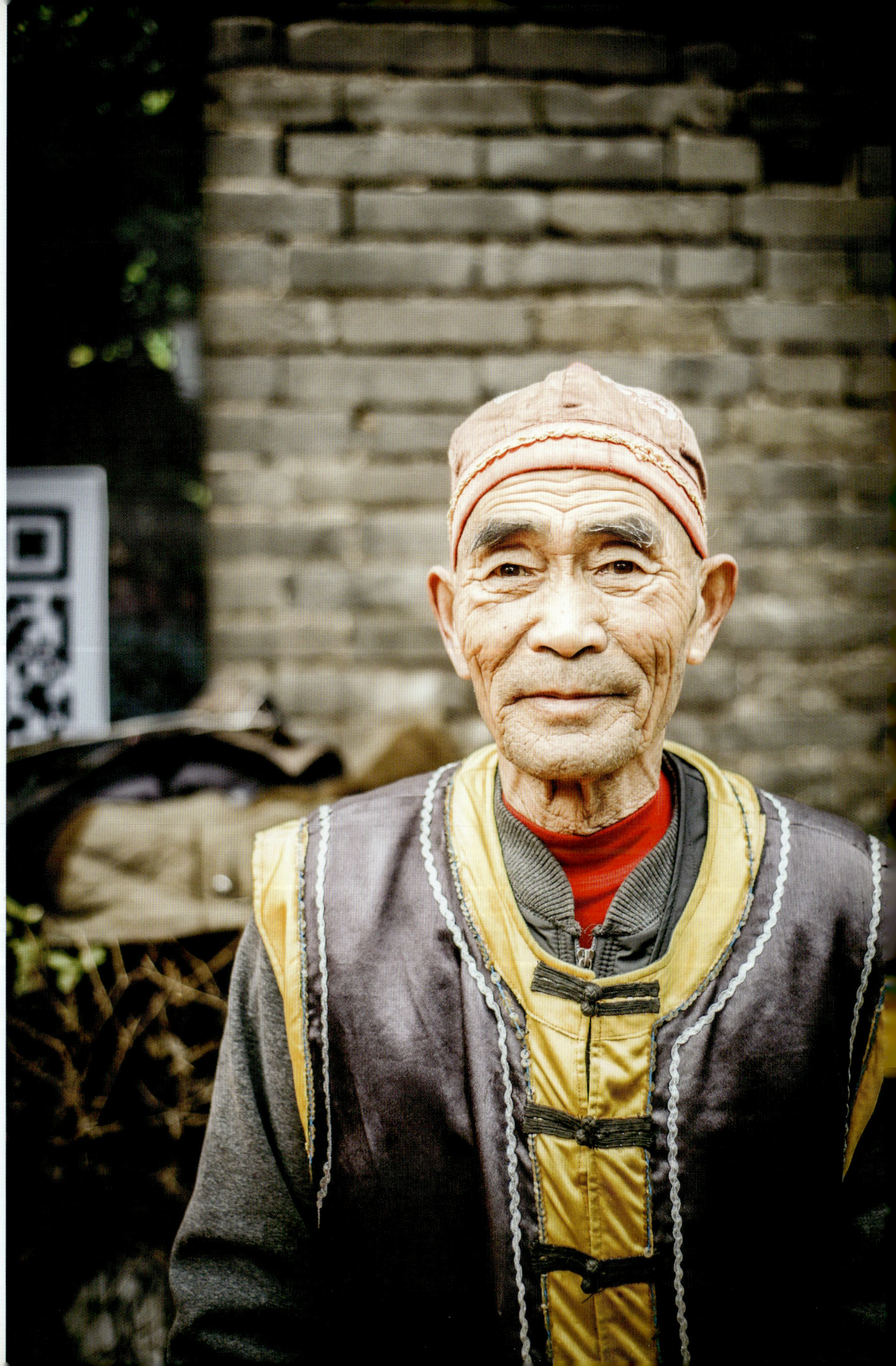

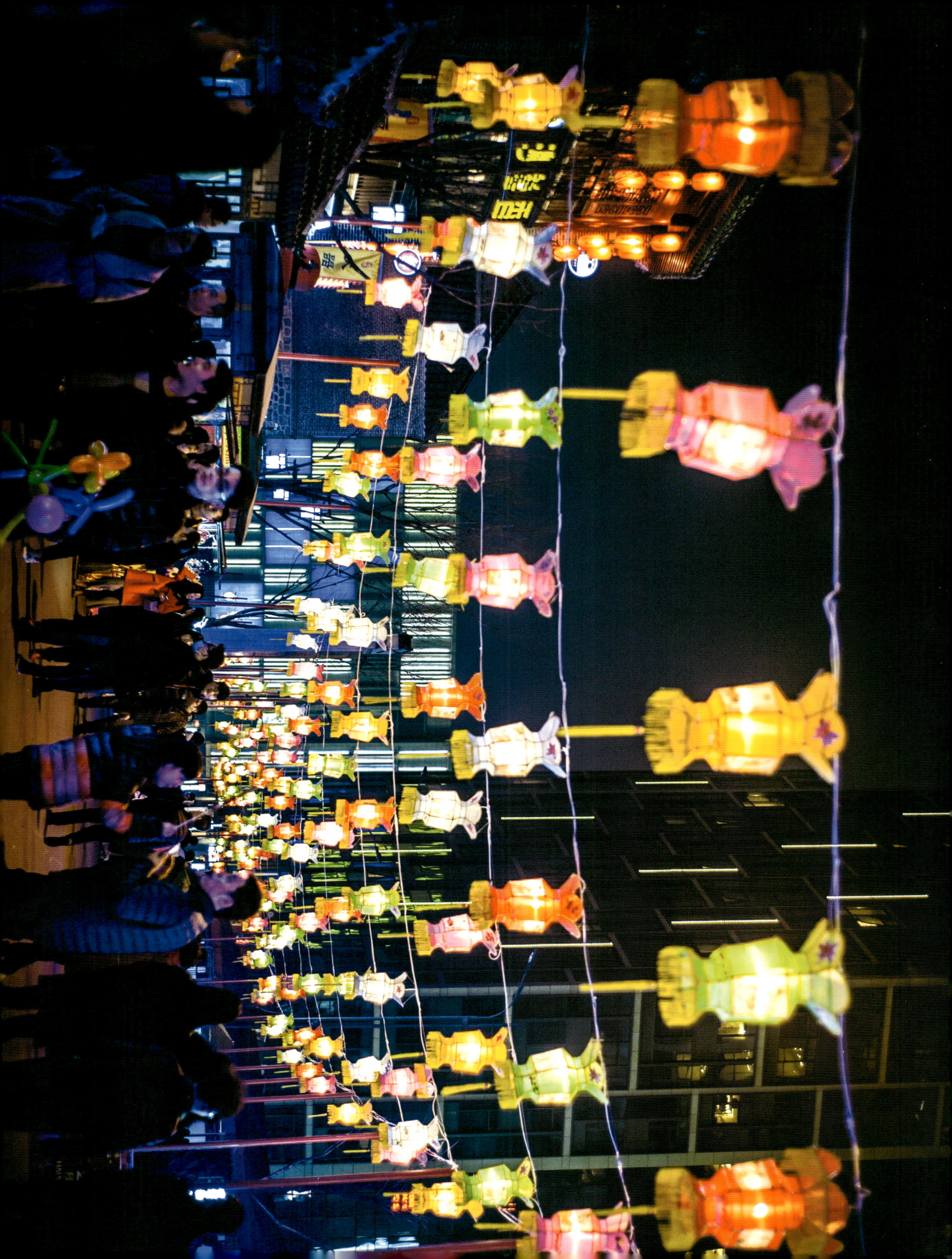

Ceremonies, Celebrations, and Traditions

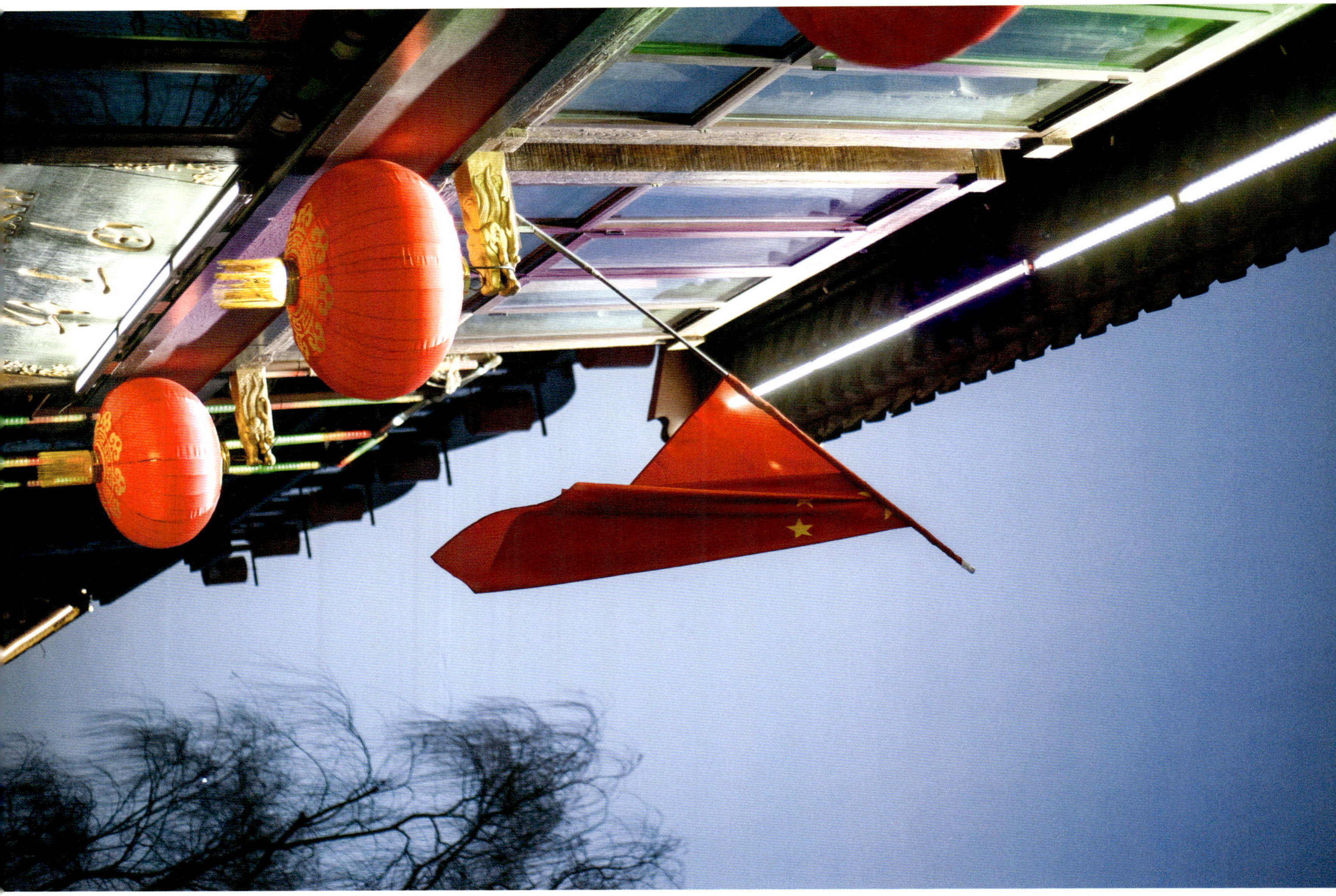

The Lantern Festival, which has been celebrated for approximately two thousand years, is held on the fifteenth day of the first Chinese lunar month. Traditionally, it marks the end of the Chinese New Year period and signals the return of spring. In 2017, it was held January 28. In 2018, it will fall on February 16, and in 2019, it will be held on February 5.

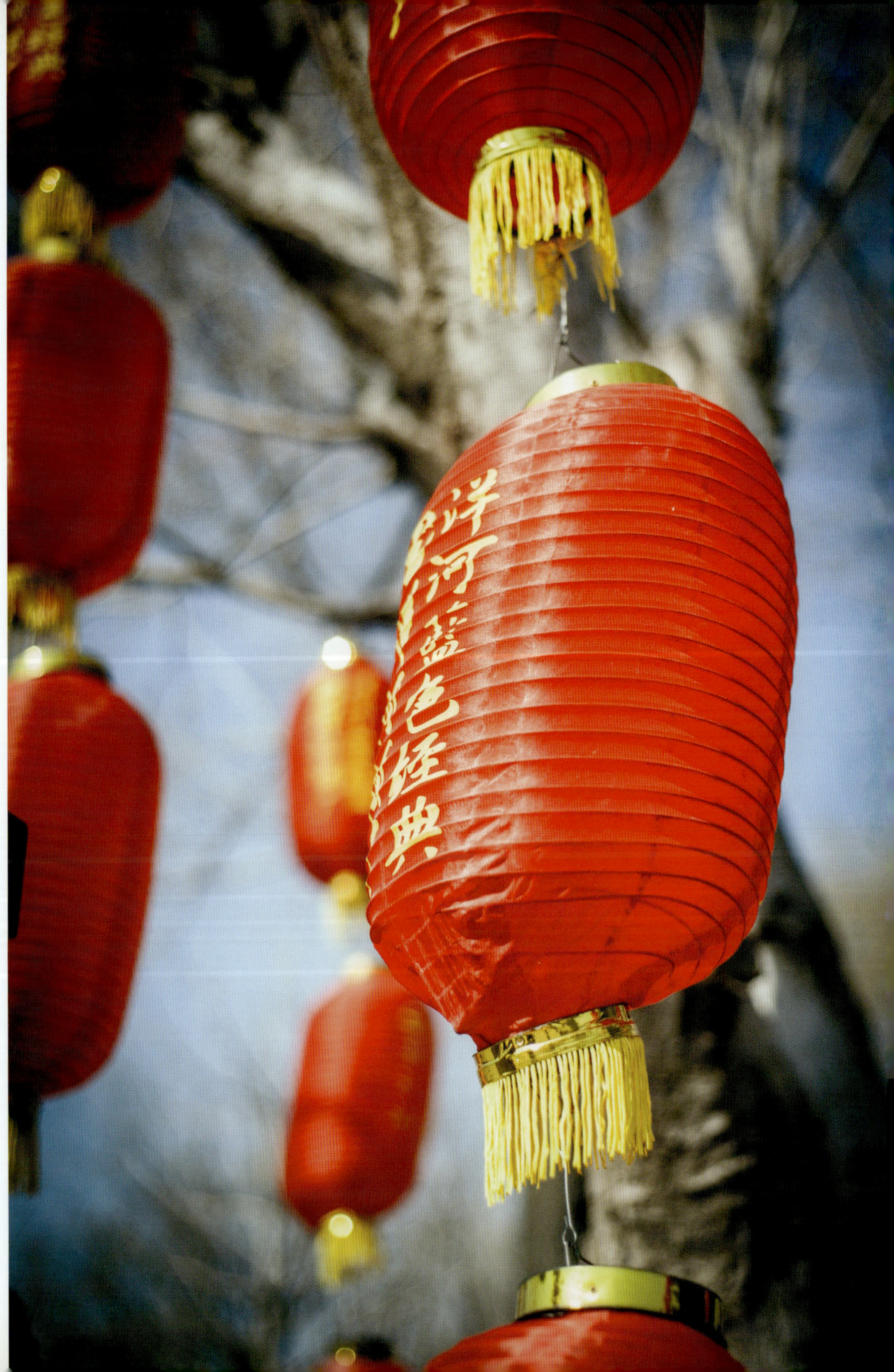

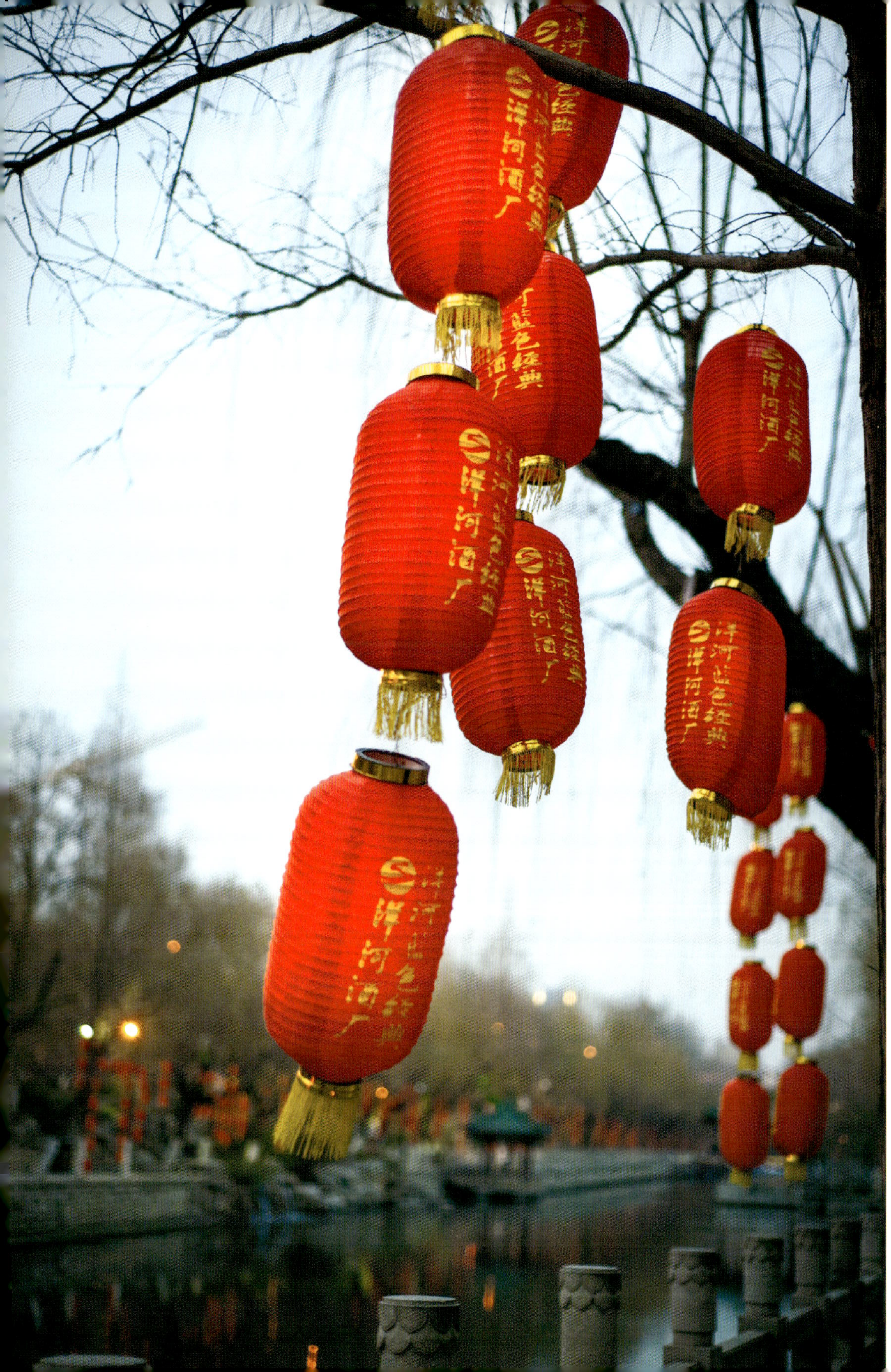

Chinese lanterns are hung across streets and in trees during the days surrounding the Lantern Festival, following the Chinese New Year. The brightly colored lanterns, which are made from thin paper, silk, or plastic, are typically used for decoration and are often adorned with calligraphy or art. Traditionally, lanterns were used to celebrate the full moon in the sky. People hung round red lanterns to create a beautiful view.

The Black Tiger Spring is one of seventy-two named springs in Jinan, which is known as the "City of Springs." Black Tiger is among the top four major springs, which includes Baotu Spring, Pear Spring, and Five Dragon Pool. An artesian karst spring, the Black Tiger Spring is located in the center of the city and emerges from the mouth of limestone caves. It is culturally significant to the people of the region.

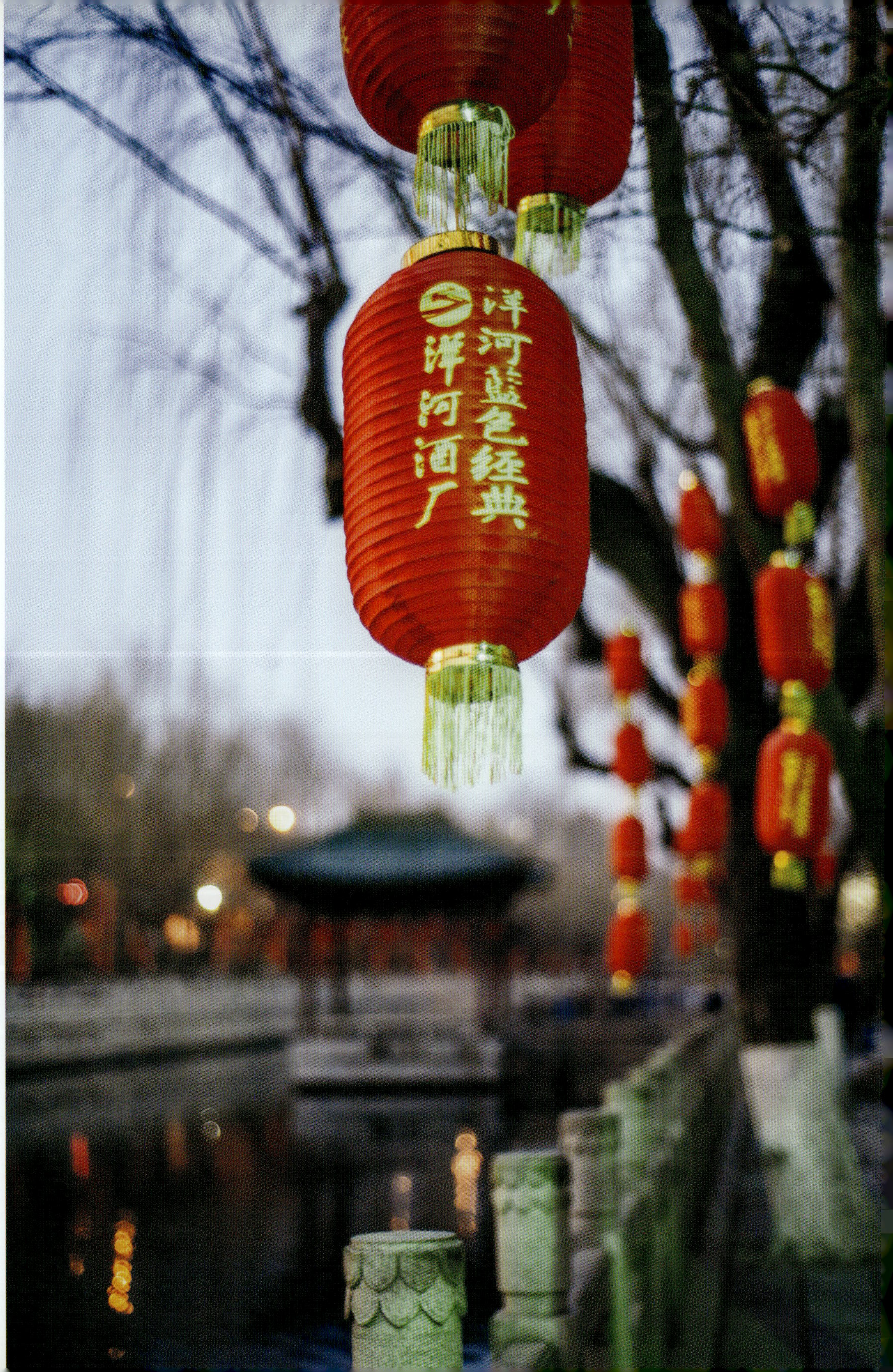

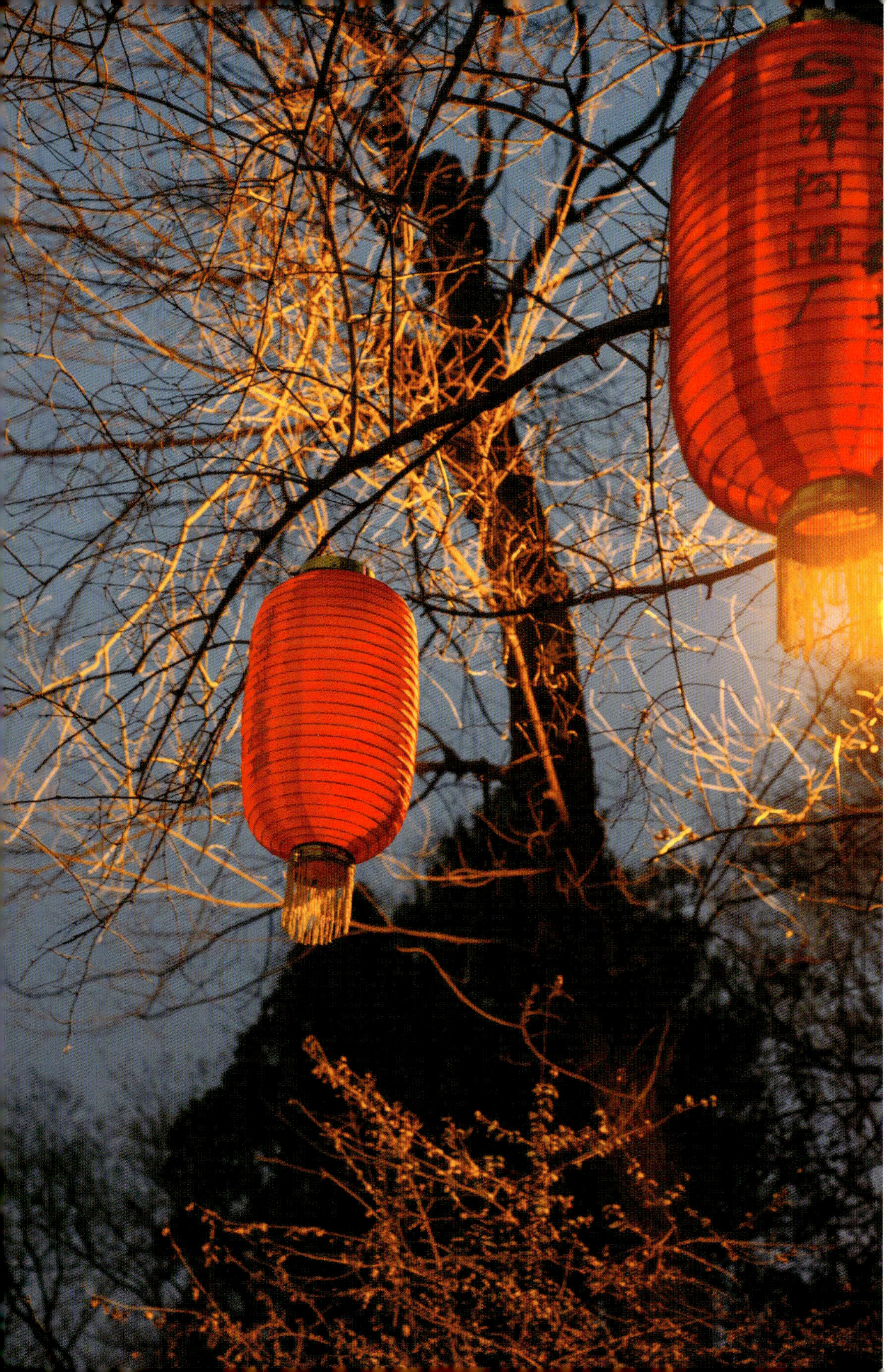

Emperor Han Mingdi, the second emperor of the Eastern Han Dynasty, is at the center of one story about the origin of the lantern festival. It is said that the emperor dreamed about a gold man who rose to the sky and disappeared just as he was about to ask the man who he was. The emperor then sent a scholar to India in search of Buddhist scriptures. Upon the scholar's return, Emperor Mingdi had a temple built where a statue of Buddha would be placed along with the scriptures. Since followers of Buddhism believe that the power of Buddha can dispel darkness, the emperor ordered the people to display lightened lanterns on the fifteenth day of the first lunar month.

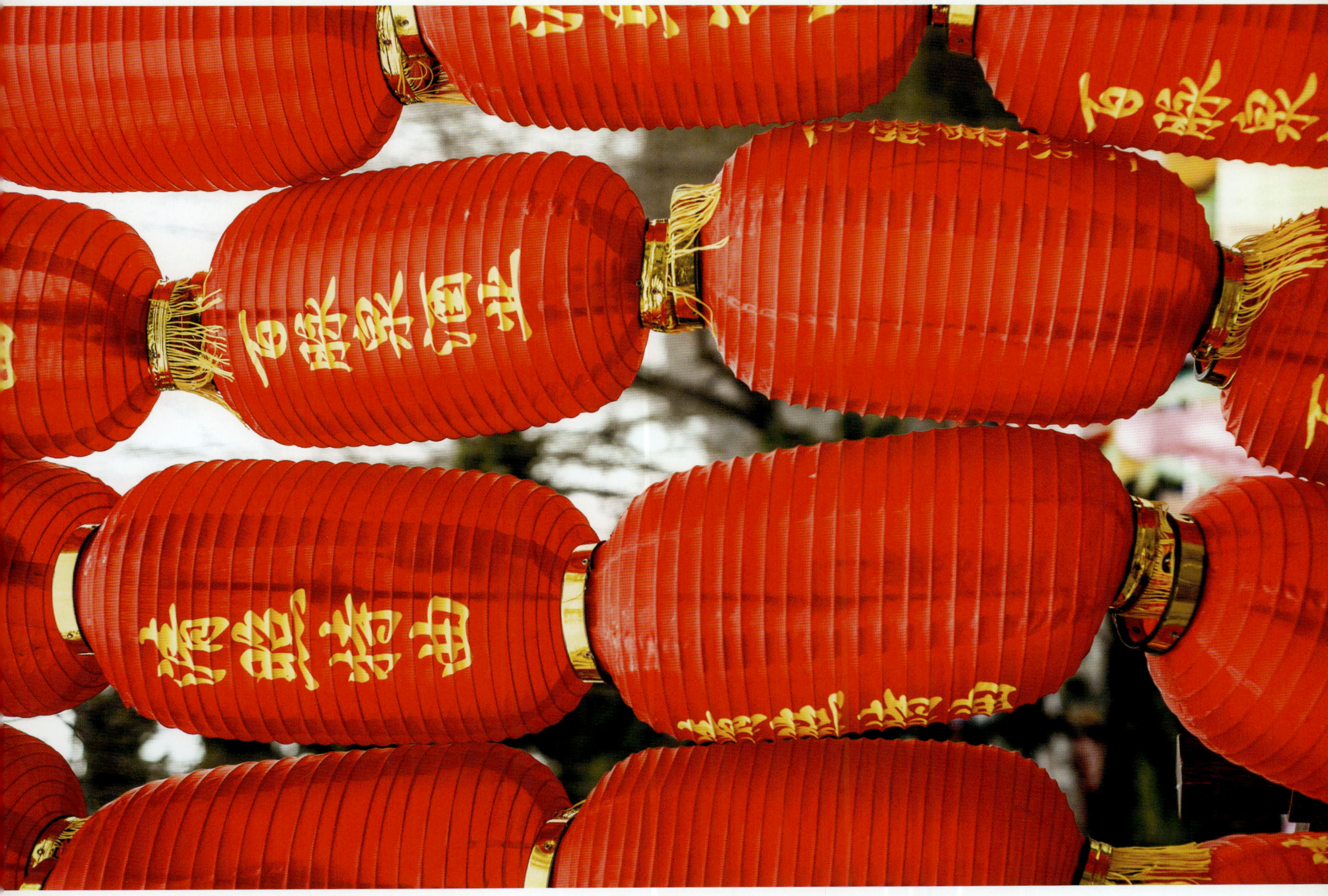

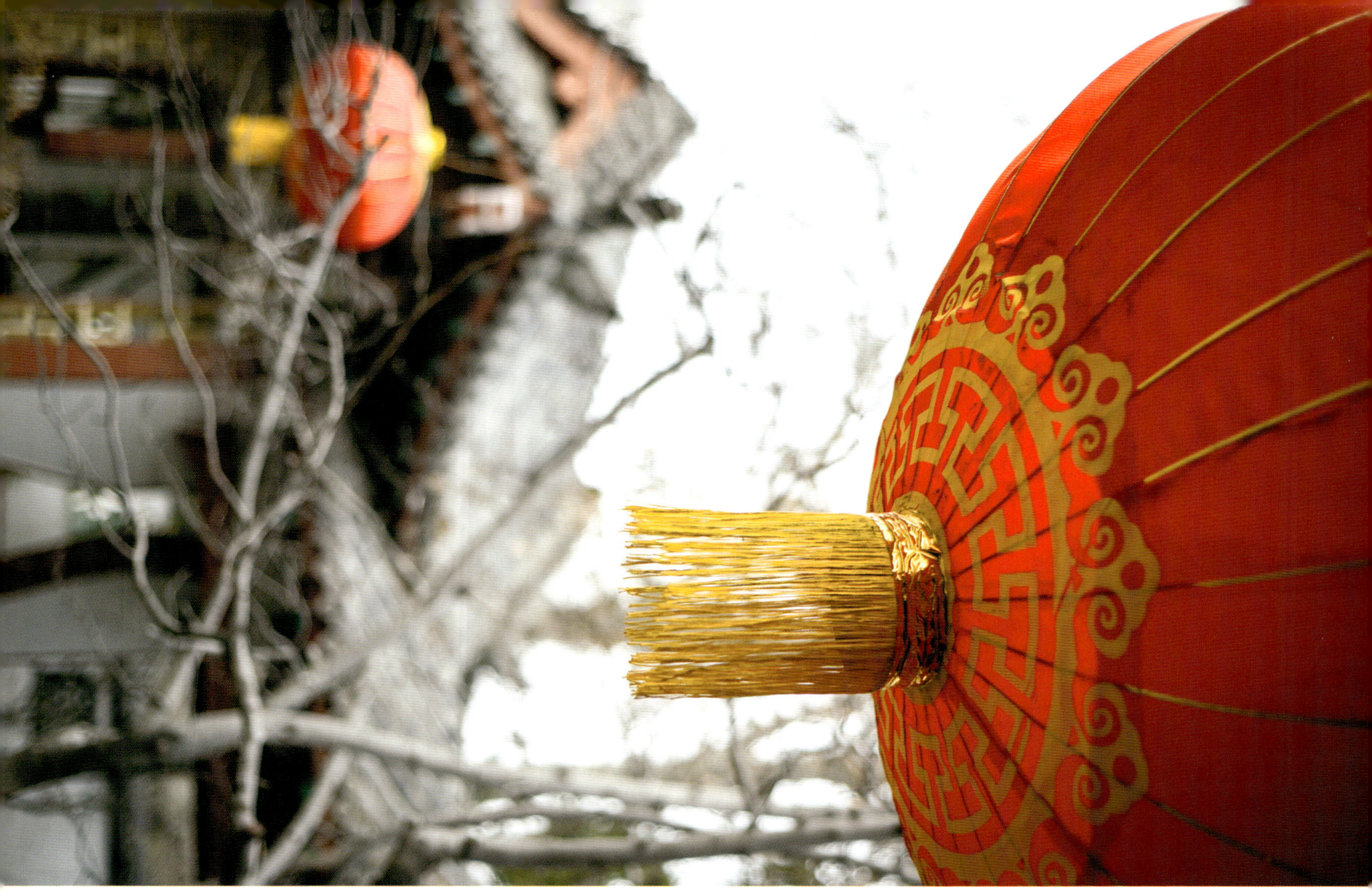

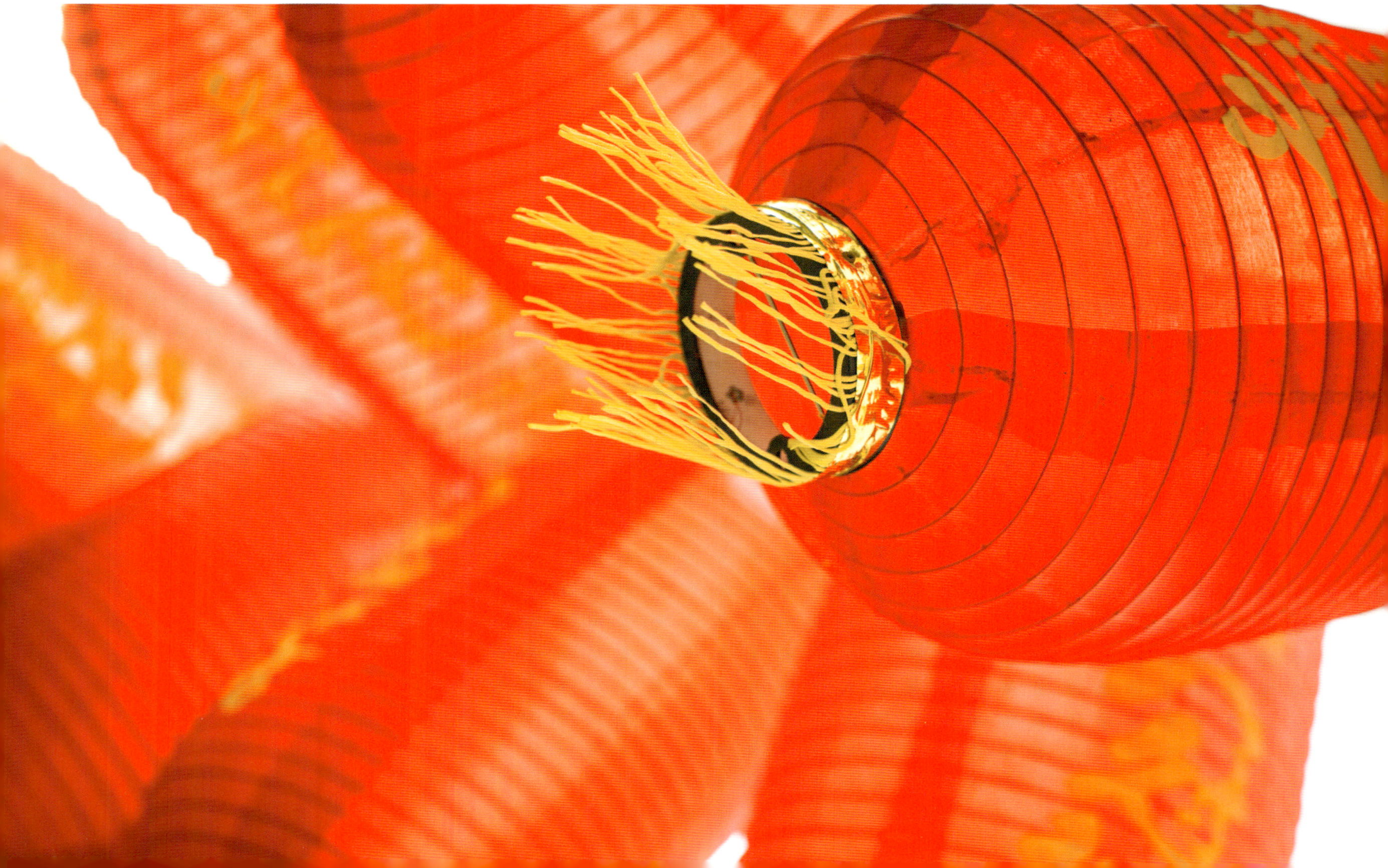

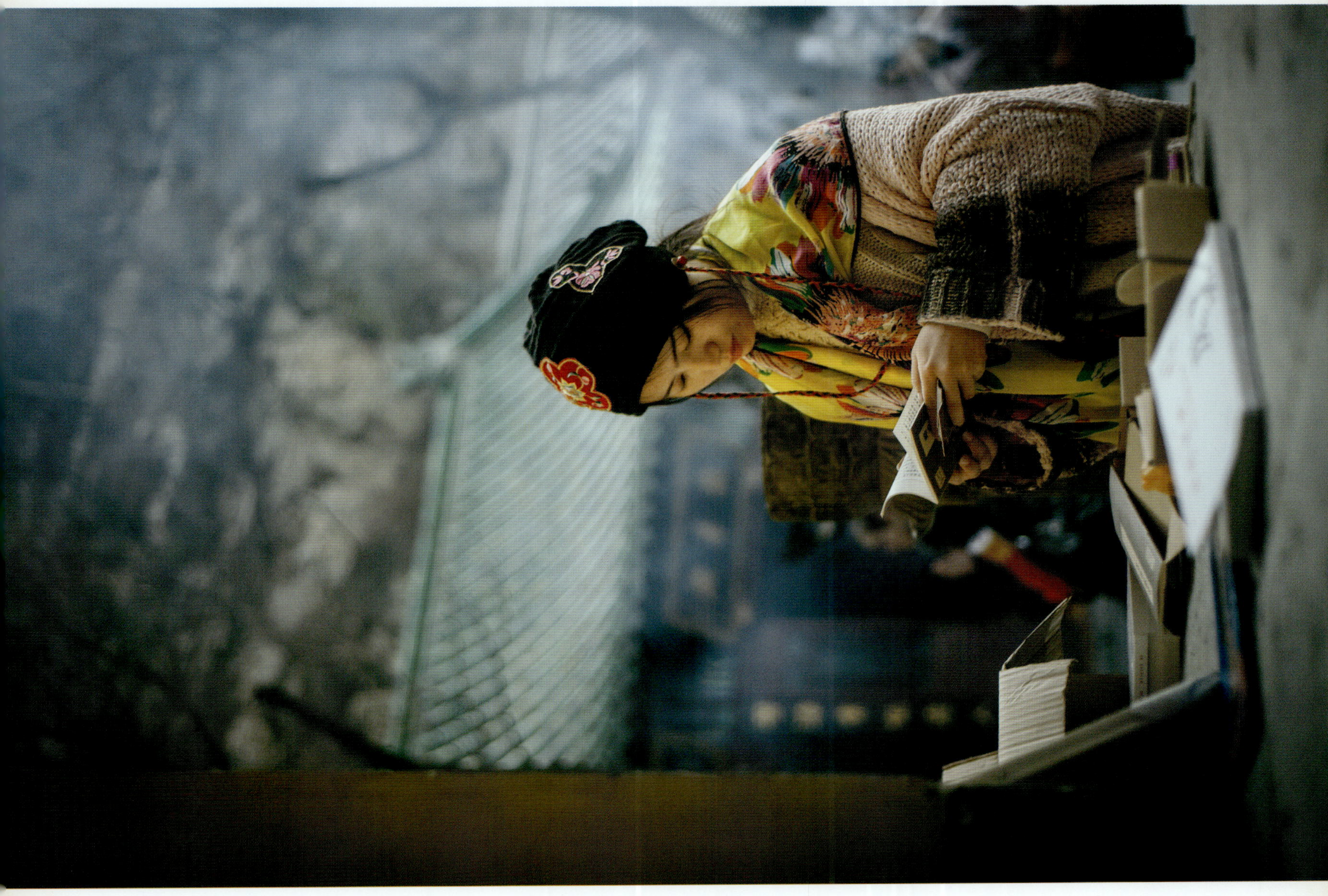

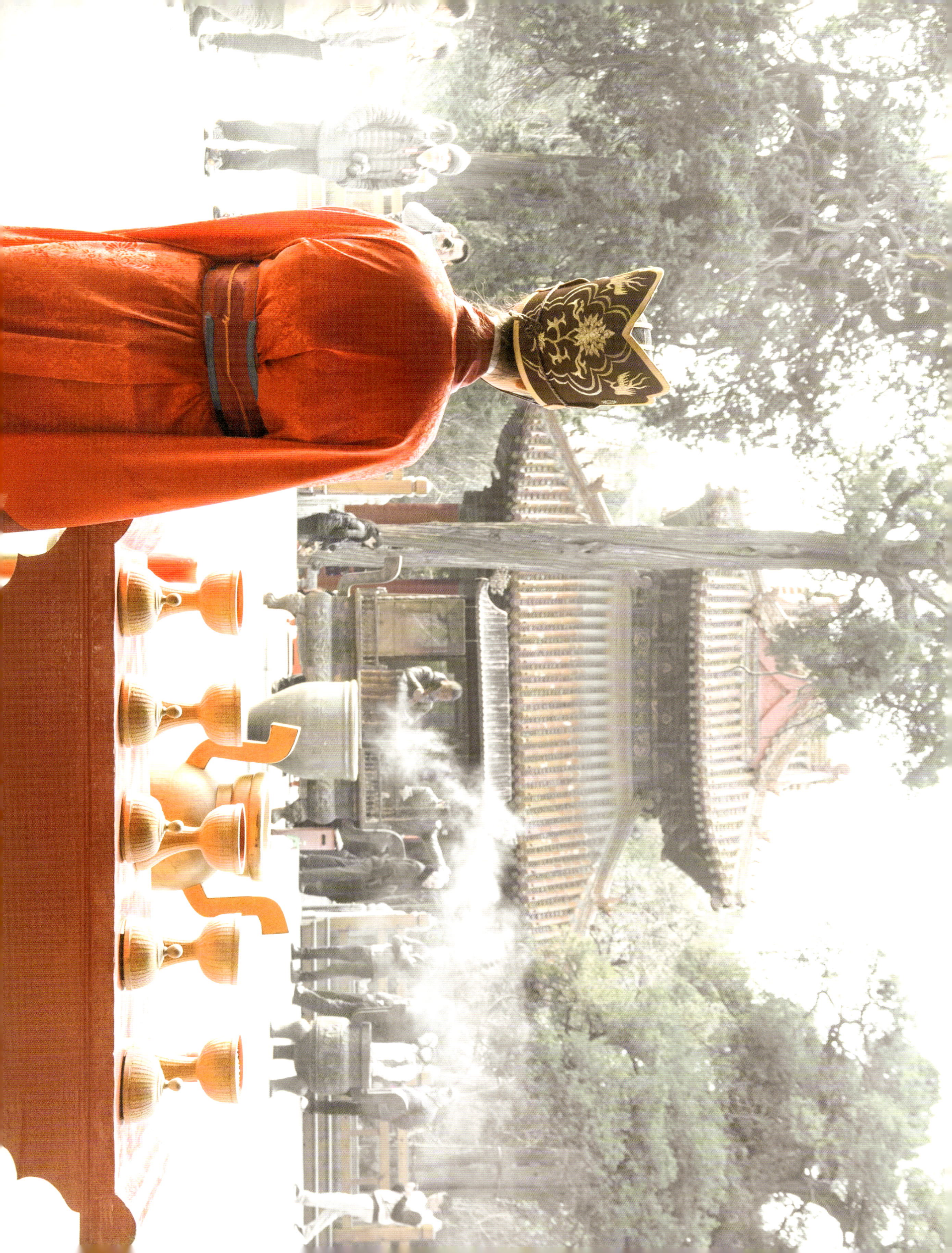

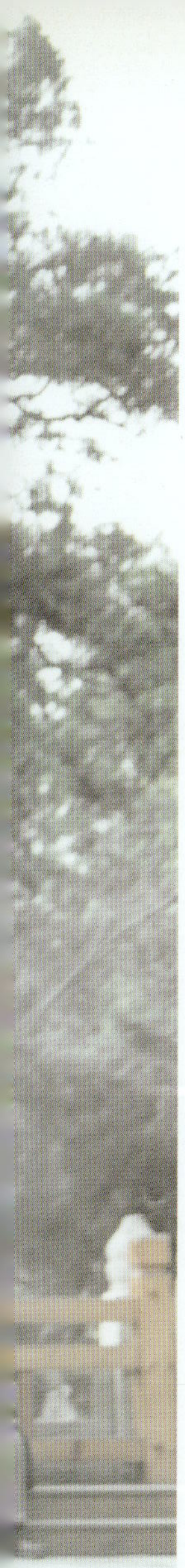

Tradition and ritual are essential parts of the Chinese culture despite the rapid modernization of the country. This series of photographs, taken in Oufu (Confucius's hometown), illustrates a religious ceremony during which locals make tributes to Heaven.

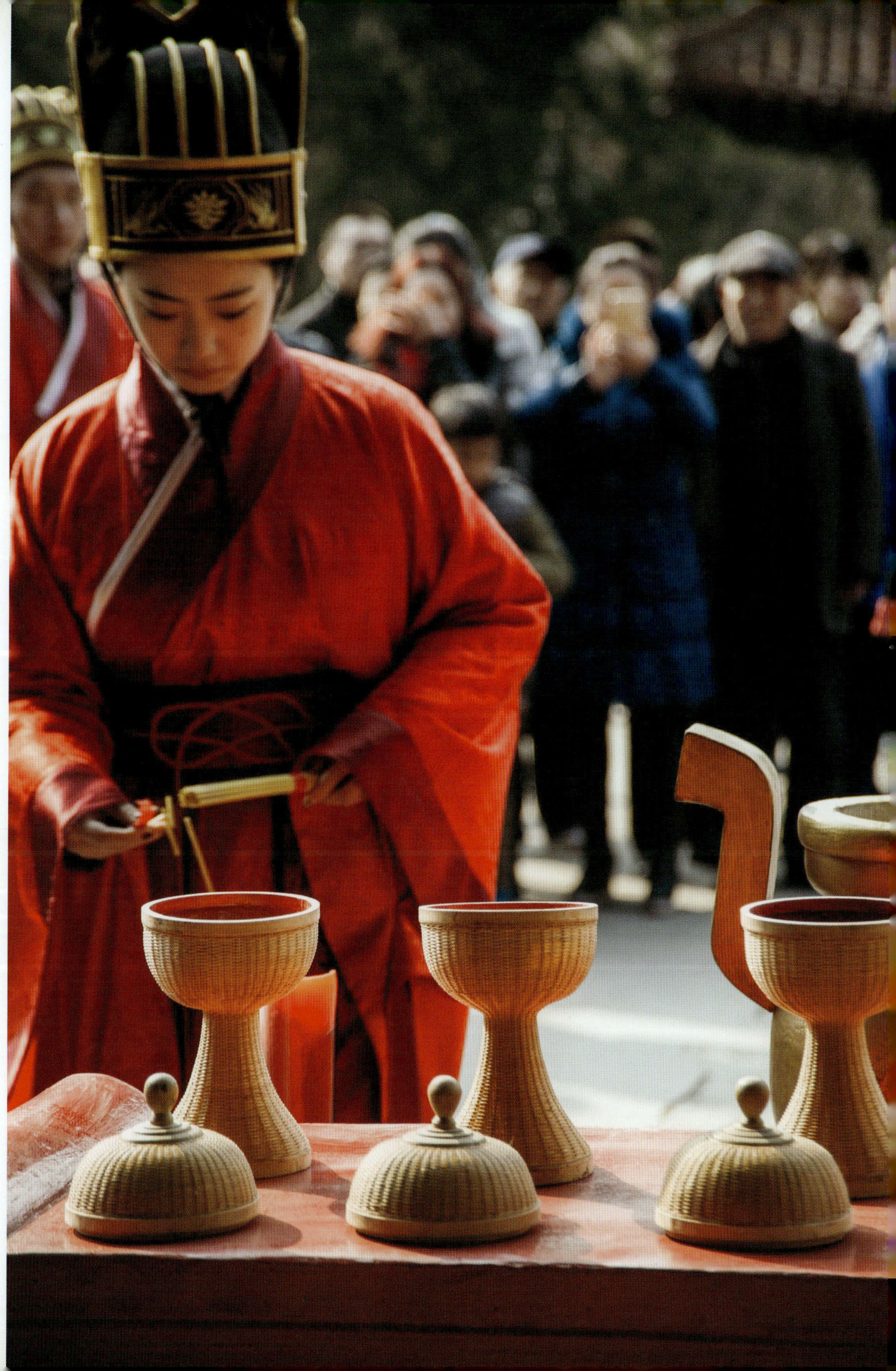

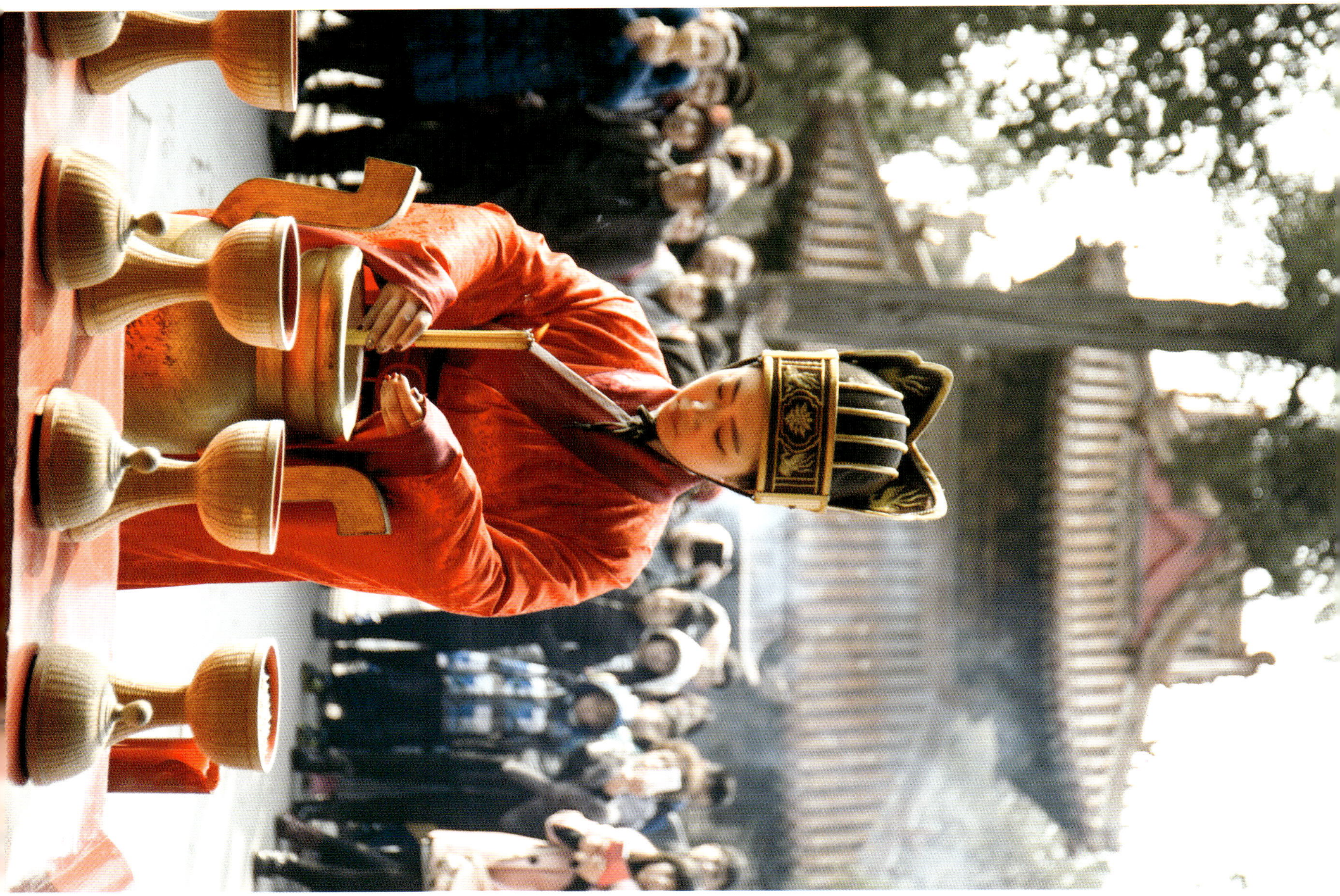

In south China, ancestor veneration is still common. The people there believe that the ghosts or spirits of their deceased ancestors are a channel of connection to the supreme power of Tiān, a Chinese term for Heaven, which has become synonymous with Shàngdi, their supreme god.

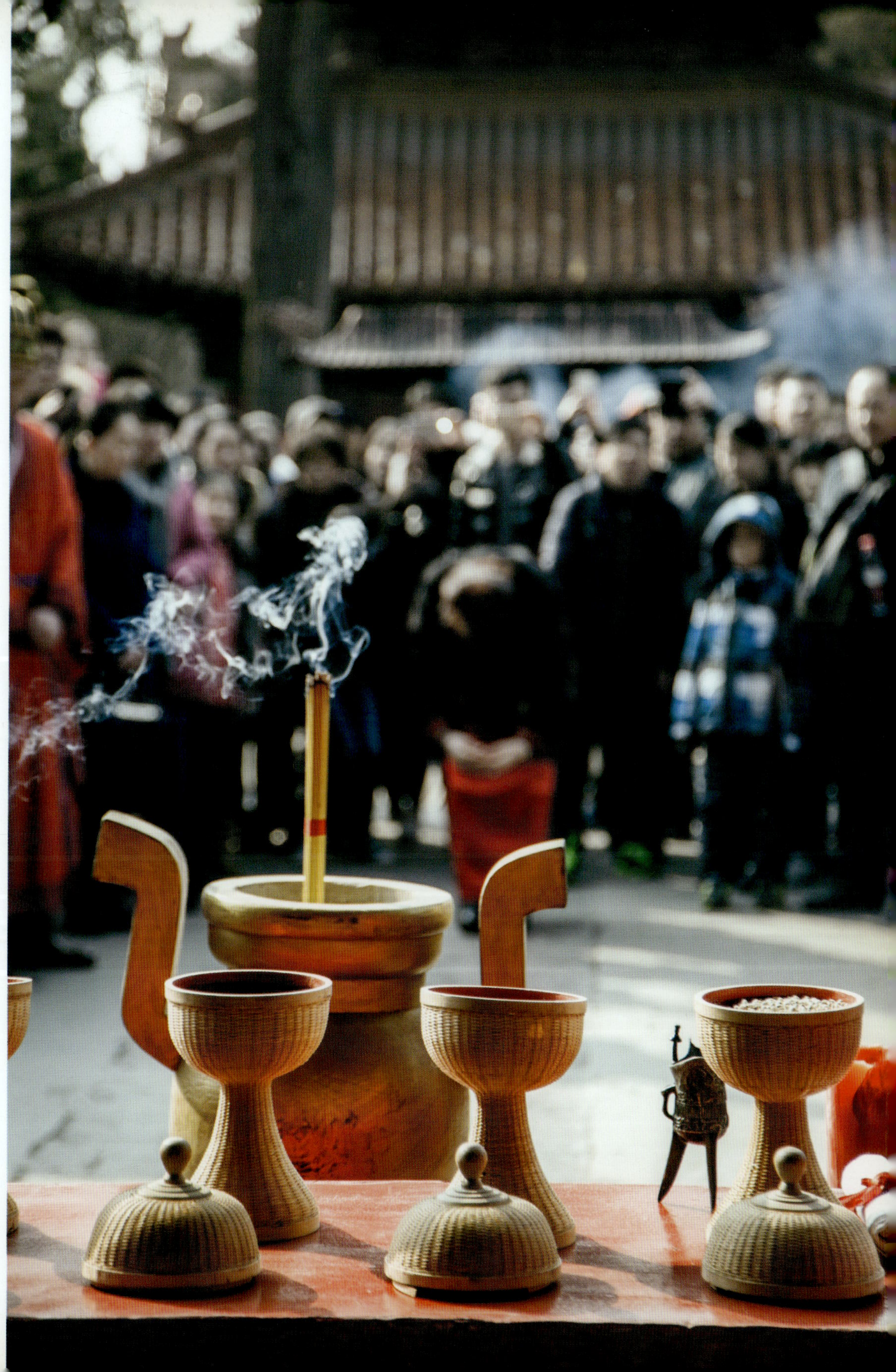

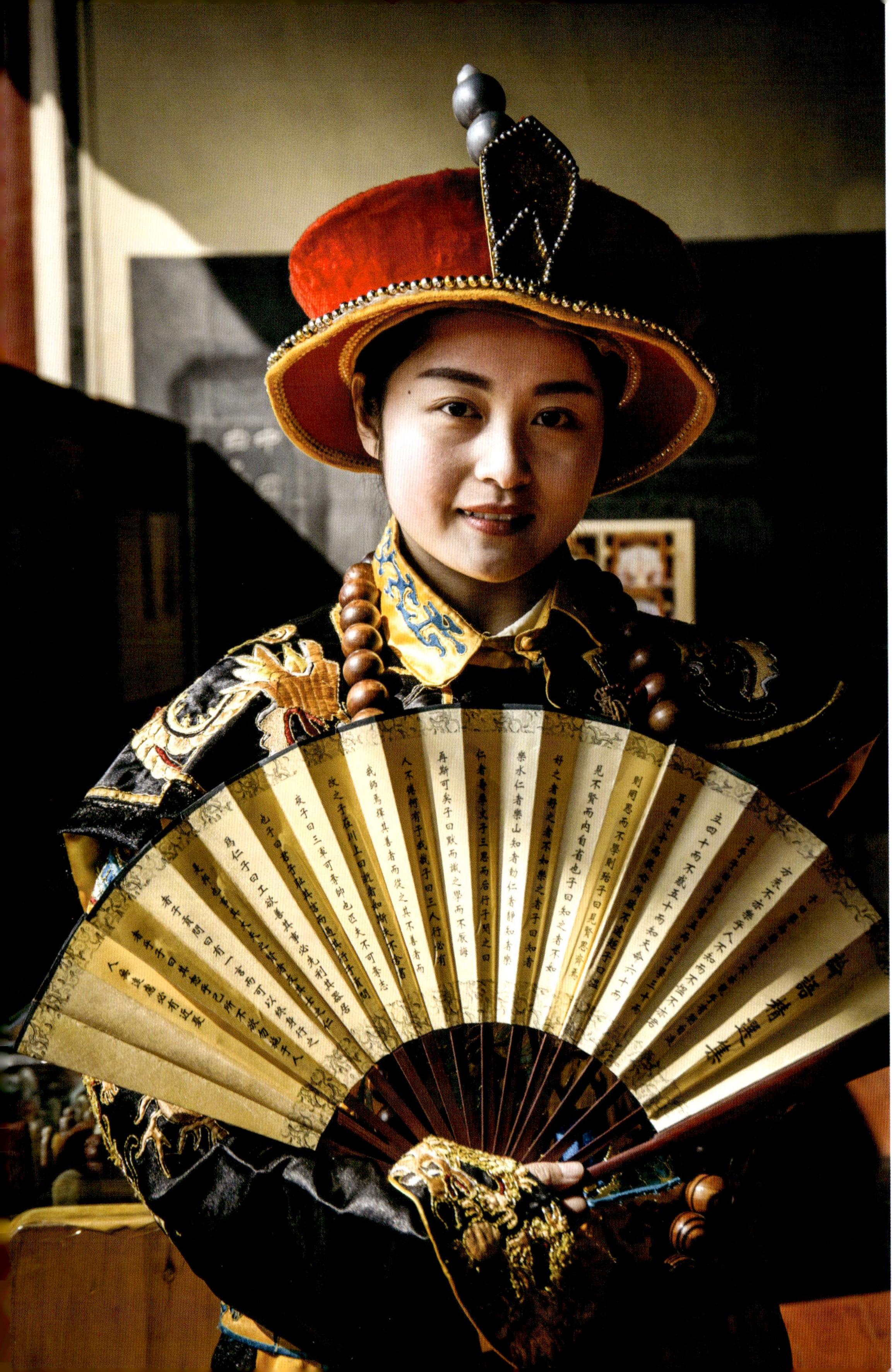

Fans are a popular handcraft in China that have been around for centuries. Fans can be made from many materials, such as silk, feathers, leaves, or thin strips of bamboo, just to name a few. Originally, they were designed to provide protection from the sun. Their use has since been extended, and fans can be used as part of a dance or other types of performances.

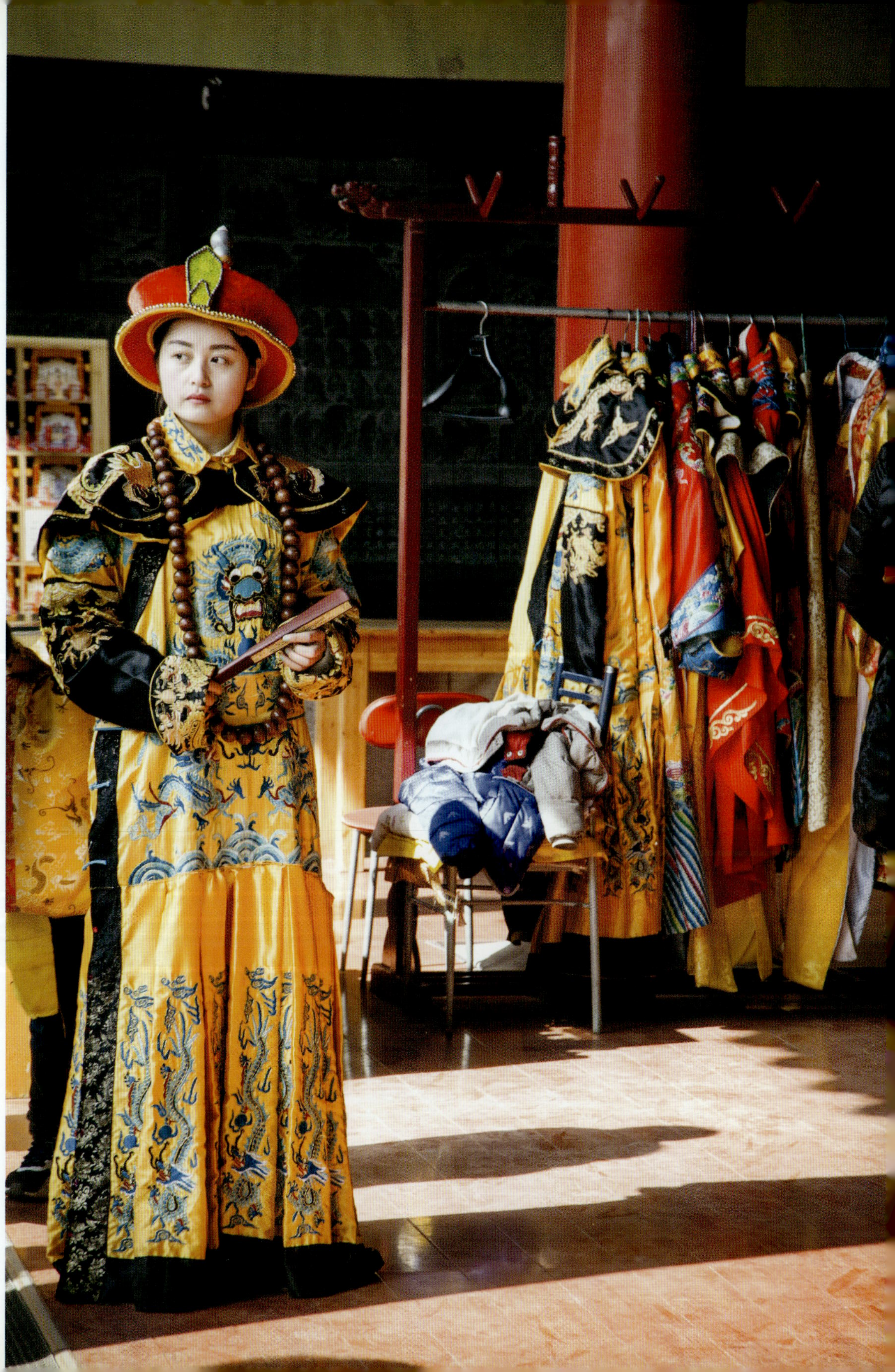

This visitor to the Wanguo Temple chose a traditional emperor's outfit to wear for her portrait. Additional traditional outfit options hang in the background behind her. Historically, only an emperor was allowed to wear this attire, but now in the modern age, anyone who visits the site can wear this outfit and feel like royalty.

This young girl wears a traditional princess costume in preparation for her portrait session at the Wanguo Temple. People of all ages enjoy this fun activity, much like Americans enjoy dressing in Wild West outfits at county fairs. Here everyone is given an elaborate costume to fit the opulence of the room.

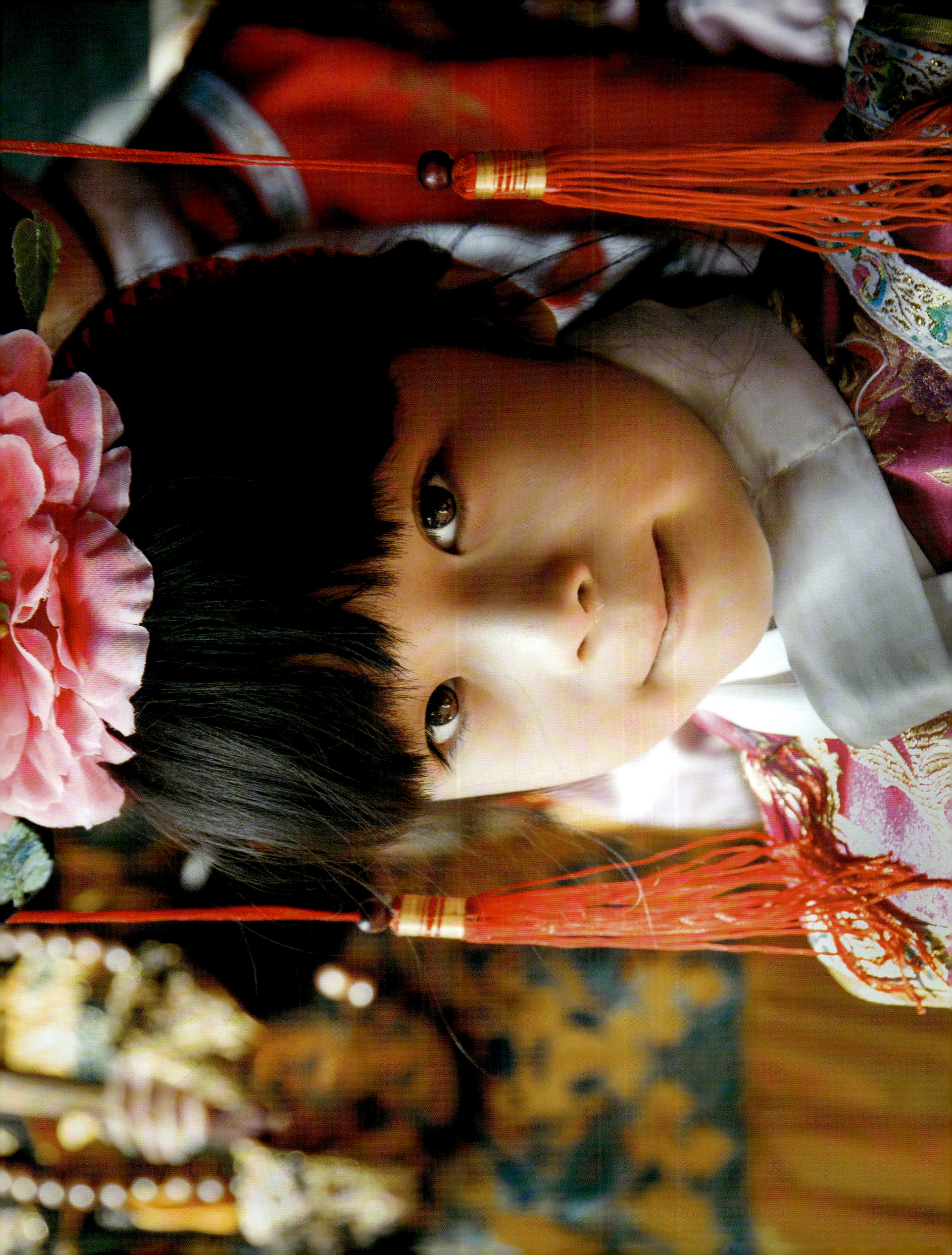

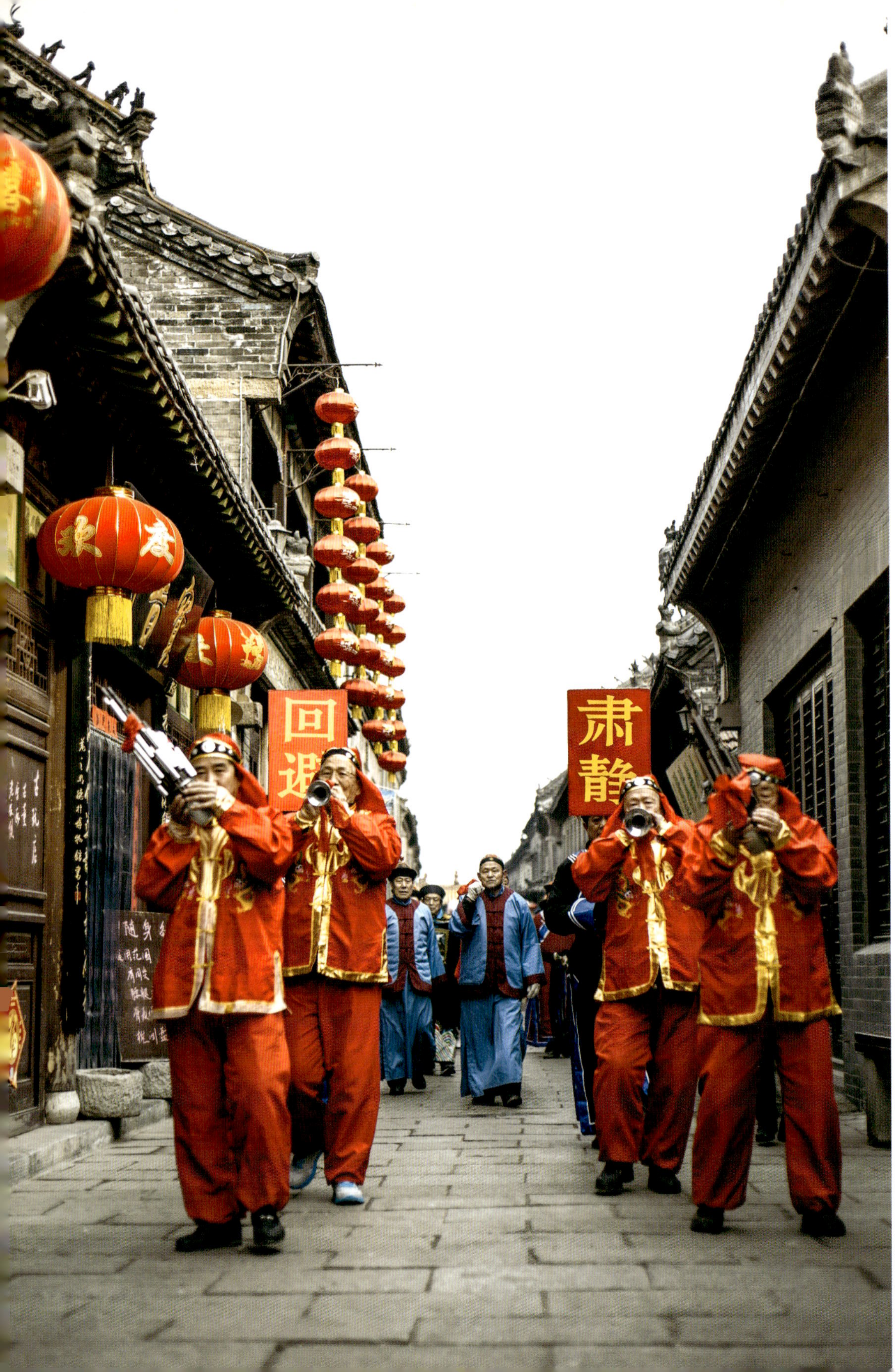

This musical procession welcomes the closing of the Lantern Festival.

The gentleman in the front plays a sheng, or a bamboo mouth organ, which is one of the oldest known instruments in China.

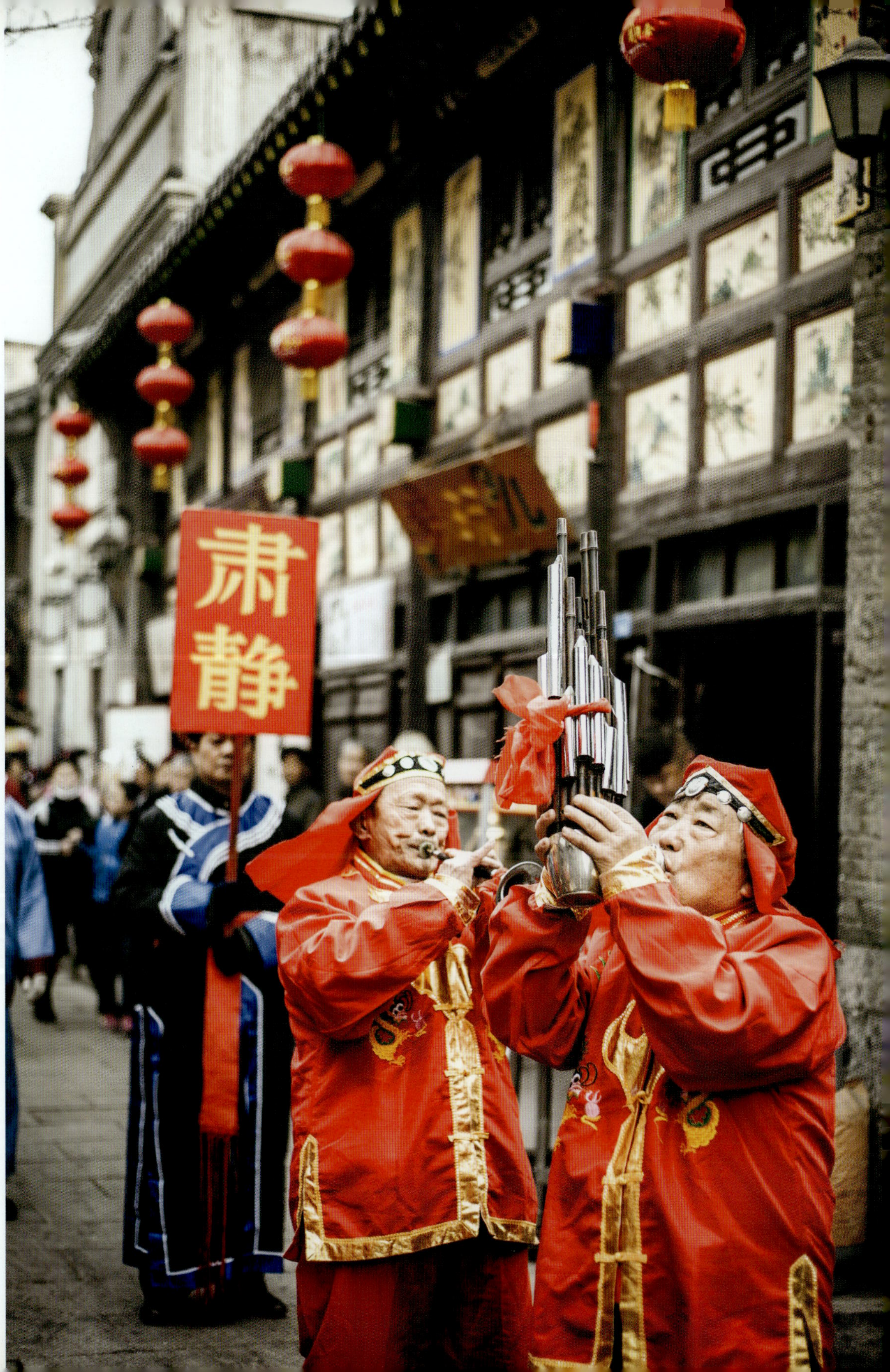

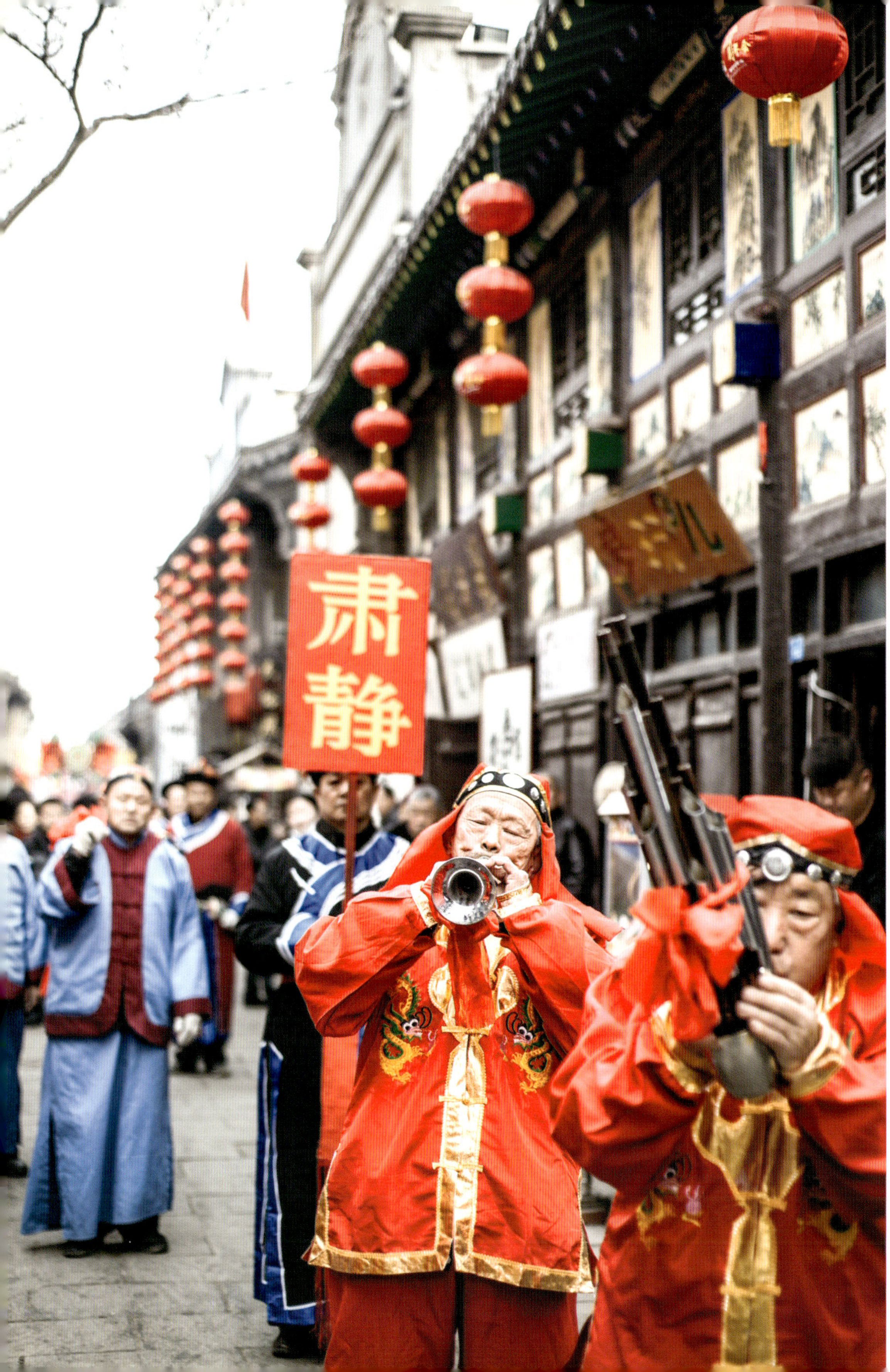

The highlight of the Chinese New Year parade at Zhoucun's Ancient Commercial Center is the music. These lively musicians play to celebrate the festival and the New Year. Though the streets date back to the Ming Dynasty, the town is known as a regional financial center, attracting merchants and time-honored silk sellers along the Silk Road.

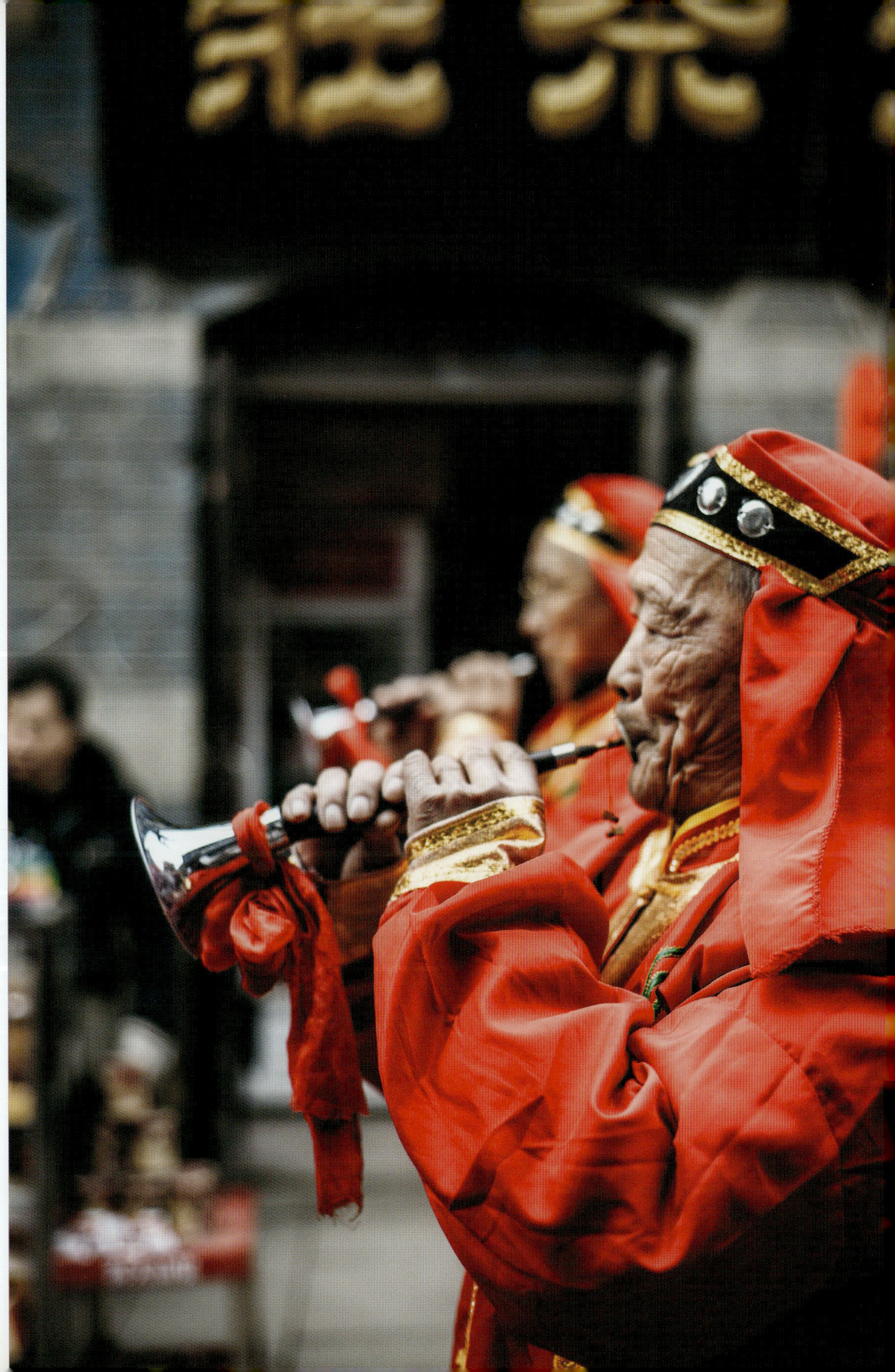

The suona, a double-reed instrument, produces bright, clear notes that are said to resemble birdcalls. It is often used in Chinese weddings to announce the arrival of the bride.

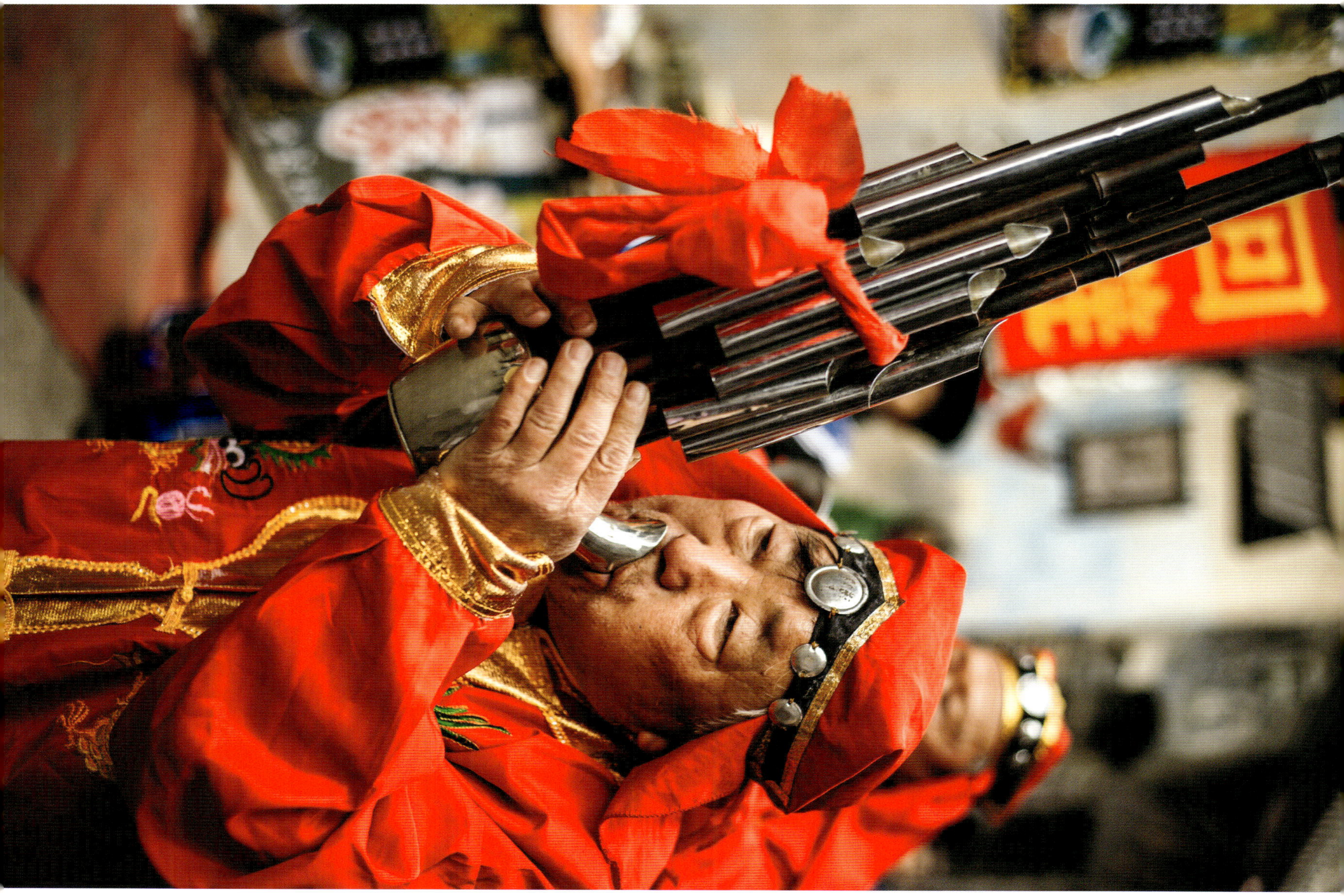

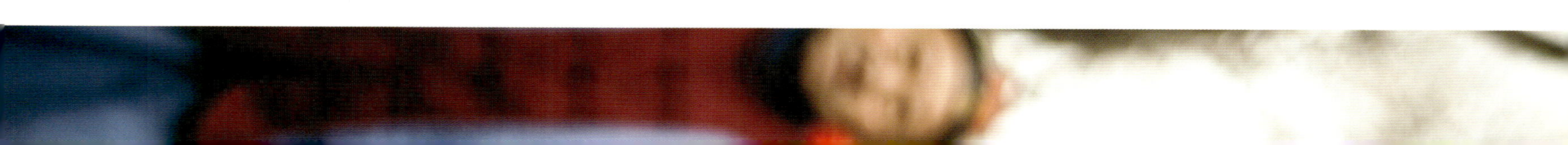

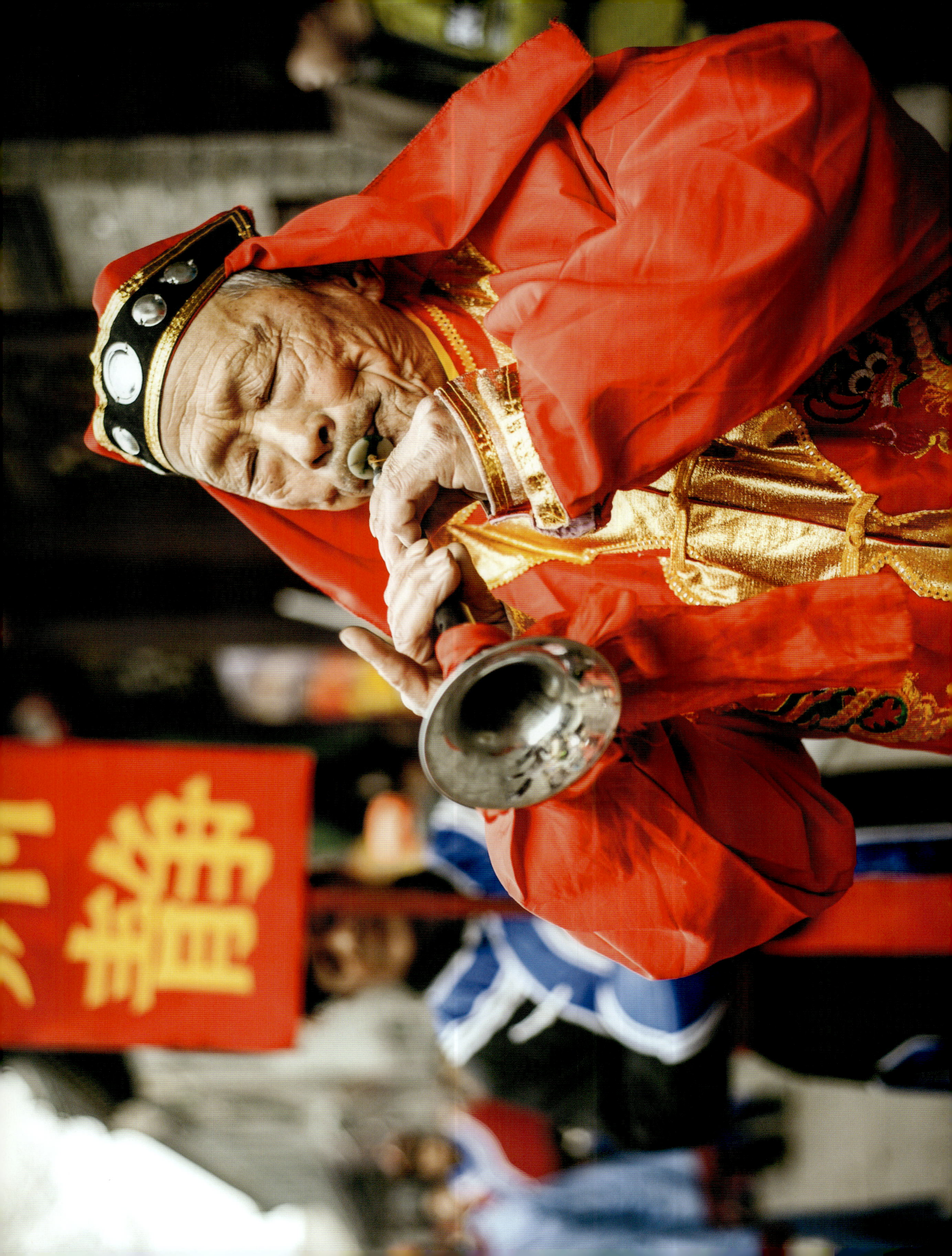

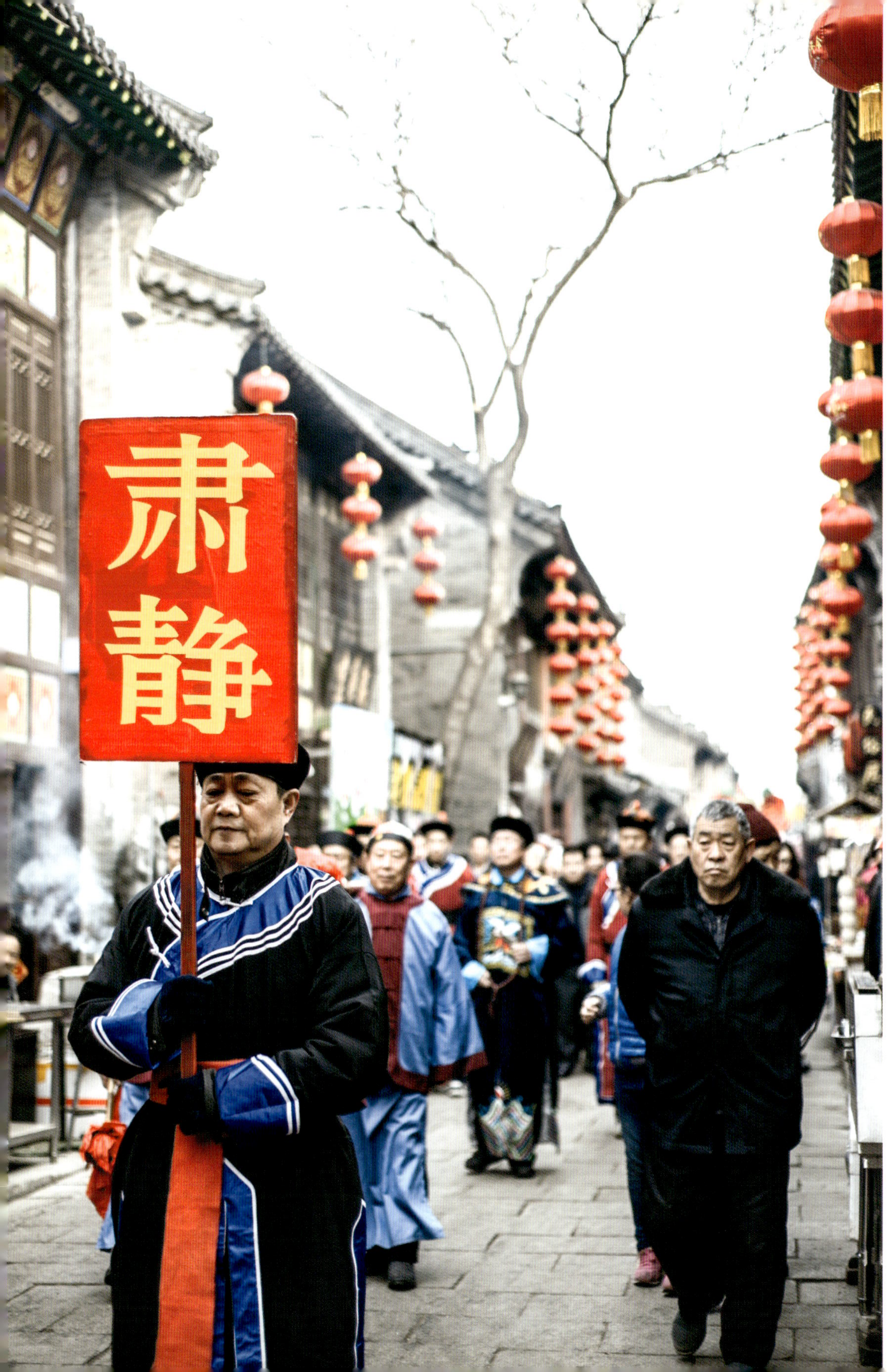

This sign, a relic of older times, says “Be quiet.” It was only used when a government official passed through the street. Now they are escorted by police instead.

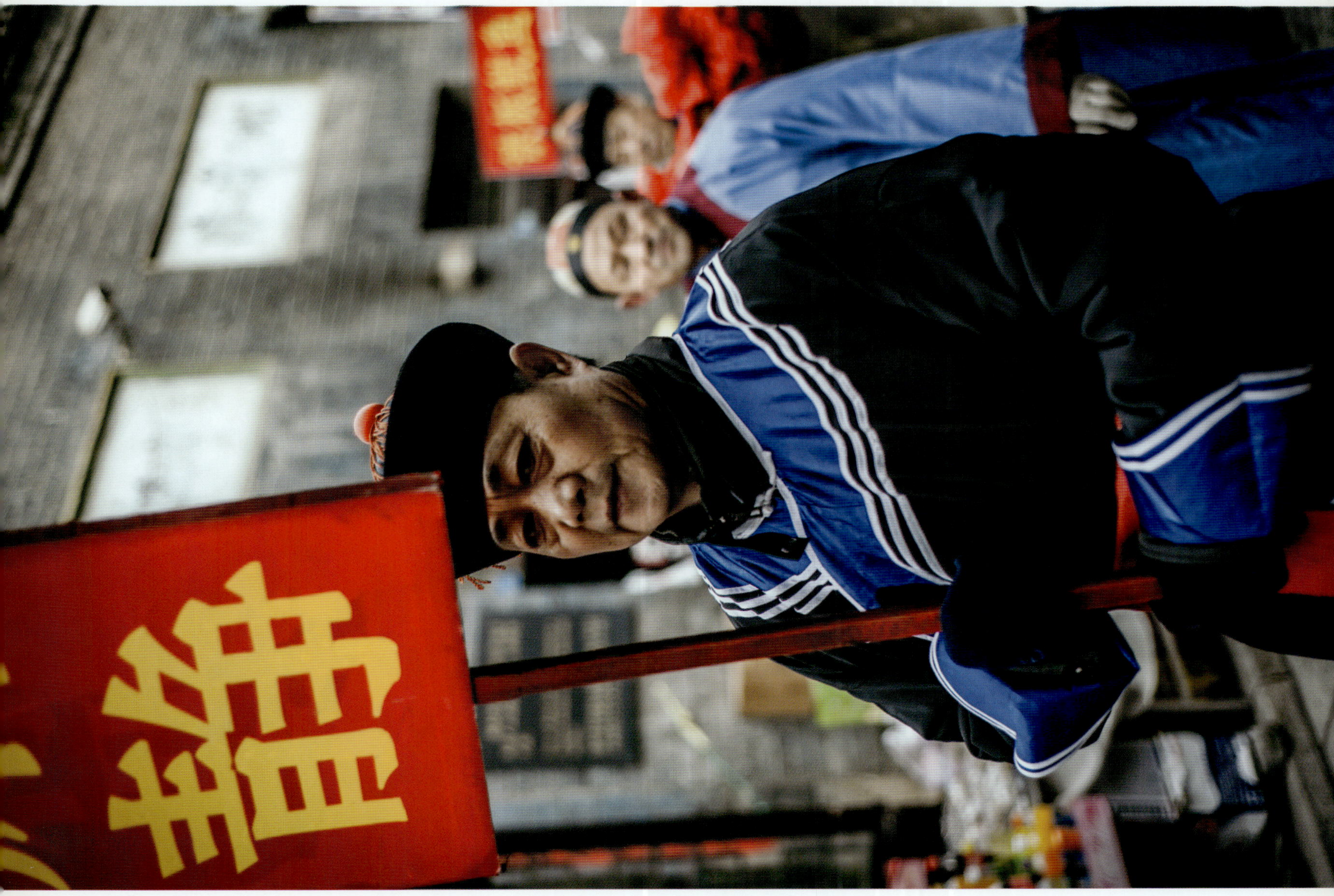

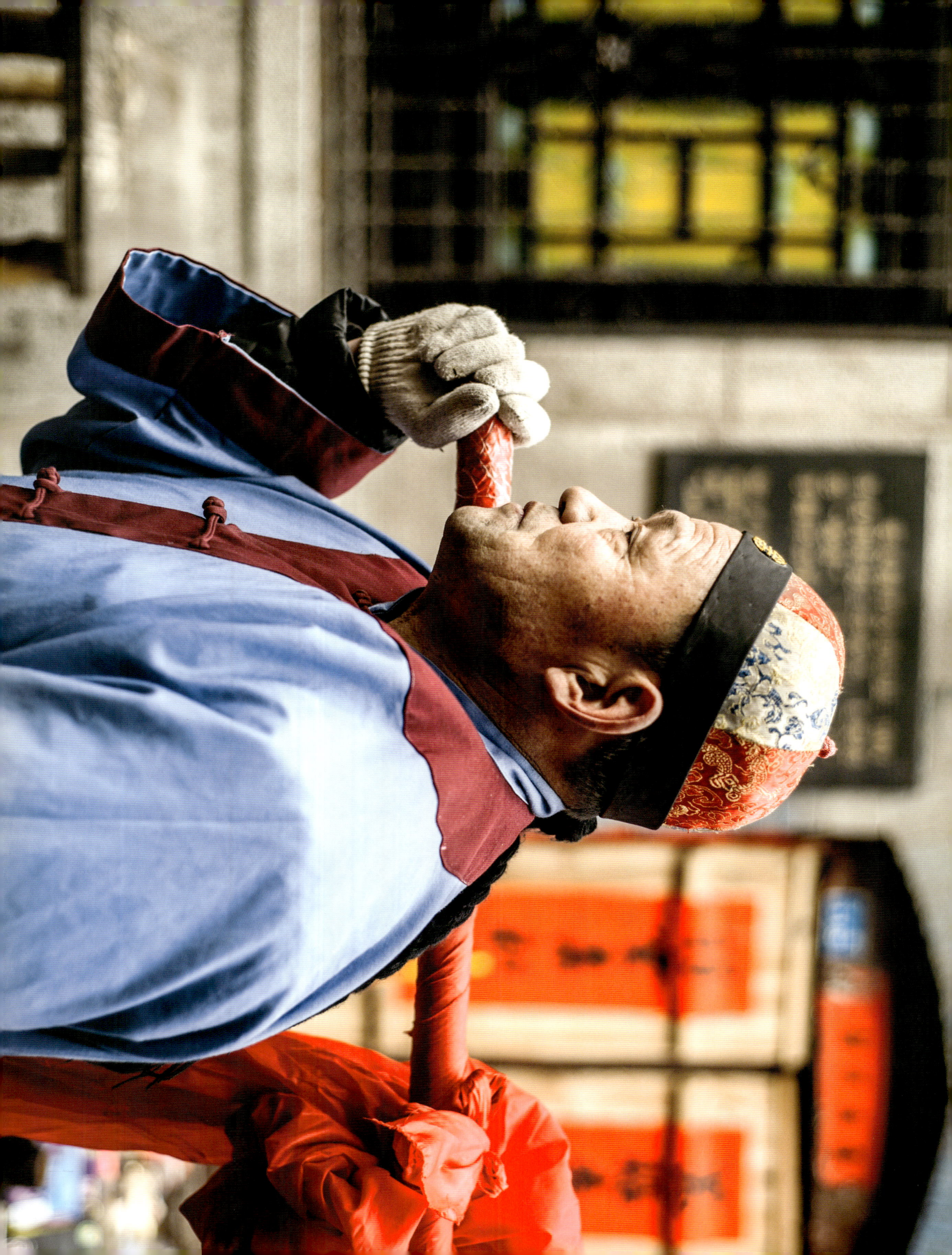

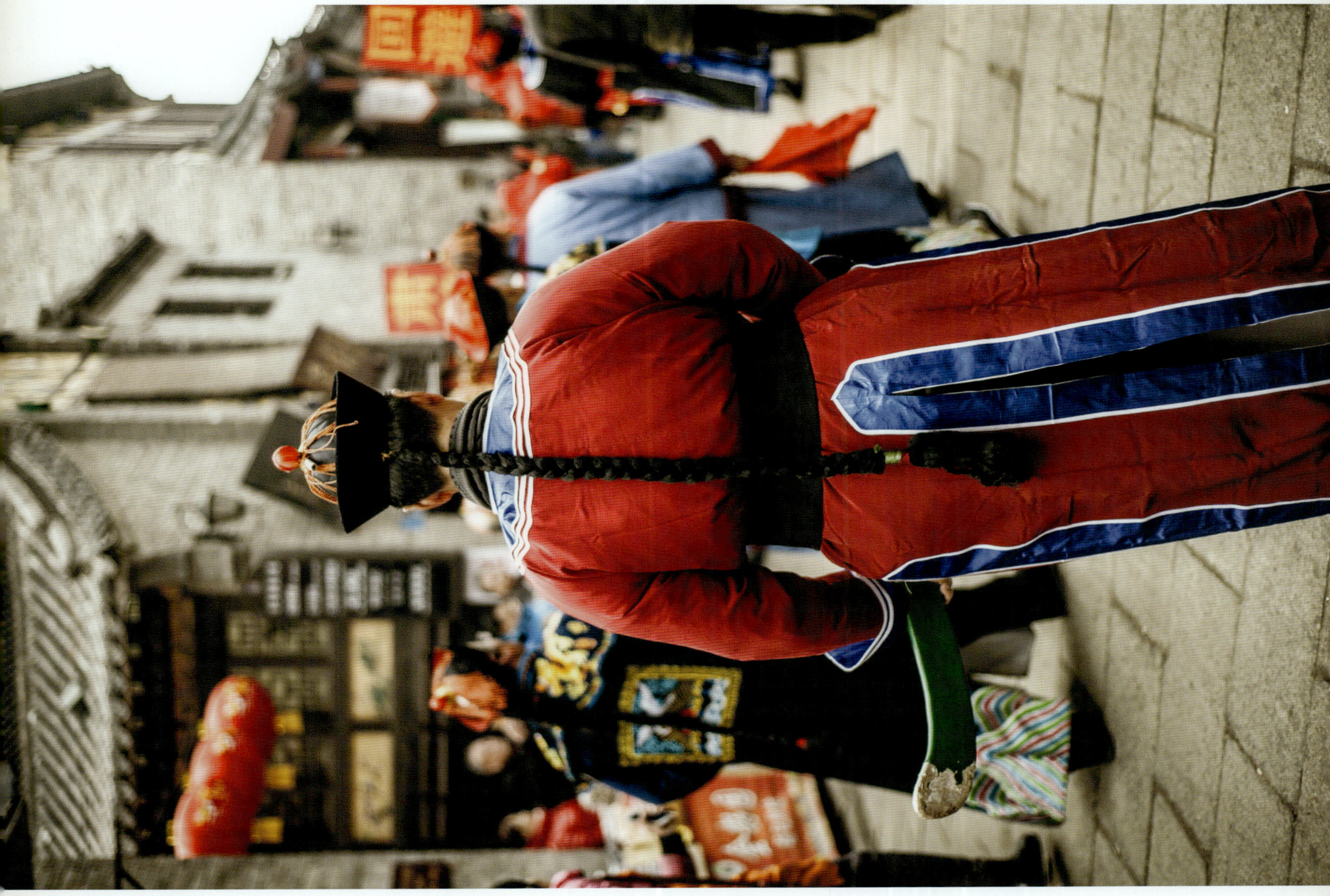

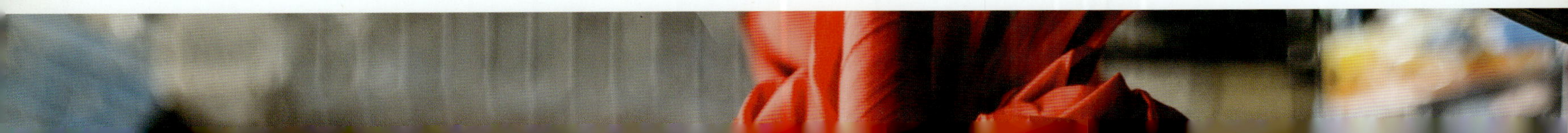

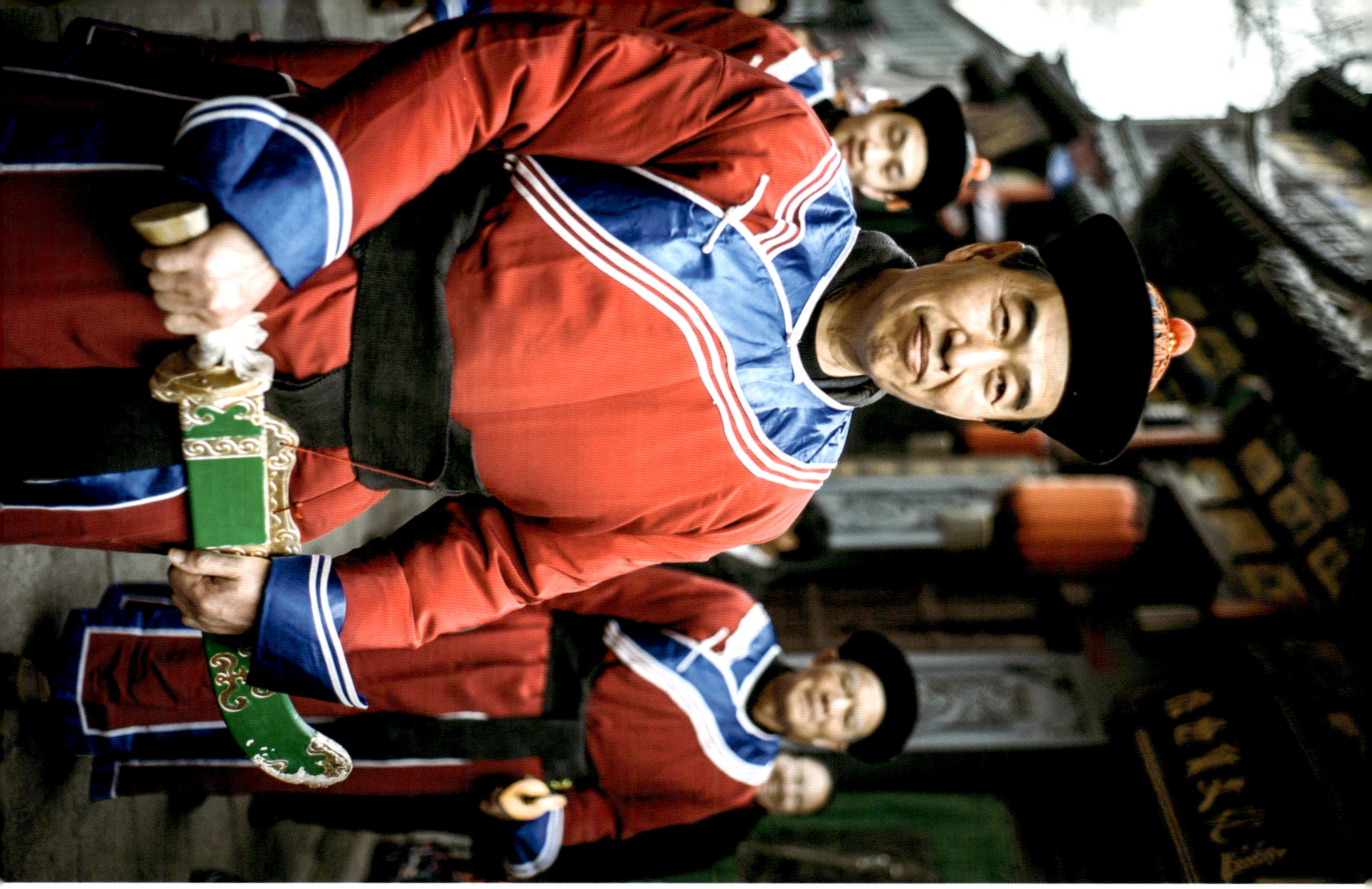

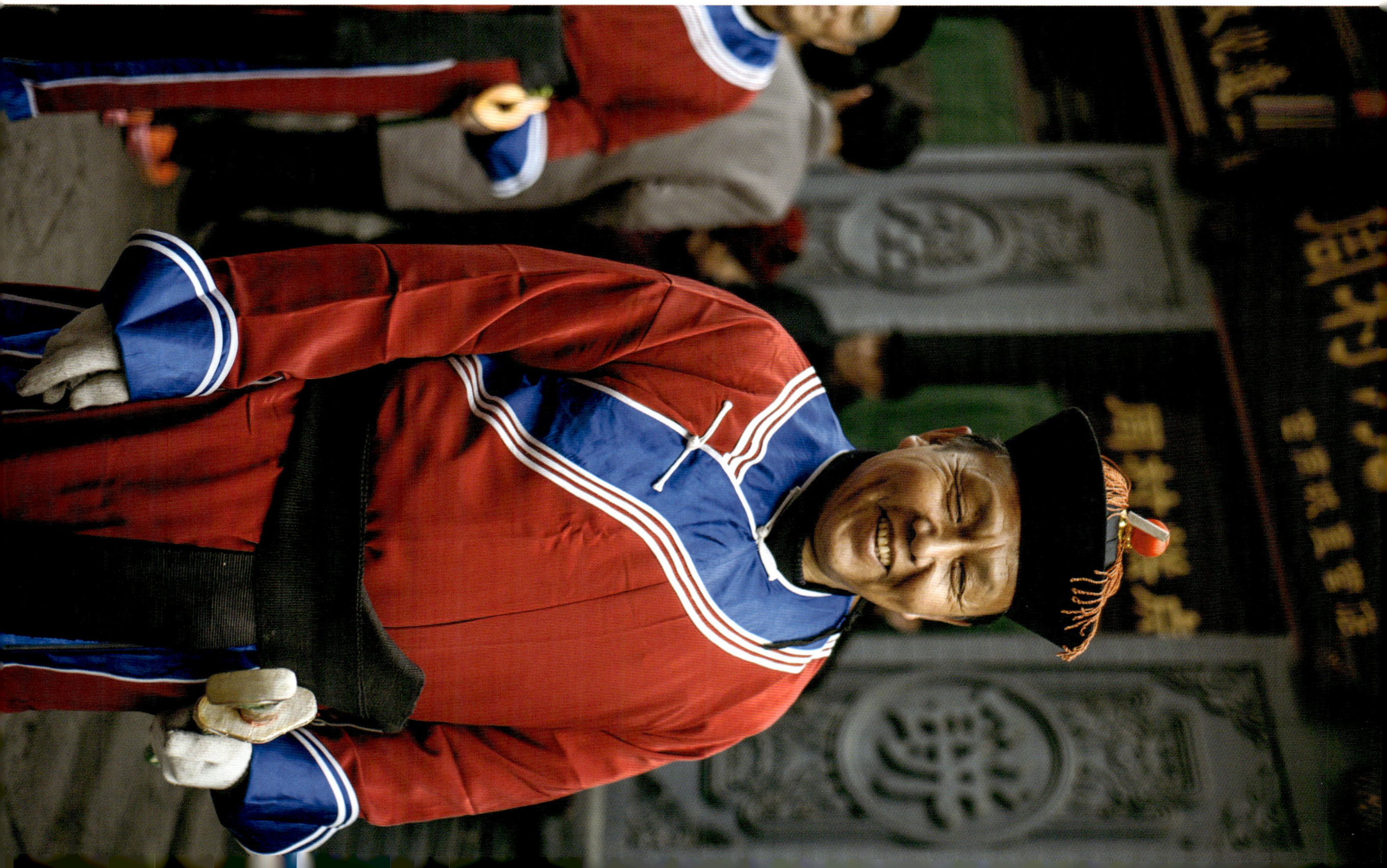

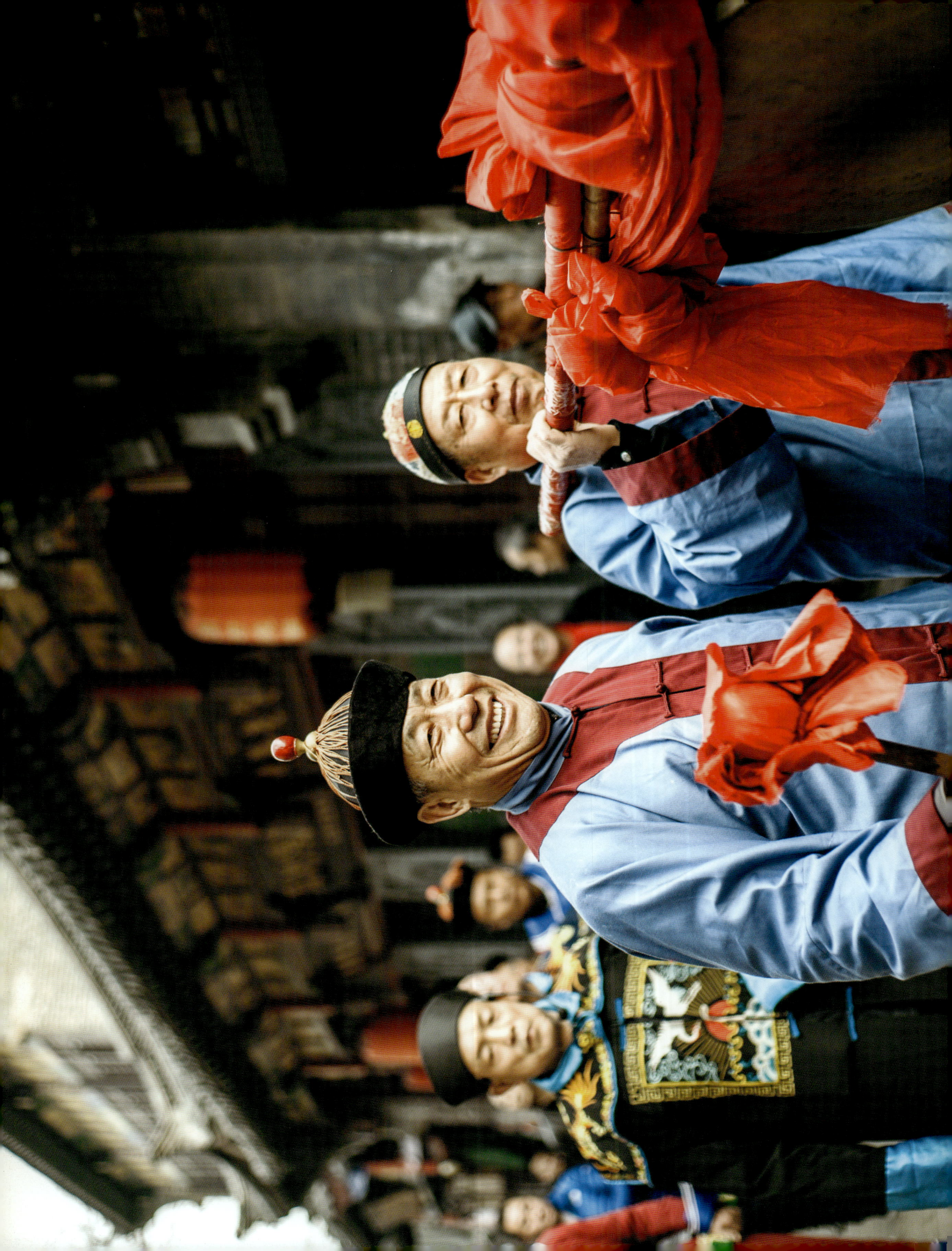

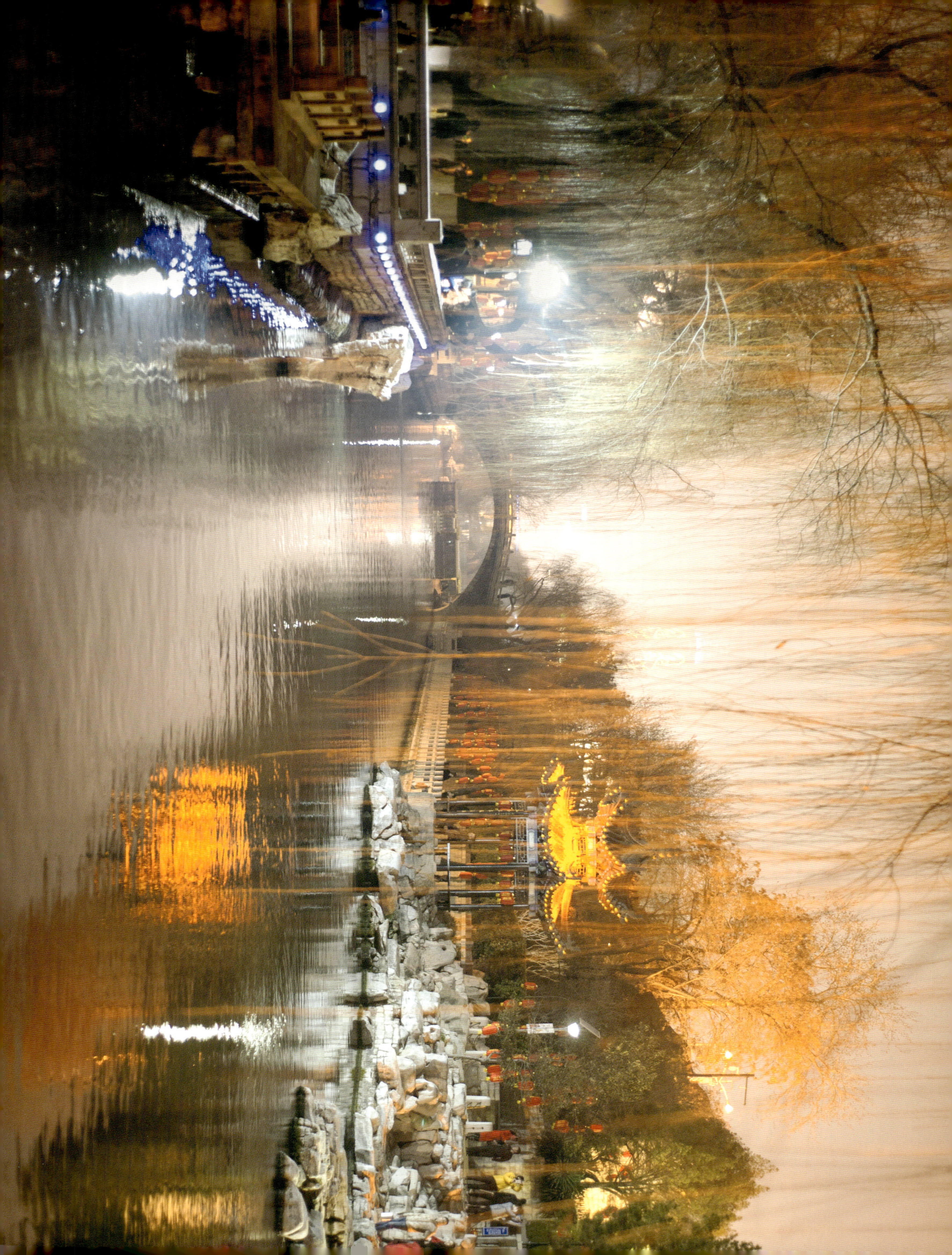

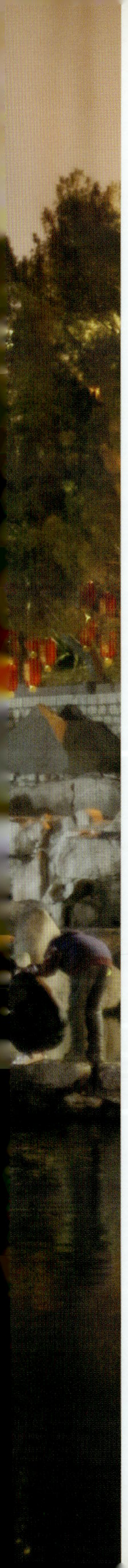

Smoke fills the air after hundreds of fireworks make a lasting impression from the Lantern Festival's climactic evening celebration over the Black Tiger Spring in the Jinan City moat.

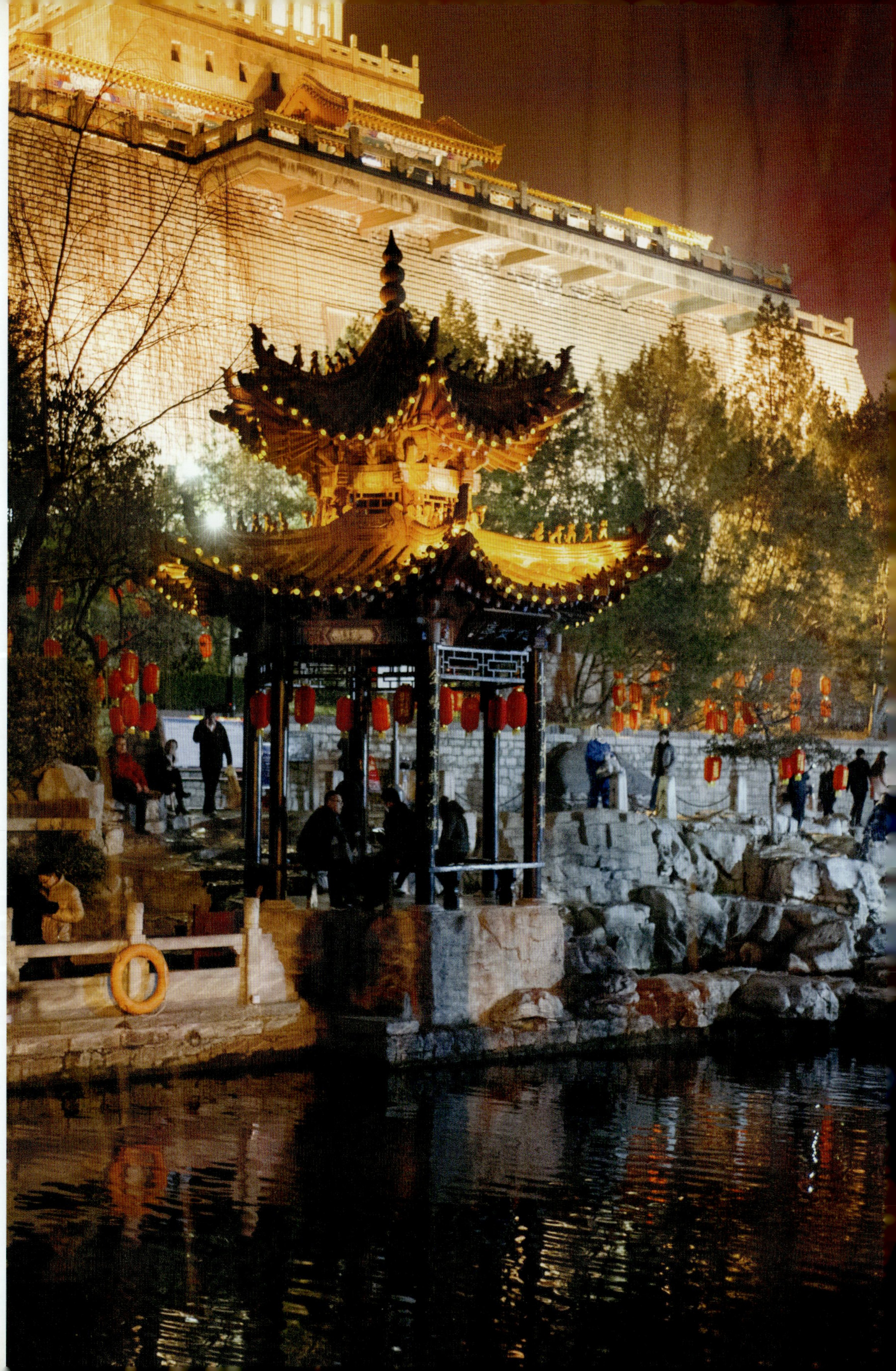

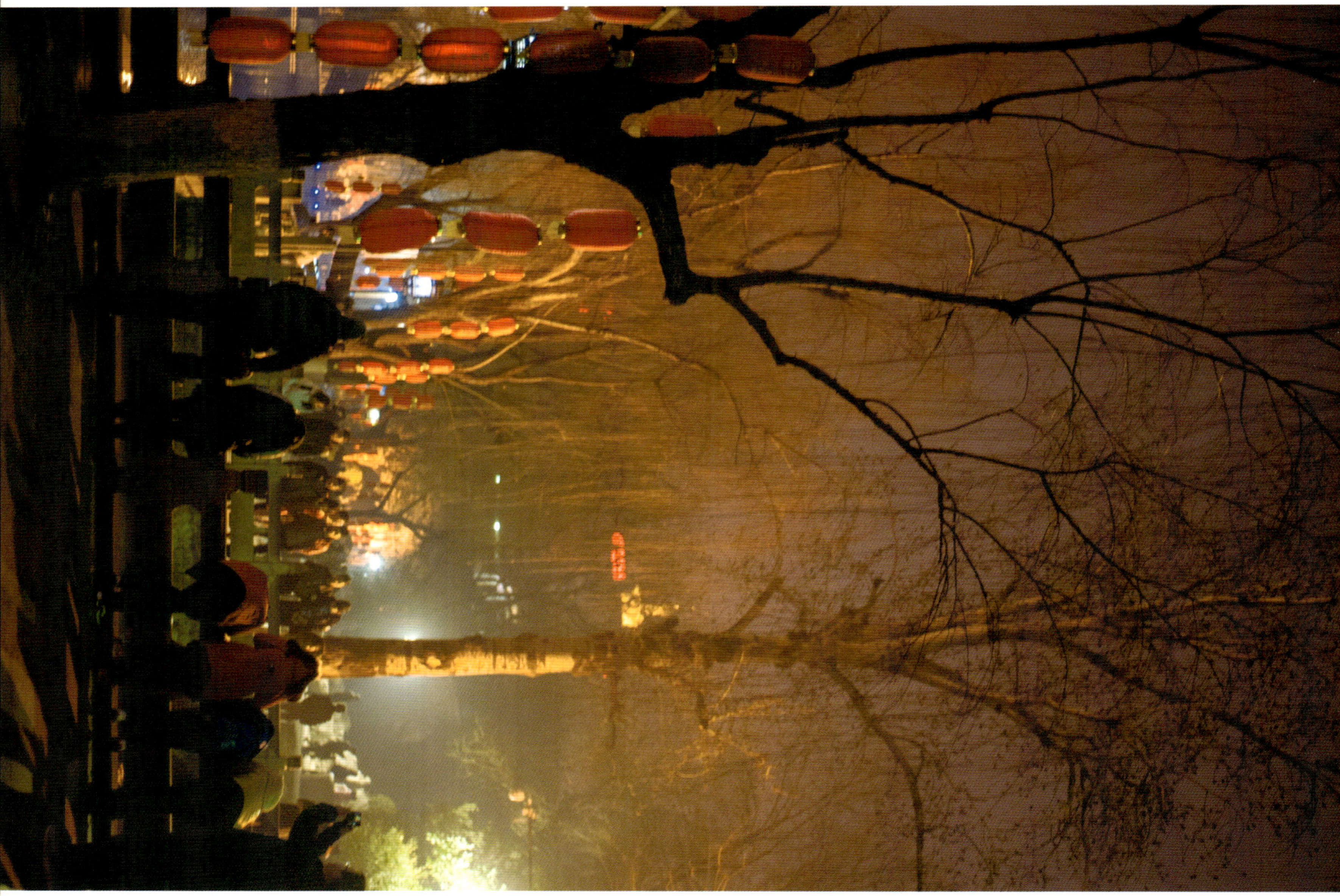

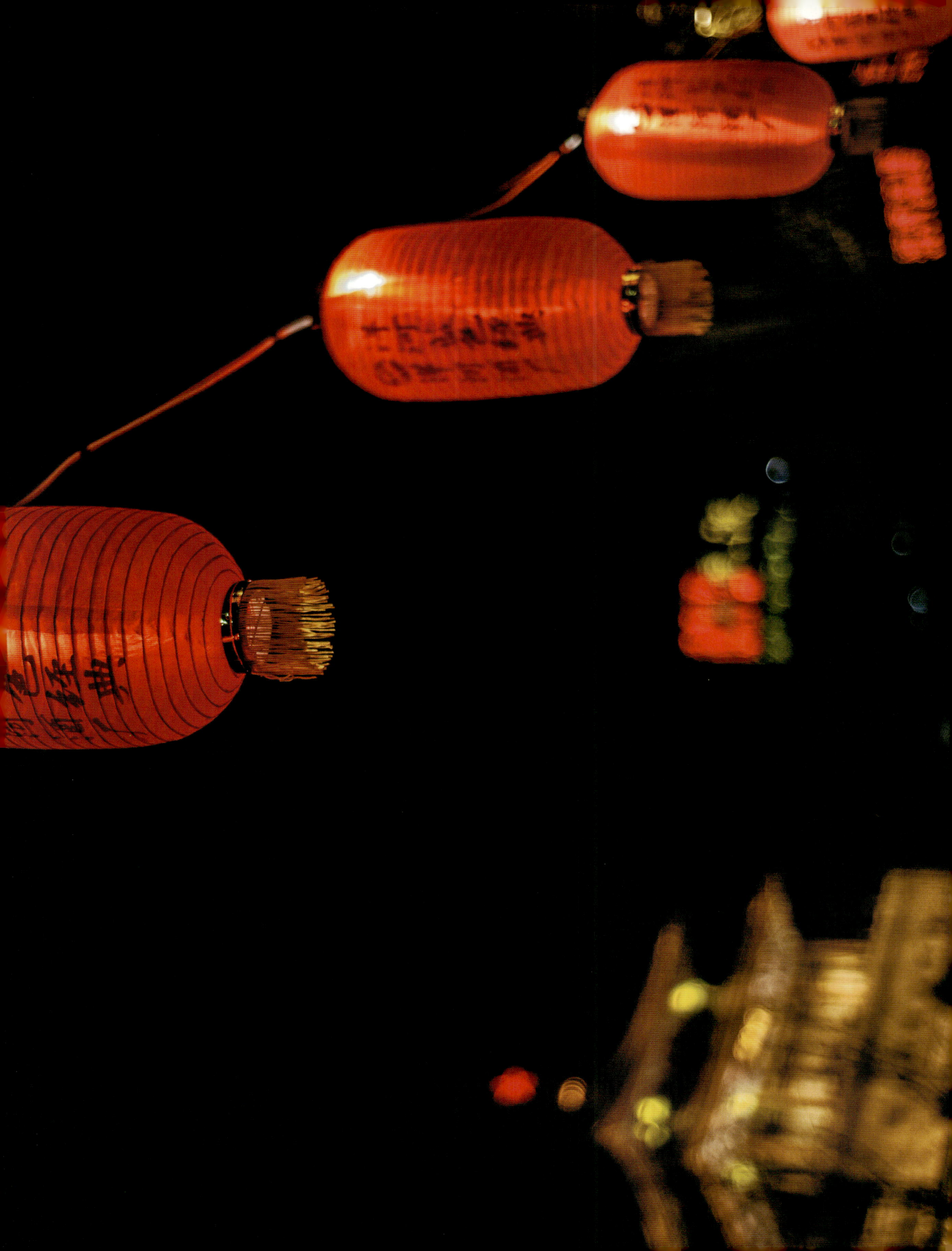

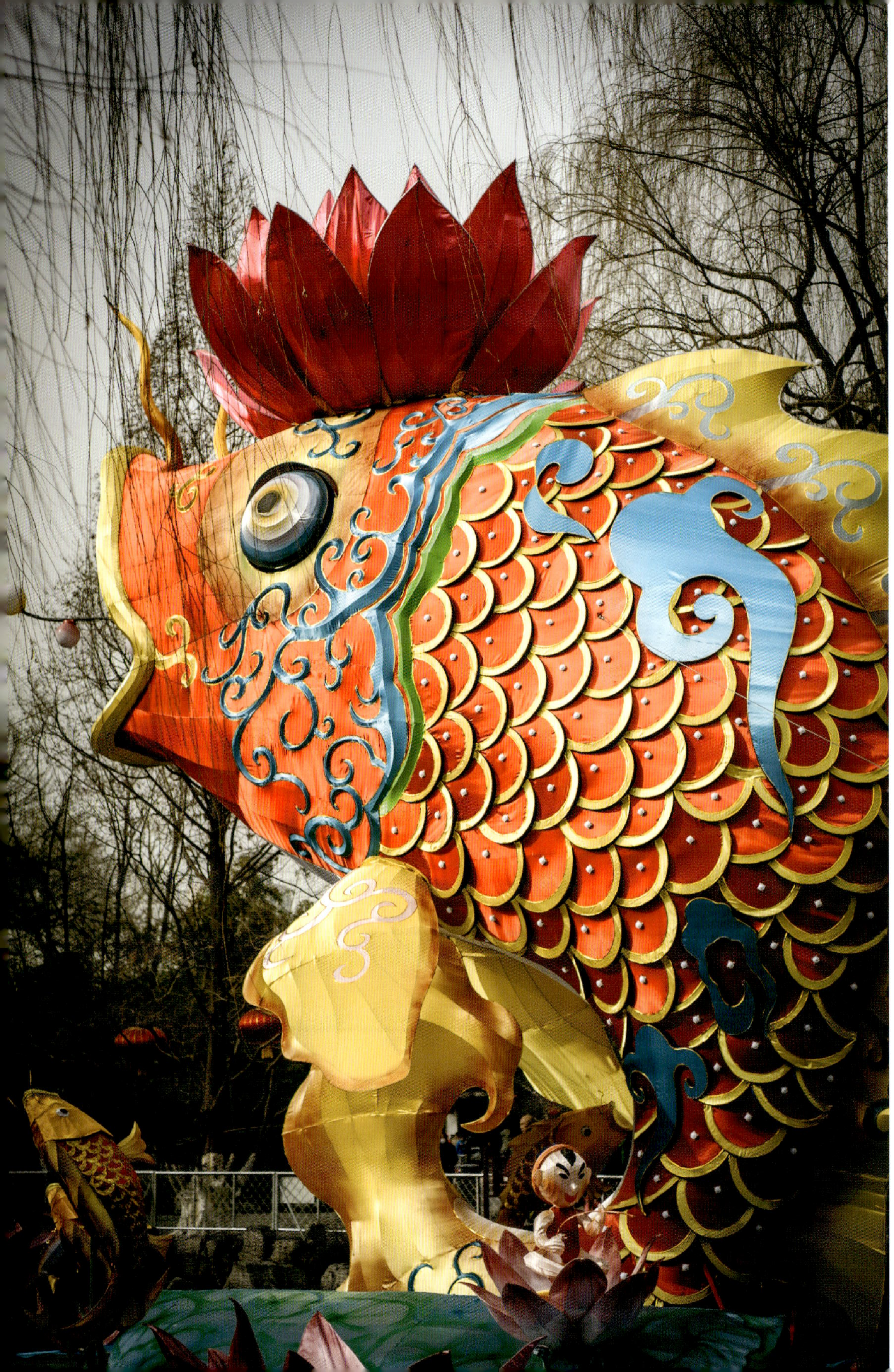

Baotu Spring Park in the Shandong Province is home to an annual celebration. This vibrant fish is one of the many colorful floats for the Lantern Festival, also known as the Shangyuan Festival. A symbol of unity and perfection, this celebration of the Chinese lunar calendar begins on the first full-moon night of the Chinese lunar year, and hundreds of lanterns of all shapes and sizes cover Baotu Spring Park. At night, each of these large luminaries glows with color.

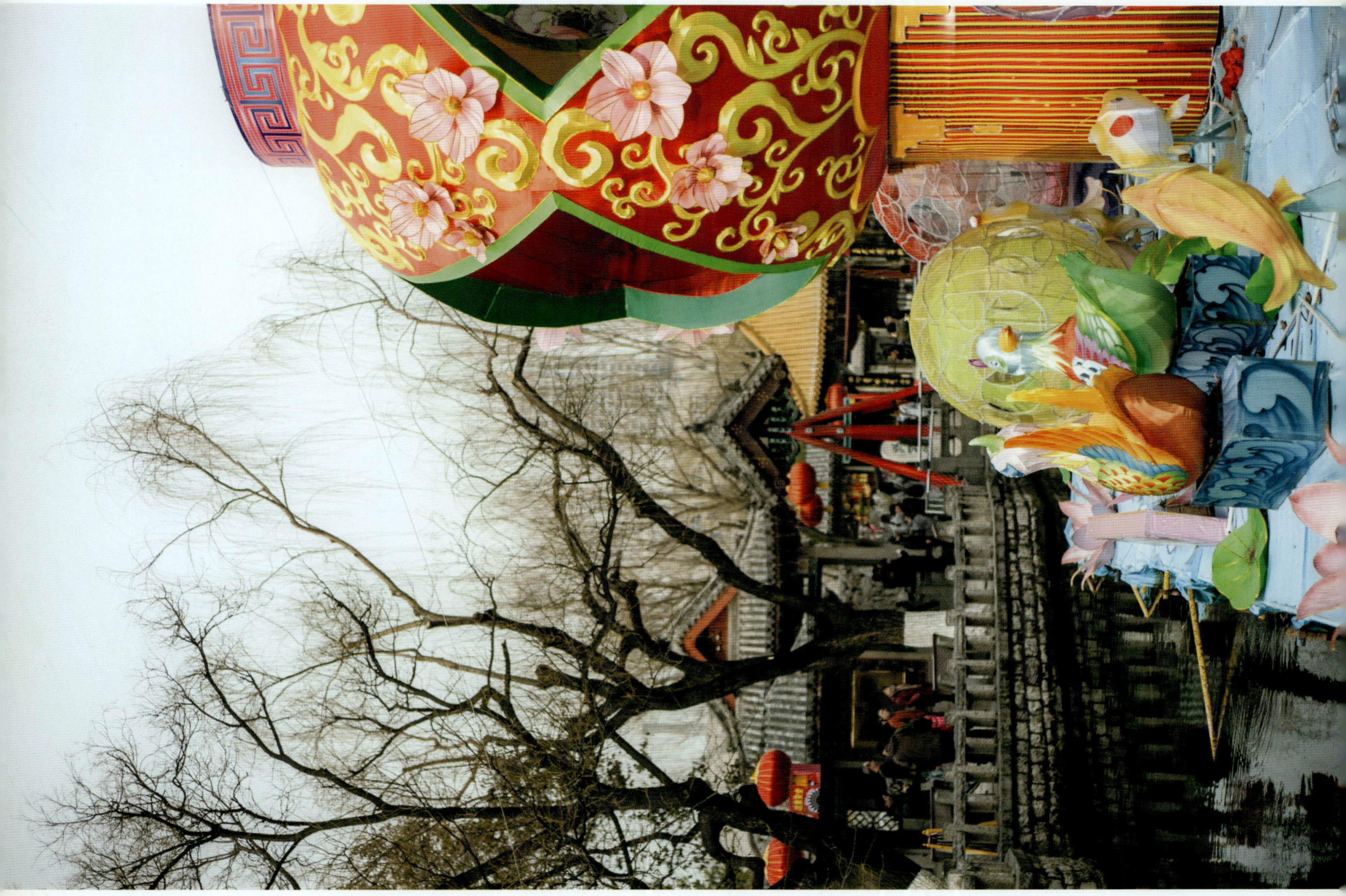

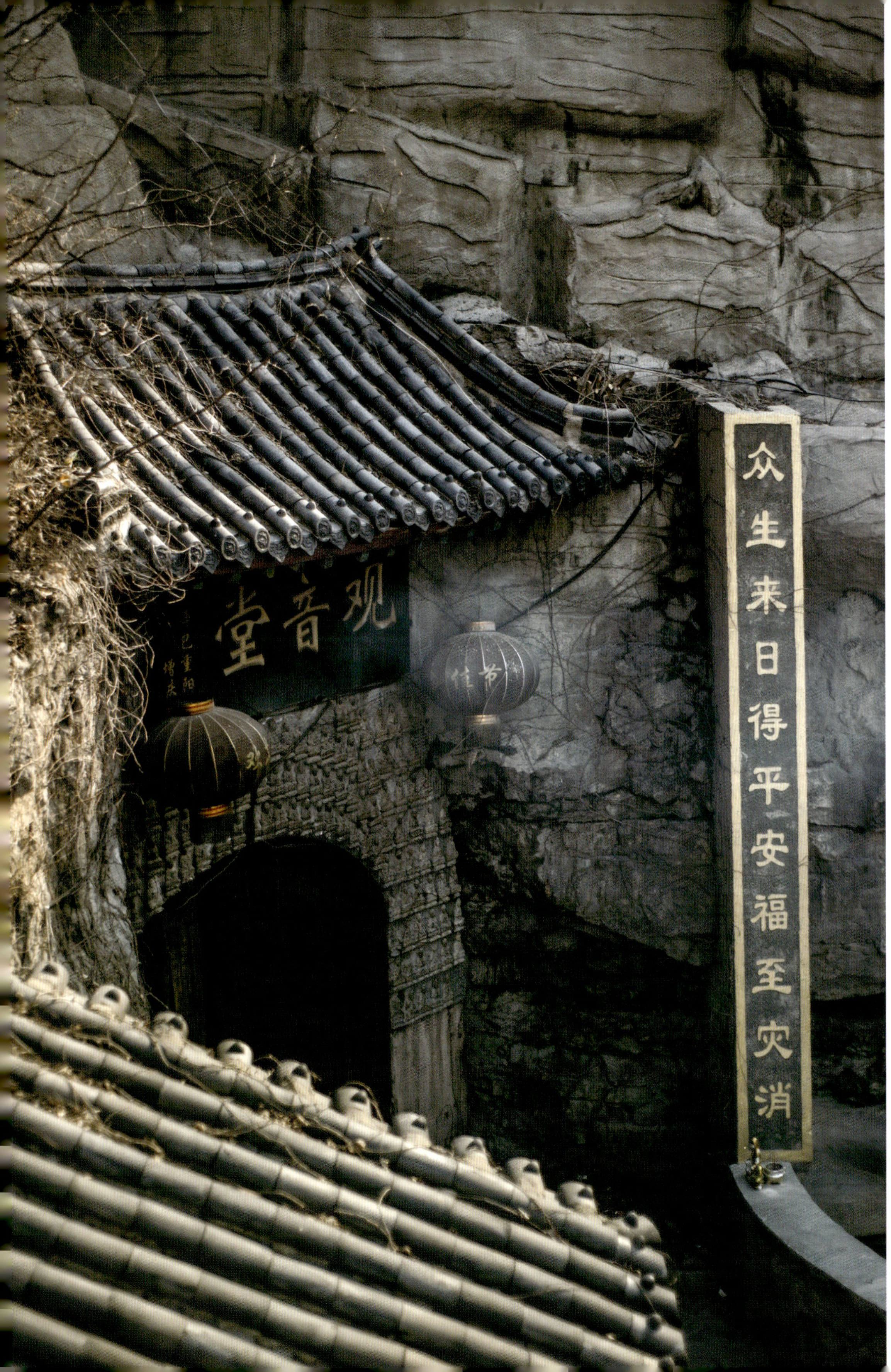
观音堂
众生来日得平安福至灾消

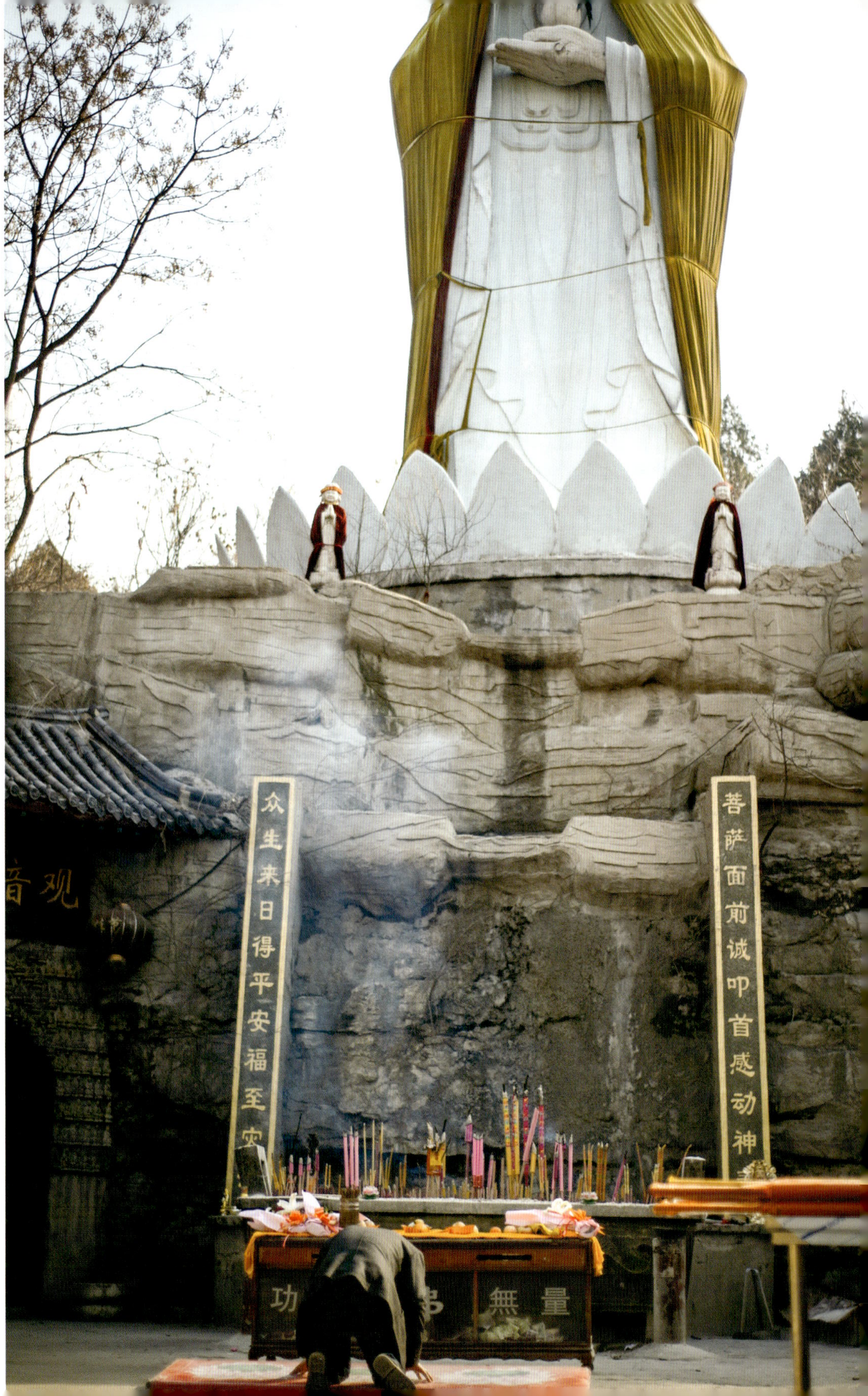
众生来日得平安福至
菩萨面前诚叩首感动神
無量

At left, a man is seen praying at the base of a Buddha at the Thousand Buddha Mountain in Jinan. These Buddhas have stood peacefully since the Sui Dynasty. Here, the scent of burning incense is prolific, as worshipers come from far and wide to pay homage to their ancestors and ask for guidance. Common in both Taoism and Buddhism, the burning of incense is steeped in thousands of years of tradition and religious ritual.

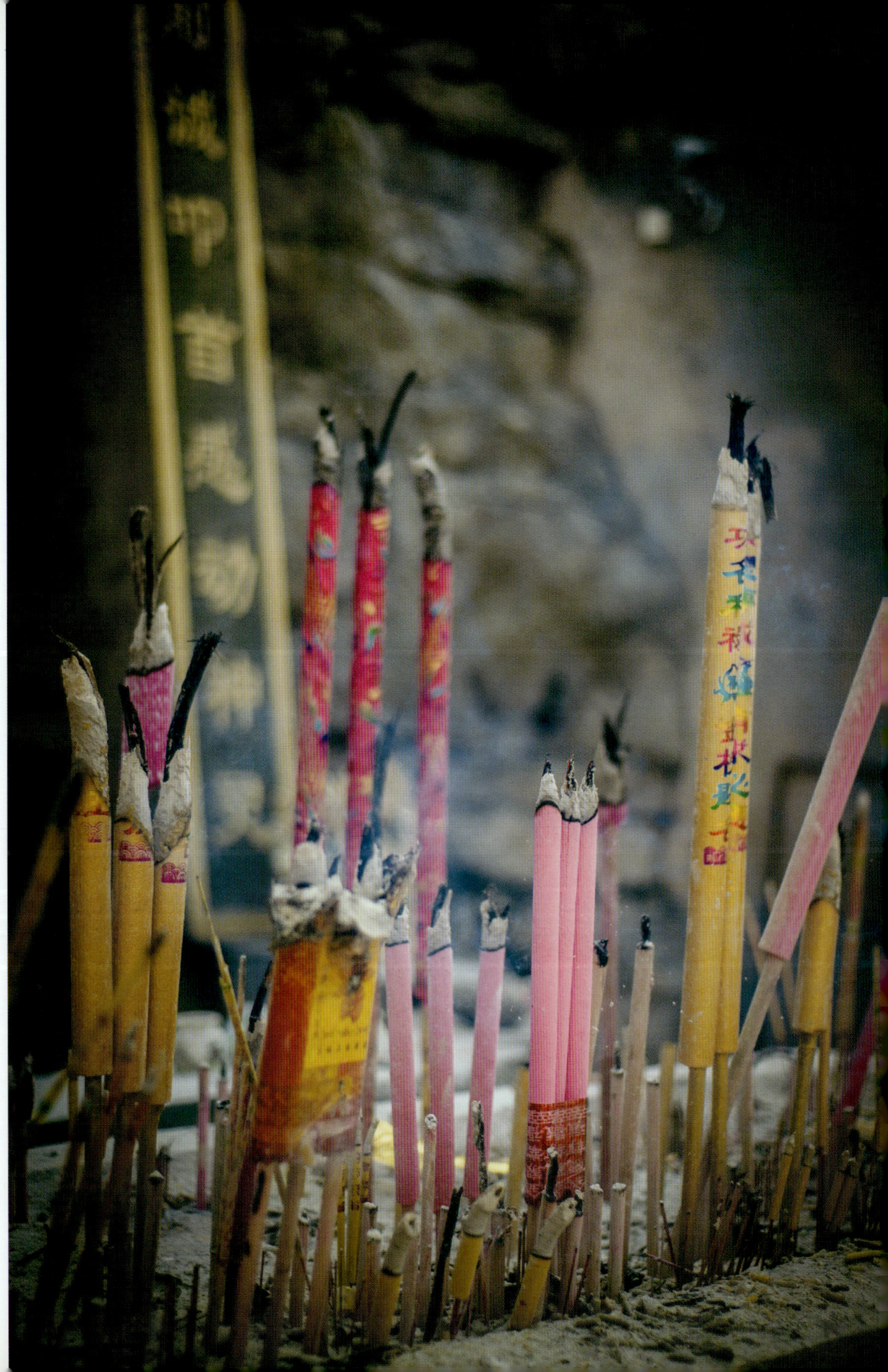

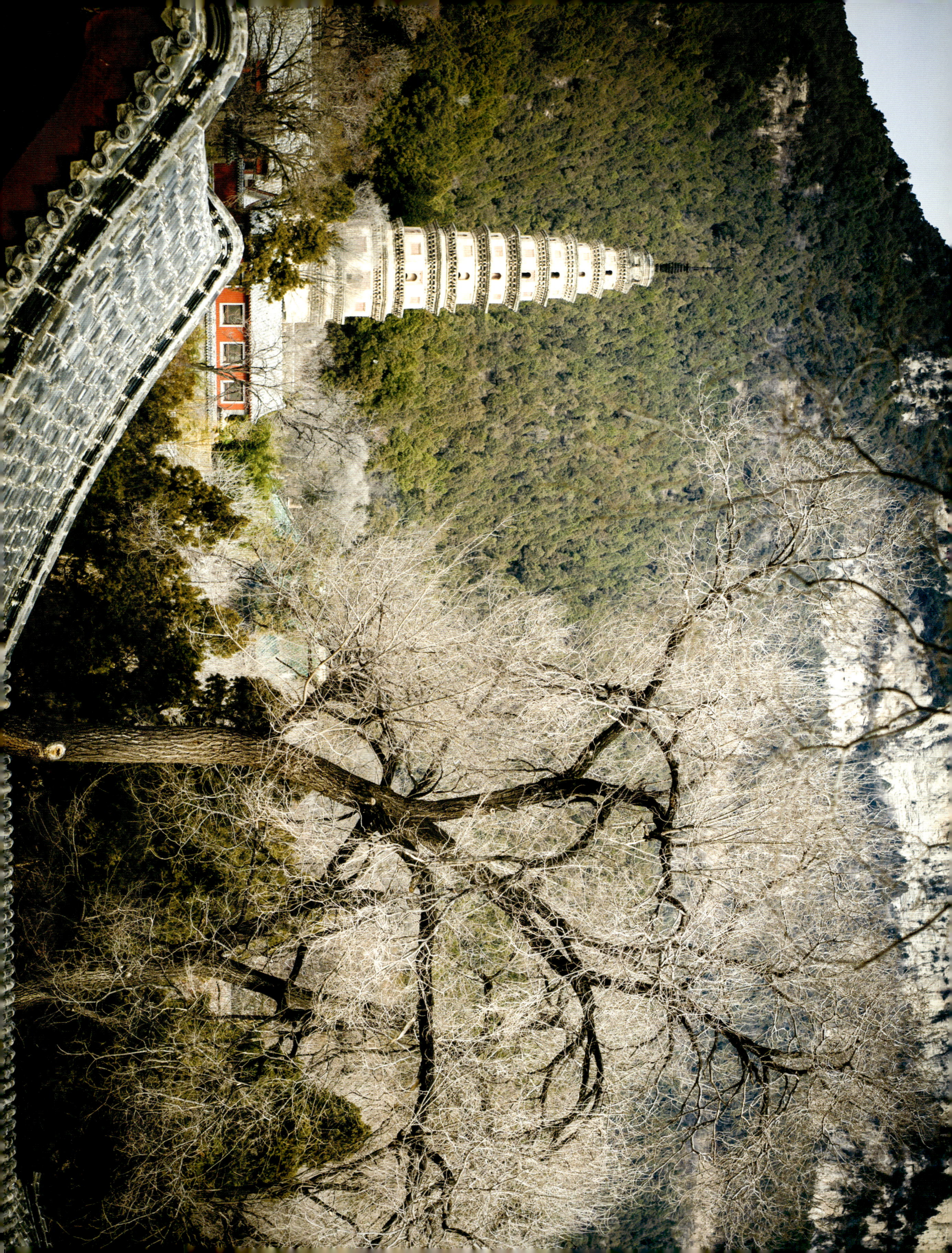

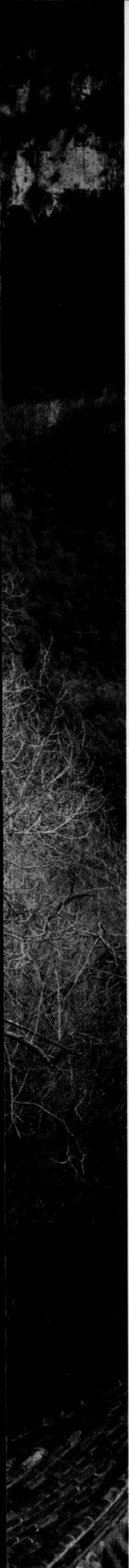

Sights Along the Silk Road

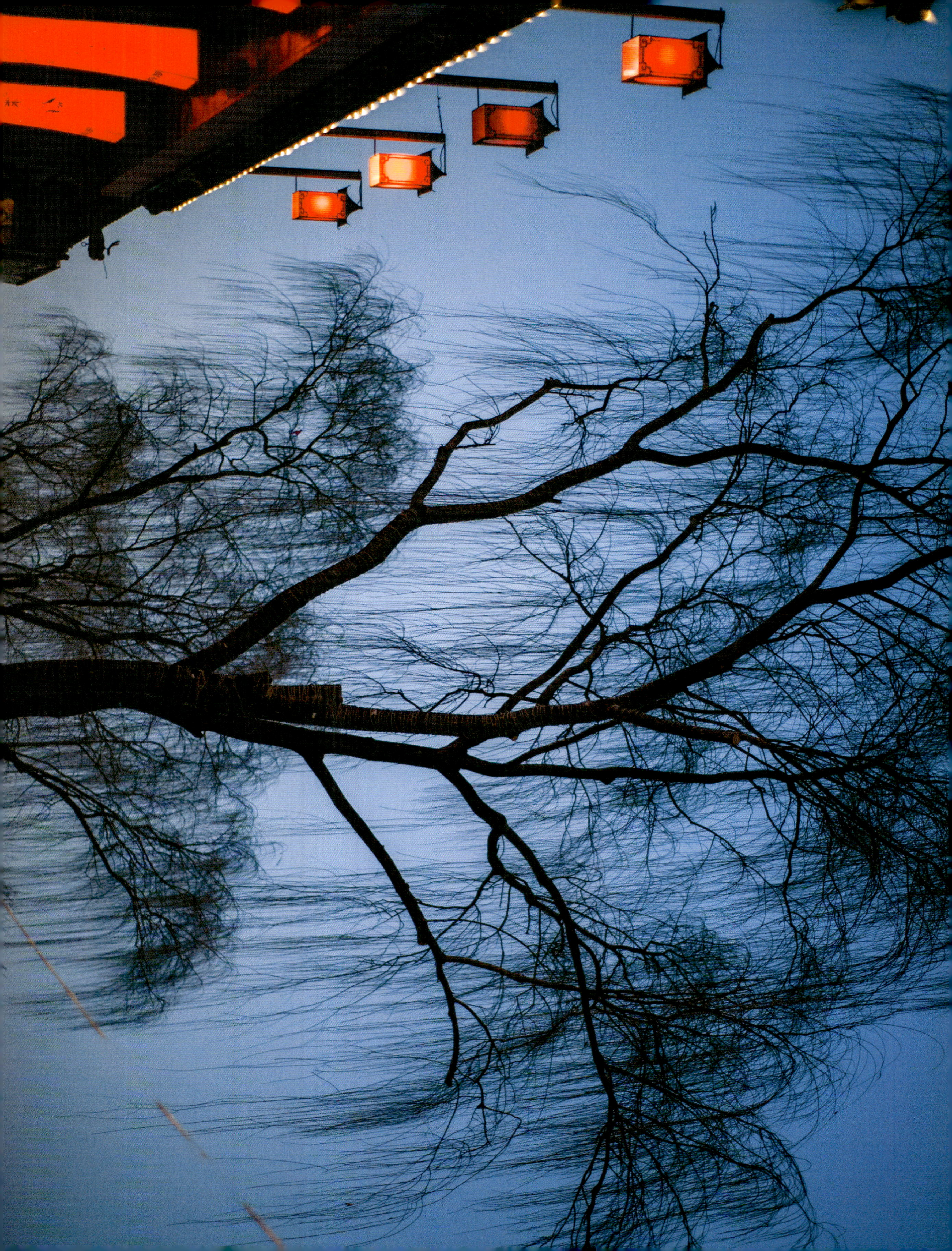

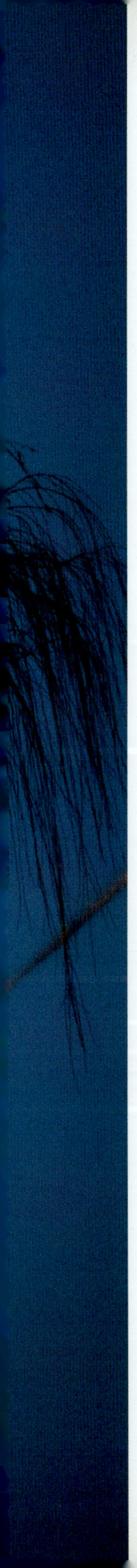

Stray cats are commonplace in China, and they have long lived in the Forbidden City. According to a 2010 report from the Capital Animal Welfare Association, there were an estimated two hundred thousand stray cats in Beijing.

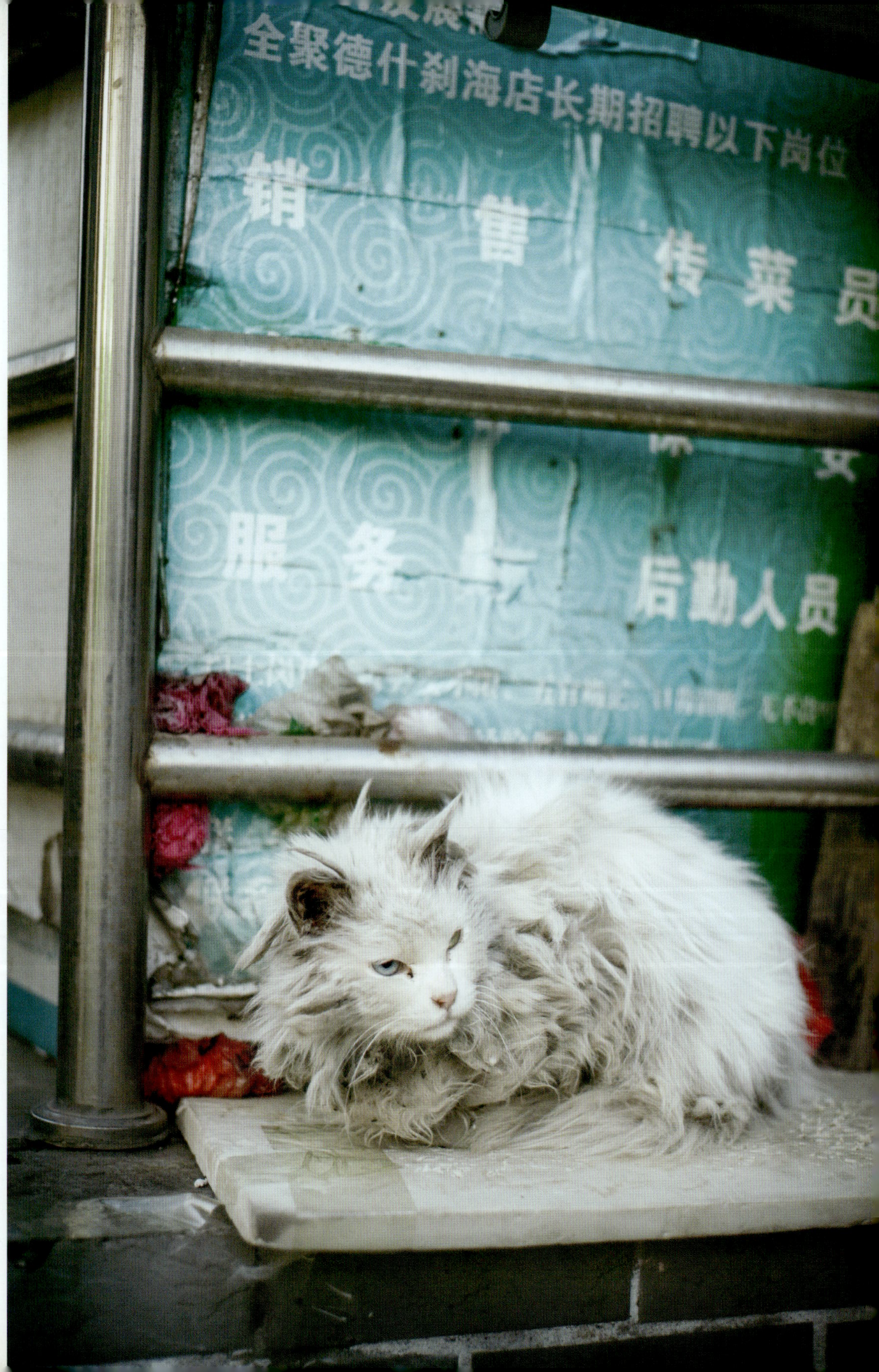

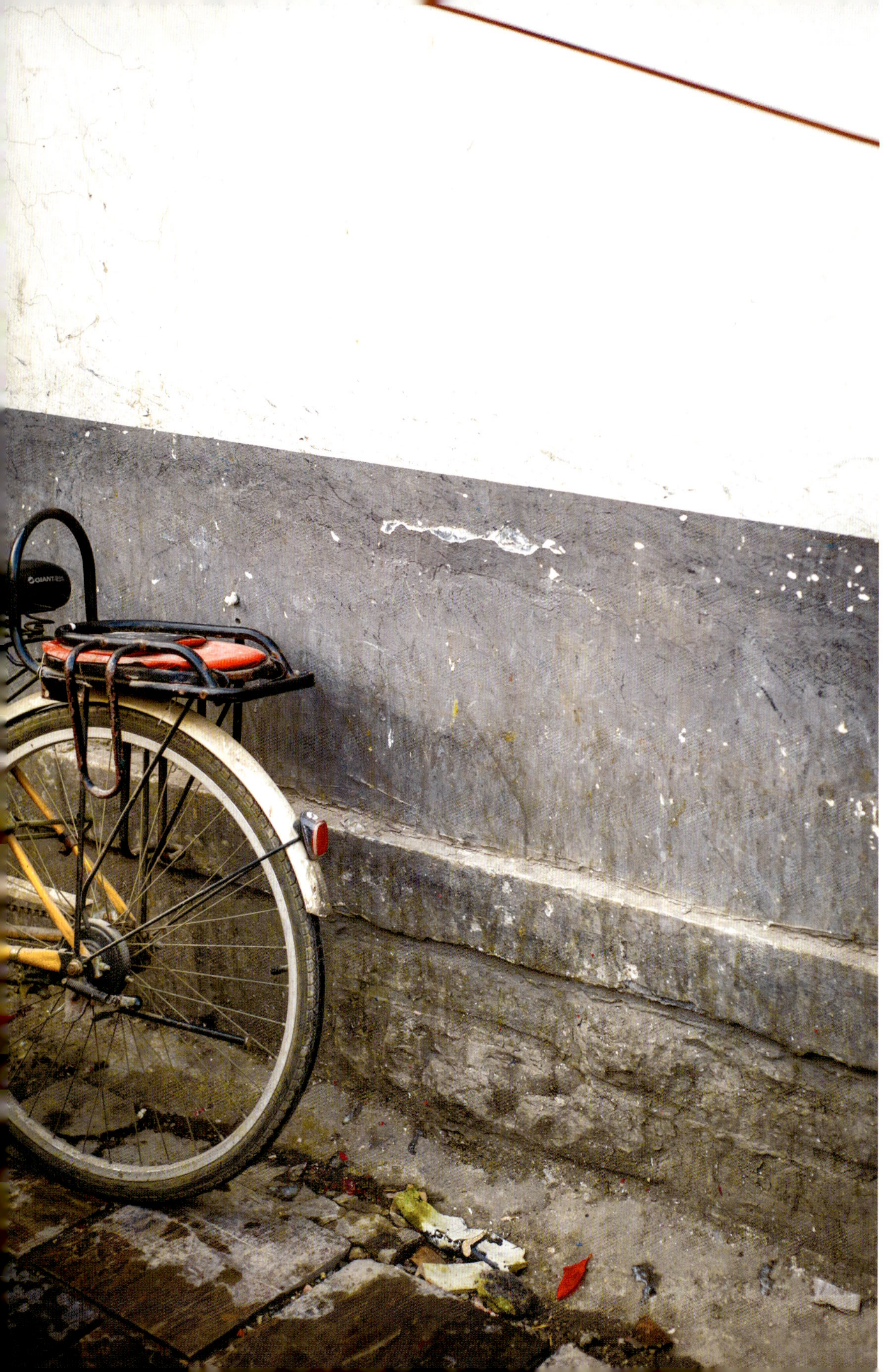

Bicycles are a common sight in China, with an estimated five hundred million in the country. Here they are mainly used for transportation, rather than for recreation.

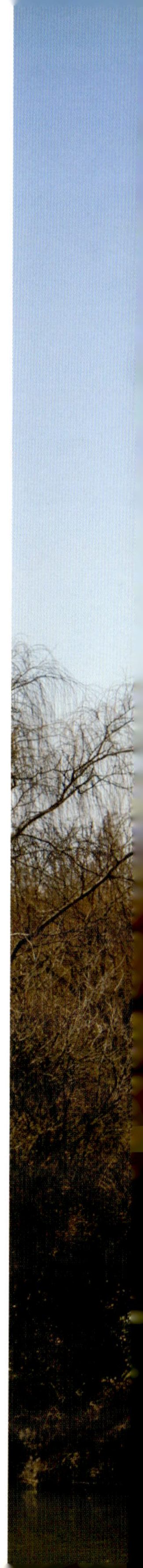

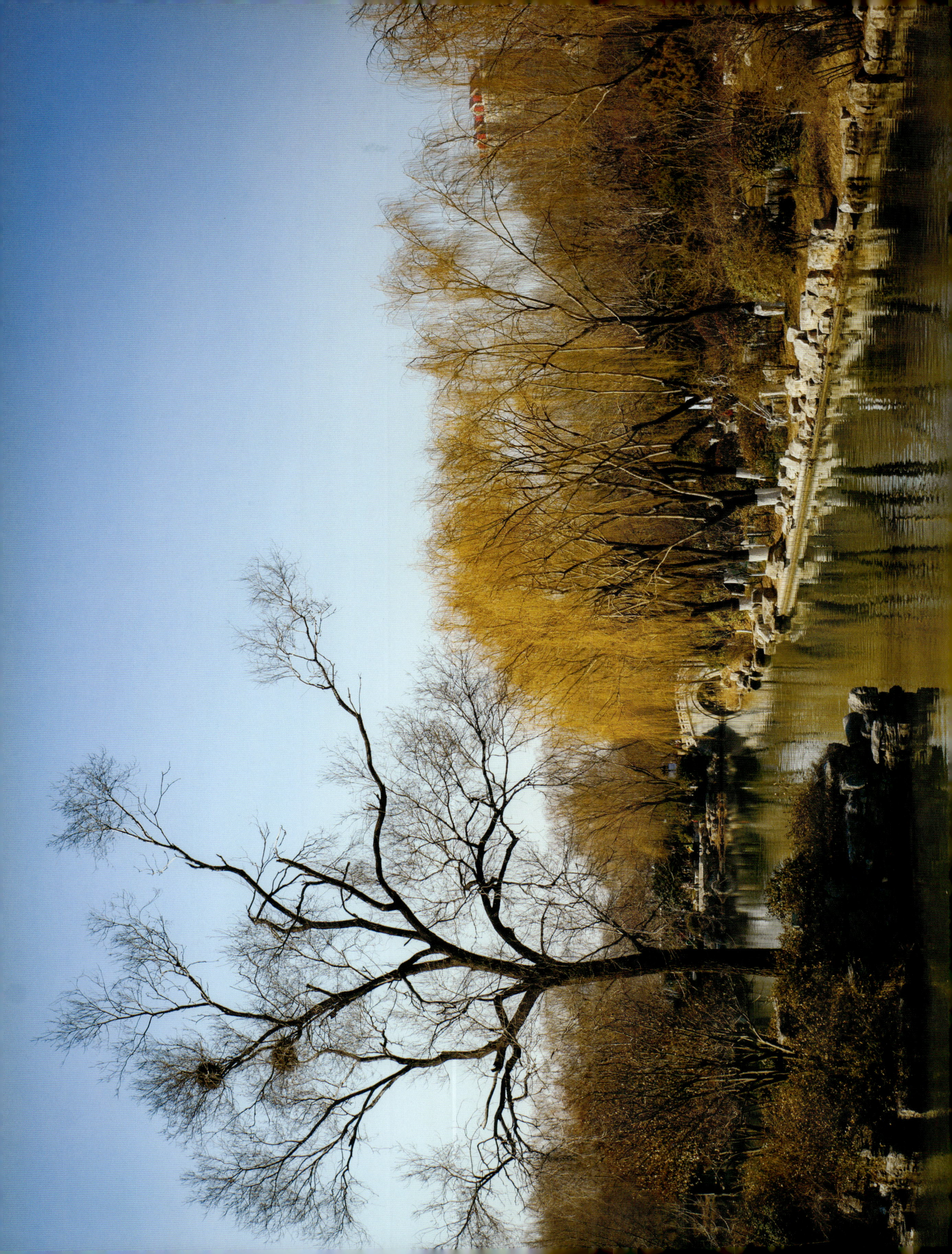

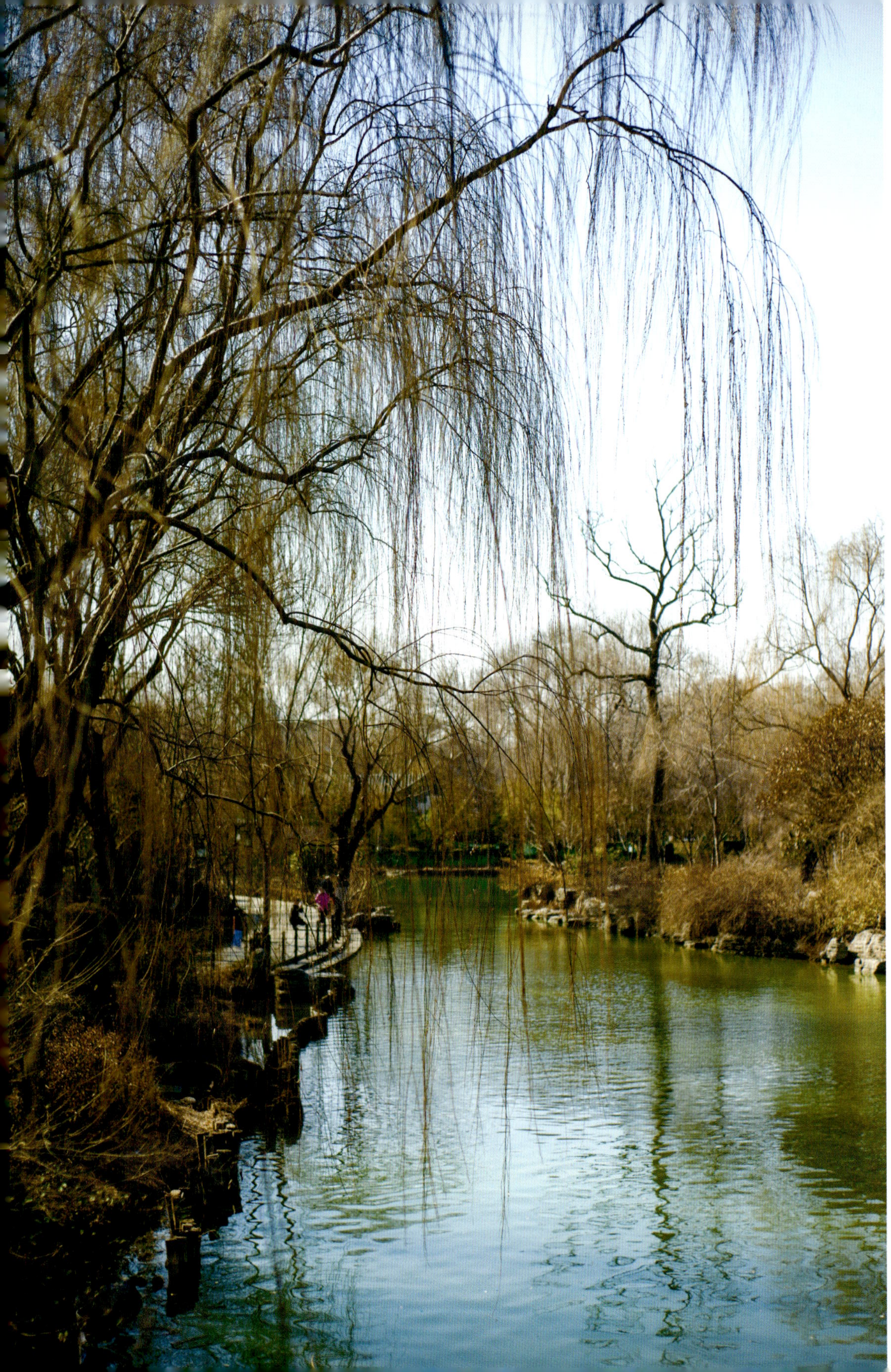

With its central location in the city of Jinan, Daming Lake and its surrounding park have played a role in many of the city's historical events. The lake is fed by the artesian karst springs of the area and covers a surface area of approximately 110 acres, making it the city's largest lake. Willow trees line three sides of the lak, which is known for the sight of these trees slowly dancing in the breeze.

One of the ancient roads in Jinan, Furong Street is a giant mecca of culture, temples, and street food that is enjoyed by locals and visitors of all ages. Weekends are packed, so weekdays are a better time to visit. It's located downtown, between the springs and the central square, where you can watch a light show at the fountain every night at eight o'clock.

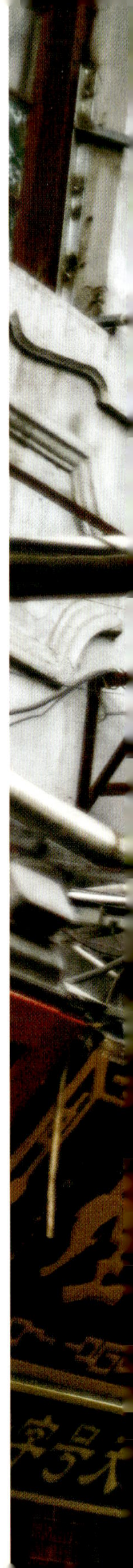

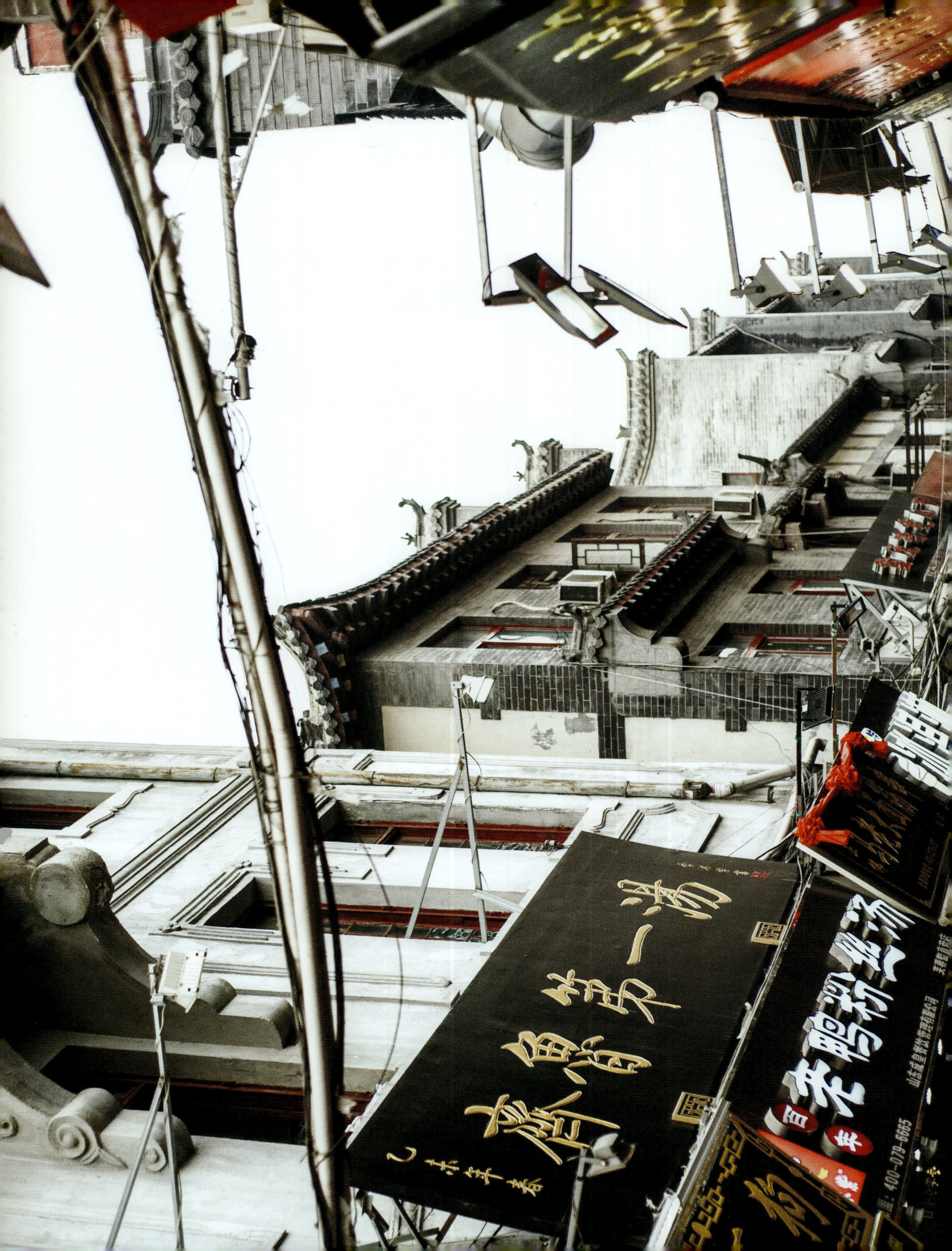
齊魯第一湯
老鴨粉絲湯
400-079-6665

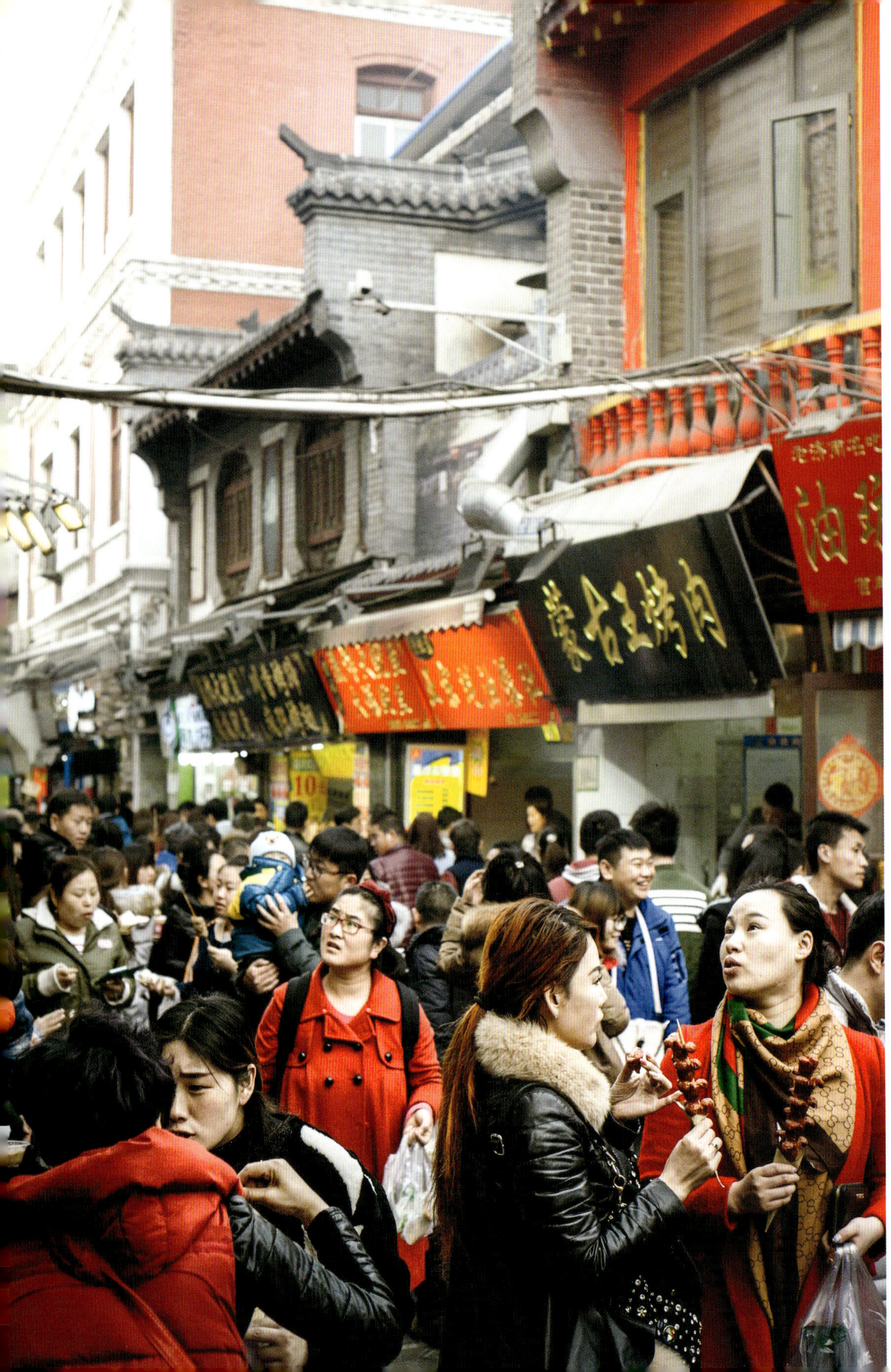

The air quality in Beijing can border on toxic, and as seen on the right, some people wear protective masks every day. On “good” air quality days, or days with less smog, you will see fewer people in masks, but you will still spot an occasional mask in the crowd. The toxic air quality in Beijing is the result of exhaust emissions from more than five million vehicles, coal burning, ongoing construction, and dust storms. China burns coal to generate electricity and provide heat in the winter. Additionally, during this period of incredible urbanization, one can pass by many construction sites every day.

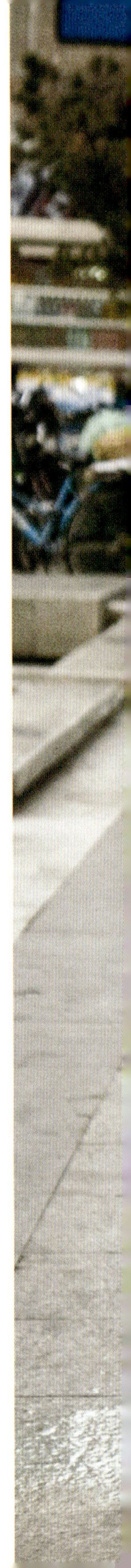

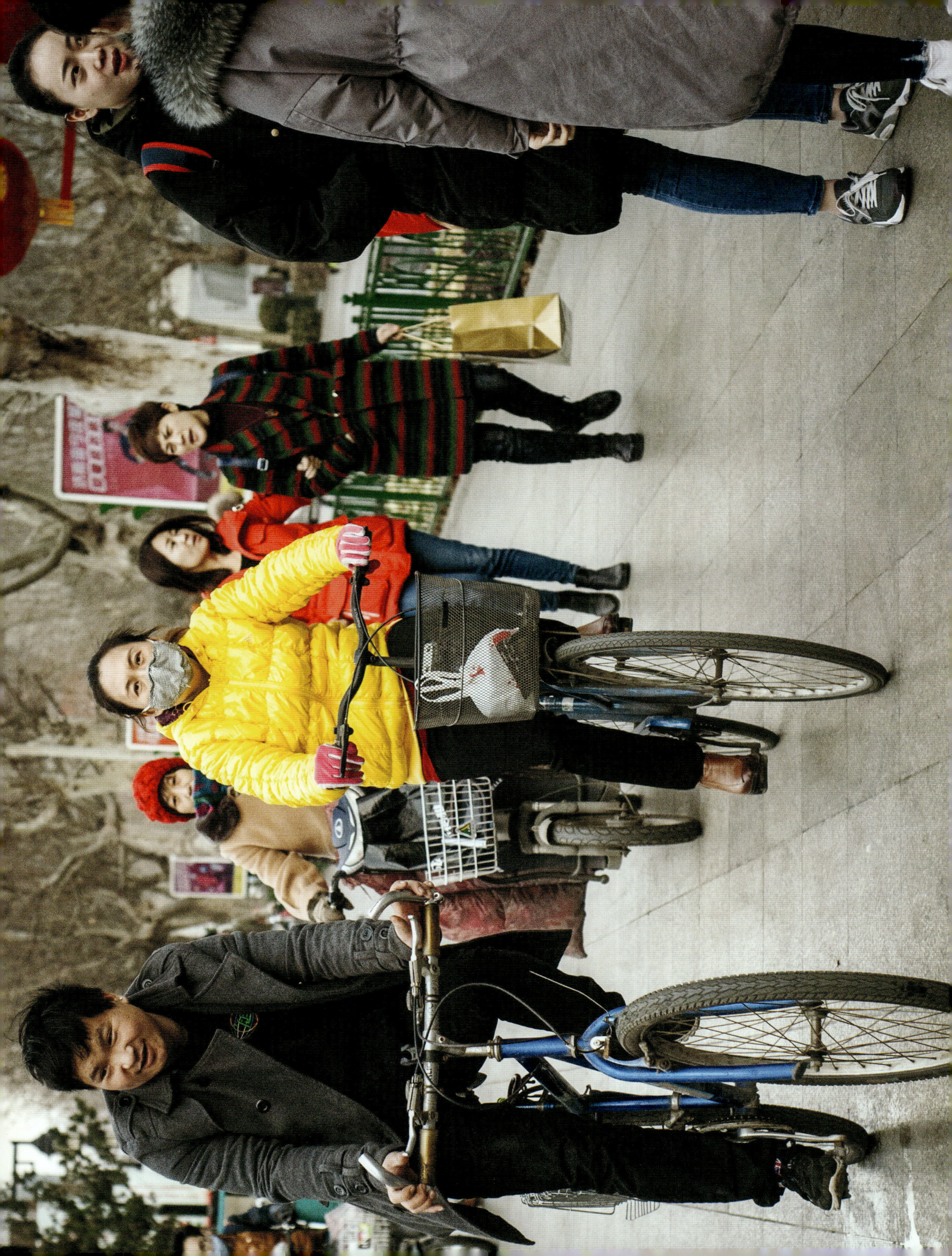

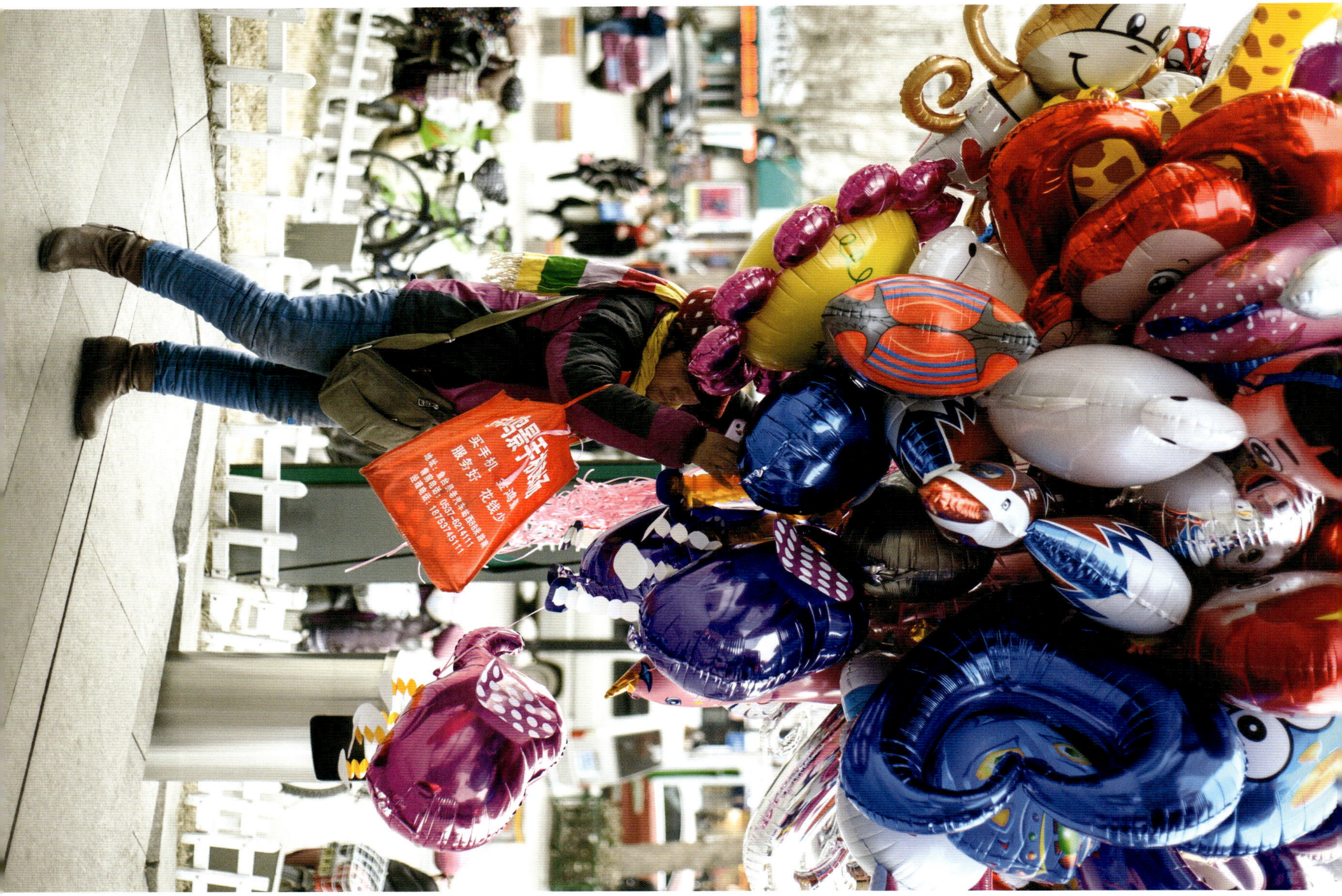
服务好 花钱少
0537-6214111
18753745111

This golden Buddha, located in the city of Jinan, the capital of the Shandong Provence, sits at the base of a hill comprised of more than one thousand Buddhas. The "Thousand Buddha Mountain" is home to Buddhas that have been carved out of the hill's rock faces by monks, as well as freestanding statues. It leads the way to a botanical garden and a cemetery to honor those who died in the the Xinhai Revolution. This is a very sacred spot, and is definitely worth a visit when touring the Silk Road. The site is open every day from dawn to dusk.

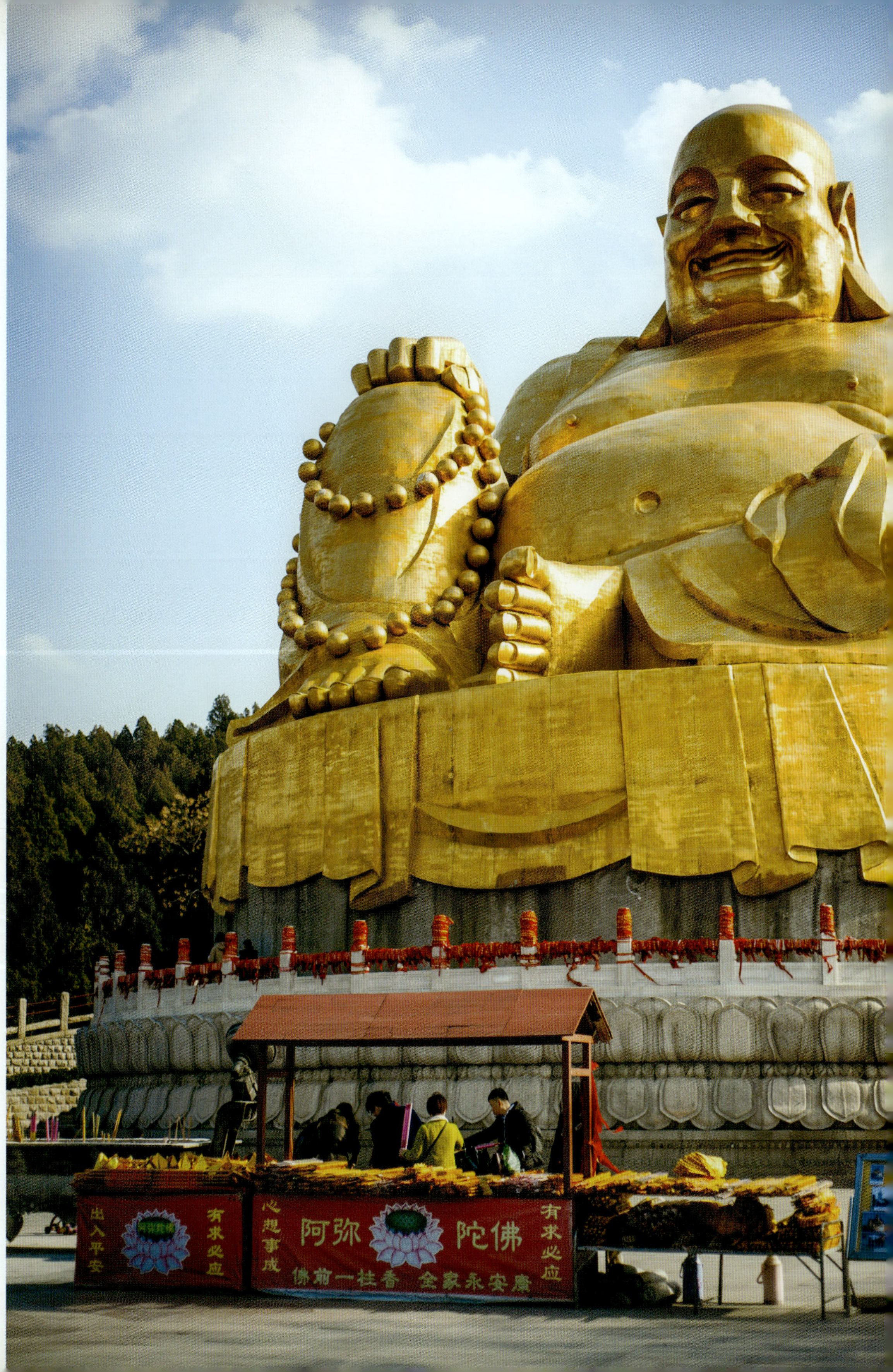

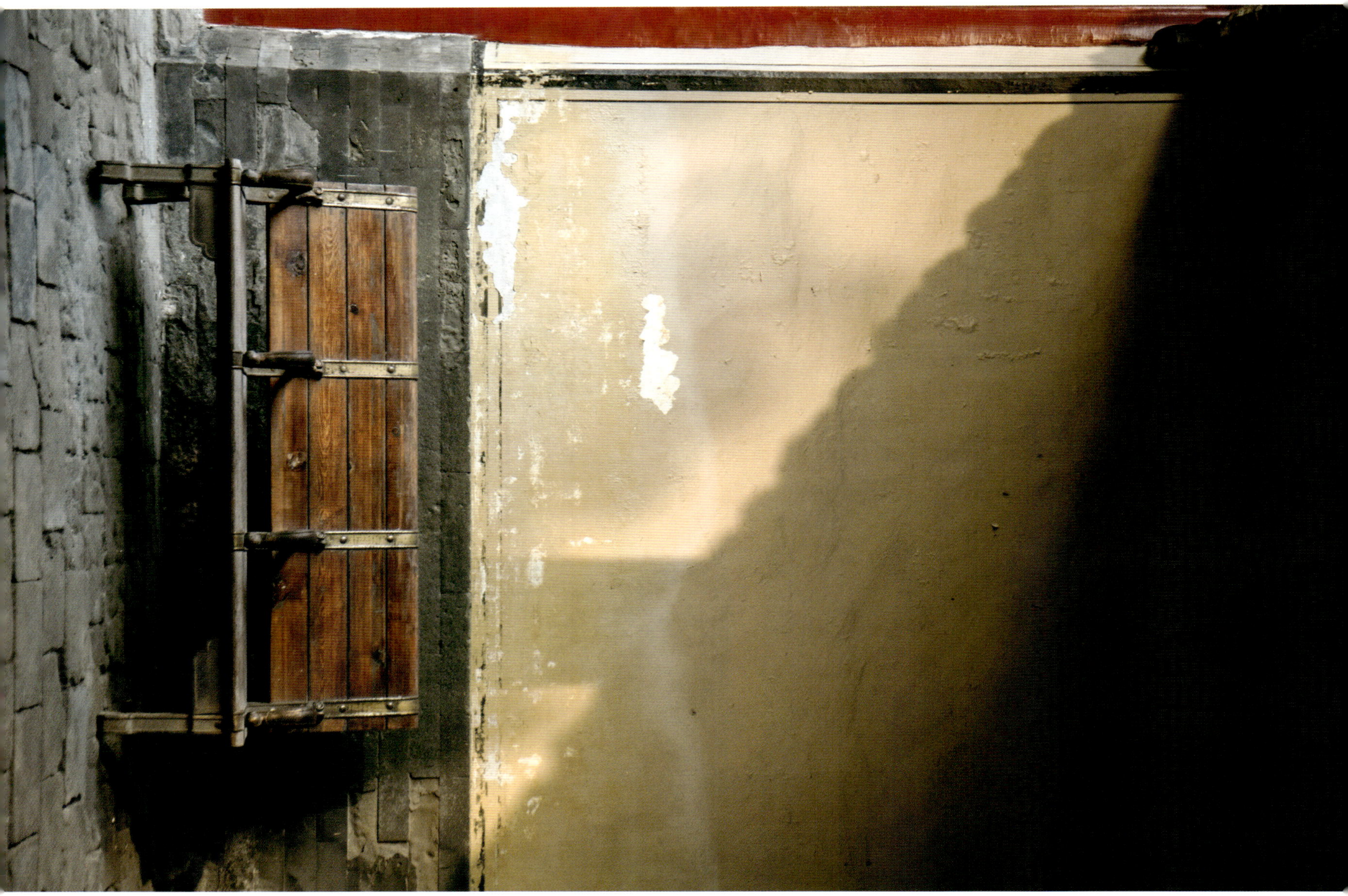

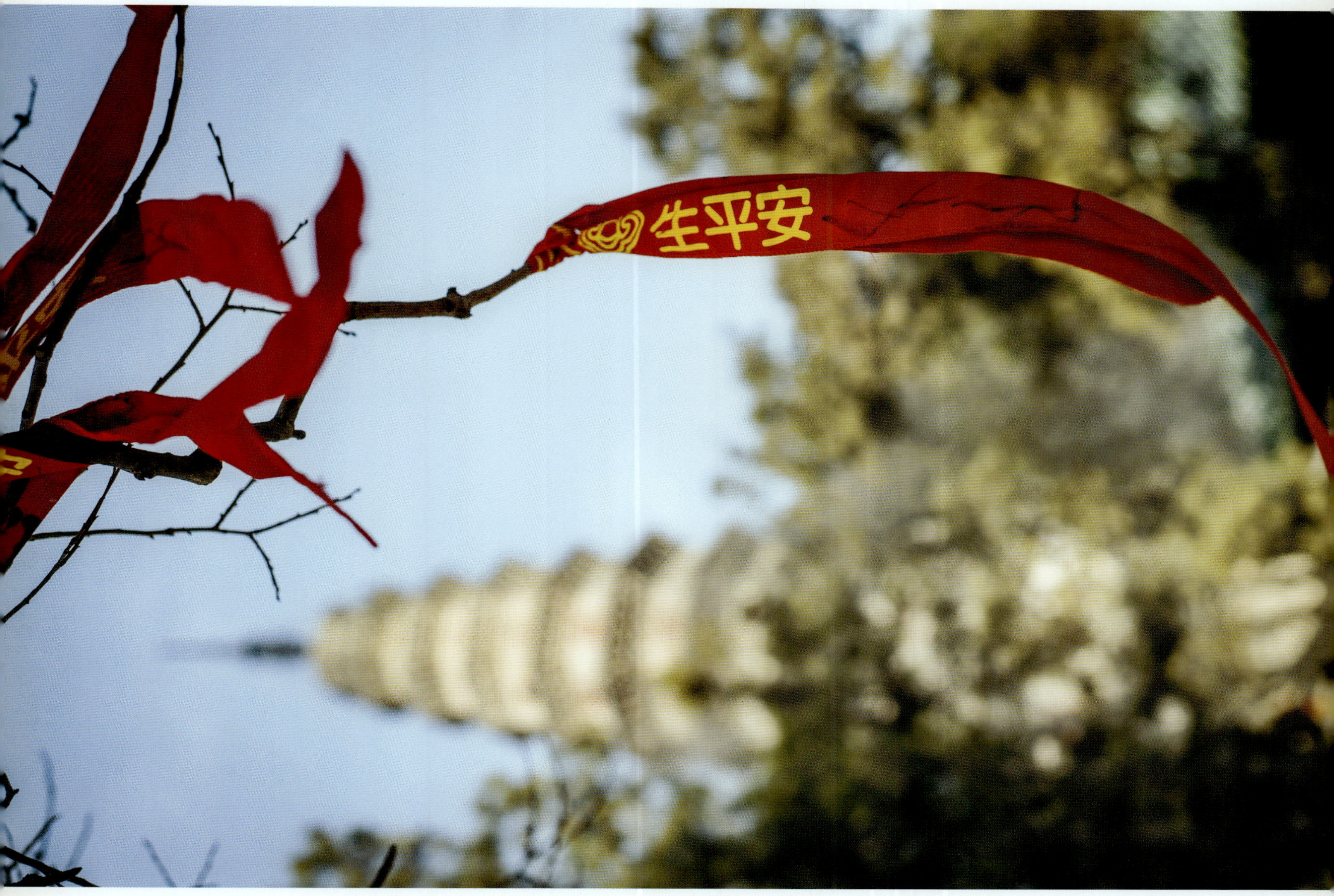
生平安

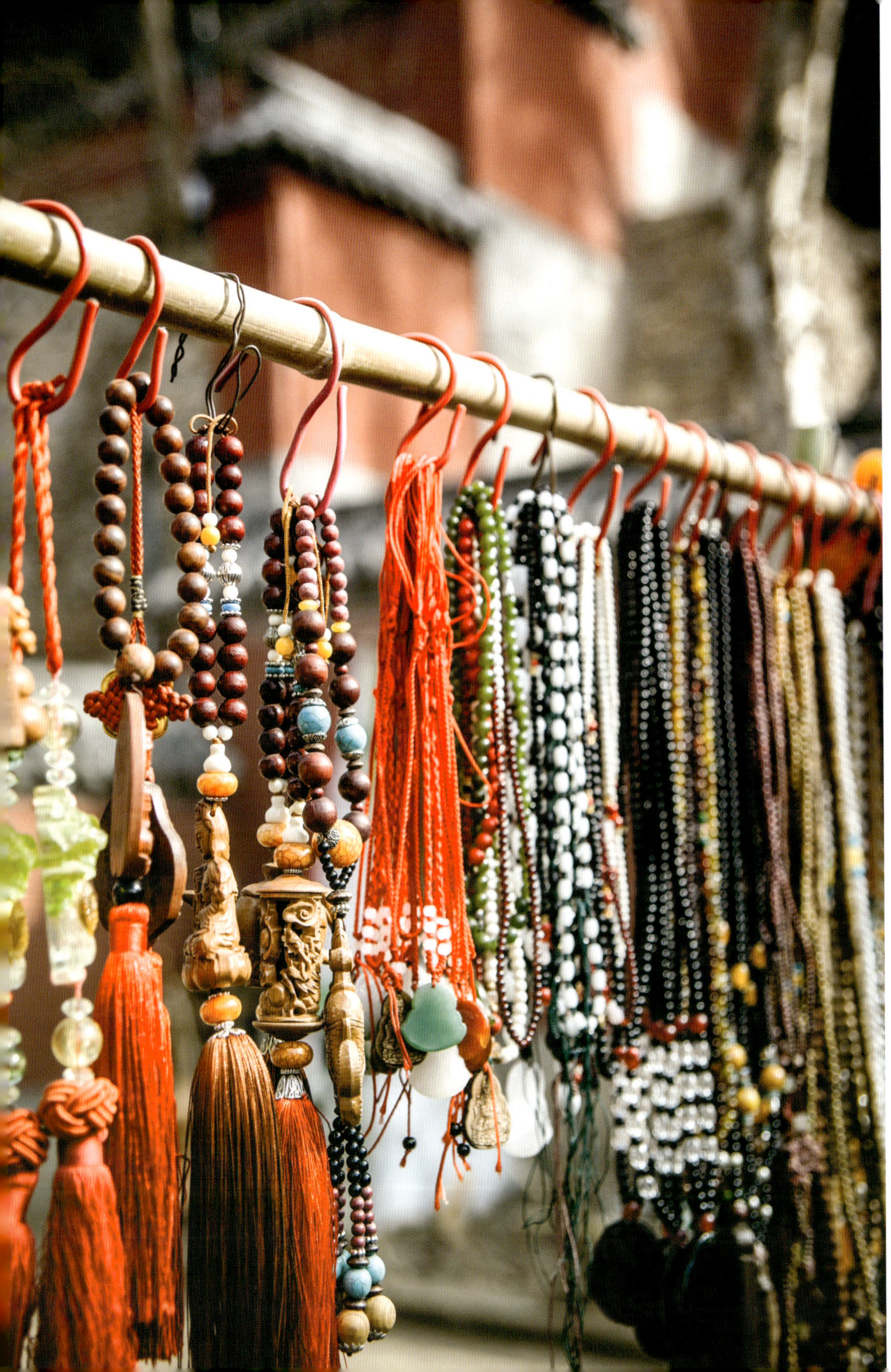

Prayer beads, which are available for purchase outside of many major temples, are part of the Buddhist culture. They are used to count the number of times a mantra is recited during meditation. A mantra can be a sound (like the familiar Om), syllable, or phrase, usually spoken in Sanskrit, that is believed to have spiritual powers. Hindus and Buddhists are among those who use mantras, but in China, Buddhists are the ones using mantras and prayer beads.

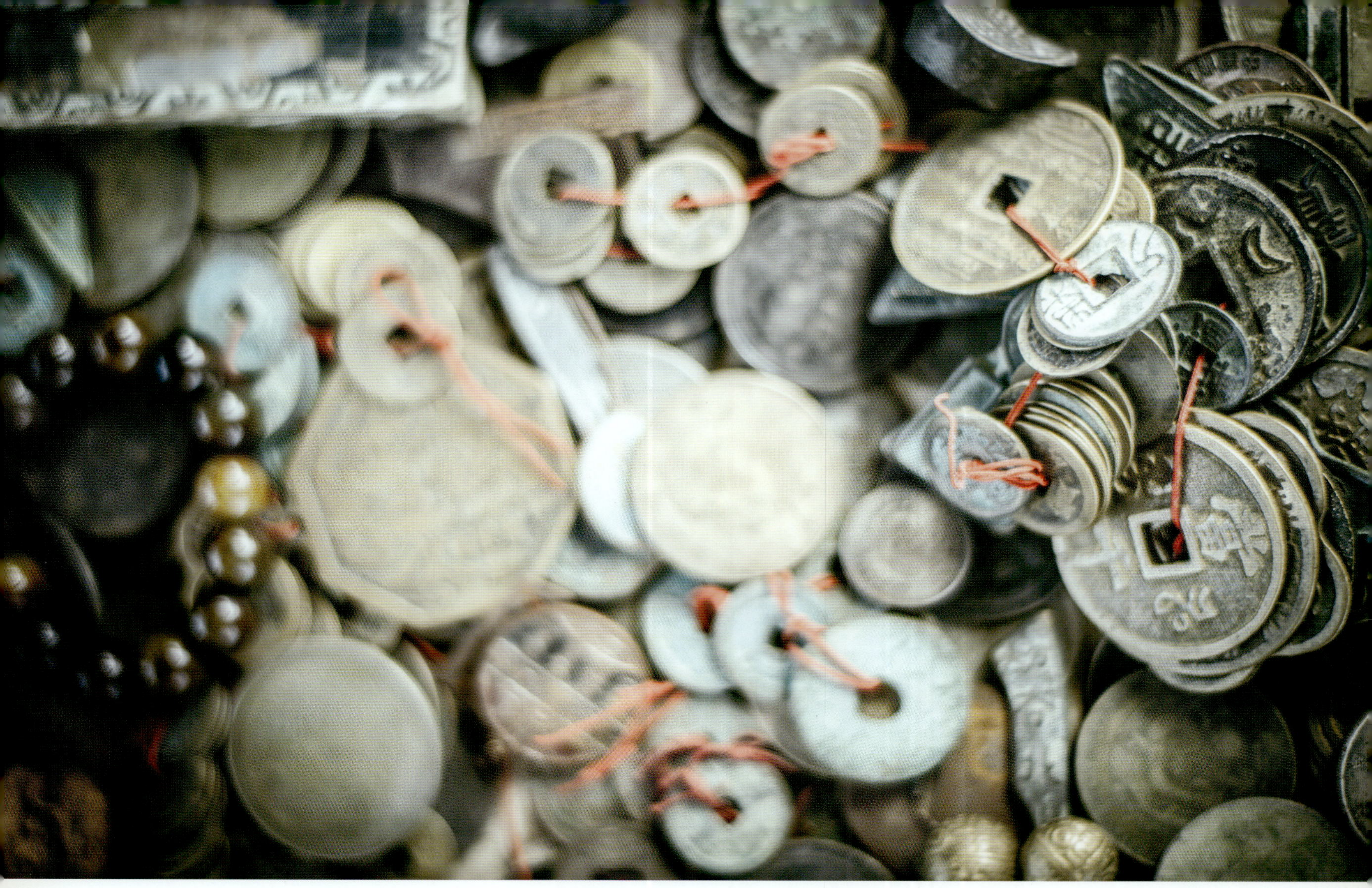

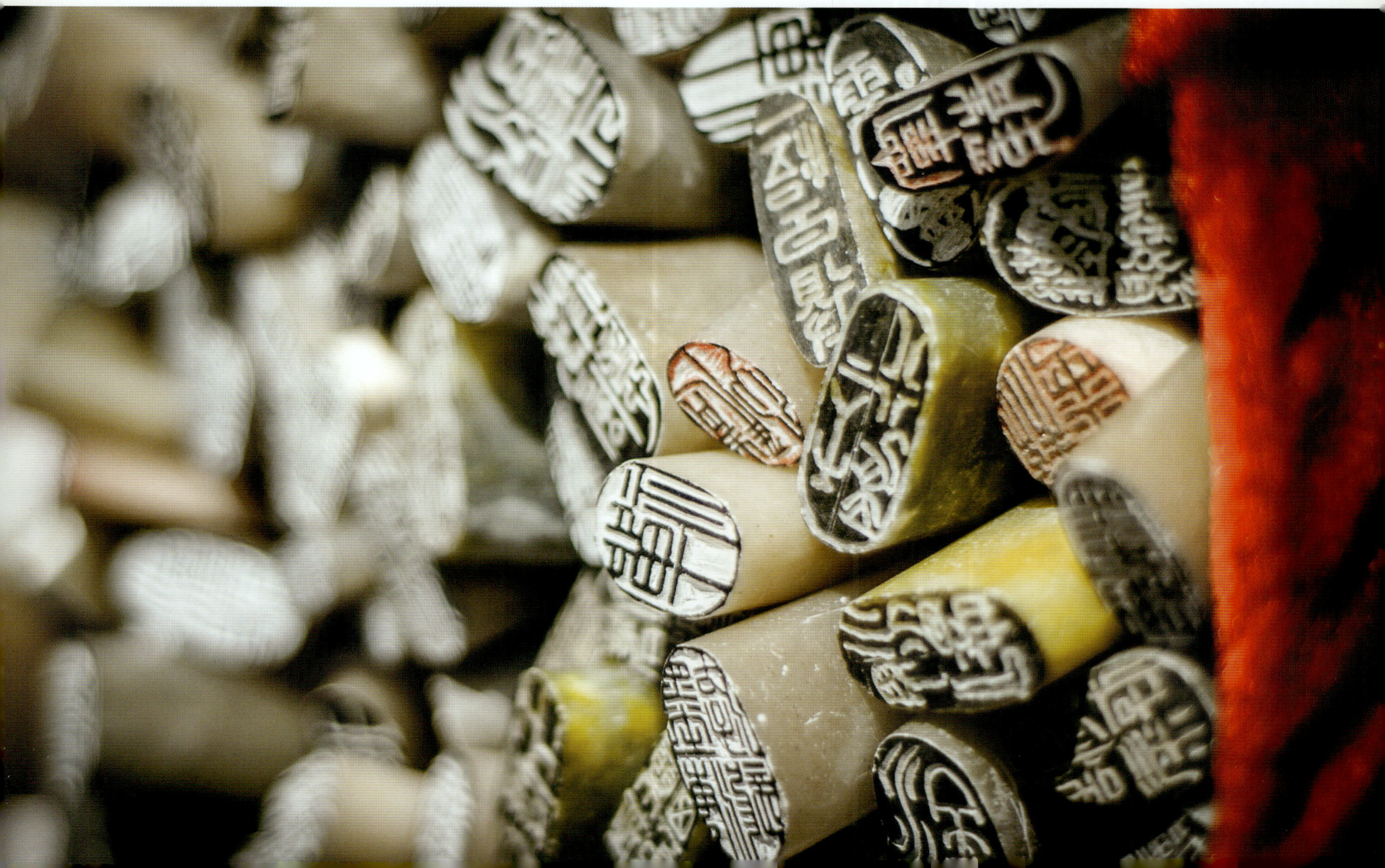

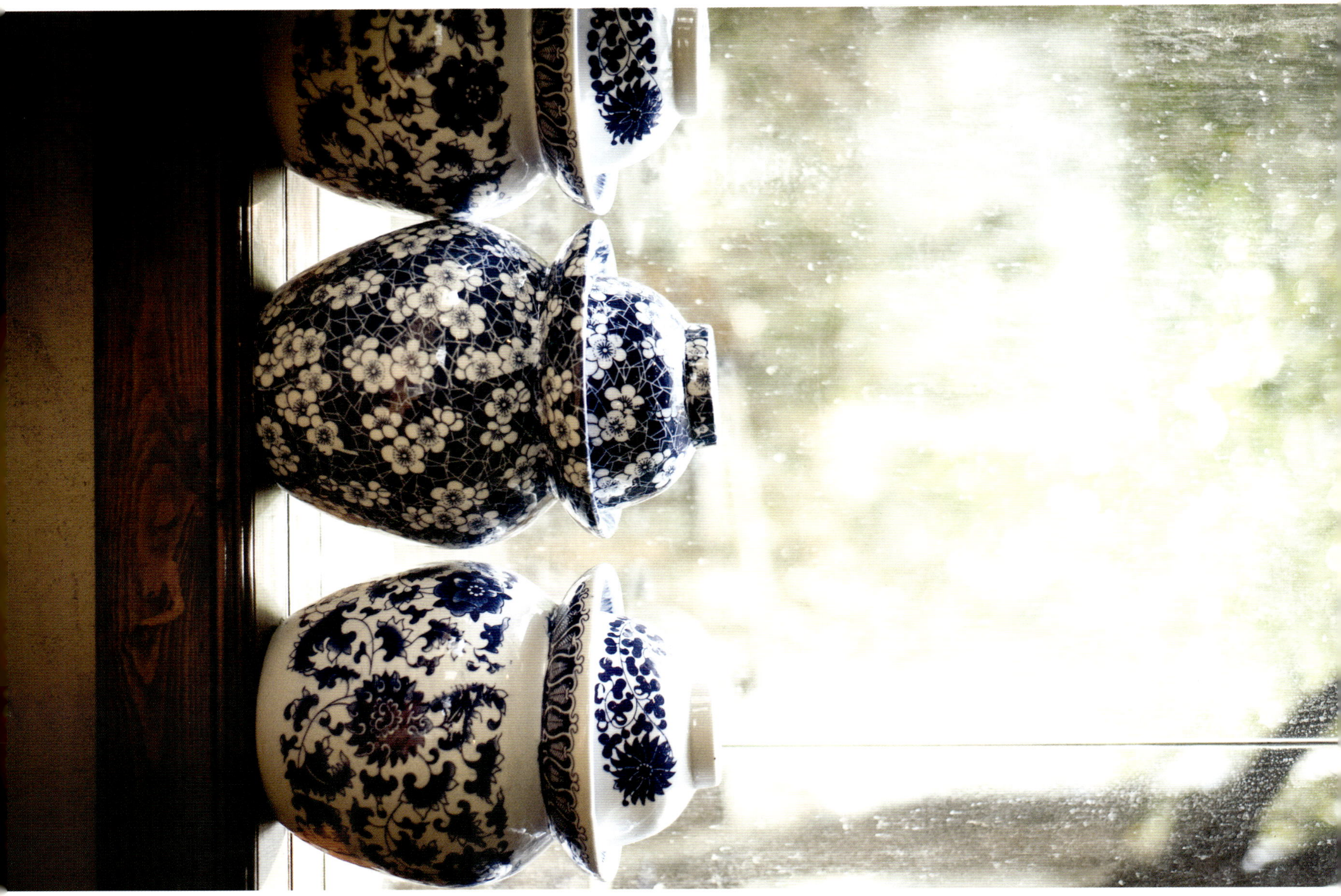

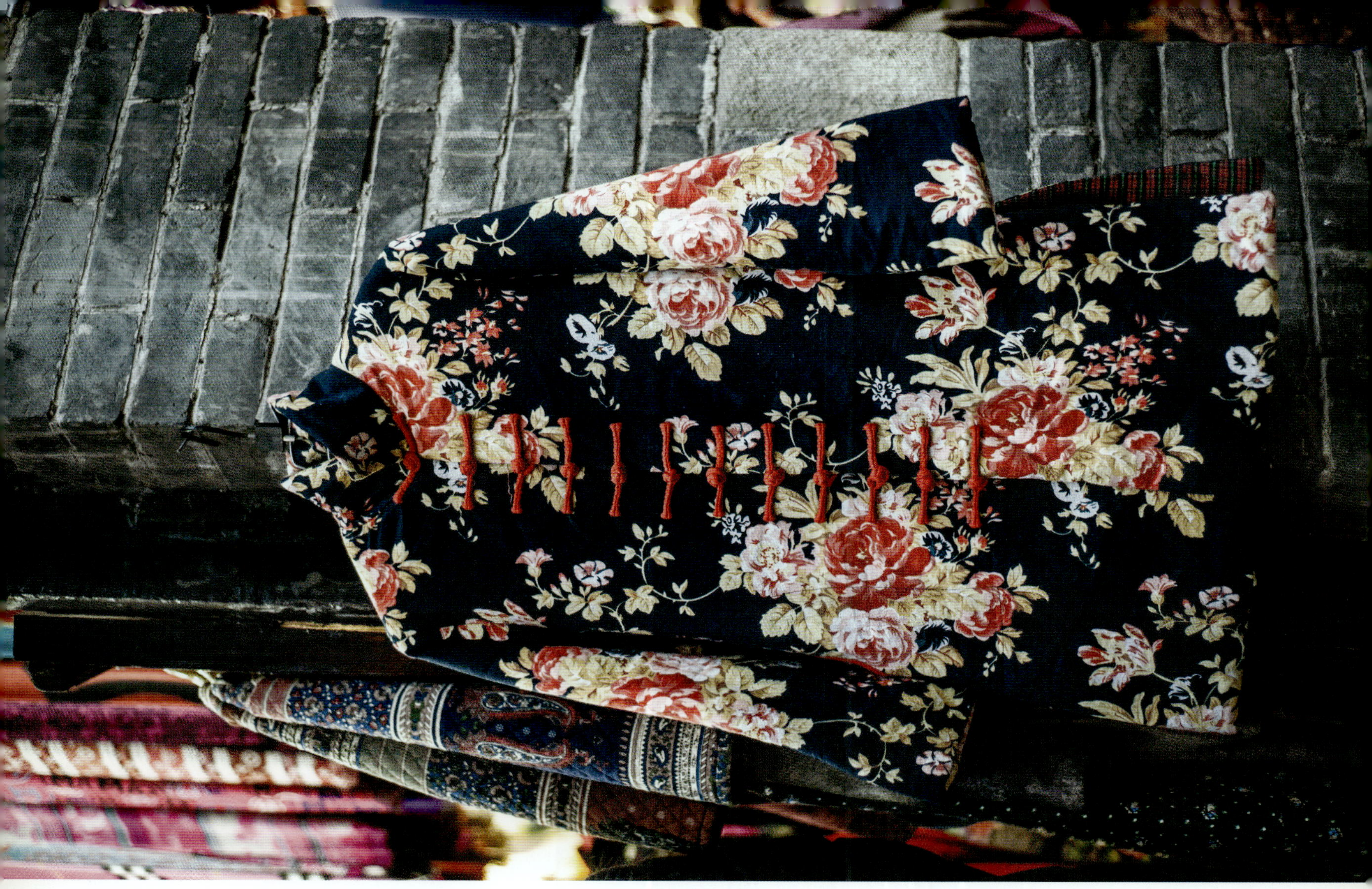

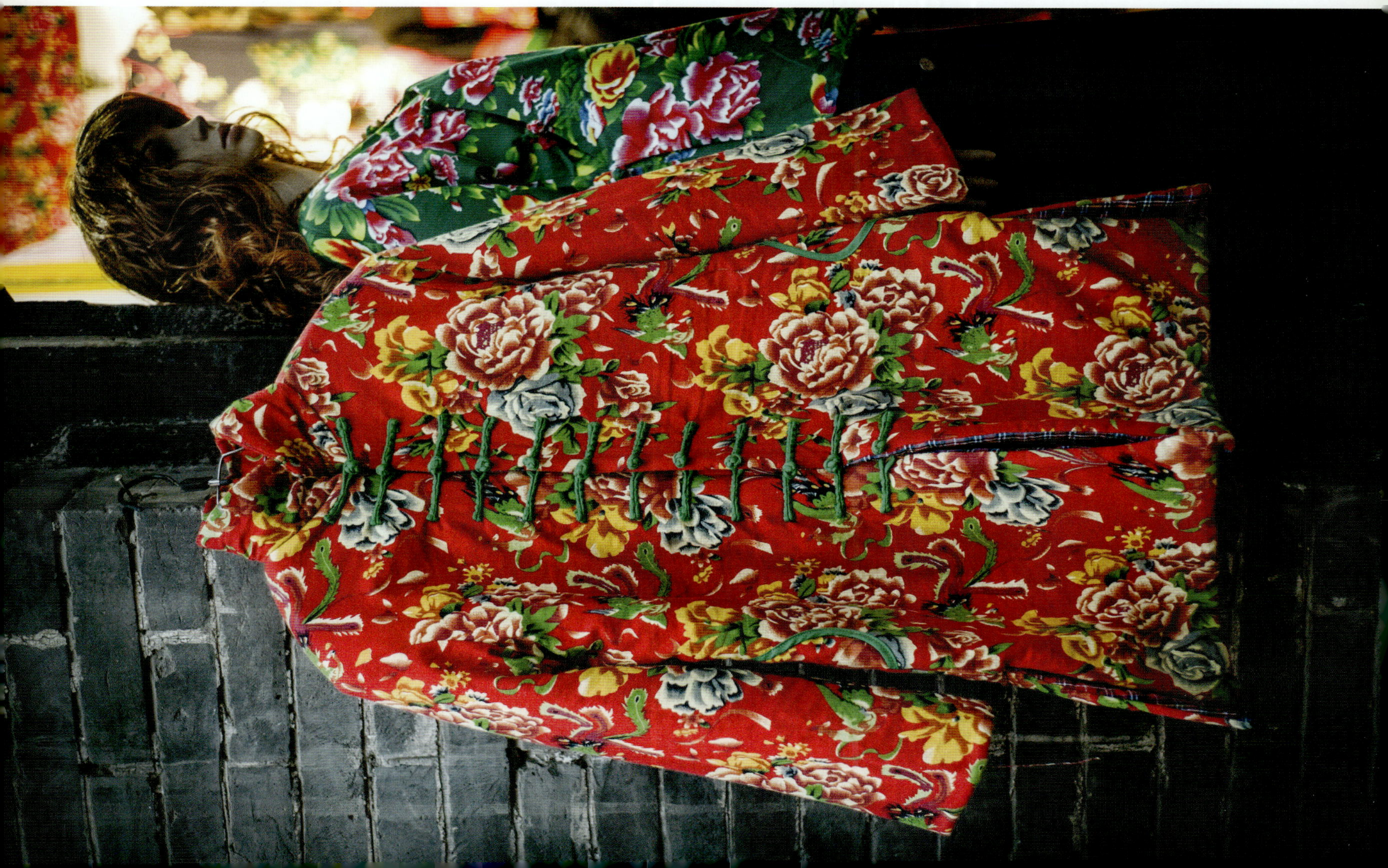

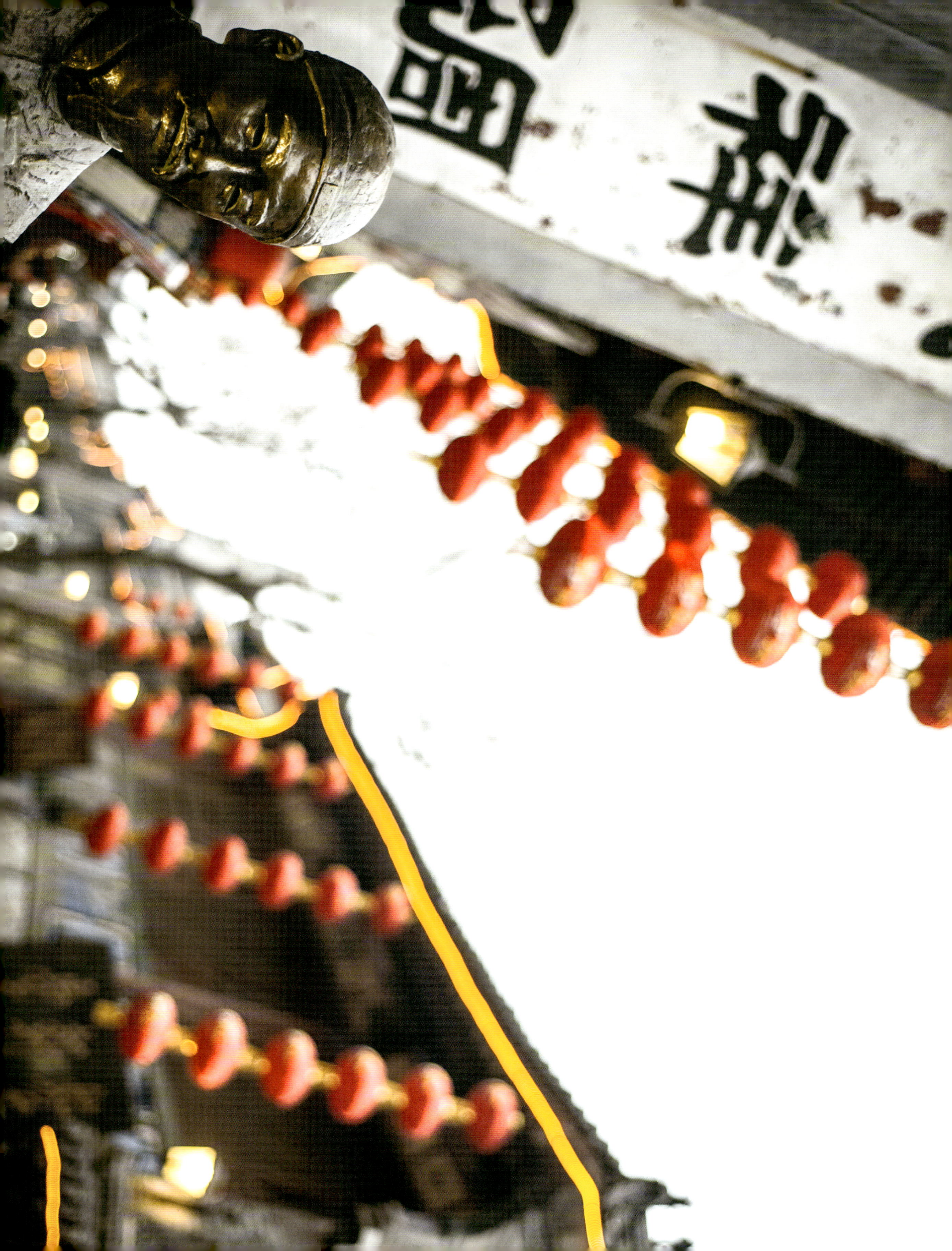

The Zhoucun Ancient Commercial Center, or Old Town in Zibo, is a living, breathing site that continues to function today. This area of ancient architecture, history, and breathtaking scenery is shared by locals and tourists alike. During Chinese New Year, brightly colored lanterns decorate the sky. Parades are also common and showcase folk art performances, music, fireworks, and fifteen-foot-long dragons.

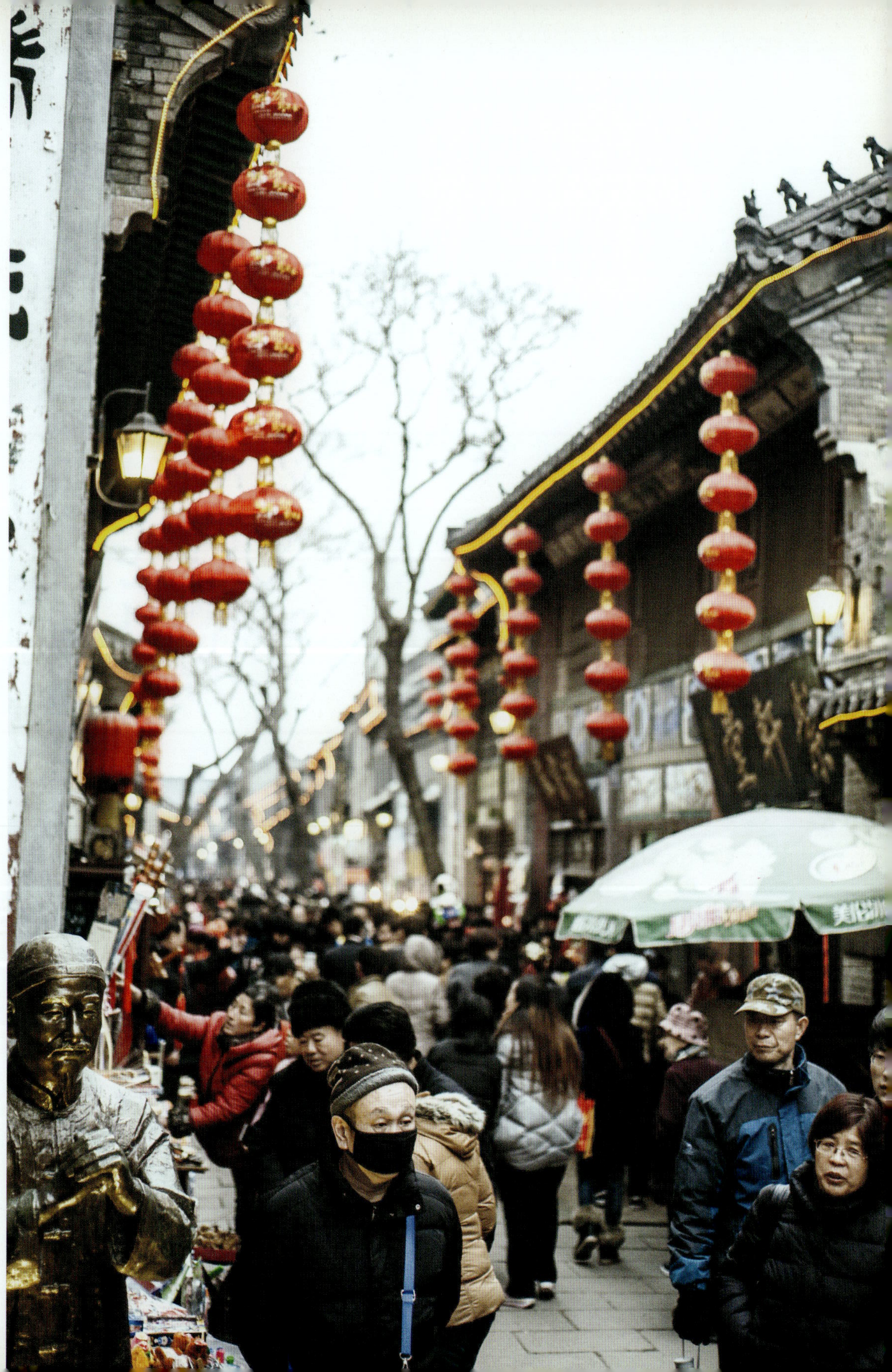

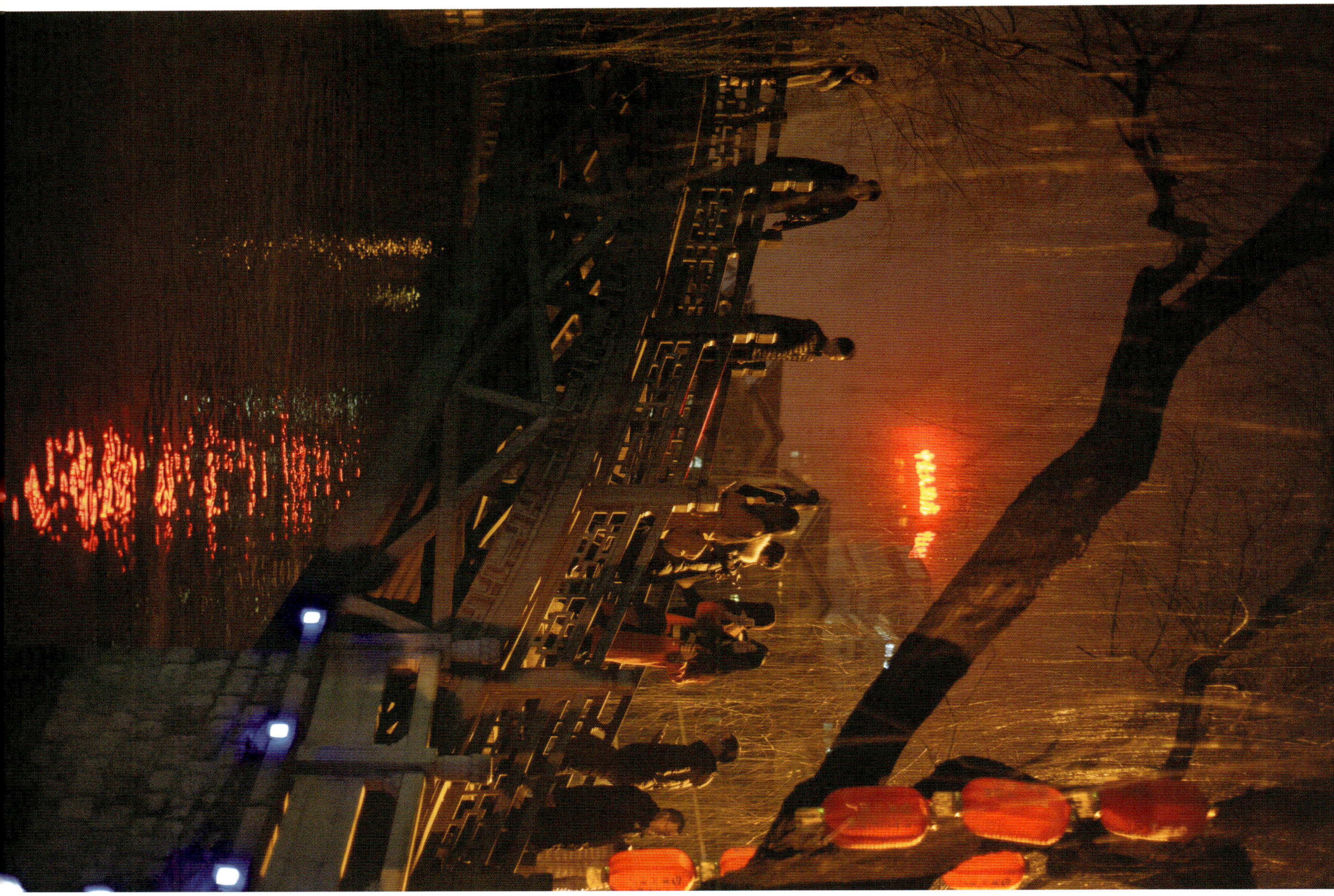

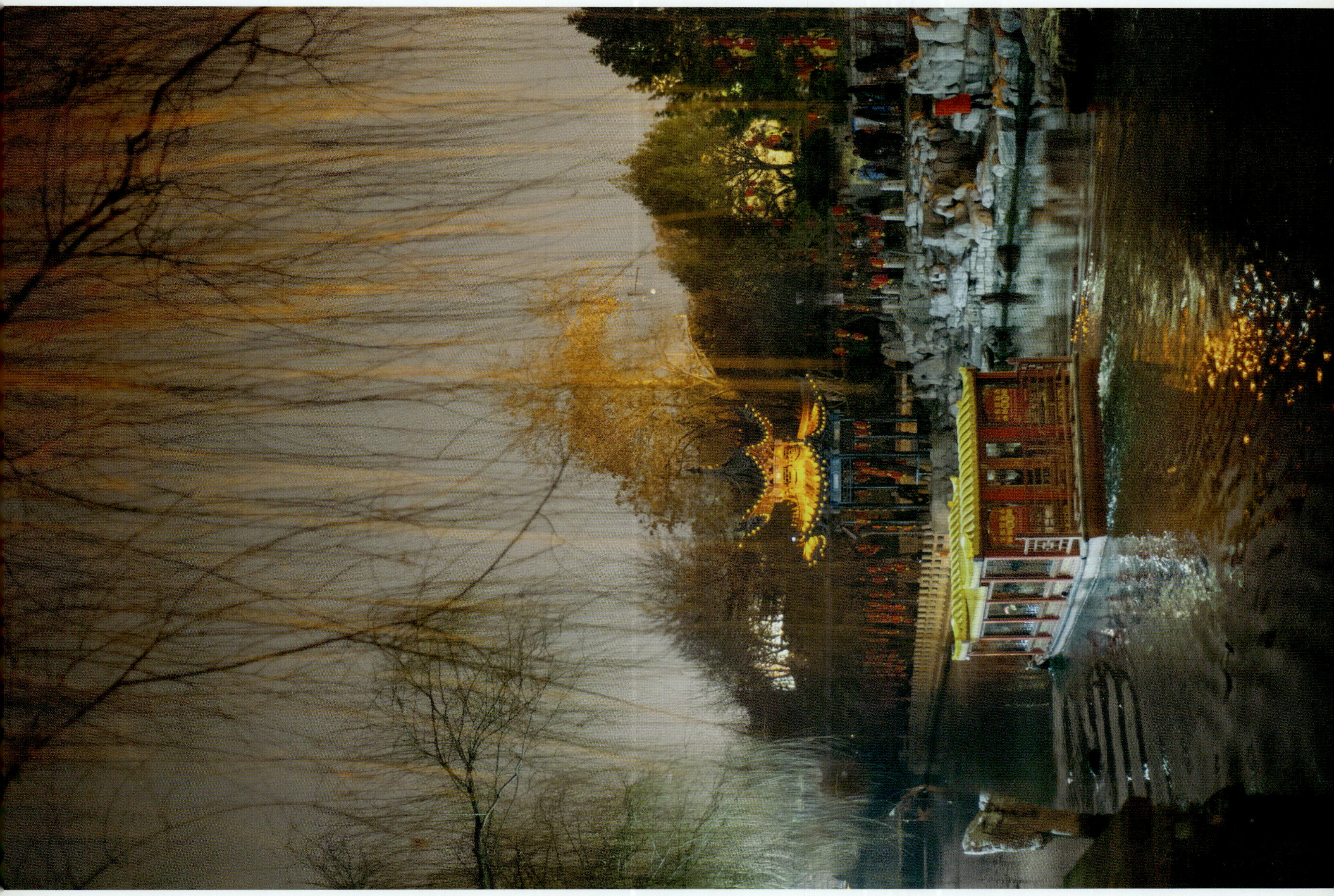

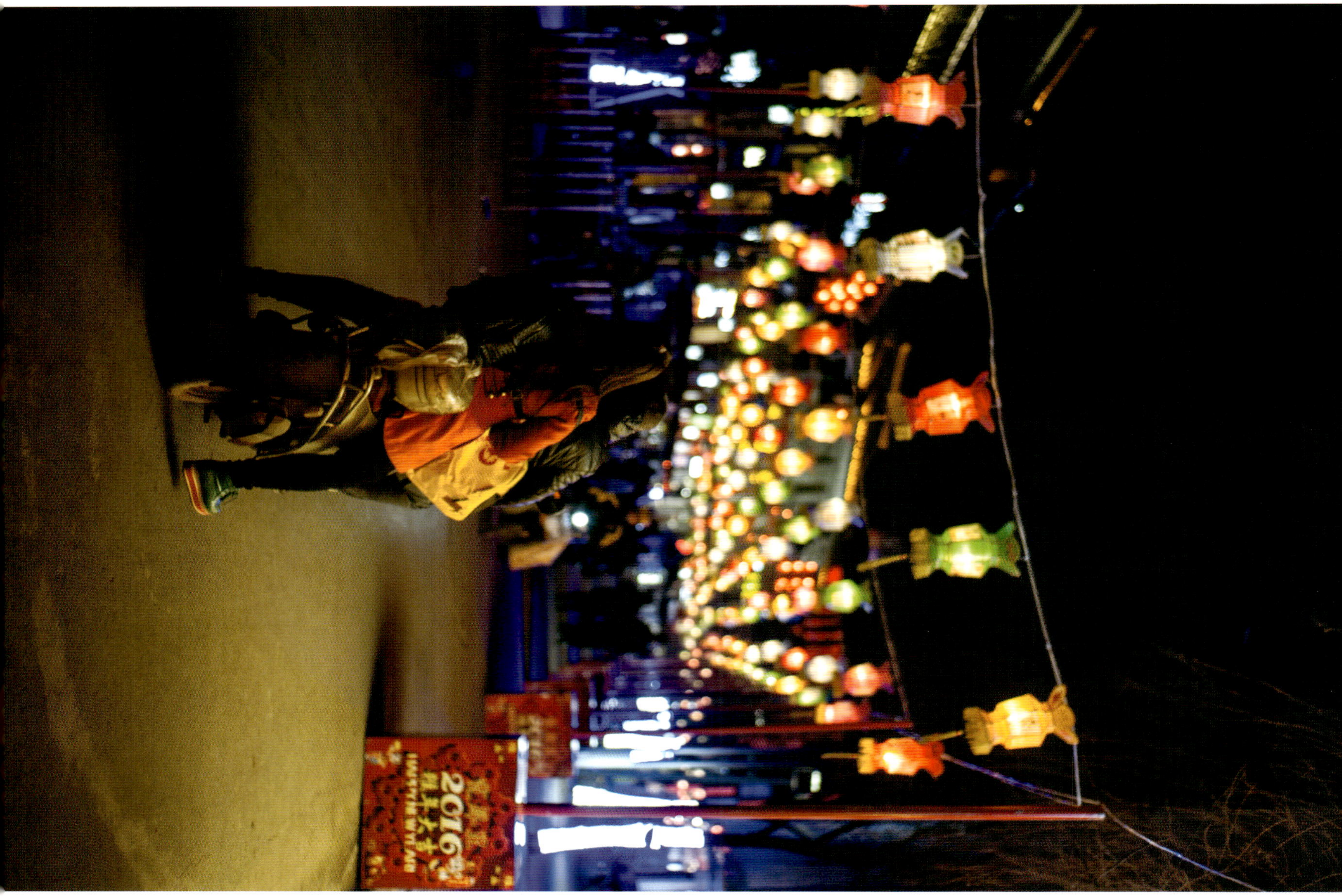

The Liberation Pavilion in Jinan commemorates the storming of the city of Jinan by the People's Liberation Army at the Battle of Jinan during the Chinese Civil War. Illuminated at night, the monument is poised above the city.

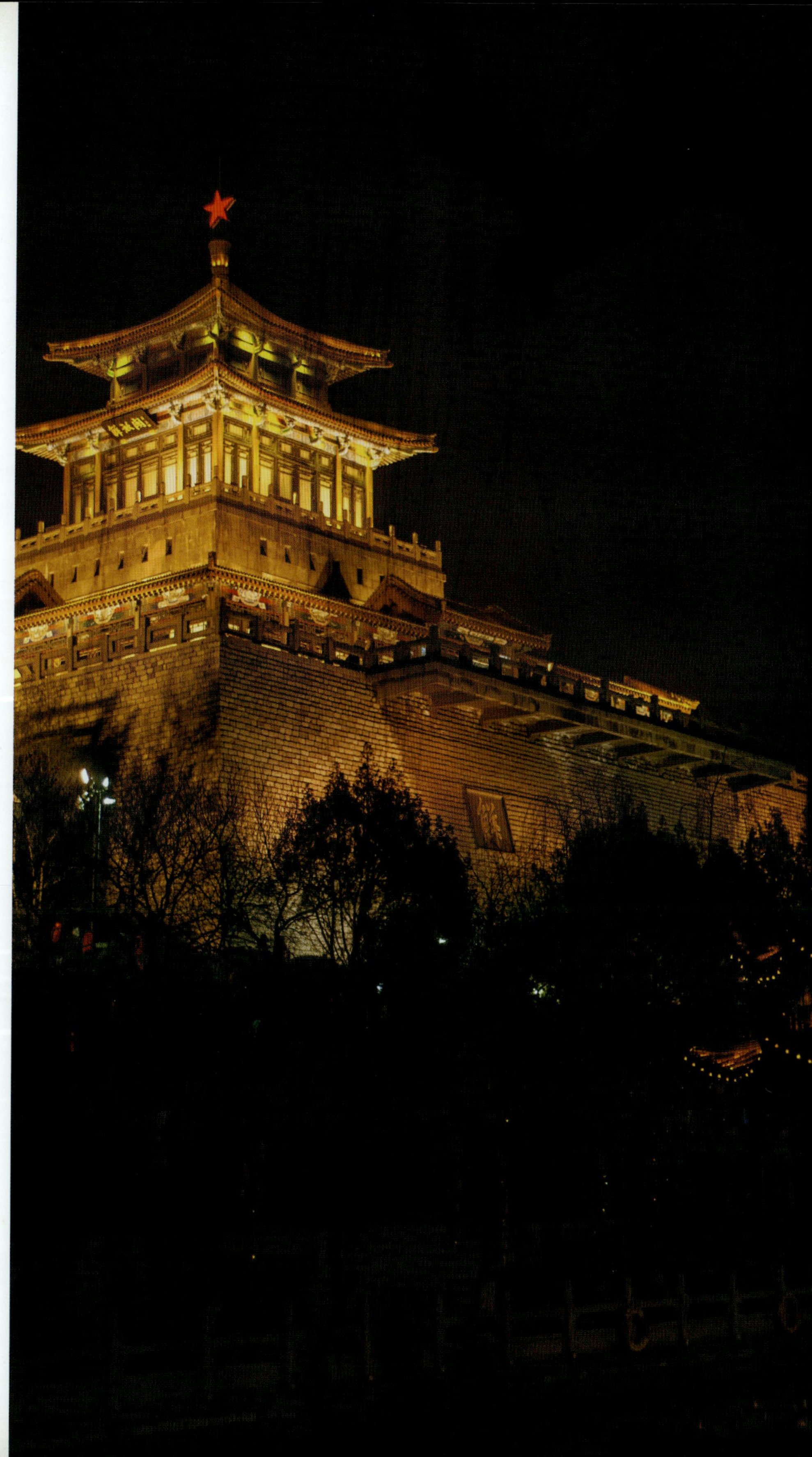

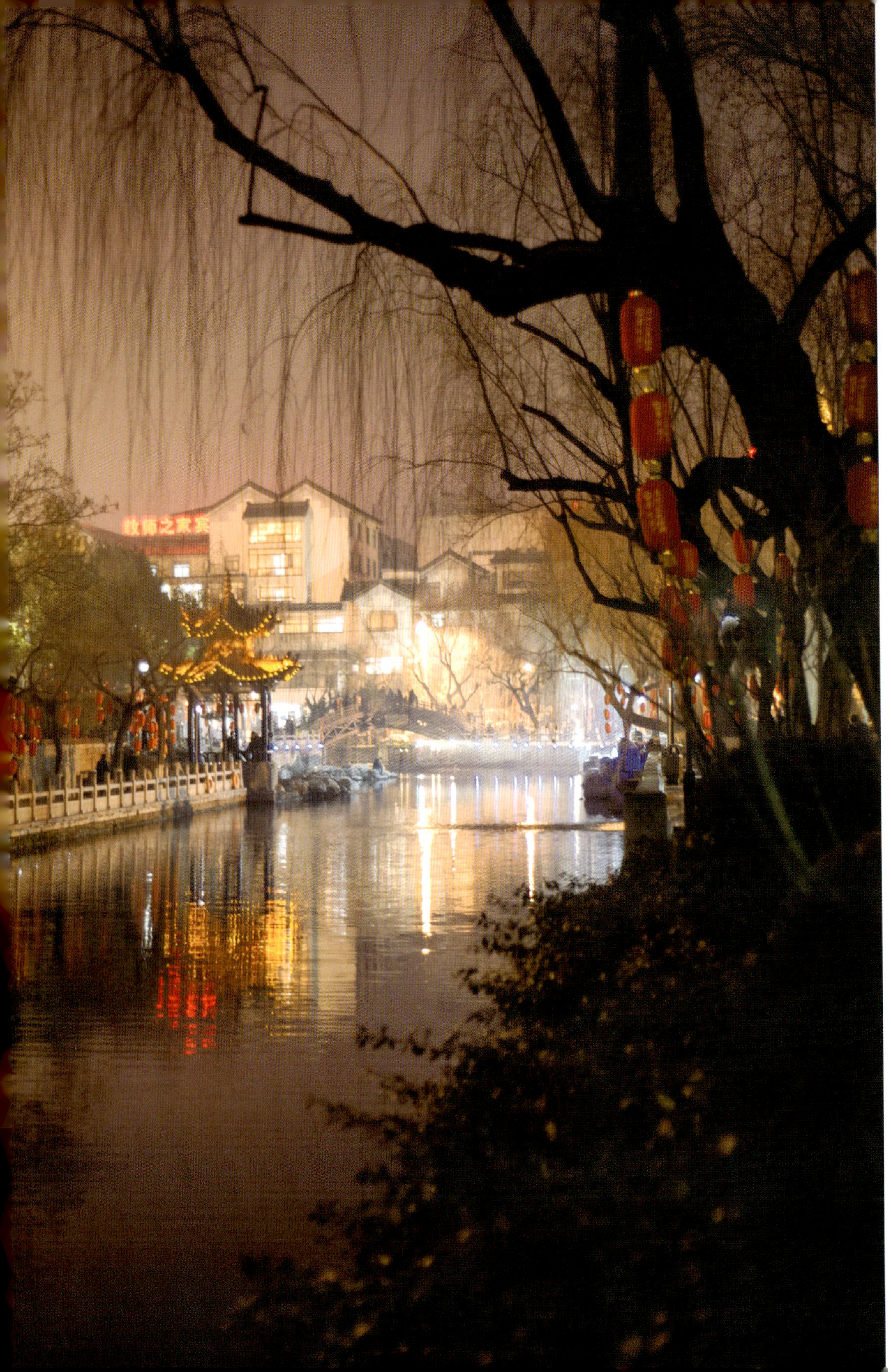

A restored ancient commercial center in Jinan is decorated with beautiful lanterns for the New Year celebration.

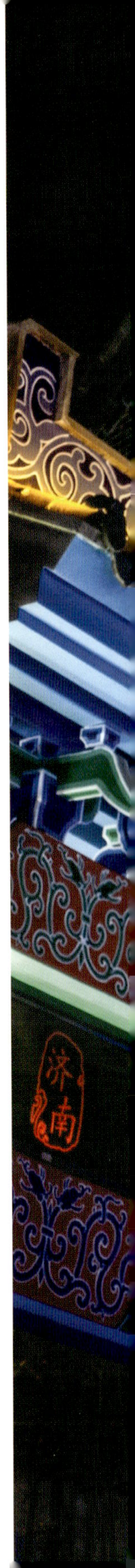

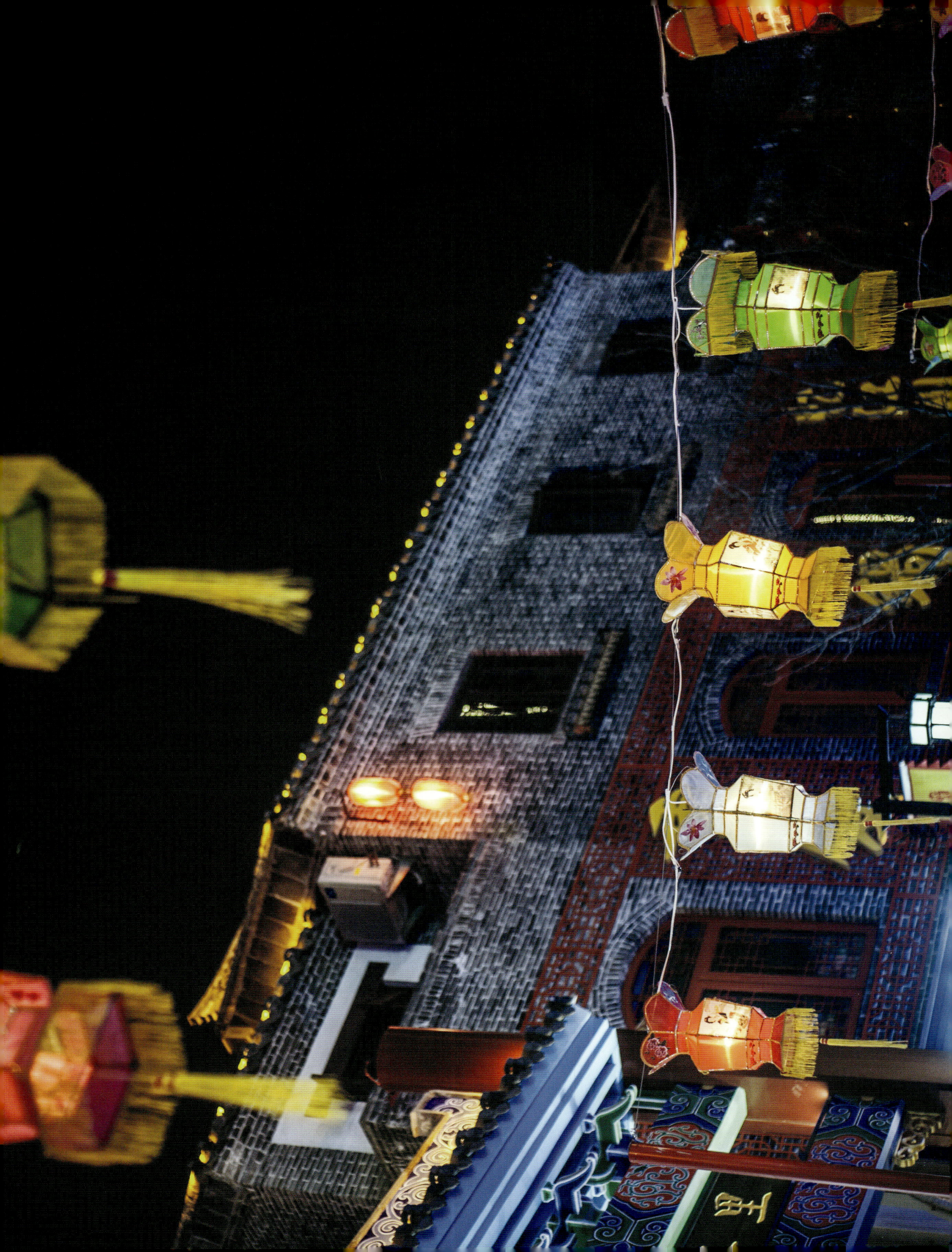

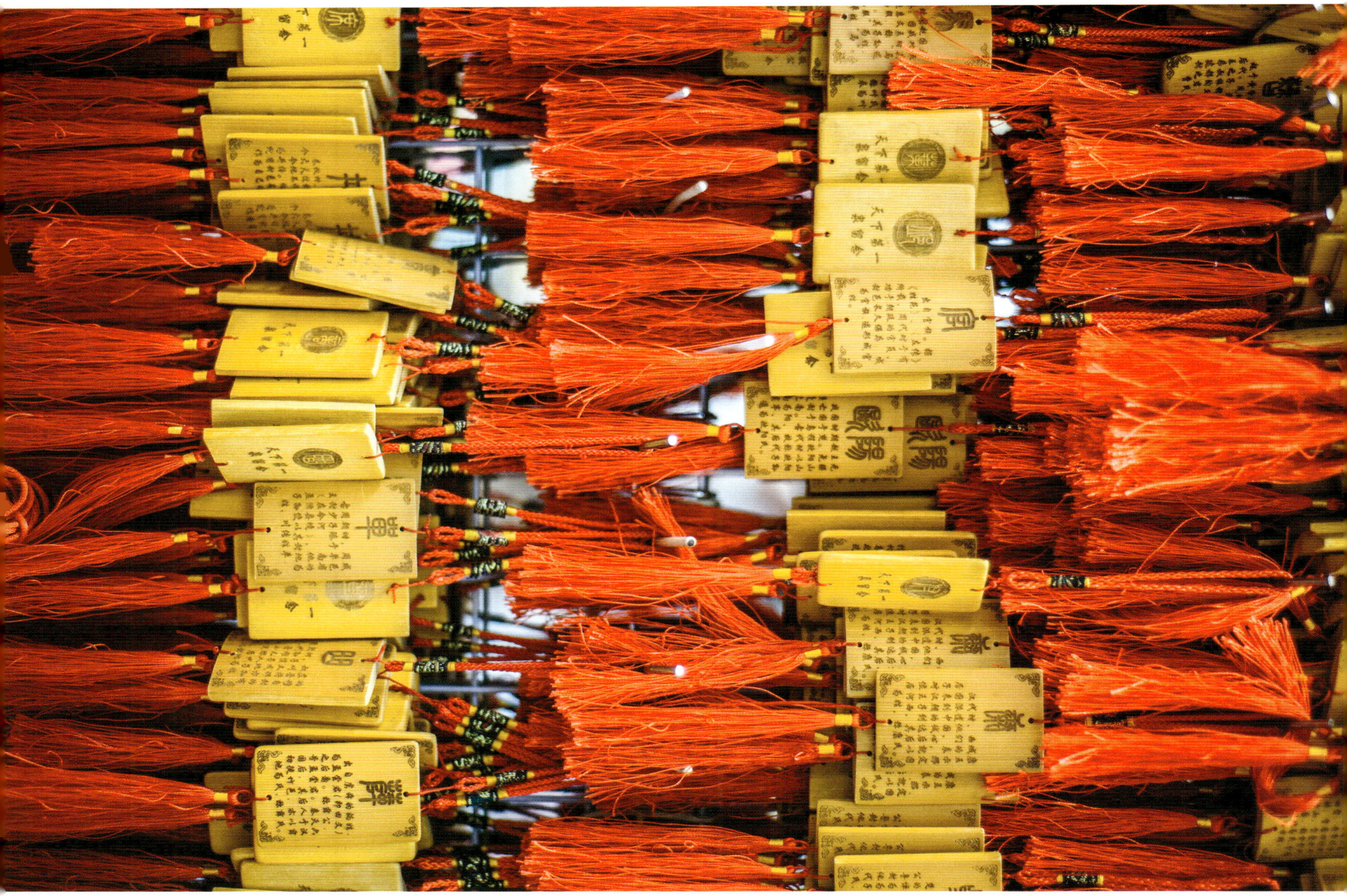

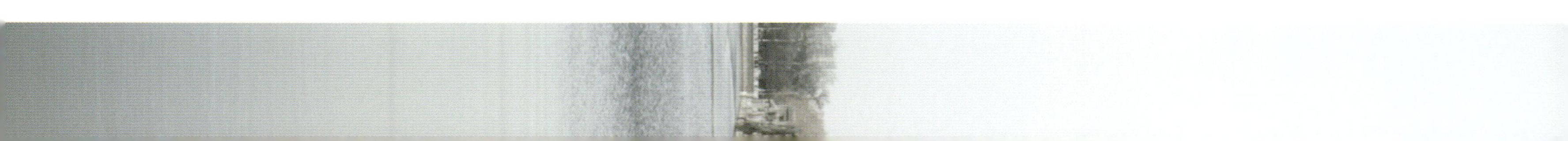

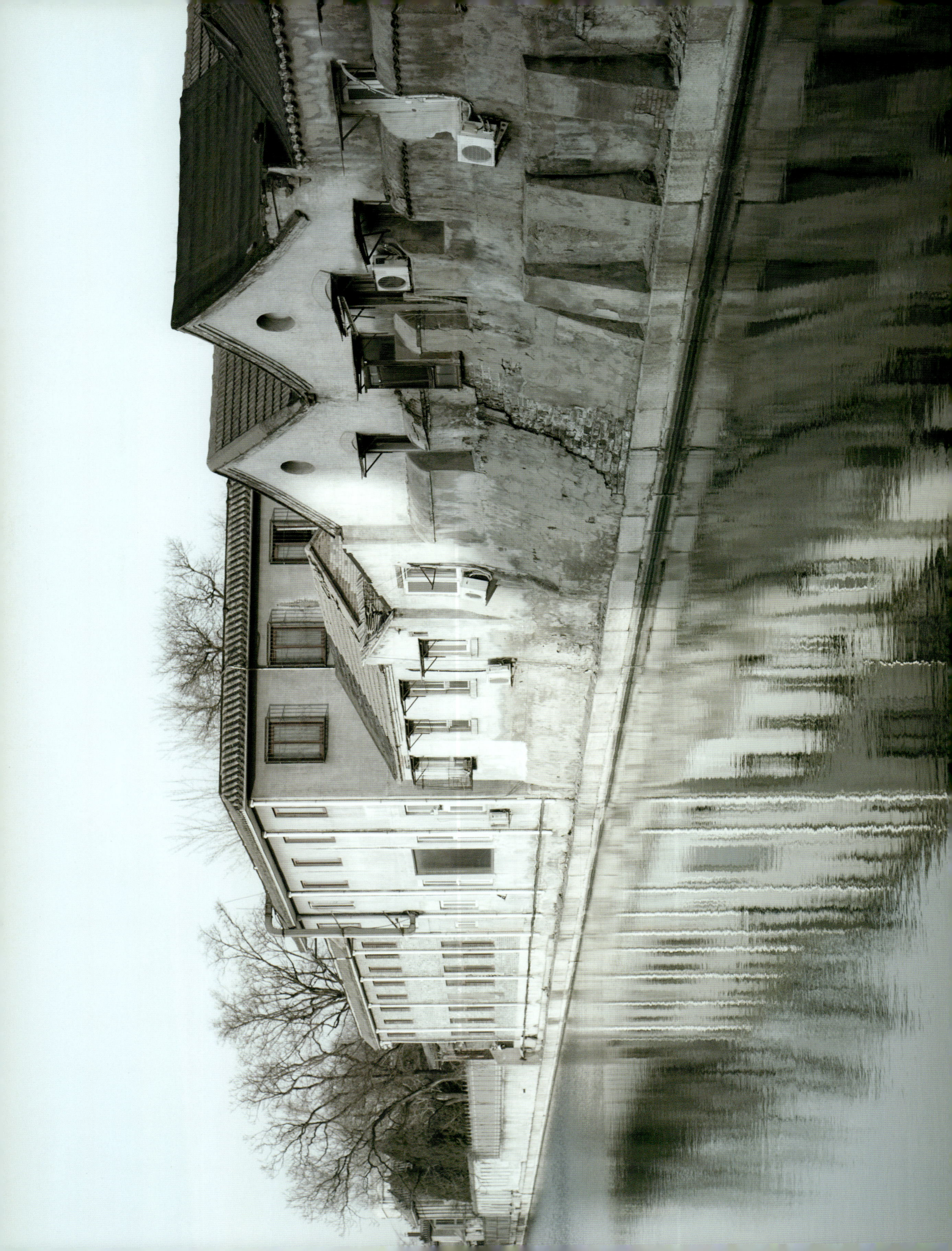

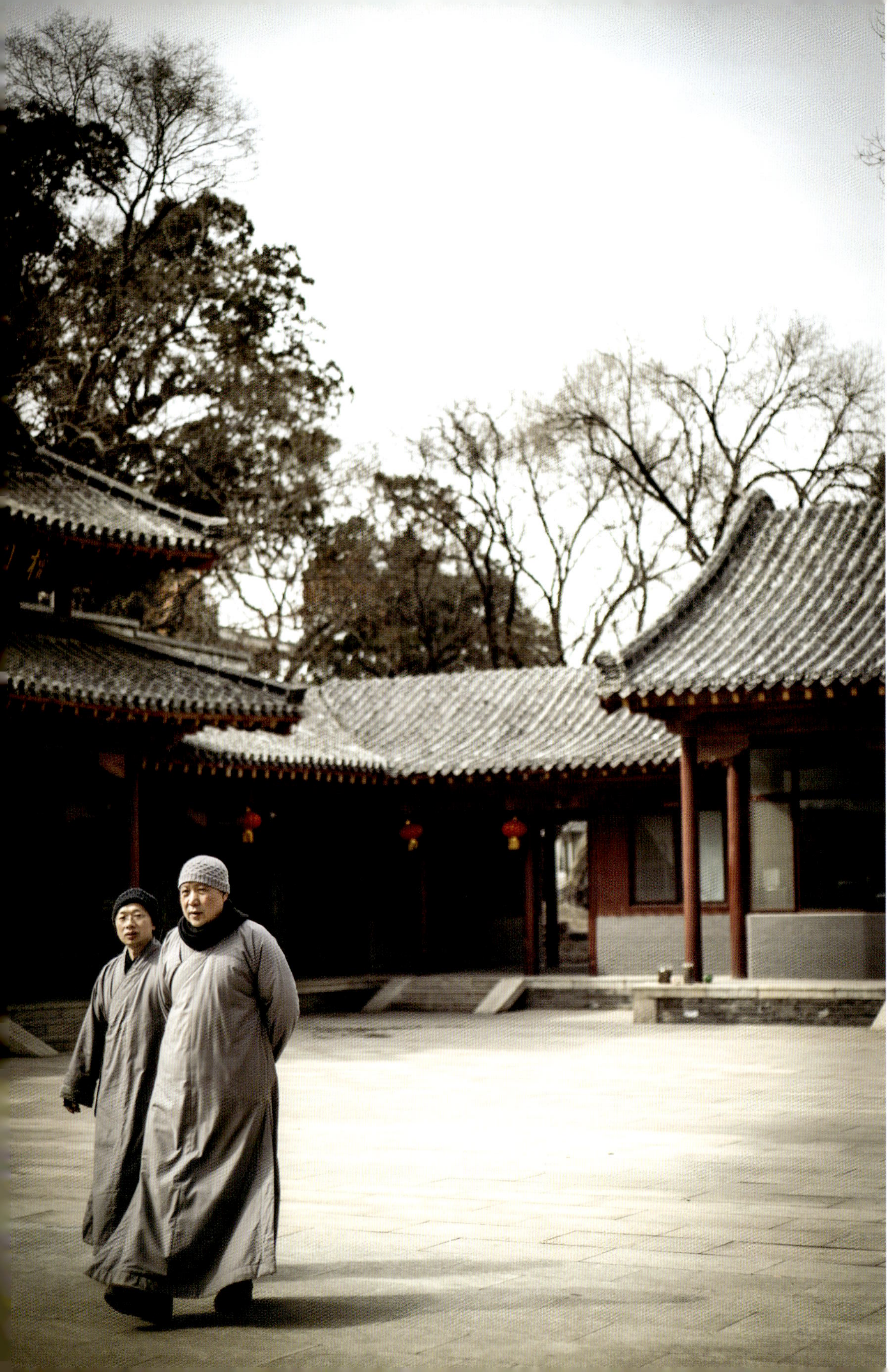

Marching on the streets of Jinan.

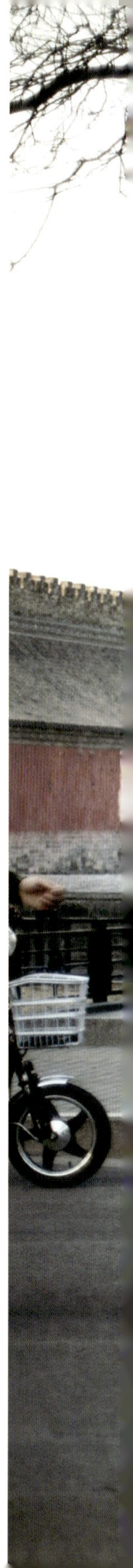

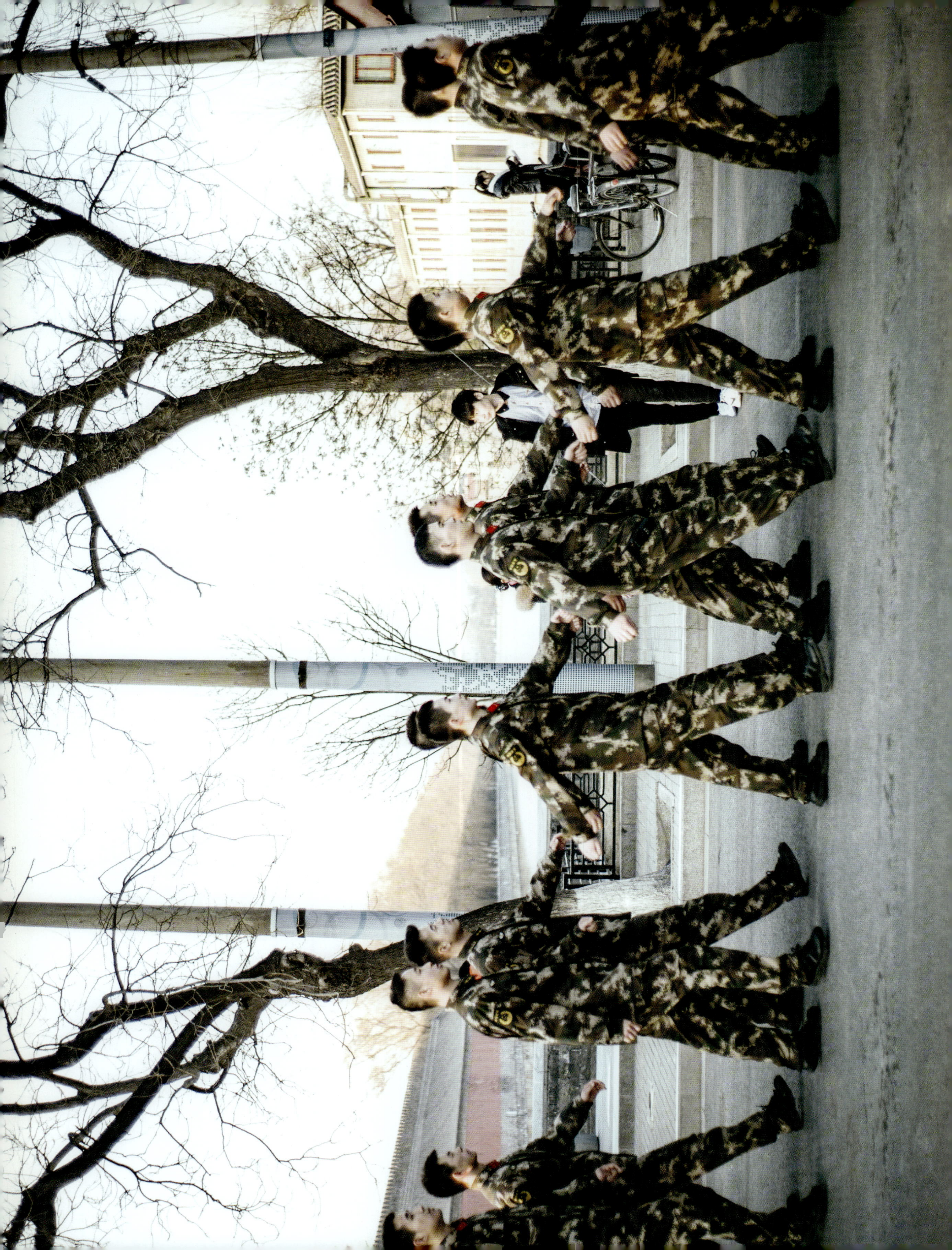

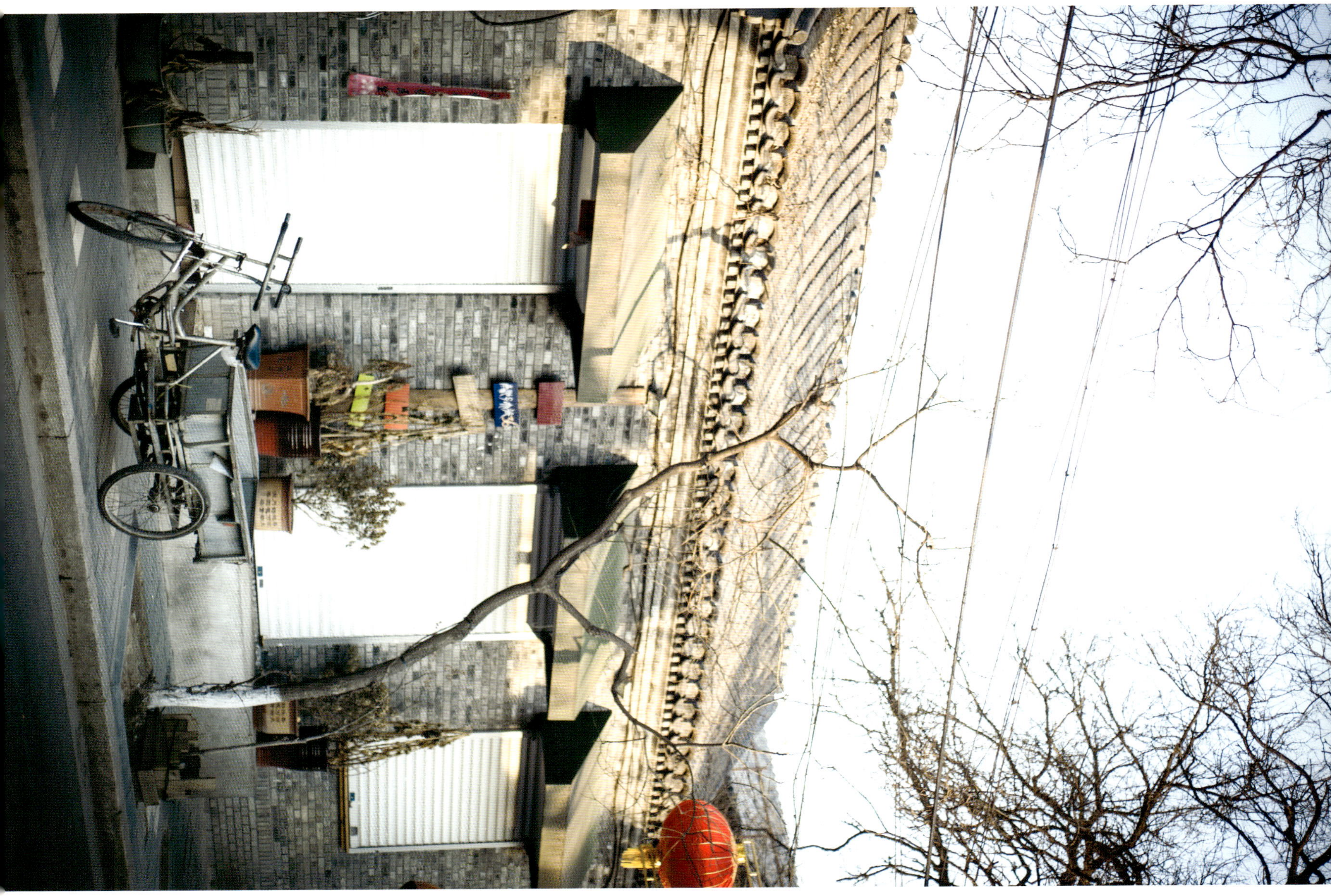

The past meets the present from this viewpoint, as Buddhas from the Thousand Buddha Mountain appear to watch over the city of Jinan, the capital of the Shandong province.

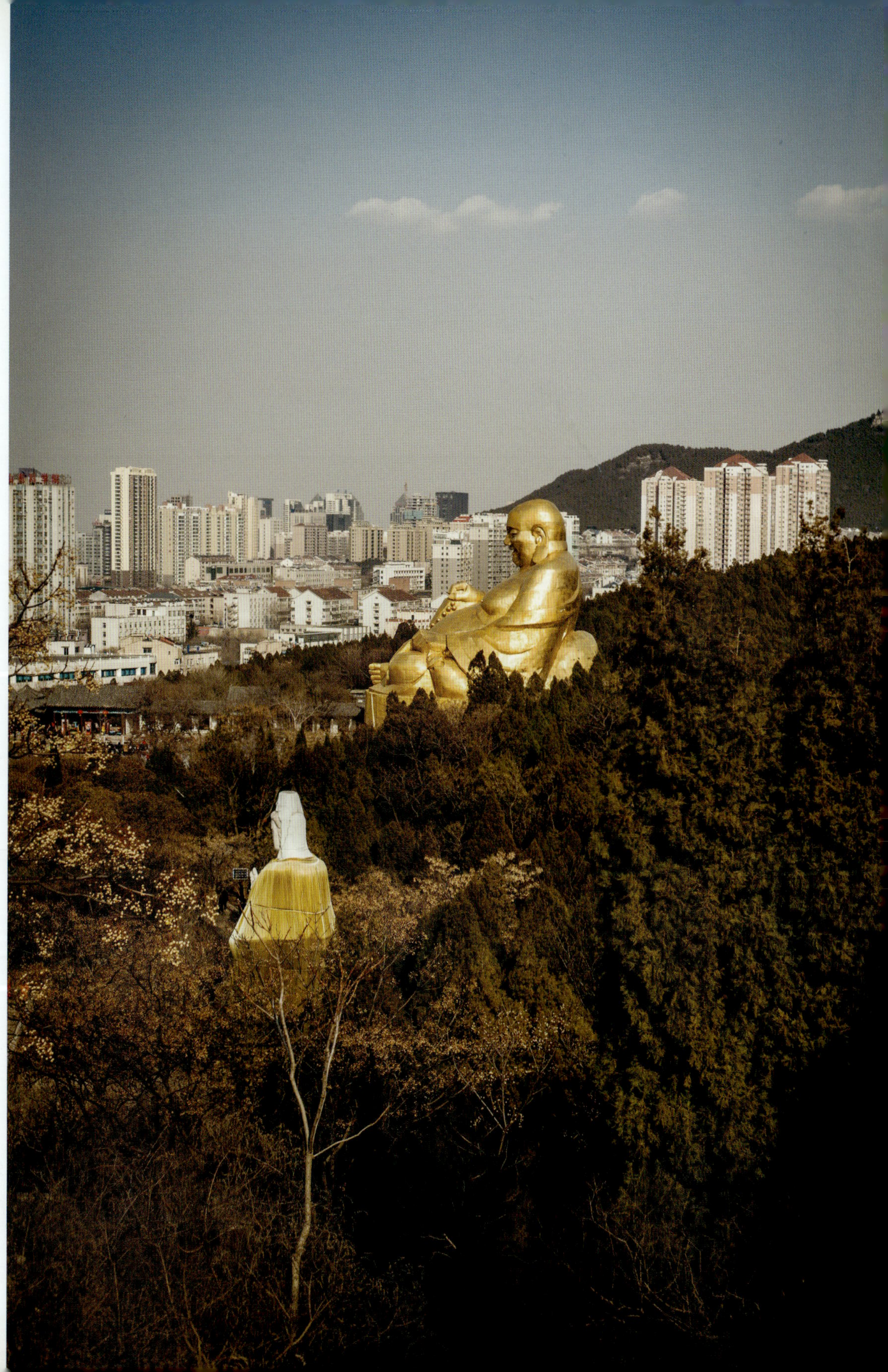

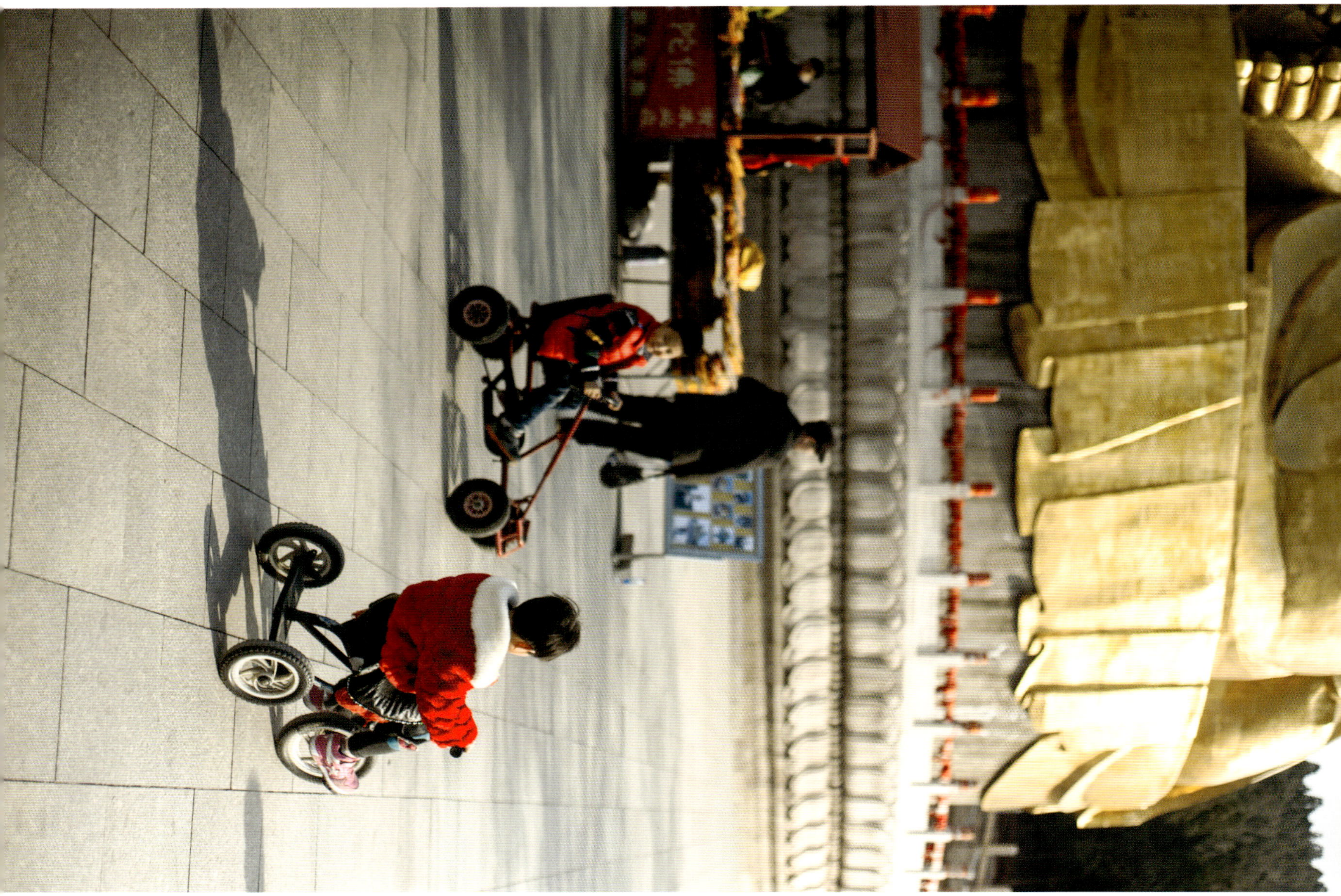

While parents are praying to one of the one thousand Buddhas, children can play on the many toys provided for them. These plush animals are the perfect size for a toddler to ride and are clearly weathered from years of loving use.

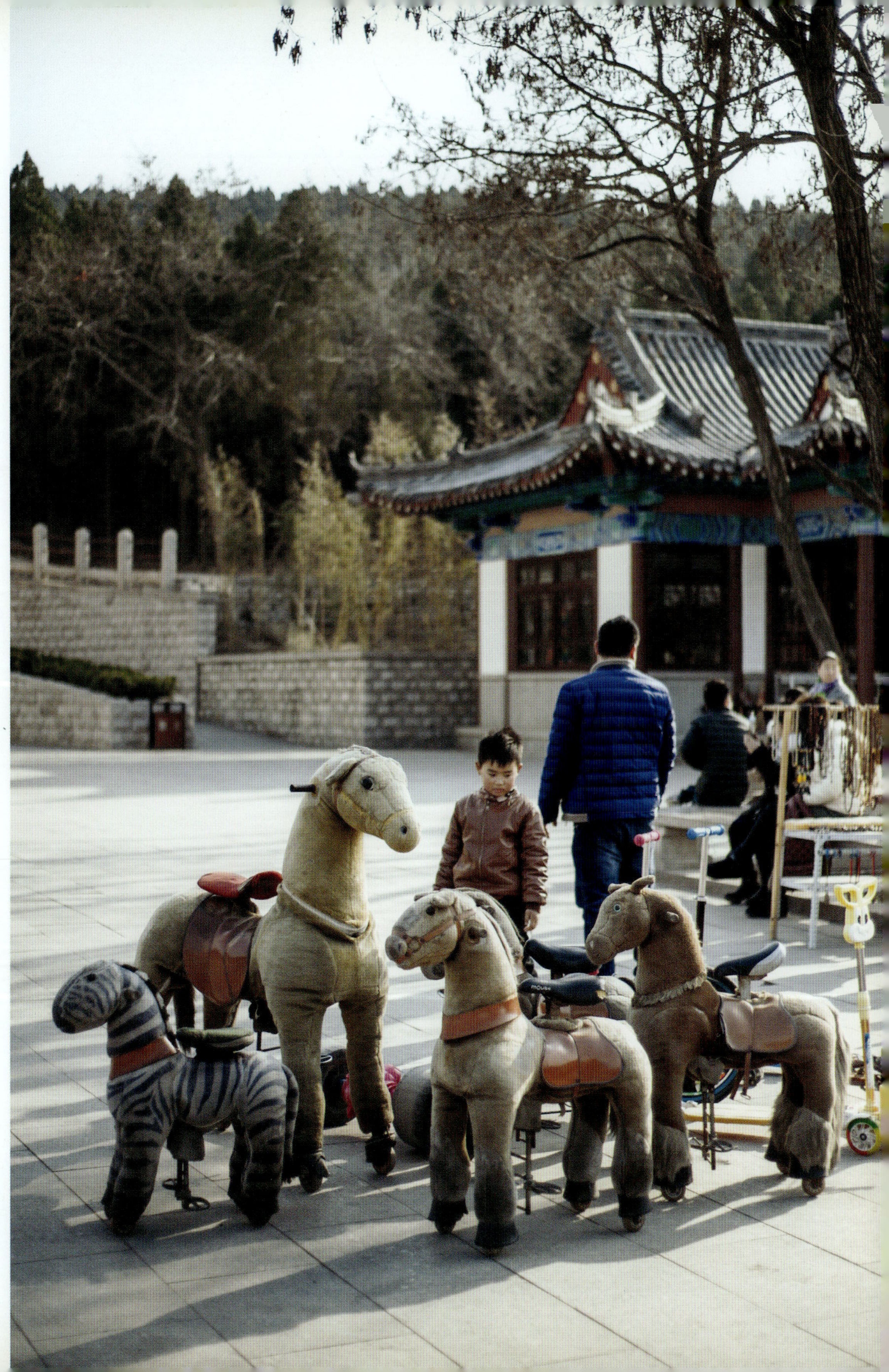

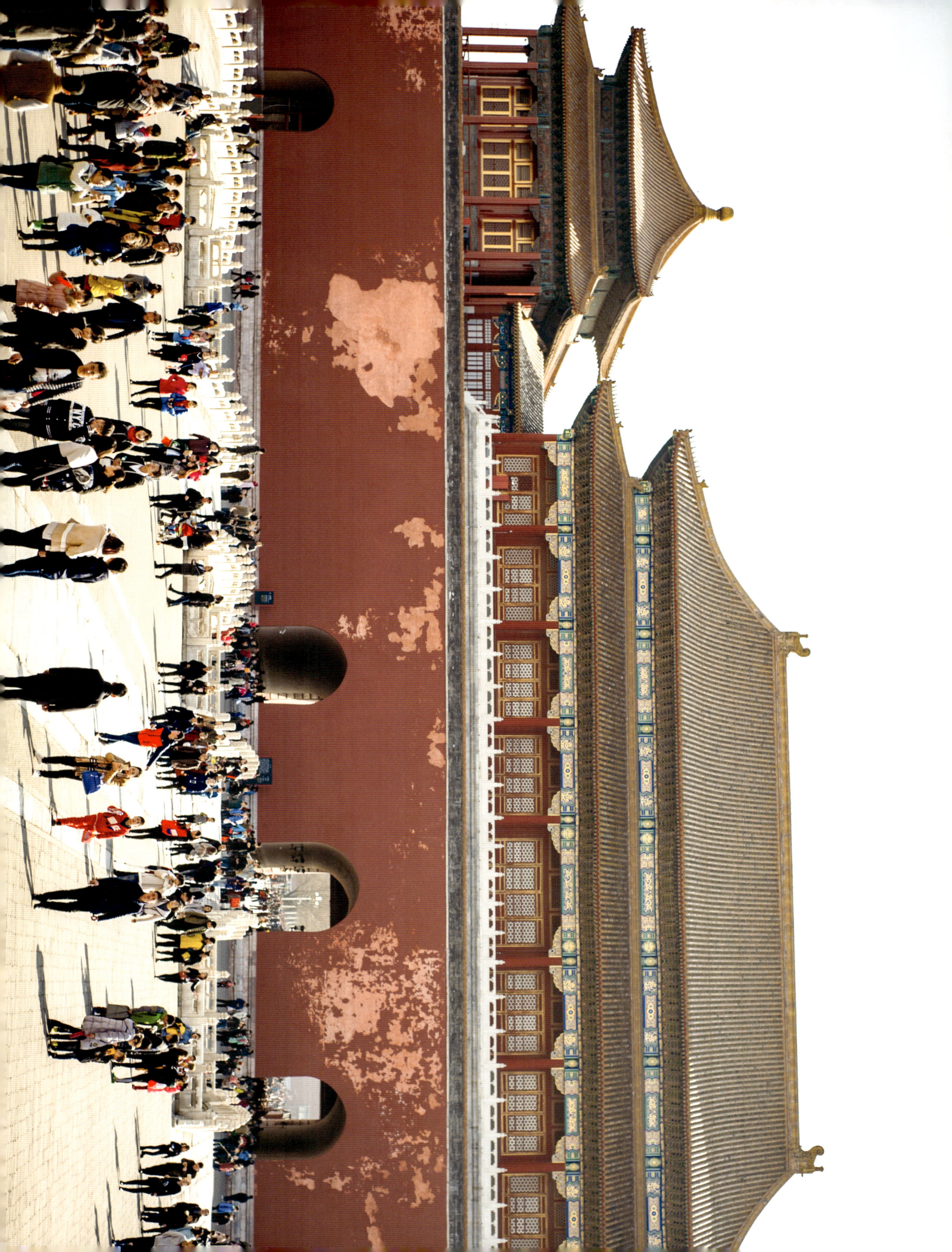

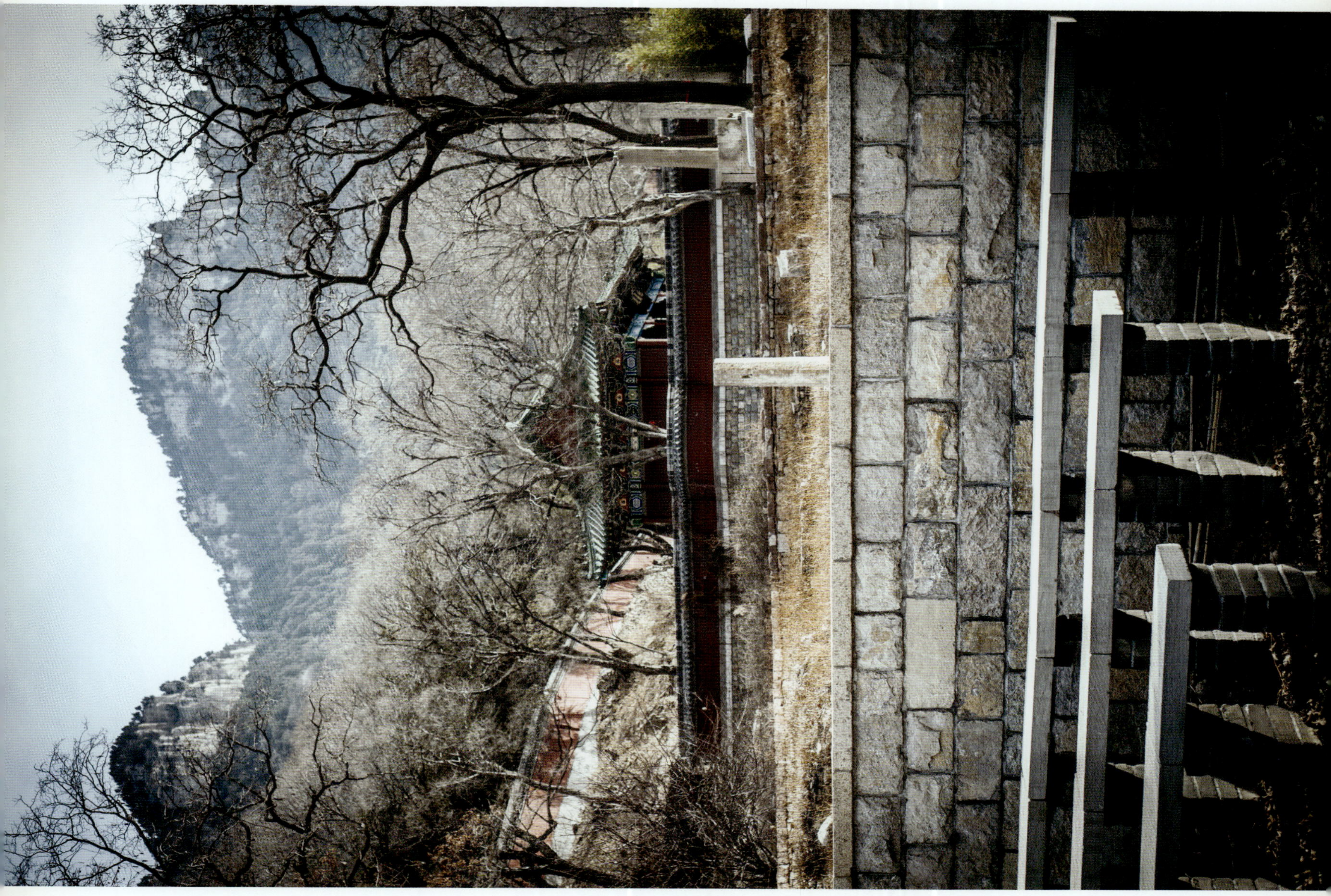

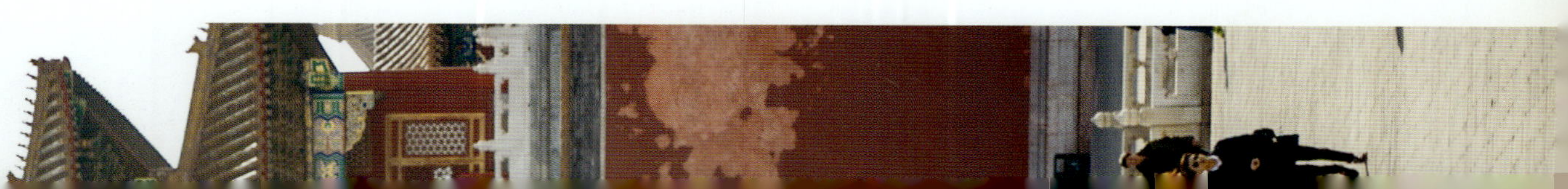

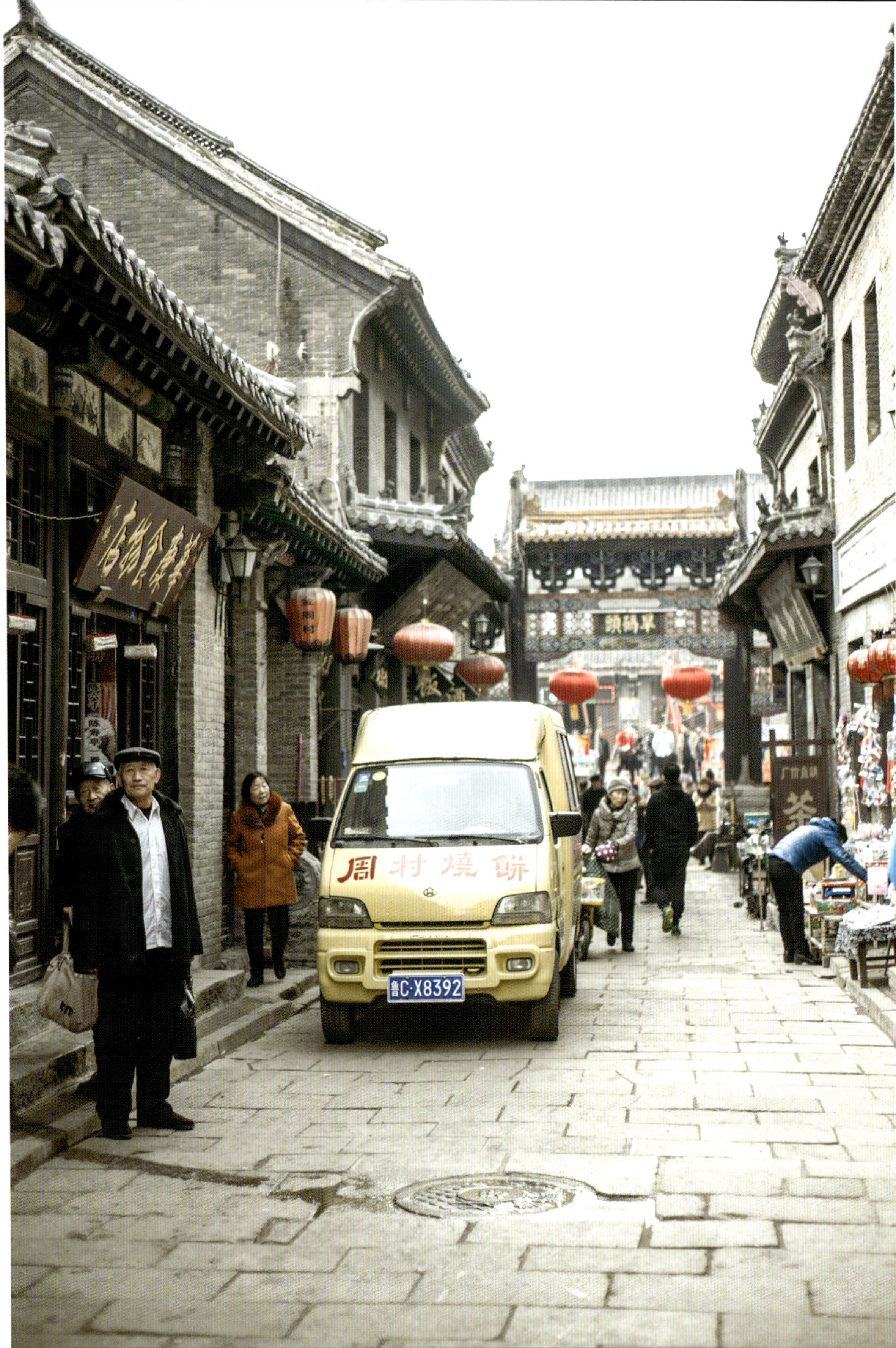
周村燒餅
鲁C·X8392

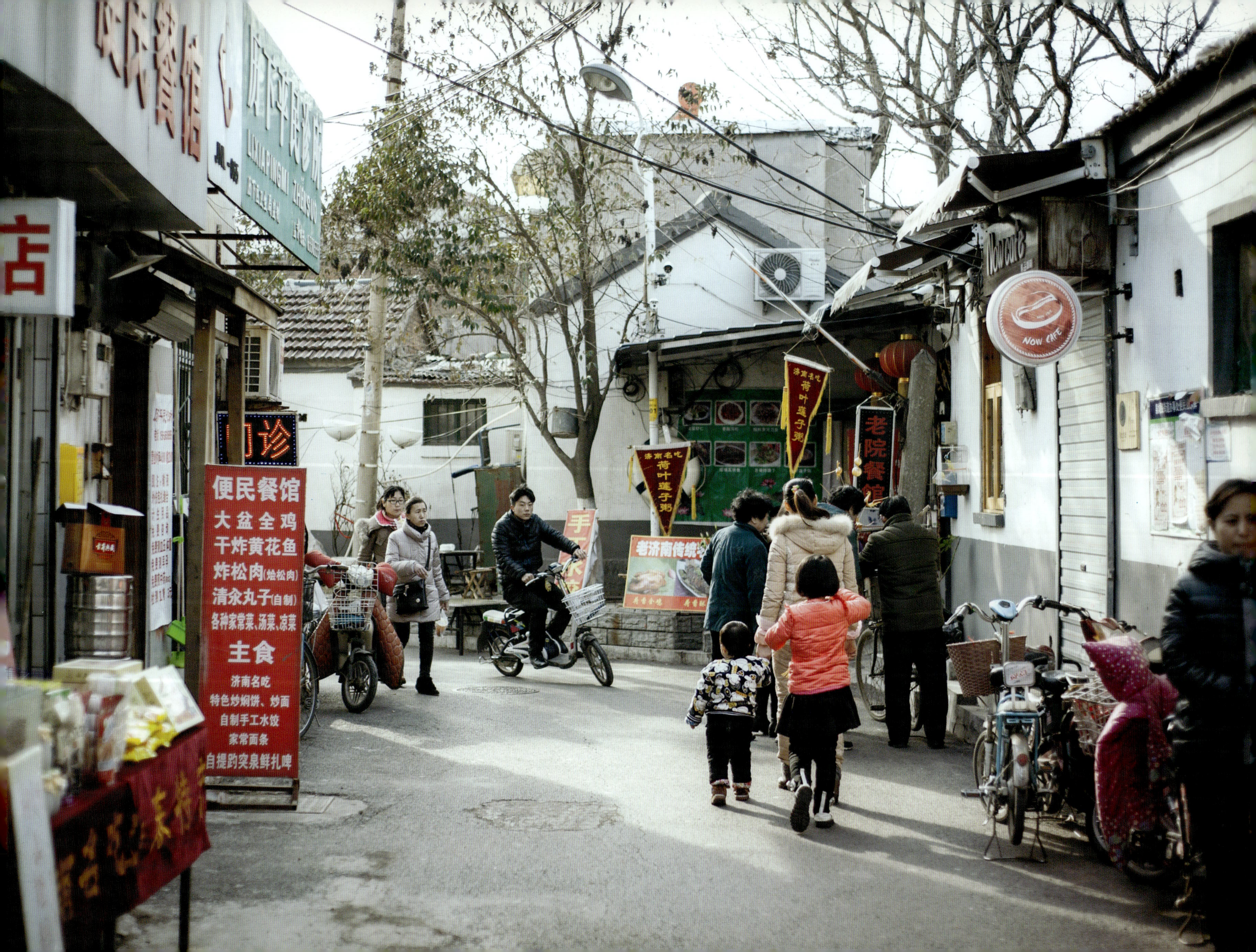
便民餐馆
大盆全鸡
干炸黄花鱼
炸松肉
主食

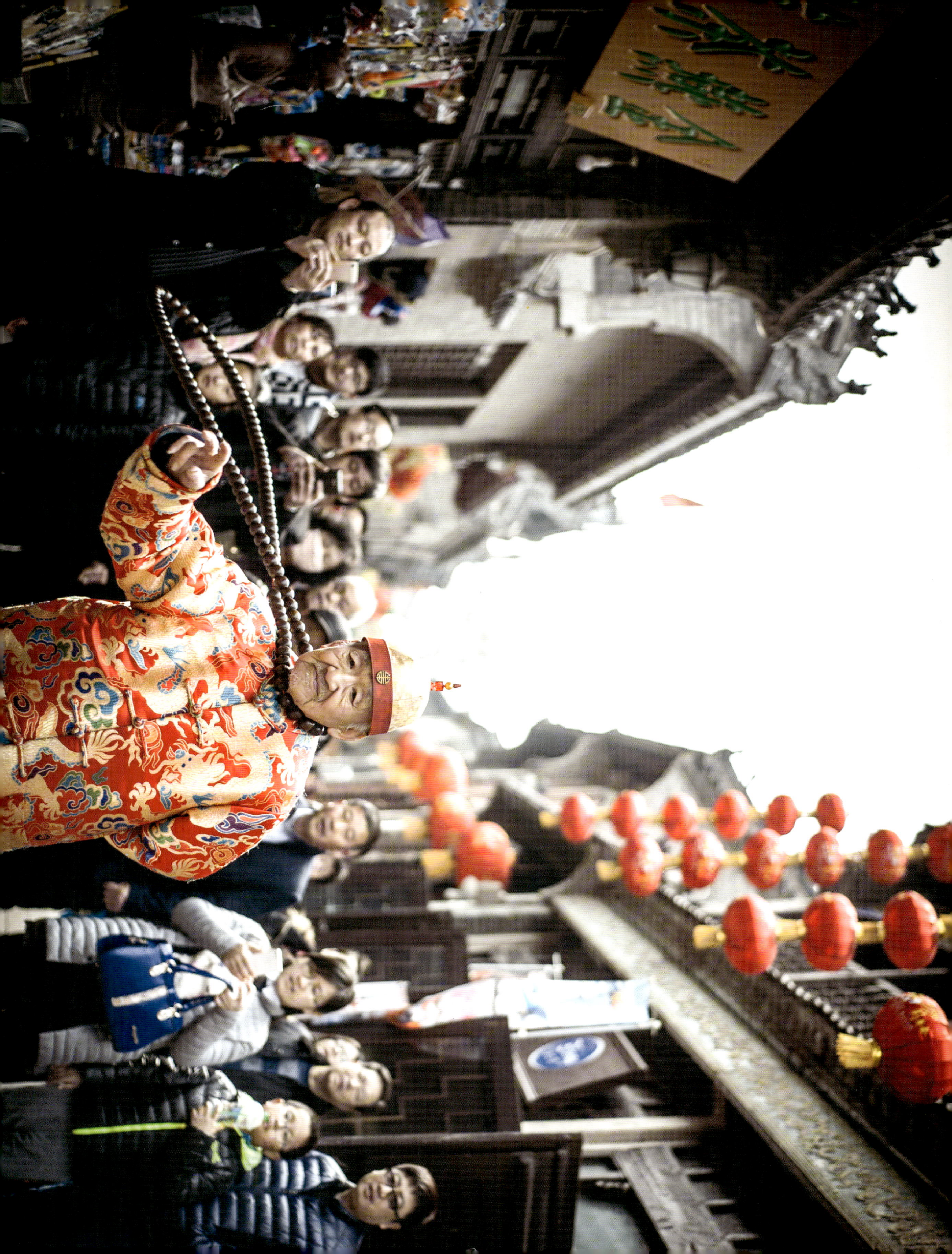

An elderly man performs for locals and tourists on the streets of Jinan. His traditional Chinese attire helps him to earn coins from passersby. His main draw is a trick in which he winds up the beads and slings them up and down his body, much like a Hula-Hoop. The crowd is enthralled by his performance.

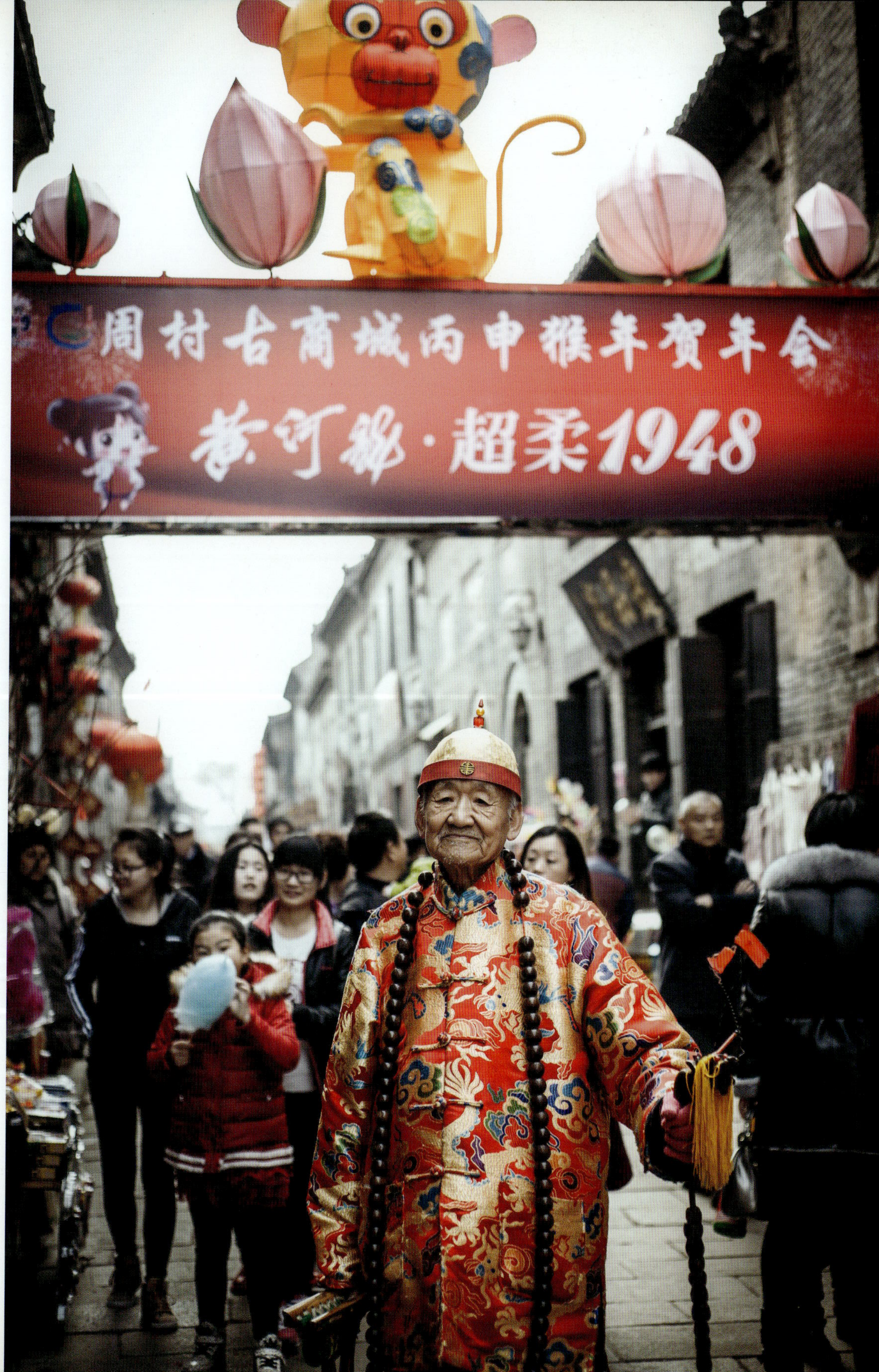

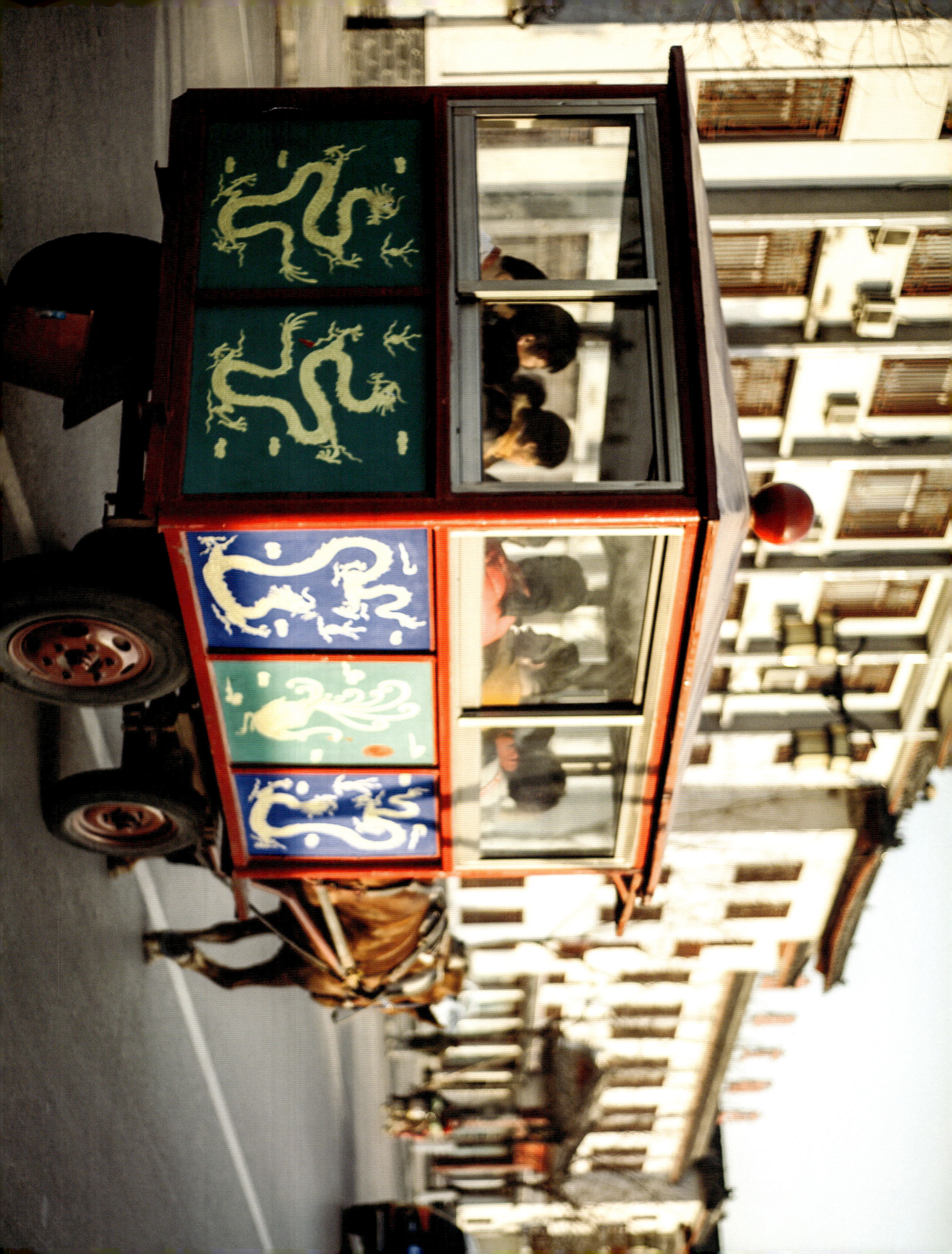

Located in one of the many gardens inside the Forbidden City, the detail on this dragon is something to be seen. Standing at approximately two feet tall, he is one of thousands of dragon representations in the city. Chinese dragons symbolize power, strength, and good luck to the Chinese people. Said to have auspicious powers, dragons are believed to control rain and water, everything from typhoons to floods.

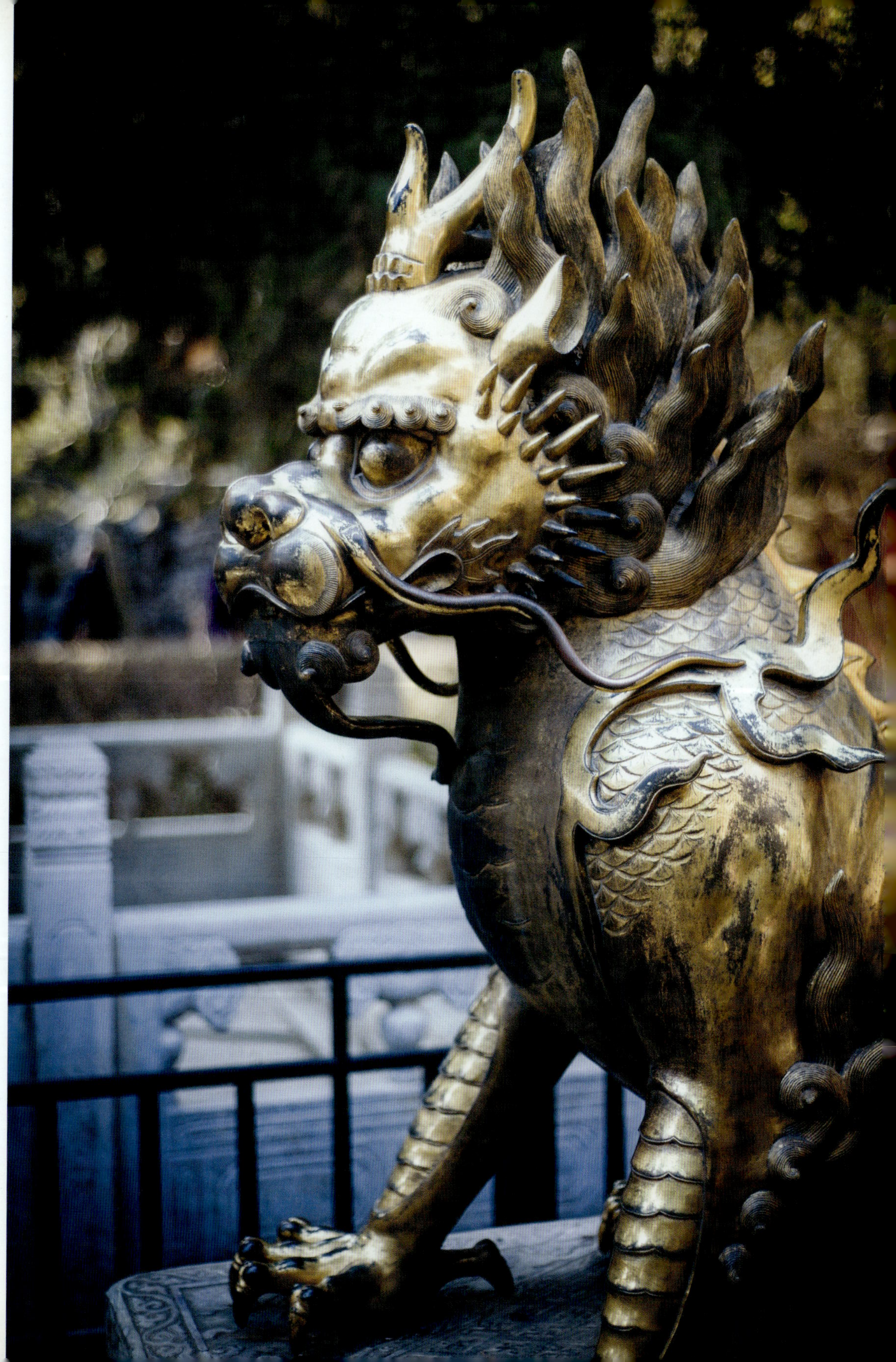

About the Author

Liza Gershman is an award-winning photographer and writer, as well as a seasoned world traveler. Passionate about food, people, and culture, Liza has had the opportunity to photograph in more than forty-three countries and forty-six US states during her career.

Liza teaches workshops, speaks, and writes articles on photography for Canon USA. She worked as the senior digital photographer for Williams-Sonoma, freelances for Restoration Hardware, is a Getty Image contributor, and has photographed and written twelve books for numerous US publishers, including Random House.

In 2010, Liza was Governor Jerry Brown's campaign photographer, and in 2014 was the lead photographer for the RedBull Youth America's Cup Team NZ2. Additional clients have included celebrity chefs, wineries, beverage brands, and restaurants.

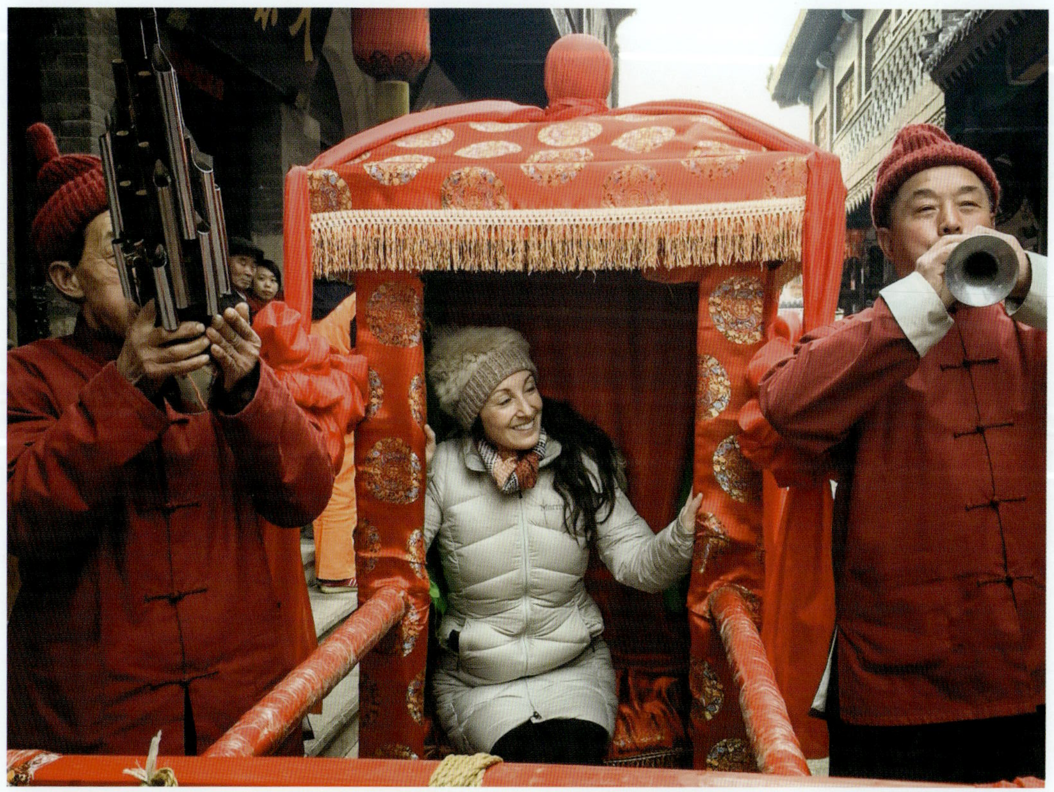